Davidson
1996

The Rhetoric of Vision

Also by the same editors

Word and Story in C. S. Lewis
A collection of sixteen critical essays
1991

The Rhetoric of Vision

Essays on Charles Williams

Edited by
Charles A. Huttar and Peter J. Schakel

With a Foreword by John Heath-Stubbs

Lewisburg
Bucknell University Press
London: Associated University Presses

© 1996 by Associated University Presses, Inc.

All rights reserved. Authorization to photocopy items for internal or personal use, or the internal or personal use of specific clients, is granted by the copyright owner, provided that a base fee of $10.00, plus eight cents per page, per copy is paid directly to the Copyright Clearance Center, 222 Rosewood Drive, Danvers, Massachusetts 01923. [0-8387-5314-0/95 $10.00 + 8¢ pp, pc.]

Associated University Presses
440 Forsgate Drive
Cranbury, NJ 08512

Associated University Presses
25 Sicilian Avenue
London WC1A 2QH, England

Associated University Presses
P.O. Box 338, Port Credit
Mississauga, Ontario
Canada L5G 4L8

The paper used in this publication meets the requirements
of the American National Standard for Permanence of Paper
for Printed Library Materials Z39.48-1984.

Library of Congress Cataloging-in-Publication Data

The rhetoric of vision : essays on Charles Williams / edited by Charles A. Huttar, and
Peter J. Schakel ; with a foreword by John Heath-Stubbs.
   p.   cm.
  Includes index.
  ISBN 0-8387-5314-0 (alk. paper)
  1. Williams, Charles, 1886-1945—Criticism and interpretation.
I. Huttar, Charles A. (Charles Adolph), 1932-   . II. Schakel,
Peter J.
PR6045.I5Z86   1996
828'.91209—dc20

95-36441
CIP

PRINTED IN THE UNITED STATES OF AMERICA

Contents

Foreword
    JOHN HEATH-STUBBS   7
Acknowledgments   10
Abbreviations   11

Introduction
    CHARLES A. HUTTAR   15

Part I. Fiction

The Athanasian Principle in Williams's Use of Images
    STEPHEN MEDCALF   27
Language and Meaning in the Novels of Charles Williams
    ALICE E. DAVIDSON   44
The Inner Lives of Characters and Readers: Affective Stylistics
    in Charles Williams's Fiction
    BERNADETTE LYNN BOSKY   59

Part II. Fiction: Individual Works

Time in the Stone of Suleiman
    VERLYN FLIEGER   75
A Metaphysical Epiphany? Charles Williams and the Art of the
    Ghost Story
    GLEN CAVALIERO   90
Charles Williams, a Prophet for Postmodernism: Skepticism and
    Belief in *The Place of the Lion*
    CATH FILMER-DAVIES   103
Complex Rhetoric for a Simple Universe: *Descent into Hell*
    JUDITH J. KOLLMANN   113
All Hallows' Eve: The Cessation of Rhetoric and the Redemption
    of Language
    GEORGE L. SCHEPER   132

Part III. Poetry

The Occult as Rhetoric in the Poetry of Charles Williams
  ROMA A. KING, JR.   165
Coinherent Rhetoric in *Taliessin through Logres*
  ANGELIKA SCHNEIDER   179
Continuity and Change in the Development of Charles Williams's
  Poetic Style
  DAVID LLEWELLYN DODDS   192

Part IV. Drama

An Audience in Search of Charles Williams
  GEORGE RALPH   217
Rhetorical Strategies in Charles Williams's Prose Play
  JOHN D. RATELIFF   238
Thomas Cranmer and Charles Williams's Vision of History
  CLIFFORD DAVIDSON   248

Part V. History, Theology, Criticism

History as Reconciliation: The Rhetoric of *The Descent of the
  Dove* and *Witchcraft*
  ROBERT MCCOLLEY   265
The Theological Rhetoric of Charles Williams: A Peculiar Density
  B. L. HORNE   277
The Caroline Vision and Detective-Fiction Rhetoric: The Evidence
  of the Reviews
  JARED LOBDELL   290
Poetry, Power, and Glory: Charles Williams's Critical Vision
  DIANE TOLOMEO EDWARDS   309

Concordances   323
Contributors   331
Index   337

Foreword

John Heath-Stubbs

It is now half a century since Charles Williams died. The present collection of essays, by a number of British, European, Australian, and North American critics, offers to the reader a comprehensive and in-depth examination of every aspect of his work and thought. To those of us who have always been his devoted readers, such a treatment might seem overdue. To others, it may come as a surprise that he should still elicit so much widespread interest. He is remembered, hostile critics might say, for his novels—and these works have been described as "theological thrillers." They belong, it would seem, to a minor strain of the English literary tradition—one that has its roots in the "Gothick" of the late eighteenth century. But Williams's handling of the supernatural and the bizarre has an inner consistency and a seriousness that, in general, we do not expect in works of this kind. The late-twentieth-century reader, tempted to dismiss such works as of secondary importance, might be persuaded to take another look at them if one were softly to whisper the phrase "magic realism." That phrase, I think, was not invented until after Williams's death, but I do not introduce it frivolously or merely to suggest that a fashionable label could be stuck onto Williams's novels. If we attempt to trace Williams's genealogy as a novelist, we soon stumble across the fictional work of G. K. Chesterton and across certain aspects of the work of Robert Louis Stevenson. And these two authors were—were they not?—among the masters gladly acknowledged by Borges.

Most of us commenced our acquaintance with Charles Williams by discovering these novels. I did myself, when I was still a student and found them in a section oddly labeled "Books for the Sophisticated" in a penny lending library at the back of a chemist's shop in a provincial English city. (One might add, not totally as a joke, that just such a venue might have found a place in one of these novels themselves.) But readers of these works soon become aware that they are finding an entry into a far wider, a far more serious, and a far more exciting world. This is also the world explored in Charles Williams's theological writings, his criticism, his plays, and above all, his Arthurian poems.

8   JOHN HEATH-STUBBS

As a student of English literature at Oxford during the 1940s, I was to find whole new worlds of imaginative experience revealed to me. Some of these were opened up to me by my teachers, others by my fellow students, among whom were a number of youthful poets whose names are still remembered. Of those lecturing in the school of English language and literature at that time, by far the most brilliant was certainly C. S. Lewis. His lectures entitled "Prolegomena to Medieval Literature" showed us that there could be ways of apprehending the universe very different from those presented by such scientific humanists as H. G. Wells, on whom my youthful thought had largely been nourished. Charles Williams's lectures, which were being delivered in Oxford during the same period, were quite another matter. I do not know that I altogether understood them then, but they were tremendously exciting. Williams is, of course, for many readers, associated mainly with C. S. Lewis and the so-called Inklings group. But it should be remembered that Williams was then resident in Oxford only through the exigencies of war and that his social and educational background was rather different from that of the rest of the group. As more than one of the present contributors point out, whereas Lewis turned away from the vision of the modern world to an older one—that of the Middle Ages—Williams looked beyond the preoccupations of the 1930s and 1940s, anticipating what may be called a postmodernist vision.

It was from my contemporaries at Oxford that I learned about modern poetry. (It was not in those days included in the syllabus.) I was to discover the work of T. S. Eliot: the *Four Quartets* were appearing during those years. So were the later poems of W. H. Auden, written during his American residence and informed by a rediscovered Christian faith. All on the margins of our awareness, but intensely exciting, were the quasi-surrealistic poems of Dylan Thomas. The poetry of Charles Williams (and one had opportunities of hearing him reading in public various parts of *The Region of the Summer Stars,* then in process of composition) seemed in some ways altogether different. Though it was with difficulty apprehended, it was somehow intensely relevant. It was much later on that I was to discover that Eliot, Auden, and Thomas were all in fact admirers of Charles Williams and were in various degrees influenced by him. Williams's verse still does not regularly find a place in the most frequently studied anthologies. But it is as a poetic visionary that we must finally assess him. He has been compared to Blake, but Blake belongs to an Illuminist tradition, rather out of the mainstream of Christian thinking, whereas Williams (in spite of his drawing on occultist learning for much of his imagery) is essentially Athanasian and Augustinian. Among Williams's contemporaries, perhaps only David Jones was working a similar seam, and one must welcome signs of a growing interest in this poet-artist. For Williams, poets—Dante and

FOREWORD 9

Wordsworth above all—were the prime exponents of the Affirmative Way. This central importance of poetry urgently needs to be restated nowadays. Some of us may fear that poststructuralist and postmodernist trends in criticism are in real danger of rendering poets so self-conscious about what they are doing as to stifle them altogether. In Charles Williams's work, so deeply rooted in tradition and yet so original, we may discover such a radical reassessment of images as may lead us out of this impasse.

Acknowledgments

We are grateful to the Executors of the Estate of Charles Williams for permission to quote from Williams's writings both published and unpublished; also to the Marion E. Wade Center at Wheaton College, Wheaton, Illinois and the Bodleian Library, Oxford, for approval to publish quotations from manuscripts in their possession. For additional acknowledgments see pages 192–93, note 2. The sources of quotations, with their publishers, are identified in the footnotes and the table of abbreviations. Those from Charles Williams are reprinted by permission of David Higham Associates.

Generous financial assistance has been provided by Hope College. We acknowledge with thanks the help and support of Provost Jacob Nyenhuis and Dean Bobby Fong.

Nancy Fleming did superb work as copy editor and taught us, by example, much about the craft. And we are deeply grateful to Myra Kohsel for her secretarial assistance, including preparation of camera-ready copy, and for her skill, patience, and graciousness throughout the lengthy process.

C.A.H.
P.J.S.

Abbreviations

For the works of Williams most commonly cited, the following abbreviations are used in references both in the text and in notes:

AHE   *All Hallows' Eve* (London: Faber and Faber, 1945)

AP   *Arthurian Poets: Charles Williams,* edited and introduced by David Llewellyn Dodds, Arthurian Studies 24 (Cambridge: D. S. Brewer, 1991)

CP   *Collected Plays* (London: Oxford University Press, 1963)
        Note: The editorship of this volume was anonymous.

DH   *Descent into Hell* (London: Faber and Faber, 1937)

Dove   *The Descent of the Dove* (London: Longmans, Green, 1939)

FS   *The Forgiveness of Sins* (London: G. Bles, 1942)

GT   *The Greater Trumps* (London: Victor Gollancz, 1932)

HCD   *He Came Down from Heaven,* I Believe Series, No. 5 (London: Heinemann, 1938)

Image   *The Image of the City and Other Essays,* ed. Anne Ridler (London: Oxford University Press, 1958)

MD   *Many Dimensions* (London: Victor Gollancz, 1931)

PL   *The Place of the Lion* (London: Mundanus [V. Gollancz], 1931)

Region   *The Region of the Summer Stars*, Editions Poetry London (London: Nicholson and Watson, 1944)

SE   *Shadows of Ecstasy* (London: Victor Gollancz, 1933)

TTL   *Taliessin through Logres* (London: Oxford University Press, 1938)

WH   *War in Heaven* (London: Victor Gollancz, 1930)

Except for those collected in *CP* and *Image,* all works by Williams are cited in their first editions. To assist readers who consult other editions than the first, a table of comparative pagination is provided at pages 323–30.

Williams was known familiarly by his initials; hence the abbreviation *CW* is used regularly in the notes in forming shortened titles of works about him and is used occasionally elsewhere.

The Rhetoric of Vision

Introduction

Charles A. Huttar

Vision is the hallmark of Charles Williams's writing. In his sensitivity to a spiritual dimension in everyday events "he was," said T. S. Eliot, "like a man who can notice shades of colour, or hear tones, beyond the ordinary range," and what he noticed he found ways of imparting to others. By a variety of means, whether he was working in poetry, drama, fiction, or the essay, Williams could slip by the barriers that we erect between "real" and "fantastic" and evoke an enlarged sense of reality. "He takes the supernatural for granted," wrote James Agee, "and has a wonderful gift for conveying, and dramatizing, the 'borderline' states of mind or Being." In an age when "the capacity for recognising [spiritual] realities . . . is numbed and almost atrophied," Williams "introduc[es] us into a real world in which he is at home."[1]

It is a world governed by principles of interrelationship—*coinherence* is the word Williams most often uses—and sacramentality. Williams rejects the simplistic model offered by absolute dualism in favor of one in which matter and spirit coinhere. Indeed, everything in the universe has its existence through what Williams habitually called a "web" of interdependence, mutually giving and receiving. Even the Self-Being which we call God chooses, in Creation and Incarnation, in mysterious fashion to enter the web—acting out a principle of coinherence already evident in the Triunity. It is not a metaphysical principle only: Williams finds it at work in epistemology—we note his regard not only for paradox and the interplay of doubt and faith but also for the "feeling intellect."[2] He finds it at work also in the ethical realm—moral choice may resolve, finally, to a decision whether to embrace one's role as a participant in the web or to reject it:

---

1. Eliot, "The Significance of Charles Williams," *Listener,* 19 Dec. 1946, 894; Agee, *Letters to Father Flye,* 2d ed. (New York: Ballantine, 1971), 207; Eliot, "Significance," 895; Eliot, introduction to *All Hallows' Eve,* by Charles Williams (New York: Pellegrini & Cudahy, 1948), xvi.

2. The phrase is from Wordsworth, but it reminds us also of the kinship Williams felt for the poetic and dramatic forms of the seventeenth century, evident especially in his work before about 1930.

16   CHARLES A. HUTTAR

whether to belong to what Williams called "the City" or to prefer aloneness, which is tantamount to destruction.[3]

The doctrine thus briefly sketched gave rise in Williams's thought to views on many aspects of life—but more, really, than views, "or a set of ideas"; rather, "primarily something imaginative,"[4] for which *vision* is the aptest term. "To study [Williams's] work with care," one critic writes, "is to be rewarded by an intellectual vision that is both sane and liberating."[5]

There is no need here to expound further on the content of Williams's vision, for it has been explicated and analyzed in a quite sizable body of scholarship that has taken shape since his death in 1945.[6] Considerable attention has been paid, as well, to the impact of that vision on matters of

---

3. The theme is ubiquitous in Williams: one succinct exposition of it is his wartime pamphlet "The Way of Exchange" (1941; reprinted in *Image*, 147–54).

4. Eliot, introduction to *All Hallows' Eve*, xiii.

5. Glen Cavaliero, *Charles Williams: Poet of Theology* (Grand Rapids, Mich.: Eerdmans, 1983), 158.

6. For an overview of the first thirty years, see Lois Glenn, *Charles W. S. Williams: A Checklist*, Serif Series, no. 33 (Kent, Ohio: Kent State University Press, 1975), 57–102. Within this period see especially John Heath-Stubbs, *Charles Williams*, Writers and Their Work, no. 63 (London: Longmans, Green, 1955); W. H. Auden, "Charles Williams," *Christian Century* 73 (1956): 552–54, and "The Martyr as Dramatic Hero," in *Secondary Worlds* (New York: Random House, 1968), 15–45; Anne Ridler, introduction to *Image*, xxx-l; Patricia Meyer Spacks, "Charles Williams: A Novelist's Pilgrimage," *Religion in Life* 29 (1960): 277–88; Charles Moorman, *Arthurian Triptych* (Berkeley and Los Angeles: University of California Press, 1960) and *The Precincts of Felicity: The Augustinian City of the Oxford Christians* (Gainesville: University of Florida Press, 1966); Mary McDermott Shideler, *The Theology of Romantic Love: A Study in the Writings of Charles Williams* (New York: Harper, 1962); Hoxie Neale Fairchild, *Religious Trends in English Poetry*, 6 vols. (New York and London: Columbia University Press, 1939–68), 5 (1962): 260–68 and 6 (1968): 122–24, 296–99, 482–88; Frederick S. Wandall, "Charles Williams," in *Minor British Novelists*, ed. Charles A. Hoyt (Carbondale: Southern Illinois University Press, 1967), 121–34; Robert J. Reilly, *Romantic Religion: A Study of Barfield, Lewis, Williams, and Tolkien* (Athens: University of Georgia Press, 1971); Chad Walsh, "Charles Williams' Novels and the Contemporary Mutation of Consciousness," in *Myth, Allegory, and Gospel*, ed. J. W. Montgomery (Minneapolis: Bethany Fellowship, 1974), 53–77. See also Jan Curtis, "Charles Williams: His Reputation in the English-speaking World from 1917 to 1985," *Inklings-Jahrbuch* 9 (1991): 127–64, esp. 134–36, 150.

Of post-1975 scholarship Curtis provides a quick survey ("Reputation," 160–64). Key studies include Karl Heinz Göller, "From Logres to Carbonek: The Arthuriad of Charles Williams," in *Arthurian Literature I*, ed. Richard Barber (Woodbridge: Brewer, 1981), 121–73; Cavaliero, *Poet of Theology;* Thomas Howard, *The Novels of Charles Williams* (New York and Oxford: Oxford University Press, 1983); A. M. Hadfield, *Charles Williams: An Exploration of His Life and Work* (New York and Oxford: Oxford University Press, 1983); Roma A. King, Jr., *The Pattern in the Web: The Mythical Poetry of Charles Williams* (Kent, Ohio, and London: Kent State University Press, 1990). In addition, there have been numerous other articles, David Dodds's recent editorial work in *AP,* and more than thirty dissertations.

INTRODUCTION

artistic technique, in such areas as Williams's use of myth, his concept of poetry, his handling of time, and his choice of genres.[7] Just emerging into view among critics, however, is the way he anticipated certain present-day attitudes about the limitations of language, of logocentric intellectual activity, and of the autonomous self. In his own day, Williams was suspicious about the Enlightenment project we now call modernism; today's climate of thought seems to be a context in which his outlook is coming to be better appreciated. That such suspicions need not always lead to a despairing stripping away of signification, but may instead harmonize with transcendence, is an implication of Williams's practice which some may welcome. Several of the essays here collected deal with such matters as these.

Also less studied, in Williams scholarship thus far, have been the rhetorical and stylistic means by which he made his vision credible—or, in the view of some critics, the faults of rhetoric which obscure or undermine it. Casual pronouncements have been thrown out *en passant*, ranging from "weird prose" and "milk-and-water literariness" to "brilliant fusion of form and content"[8] and, as regards the poetry, using such terms as "dazzling," "strict," "Pindaric"—and "bathos."[9] More methodical rhetorical analysis, leading to specific, supported evaluations, may be found in some of the studies of Williams's ideas listed above;[10] in addition, there is significant

7. See, for example, George P. Winship, Jr., "This Rough Magic: The Novels of Charles Williams," *Yale Review* 40 (1950): 285–96; James Roy King, "Christian Fantasy in the Novels of C. S. Lewis and Charles Williams," *Journal of Religious Thought* 11 (1953): 46–60; John P. Gigrich, *An Immortality for Its Own Sake: A Study of the Concept of Poetry in the Writings of Charles Williams* (Washington: Catholic University of America Press, 1954); Dorothy L. Sayers, "Charles Williams: A Poet's Critic," *The Poetry of Search and the Poetry of Statement* (London: Gollancz, 1963), 69–88; William V. Spanos, *The Christian Tradition in Modern British Verse Drama: The Poetics of Sacramental Time* (New Brunswick, N. J.: Rutgers University Press, 1967); J'nan Sellery, "Fictive Modes in Charles Williams' *All Hallows' Eve*," *Genre* 1 (1968): 316–31; Gunnar Urang, "Charles Williams: Fantasy and the Ontology of Love," chap. 2 in *Shadows of Heaven: Religion and Fantasy in the Writing of C. S. Lewis, Charles Williams, and J. R. R. Tolkien* (Philadelphia: Pilgrim Press, 1971): 51–92; and W. R. Irwin, *The Game of the Impossible: A Rhetoric of Fantasy* (Urbana, Chicago, London: University of Illinois Press, 1976), 167–74.

8. Winship, "This Rough Magic," 288; H. D. Hanshell, "Charles Williams: A Heresy Hunt," *Month* 9 (1953): 15; Spacks, "Novelist's Pilgrimage," 278.

9. Vernon Watkins, "Three Sonnets for Charles Williams" (first published in *The Wind and the Rain*, 1951), sonnet 3: "revealed in the window-glass / Of your dazzling verse"; "For you the immediate thing / Has true dimensions; . . . / . . . Through strictness the pictures stay, / Caught by the voice, and held" (*Collected Poems* [Ipswich: Golgonooza, 1986], 292–93); *Pindaric:* C. S. Lewis, review of a reissue of *TTL, Oxford Magazine* 64 (1946): 248; *bathos:* John Press, *The Fire and the Fountain* (London: Oxford University Press, 1955), 151.

10. See, for example, Cavaliero, *Poet of Theology*, 159, 162-64, 167-72.

18 CHARLES A. HUTTAR

work devoted primarily to such detailed analysis.[11]

There have also been efforts to go beyond the details and generalize Williams's characteristic rhetoric under some broad label having ideological and not merely technical implications. One critic, in an essay unfortunately marked by its own strong, ideologically based animus, blamed Williams for being too iconic in his poetry, substituting verbal counters for the work of the imagination; another chose Williams to exemplify what he called a "rhetoric of certitude," a category which, had it been defined technically with greater care, might have been found not so applicable to Williams.[12] Both these pieces are related, one of them explicitly, to an earlier attack which (though not arguing from rhetorical considerations) labeled Williams's outlook "totalitarian."[13] Both describe elements of a rhetoric which might be called one of "dominance" or "imposition," a vehicle for achieving one's ends by means that are intellectually violent.

Such a conclusion, however, seems diametrically opposed to those of other scholars who emphasize the paradox, tension, irony, skepticism, and heightened imagination that all characterize Williams's prose rhetoric,[14] as well as to the conclusion of a more recent inquiry which finds a rhetoric of "risk" underlying Williams's earliest fiction.[15] Any writer as sensitive as Williams is to good and evil runs the danger of having his views oversimplified, but there is a nice parallel between the complexity of Williams's rhetoric, as it is understood by the latter group of critics, and his vision of a social structure marked by hierarchy blended with mutuality, in a dance of ever-exchanging positions of dominance and submission.[16]

In the study of Charles Williams's rhetoric there remain debates to be

11. See Patricia Meyer Spacks, "Charles Williams: The Fusions of Fiction," in *Shadows of Imagination: The Fantasies of C. S. Lewis, J. R. R. Tolkien, and Charles Williams*, ed. Mark R. Hillegas (Carbondale and Edwardsville: Southern Illinois University Press, 1969), 150–59; Angelika Schneider, "A Mesh of Chords: Language and Style in the Arthurian Poems of Charles Williams," in *Arthurian Literature V*, ed. Richard Barber (Woodbridge: Brewer, 1985), 92–148.

12. Roger Sale, "England's Parnassus: C. S. Lewis, Charles Williams and J. R. R. Tolkien," *Hudson Review* 17 (1964): 203–25, esp. 210–15; Winston Weathers, "The Rhetoric of Certitude," *Southern Humanities Review* 2 (1968): 213–22. Critiques of the latter are undertaken in the essays by Bosky and Kollmann which follow.

13. Robert Conquest, "The Art of the Enemy," *Essays in Criticism* 7 (1957): 42–55 (cf. Sale, "England's Parnassus," 213).

14. Cf. Patricia Meyer Spacks, "Critical Forum: 'The Art of the Enemy,' II," *Essays in Criticism* 7 (1957): 335–39; Sellery, "Fictive Modes," 325–28; Cavaliero, *Poet of Theology*, 164; Howard, *Novels of CW*, 219–20.

15. Charles A. Huttar, "Williams's Changing Views of Milton and the Problem of *Shadows of Ecstasy*," *Inklings-Jahrbuch* 5 (1987): 234. Cf. Cavaliero, *Poet of Theology*, 165.

16. Cf. Charles Williams, "A Dialogue on Hierarchy" (1943), in *Image*, 127–30; Shideler, *Theology of Romantic Love*, 81–83, 181; King, *Pattern in the Web*, 122, 155.

INTRODUCTION 19

resolved and questions to be answered, many of them having greater than technical import. No attempt has been made in the collection which follows to take up all the possible questions. We do seek to offer a range of essays using various approaches to deal with Williams's rhetorical practice and with the theory (drawn from his study of theology and of the literary tradition) which guided his practice. We hope that the studies offered here will encourage yet further inquiry along these lines. Contributing scholars include both well-established Williams critics and fresh voices. Some concentrate on rhetorical strategies found in particular portions of Williams's writing, including such seldom-studied genres as his book reviews and books of history and of theology, or in single works; others take a more general or sweeping view.

A complicating factor in the consideration of rhetorical means and theory is the double-edged nature of the word "rhetoric" itself. Since the Sophists, it has connoted manipulative technique, isolated from any questions of goodness or truth. Even viewed more positively, it still seems an officious go-between separating speaker from hearer, and there is a great temptation to long for some ideal state in which the intermediary were not necessary —in Williams's words, for "the recovery of that ancient validity, our unfallen speech."[17] Indeed, in one essay below George L. Scheper traces Williams's own negative statements about "rhetoric" and Williams's vision of that ideal state: of a redeemed language in which speech and act would be one. On the other hand, by a different definition rhetoric comprises the entire repertoire of the speaker's or writer's approach to both theme and audience, and therefore in our present less-than-ideal human condition, if we may borrow a phrase from Donne, without rhetoric "a great prince in prison lies." And a recurrent theme in this book is how Williams managed to use rhetoric not only to present but at the same time to embody that vision of coinherence which rhetoric in the conventional sense often threatens to violate.[18]

The essays in the first group deal generally with Williams's fiction. Stephen Medcalf undertakes to work out the theory underlying his creation and use of imagery. Beginning with the acknowledged tension between the ideal forms of things and their particular manifestations in the world of the senses, he traces Williams's progress, across twenty years of fiction writing, from the intrusively supernatural as a vehicle for ideal presence to the stubbornly natural which nevertheless incarnates its own higher essence. He thus finds Williams working toward a parallel, in the aesthetic realm, to the

---

17. Williams, "The Index of the Body" (1942), in *Image,* 82.

18. One manifestation of coinherence being the mutuality of exchange which was mentioned above as a vital aspect of Williams's view of hierarchy, it will be evident that some of the essays which follow carry on a debate already begun in the scholarship, without having set themselves to do so explicitly.

theological formulation known as the Athanasian Creed: the image, without losing its own identity, is taken up into the reality it represents. In the search for a rhetoric by which to present a spiritual vision, there is what might be called an Arian temptation to reduce the vision by means of shortcuts, such as magic or verbal formulae. After acknowledging that this did sometimes happen in Williams, Medcalf goes on to analyze several passages which powerfully succeed in presenting a higher reality while at the same time preserving the reality of the image in which it inheres. Rhetoric and vision alike battle the reductionist pressures of the age, the rhetoric modeling coinherence as well as presenting it.

The next two essays look closely at aspects of Williams's use of words. For Alice Davidson, his theory of language as inherently meaningful led him to a "rhetoric of precision" marked by unusual attention to diction—for example, the use of words in archaic, extended, double, or hyperliteral meanings—and by character portrayal which valorizes verbal integrity. Bernadette Bosky is interested in Williams's affective stylistics, particularly the methods by which he offers "subjective correlatives" for heightened states of consciousness. She finds that he has a special way of using pronouns which hints at transcendence. Through paradox he achieves a rhetoric that delicately combines "certitude" and "mystery," and through attention to words' "multivalence" he suggests a larger principle of coinherence; both devices are verbal counterparts of Incarnation.

The essays in the next group deal with individual works of fiction, arranged nearly in chronological order (though the one short story is placed after the novel with which it is associated). In "Time in the Stone of Suleiman," Verlyn Flieger examines a particular instance of the rhetoric of "dislocation" which Williams uses to arouse readers' awareness. To be effective, the "discordant element" must not be arbitrary but harmonize with the primary world according to a coherent rationale. (Flieger believes that Williams was here using a Wordsworthian rather than a Tolkienian approach to mythopoesis.) Taking a cue from the title of *Many Dimensions*, in the light of contemporary interest in Einsteinian space/time and particularly in J. W. Dunne's 1927 best-seller, *An Experiment with Time*, Flieger explains the Stone around which the novel's action revolves in terms of such a coherent rationale. A major character in *Many Dimensions*, Lord Arglay, reappears in "Et in Sempiternum Pereant," the ghost story which is the subject of Glen Cavaliero's essay. Perhaps the first rhetorical choice that an author makes in shaping an idea for a conceived audience is the choice of genre, but for Williams it was not a simple matter of selection from a menu: neither realistic fiction nor romantic fiction, as each had developed by his time, offered exactly the vehicle he needed, and so, as T. S. Eliot observes, he had to invent his own forms (introduction to *All Hallows' Eve,* xiii). Using Jakobsonian categories of linguistic analysis to understand Williams's achievement, Cavaliero shows how he could take a popular form, one

INTRODUCTION   21

commonly used with little serious intent, and, while respecting its generic distinctives, at the same time infuse it with his vision.[19]

In a close study of chapter 1 of *The Place of the Lion*, Cath Filmer-Davies detects a poststructuralist quality in the tone of skepticism which Williams achieves and the means by which he achieves it. The skepticism is part of the dialectic of doubt and faith which was integral to his vision. The "proto-deconstructive turn," as she calls it, can be recognized in Williams's use of such now-familiar devices as aporia, to keep postponing closure, and intertextuality to position himself in a tradition of Christian thought outside the orthodox mainstream. Judith J. Kollmann's study of *Descent into Hell* concentrates on selected stylistic devices to show how Williams enacted on the verbal level elements of his vision, especially the concept of coinherence. Kollmann's attention to Williams's diction, picking up a topic developed earlier by Bosky and Alice Davidson, looks forward to George L. Scheper's discussion of the moral implications of using words without regard to their integrity. Scheper focuses on *All Hallows' Eve* as he explores the distinction on which Williams insists between the falsified language that too often characterizes daily life and a more "pure" language such as that exemplified in liturgical speech acts. In maintaining a similar distinction between magic and mystery, as radically opposite in perspective though often muddled together, he returns to a point made by Medcalf earlier in this book.

In the first of three essays on Williams's poetry, Roma A. King, Jr., explores the same distinction more extensively as he investigates the question of Williams's use of the popular occult—an issue also at stake in the works of fiction discussed by Flieger and Cavaliero. This topic has attracted considerable interest in recent years; King argues that Williams's use of the occult in his writings was on the level of rhetoric rather than, as is often supposed, on that of belief (except in the general sense of a belief in "hidden things" beyond the world of *phenomena*). He used the occult as a mode of imagining. King identifies five occult themes and describes how Williams adapted them: how such recurrent images as the heavenly bodies, the human body, correspondences, magic, pentagram, tree, and stair all serve to communicate the vision of a radically monistic, coinherent universe.[20]

Angelika Schneider, also, studies the patterns of imagery in Williams's

---

19. Patricia Meyer Spacks has already commented on Williams's "serious" use of the ghost story. She notes that he was willing to "risk . . . having his work classed as . . . sub-literary . . . because his special vision of the world require[d]" such a genre: "his ghosts are part of his effort to objectify a sense of the constant encroachment of the unexpected" ("Critical Forum," 337).

20. Other scholars who find a qualified occultism such as Williams's fully compatible with Christian faith include Francis King, *Ritual Magic in England, 1887 to the Present Day* (London: Neville Spearman, 1970), 94–95, 112, and Elisabeth Brewer, "Charles Williams and Arthur Edward Waite," *Seven* 4 (1983): 61–66.

poetry and finds the notion of coinherence central to Williams's vision. Further, she claims Williams as a visionary in a larger sense, fraught with social significance: one who astonishingly adumbrates a postmodern appreciation for ecological ways of thinking about the world and the place of humans in it. She analyzes how his vision is, in his poetry, not only expressed but embodied in the rhetorical fabric, through images—the human body, myths, magic, the hazel, and others—and through the resources of language: sounds and rhythms, diction, syntax.

The vision found in Williams's poetry, while it owes much to the poets of earlier centuries, is peculiarly his vision. After five volumes of verse uttered largely in the voices of past cultures, Williams broke free of these trammels and, in his late forties, began to evolve a style of his own that could express such a vision. David Llewellyn Dodds traces the literary and personal influences on that evolution and identifies the elements of the change as it continued across a dozen years to Williams's last published volume and beyond. By using previously unpublished drafts and intermediate versions Dodds is able to reach firmer conclusions on matters which until now have been largely conjectural.

Three essays treat Williams's dramatic works. George Ralph's experience in the theatrical presentation of Williams leads him to examine what this playwright typically expected of his audiences and performers. Williams made heavy demands of viewers, Ralph believes, with his morality-play device of personified abstractions, his frequent reliance on a fairly high level of religious knowledge and even religious sympathy, and his highly compact and figured language. He called to his aid a rhetoric borrowed from medieval drama, which proved instrumental in alleviating these difficulties and making his vision accessible.

Next, the rhetoric of two particular plays is studied. A radical departure from earlier styles is found in the prose play *Terror of Light* (1940), which John D. Rateliff argues exists in prose by a rhetorical choice and not, as critics have heretofore supposed, because the author didn't get around to revising it into verse. Rateliff considers *Terror* Williams's best play, an achievement made possible in part by the decision to relate to his audience by means of a rhetoric radically different from that used in his verse plays. Clifford Davidson looks back at Williams's first dramatic success, *Thomas Cranmer of Canterbury*, which Williams was commissioned to write for the Canterbury festival the year after T. S. Eliot's *Murder in the Cathedral*. He considers the necessity of ambiguity and the role of skepticism in religious knowledge to be key themes in this play. Williams's sacramental vision led to a meticulous handling of historical texts and to taking seriously the role of theological issues in history. His Cranmer emerges as very different from Eliot's Becket.

Williams described his Nativity play *Seed of Adam* as "not so much a

INTRODUCTION 23

presentation of the historic facts as of their spiritual value" (*CP,* 173). Historian Robert McColley discovers in Williams's two most ambitious historical writings the same awareness of *species aeternitatis*. In the balance, caution, and courtesy of Williams's rhetoric he finds the doctrine of coinherence exemplified as well as taught, thus increasing the persuasive effect. It is in H. Richard Niebuhr, more than in C. S. Lewis, that McColley finds a parallel vision.

Like McColley's essay, the last three deal with Williams's discursive prose. Through a close analysis of the style of *The Forgiveness of Sins*—the unusual ways Williams employs adjectives, metaphors, and the structural devices of parenthesis and antithesis—B. L. Horne identifies a "peculiar density" of style: Williams here is writing prose like a poet. It is a style carefully crafted to reinforce his correspondingly "dense" theological vision, with its uncompromising rejection of dualism. Jared Lobdell, on the other hand, deals with a very prosaic sort of literary criticism, the outpouring of book reviews by which Williams supplemented his income for about five years in the early 1930s. Lobdell's study has a double focus: on Williams's ability, as a reviewer of detective fiction for the popular press, to achieve an unusual level of serious comment, and on his understanding of the detective genre itself, as revealed in his reviews and exemplified in some of his fiction.

The prose style more typically found in Williams's literary criticism, however, was a style markedly poetic in quality. Diane Edwards shows how perfectly that rhetorical choice accords with his conception of poetry, which he valued for its power to reveal vision and put readers in touch with the numinous. Analysis and theory, necessary as they might be, are inevitably reductive; a higher role for the critic is to reenact, within his or her own frame of reference, the poet's visionary experience. Edwards sees an incarnational principle at work: poetry (to adapt the Athanasian formula which Williams was fond of quoting) is not brought down by the critic to the everyday world, but the everyday world is elevated to the realm of the divine which poetry represents.

The arrangement of the essays in this book according to the genres with which they deal requires us, if we are to appreciate the unity of Williams's *oeuvre* in respect to both vision and rhetoric, to make a special effort in tracing recurrent themes. One strand is the incarnational, sacramental, monistic, and antireductionistic nature of Williams's vision, with the idea of coinherence at its center. Another is his concern for affect and his tendency to adopt a poetic stance, even when writing prose; another, his commitment to skepticism, ambiguity, multivalence, and paradox. In listing these themes it becomes impossible to distinguish sharply which ones have to do with Williams's rhetoric and which with his vision; indeed, a fourth key theme of the whole collection is Williams's striving for, and achieving, a rhetoric

24   CHARLES A. HUTTAR

that would not only communicate, but itself embody, his vision. Which might, in a world where the rapport between speaker and audience is not immediate and therefore rhetoric is still required, be as near as rhetoric can get to becoming honest. Manipulative it remains, but not isolated from veridical or moral concern.

Moreover, if rhetoric is inescapably manipulative, Charles Williams at least resisted the more obvious temptations by purposely employing off-putting strategies that would allow unwilling readers an easy escape. He must have known that many readers would encounter his vision with hostility or indifference—for the culture characterized at mid-century by Dorothy L. Sayers was equally that of Williams's time and is still recognizable today: "a world which, with greater ease of communications, is rapidly losing its coinherence, and which, while insistently making larger demands upon life, appears at times most singularly lacking in largesse"—and that because of this hostility or indifference, his vision, although, as Sayers says, "traditional and perennial," not private, would have little chance of commanding prompt and widespread assent.[21] Such assent might be sought at the cost of the vision itself—an unacceptable price: given the complexity of the vision, a rhetoric that made it more casually accessible would be a betrayal. Nor did Williams care about the trivial activity of preaching to the already converted. Thus he adopted instead the risky course of a "presentation . . . so individual as at a first encounter to disconcert, perplex, or even antagonise" many; still, there would be those "on whom it [would] break as a sudden light to them who had sat in darkness."[22] That sudden rapport marks, perhaps, a stage (momentary, at least) beyond rhetoric. If one's vision is, in its fullest realization, "beyond the resources of language,"[23] then failures are perhaps no disgrace, nor should rhetoric receive all the credit for successes. Still, rhetoric will have had a role in finding those readers who are capable of response: the moment of grace requires the cooperation of art. That artistry is what the essays which follow explore.

21. Dorothy L. Sayers, introduction to *James I,* by Charles Williams, 2d ed. (London: Arthur Barker, 1951), xiii, ix. Some of the strong negative responses to Williams are cataloged by Curtis, "Reputation," 127–31, 140–45.

22. Sayers, introduction to *James I,* ix.

23. Eliot, introduction to *All Hallows' Eve,* xi. As Williams himself understood: "The fear is in making statements about God. There both the possibility of truth and the possibility of communication fail. Neither rhetoric nor meiosis will serve; the kingdom of heaven will not be defined by inexact terms, and exact terms. . . . Exact terms! It is not altogether surprising that we are driven back sometimes on irony" (*FS,* 2; ellipsis points in original). In a slightly different context, he wrote: "All that can be hoped [for] is . . . a not too incorrect approximation" ("The Cross" [1943], in *Image,* 131).

PART I

Fiction

The Athanasian Principle
in Williams's Use of Images

Stephen Medcalf

One, not by conversion of the Godhead into flesh:
but by taking of the Manhood into God.

Throughout Charles Williams's writings appears, in various forms, the sense that everything and every person is haunted by its own perfection; that that perfection not only is possible but exists actually; and that in certain states of consciousness, conspicuously—but by no means only—in falling in love, we are immediately aware of the perfect forms of things, of other people, and of ourselves. Williams was clear that there is an analogy to the incarnation in this. One of his earliest notes, for example, is "The incarnation-like love in a lady's eyes, localising and unifying the whole face,"[1] and in his early poems and in the little book *Outlines of Romantic Theology*[2] he tried to develop such intuitions into detailed comparisons between the process of falling in love and the life of Christ from Annunciation to Resurrection. Some of this can appear grotesque and mistakenly concrete, in the way that he calls in his later Arthurian poetry "Caucasian"; but some of it makes good sense.

Williams was, of course, well aware that he was not the discoverer of either these experiences or the theory he attaches to them, and that the experiences are perhaps universally human, while the theory goes back at least to Plato, in particular to his *Symposium* and *Phaedrus*.[3] In the *Symposium* Socrates completes a set of descriptions, by various people, of love, with a description of falling in love as the means by which we recognize what *kalos* 'beautiful, good-as-attractive' actually is in one person, after which, and only after which, we can recognize it wherever it exists, whether in

---

1. Williams, Arthurian Commonplace Book (c. 1911 onward). Oxford, Bodleian Library, MS. Eng. e. 2012.

2. Williams, *Outlines of Romantic Theology*, ed. A. M. Hadfield (Grand Rapids, Mich.: Eerdmans, 1990). The date of composition was 1924.

3. *Symposium,* especially 201D–12C; *Phaedrus,* especially 244A–57A.

people, or in physical objects, or in laws and institutions, never losing the passionate excitement it arouses, until finally in a mystical flash we perceive the beautiful itself. To Socrates' speech, itself powerfully attractive, everyone who has previously spoken assents, except Aristophanes, who however is prevented from speaking by a noise of knocking and flute playing as Alcibiades enters, drunk, to talk about his own amorous relations with Socrates. This may be a hint on Plato's part that more attention could be paid to Aristophanes' earlier speech, which is indeed incompatible with Socrates', although in its own way as attractive. For Aristophanes' theory is that in our present state every individual is really only a half-individual, the result of Zeus' division of beings twice as strong as we are, in case we should conquer heaven: each half is now in quest of the other, union with whom is love. In this theory, the union of two people is the consummation of love, whereas for Socrates that union is something to be transcended in the search for what was revealed in it.

That these two theories represent a permanently valid tension may be seen in connection with Charles Williams in Lois Lang-Sims's account of her relation with him, *Letters to Lalage,*[4] incorporating his letters to her, and in the still more poignant book which Williams's friend C. S. Lewis wrote after the death of his wife, Joy Lewis, *A Grief Observed.*[5]

In quite another sense, the Platonic tension probably influenced, and was resolved in, the doctrine of the incarnation itself. Jesus is understood as the one person love for whom is not left behind by the achievement of the mystical perception of the beautiful-in-itself, that is God, and the one person in whom dwelt all the fullness of the Godhead bodily. But even in the case of Christ, the resolution is achieved by the formula which Williams thought governed all the analogous cases also, the formula of the Athanasian Creed that God and Man were united "not by conversion of the Godhead into flesh: but by taking of the Manhood into God." The technical reason for this formula was probably to ensure that there was no danger of believing that God was altered by the incarnation. God is not made less perfect, but humanity has open to it the possibility of perfection. God is not divided into the moments of time, but humanity is made conscious of the fullness of eternity. God is not subjected to mechanical causation, but humanity fulfills God's purpose. Christ's humanity has all the limitations of humanity—is subjected to chance, compulsion, ignorance, and death—but it is taken into God, and with it, if we accept the possibility, so are we.

4. Lang-Sims, ed., *Letters to Lalage* (Kent, Ohio, and London: Kent State University Press, 1989).

5. N. W. Clerk [pseud. for C. S. Lewis], *A Grief Observed* (London: Faber and Faber, 1961).

ATHANASIAN PRINCIPLE IN WILLIAMS'S USE OF IMAGES   29

The Gospels have various ways of expressing this situation—the mystery of Mark, the explicit fulfillment of prophecy of Matthew, the exaltation of human motive of Luke, and the symbolism of John that draws into itself the physical circumstances surrounding Jesus, above all, light. If we may revert to the *Symposium,* these are all ways of doing justice both to Socrates' sense of the difference, transcendence, and perfection of the beautiful-in-itself and to Aristophanes' sense of perfecting the individual and personal without putting anything aside.

Since Williams believed in the analogy between the incarnation and the haunting of everything and every person by its own perfection, we may comparably expect to find in his writing various ways of expressing that haunting. In fact, in their way of dealing with the dialectic of perfection and the individual, his novels fall into three groups, not only formally but chronologically.

The first group, *Shadows of Ecstasy, War in Heaven,* and *Many Dimensions,* was composed between 1925 and 1930. (Although *Shadows of Ecstasy* was not published until 1932 and was then heavily revised, it was the first written, and the revision does not seem to have changed its essential themes.[6]) In this first group, a part of the natural which is particularly transparent to the supernatural (either poetry, or the means of religious ritual, that is the Grail, or the means of magical ritual, that is the Stone of Solomon) grows huge and monstrous and invades the rest of the natural.

In the second group, those written from 1931 to 1932,[7] *The Place of the Lion* and *The Greater Trumps,* Williams uses mechanisms of expression close to Platonism. The whole nature of reality as we know it is threatened by the entry into the level of ordinary experience of the principles that ordinarily undergird and pattern it. They are something like the archetypes of Plato, although neither their common nature nor the list of their separate characteristics corresponds exactly with those. In *The Place of the Lion,* there are said to be nine principles, corresponding to the nine orders of angels, principles which are more or less purely revealed in the kinds of animals but are combined and united in man. It is man's business to rule them, as is imagined in the myth of Adam naming the beasts, or else to put them all utterly away, to return to the unimaginable and unimaged beyond them. But they are never fully listed in the novel. They are grouped as four, one, and four. The first four are manifested as strength, beauty, subtlety, and speed: the lion, the butterfly, the serpent, and the horse. The one is balance, the eagle. Beyond it are a more mysterious four, of which

---

6. A. M. Hadfield, *Charles Williams, An Exploration of His Life and Work* (Oxford and New York: Oxford University Press, 1983), 45–46, 81–82, 92–93, 96–97.

7. Hadfield, *Exploration,* 93–99.

only three are named: the lamb, which is innocence, balances the lion; the phoenix, which is "the life of truth . . . momently consumed, momently reborn," corresponds to the serpent, though also in some way to the eagle, which is "the measure of truth"; and the unicorn, which seems to be the speed of return from the whole world of images to the unimaged, balances the horse (*PL,* 159, 256–59, and passim [the quotations are from 257]). Other beasts correspond further with these nine as their corruptions—the dragon with the lion, the pterodactyl with the eagle. Nothing seems to be mentioned (either among the principles beyond the eagle or among the corruptions) that corresponds to the butterfly, yet, as suits with beauty, of all the epiphanies that of the butterfly is given the finest and most detailed description. But the power of the book is inseparable from its sense of only partly, though richly, revealing mysteries, of which the four beyond the eagle are the most removed from everyday and active life.

In *The Greater Trumps,* the world is a dance, a dance revealed in shapes made by some man long ago "for resemblance and for communication," each of them "some step, some conjunction, some—what we call a fact— that is often repeated in the infinite combinations" (*GT,* 118). These shapes are the four suits, each with its four court cards, and the twenty trumps of the Tarot pack; they are more defined and more richly detailed than the principles of *The Place of the Lion* and seem only incidentally to correspond with them. *The Place of the Lion* is the more heraldic and medieval—there is a grand simplicity about the animals in it, which are also emblems, like that of the medieval Bestiary. *The Greater Trumps* is more alchemical, hieroglyphic, Renaissance, wisdom reached through accumulation and intricacy of signs, as befits the Tarot pack, which is indeed probably a creation of the early Renaissance. Both books embody the opposition of the *Symposium* between vision of a principle and personal love, and the opposition is felt as that tension which Plato avoids. For in both novels what is primarily threatened by the invasion of the principles is the existence of persons and of personal relations, and in both novels the principles are finally returned to their place by someone motivated by love for particular people, while those who devote themselves to the principles do it at the expense of personal relation.

But there is a difference here, which begins by being a contrast of Old Testament to New. Anthony the restorer in *The Place of the Lion* is compared to Adam naming the beasts (277–86), Nancy in *The Greater Trumps* to Messias, Christ, (287), in his self-sacrifice. Anthony, therefore, simply restores the work of Adam and reestablishes the world as we know it by understanding, and therefore controlling, its principles. He is seen in a vision as Adam in Paradise with the animals about him (*PL,* 281–82), but we are not asked to explore the relation between the present-day Anthony and primeval Adam any further. But at the end of *The Greater Trumps*

ATHANASIAN PRINCIPLE IN WILLIAMS'S USE OF IMAGES   31

there is a new revelation: something that could never be understood from the Tarot pack itself—the function of the most fundamental of the Trumps, the Fool—is revealed as the Fool appears himself, "all-reconciling and perfect" (*GT,* 285). In the Tarot scheme, he is like the beautiful-itself in the *Symposium* and the unmoved Mover who is God in Aristotle's picture of the world: he may be the center of everything, but he moves the world, if he does, by being loved rather than loving; he does not move. But in the end of the novel, his appearance is simultaneous both with the destruction of the magical appearances of the Tarot principles round which the novel is built and with the realization that there is in Nancy something of his power to move. The end of the book is, as it were, a note that from now on the exploration of the relation of natural to supernatural in Williams's novels must be carried on not in the world of objects, of things outside a human personality, but within some human personality like Nancy's. It is a close approximation to the incarnation and even is like the effect of the incarnation in history; the divine is no longer to be apprehended by epiphanies appearing in and through the objects of the world, or not only so, but also within the human mind and heart.

This is in fact what the remaining pair of novels explores. The haunting of things by their own perfections does still have an objective embodiment in *Descent into Hell,* in the place where it is set, a satellite of London called Battle Hill, which closely corresponds to Charles Williams's own childhood home of St. Albans. It is haunted by its history, its destruction by Boadicea, a battle in the Wars of the Roses, the death of a Marian martyr, and through these mortalities by the hill of Calvary itself. The world the other side of death is very close in Battle Hill. But the haunting central to the plot is that of a girl called Pauline, literally by herself, by a doppelgänger which has been drawing nearer to her as her life has gone on and which she is terrified of one day meeting. In the secondary plot a man (Lawrence Wentworth) beginning with advancing middle age to withdraw into himself parodies Pauline's situation by adoring what he persuades himself is the perfect form of another girl, Adela, although it is nothing but a projection of himself, a kind of other self, a *succubus.* It is the only novel in which Williams does not use magic—in the sense of ritual techniques and objects intended to procure power for their employers—as part of the machinery of expression. It is no accident that, in most readers' view, it probably is by far his best novel, not because it avoids offending twentieth-century habits of mind in requiring imaginative belief in magic—for in the end, there are events in *Descent into Hell* fully as strange as the magic of the other novels (the existence of the succubus, the behavior of the Marian martyr on a day in the 1550s being affected by the choice of his descendant Pauline on a night in the 1930s)—but because it avoids the artistic dangers

STEPHEN MEDCALF

of magic in offering the novelist shortcuts. Williams has done harder work in establishing a self-consistent world in *Descent into Hell* than he does in any of the other novels, and the result is felt in its much greater power.

This is true even in comparison with his last novel, *All Hallows' Eve,* which he assured his publisher T. S. Eliot "went on from the point at which *Descent into Hell* left off."[8] It undoubtedly does this: it penetrates deeply into the world beyond death, whose borders appeared in *Descent into Hell;* the relation of the city of London to its unearthly counterpart is more extensively and more powerfully developed than is the double nature of Battle Hill; and the haunting by a person's other self is most powerfully rendered by the development of an earthly self into a self ready for heaven. It is a disturbingly powerful book: taken in isolation, its first chapter is possibly more powerful than any other passage in Williams's novels. Nevertheless, *All Hallows' Eve* as a whole is not quite so powerful or consistent as *Descent into Hell,* in part because too much is taken for granted and not enough is done about aspects of the magician's power. Yet the magician is a powerfully drawn figure, and the means of his defeat is interestingly related to the very objection that magic is an aesthetic shortcut. For circumstances oblige him to use techniques which are not appropriate to him— crude acts which are said to be, in the terms of magic, shortcuts—and his inability to control these brings him down (*AHE,* 182–83).

Analogously, the reliance on formulae is primarily what hinders Williams from being quite as great a writer as his insight and imagination demand. It is a weakness apparent in areas other than his use of magic. Even in *Descent into Hell,* for example, the phrase "the Republic" assumes a weight of meaning and an intricacy of context which simply do not exist for someone who has not read a number of his other books. That is, it is present to him but not established by the context of the novel itself nor given in common language; therefore it is a denial of the very sense of community and shared usage and constitution that the phrase "the Republic" conveyed for him.

In *War in Heaven,* the chat of a clergyman called Batesby imports to parish councils "a high eternal flavour which savoured of Deity Itself." That they were "taken into God was normal and proper: what else . . . could one do with parish councils? But . . . to Mr. Batesby they were opportunities for converting the Godhead rather firmly and finally into flesh" (*WH,* 62–63). Mr. Batesby's temptation is one to which Williams himself is subject: his visions become for him embodied in certain words, and the words sometimes substitute themselves for the visions. It will be

---

8. Quoted in Hadfield, *Exploration,* 228.

profitable now to see how in some of his greater passages he rises above this temptation.

We may begin with one of his most memorable pieces of writing, the vision of the butterflies in *The Place of the Lion.* It is perhaps his most Platonic passage, if we interpret it as we would the myths at the end of the *Phaedo* or the *Republic,* as a story that in literal reality is almost but not quite possible and that in symbolic expression is intended as the probable truth. Since in the scheme of the book the butterfly corresponds to beauty, it is an expression of the vision of the beautiful, close to that in the *Symposium.* T. S. Eliot observed, with special reference to "certain passages in *The Place of the Lion,*" that Williams "knew, and could put into words, states of consciousness of a mystical kind, and the sort of elusive experience which many people have once or twice in a life-time."[9] This passage may well be one of those he has in mind, and indeed the sense in it of a garden in autumnal heat and color, where a dislocation of reality might and does occur, calls to mind the first movement of Eliot's own *Burnt Norton.* It has no audible music such as that found in *Burnt Norton;* few words draw attention to themselves, there is no patterning of vowels and consonants, the rhythms are prosaic, and even the syntax is simple and mostly additive, though it slightly increases in complexity where speed is expressed. In short, it is simple prose, and its power is in what it describes. What is described is, however, more patterned, in three movements separated by Anthony, the observer, twice turning his attention from the behavior of the butterflies to the ecstatic reaction of the butterfly collector, Mr. Tighe.

There is first an introduction, which begins with a discussion about the subduing of the rest of the beasts to man, with Mr. Tighe's expression of regret that their independent manifestation of the qualities of the universe should vanish, although Anthony suggests that all these qualities exist sufficiently in humanity. This vanishing is reflected visually in the garden, although we are first reminded that we have already seen a vision of strength rising out of human control in the form of a lion, and are thus prepared for the realization that what has happened in the garden is the removal not only of strength but of beauty. Beauty is beginning to exist by itself, the very reversal of Mr. Tighe's fears:

> Anthony's eyes, passing over the garden, remained fixed where, two nights before, he had thought he saw the form of a lion. It seemed to him now, as he gazed, that a change had taken place. The smooth grass of the lawn was far less green than it had been, and the flowers in the beds by the house walls, on either side of the door, were either dying or already withered. Certainly he had not

---

9. T. S. Eliot, introduction to *All Hallows' Eve,* by Charles Williams (New York: Pellegrini & Cudahy, 1948), xvii.

been in a state to notice much, but there had been left with him a general impression of growth and colour. Neither growth nor colour were now there: all seemed parched. Of course, it was hot, but still. . . .

There was a sudden upward sweep of green and orange through the air in front of him: he blinked and moved. As he recovered himself he saw, with startled amazement, that in the centre of the garden, almost directly above the place where he had seen the lion, there floated a butterfly. But—a butterfly! It was a terrific, colossal butterfly, it looked as if it were two feet or more across from wing-tip to wing-tip. It was tinted and coloured with every conceivable brightness; green and orange predominating. It was moving upward in spiral flutterings, upward to a certain point, from which it seemed directly to fall close to the ground, then again it began its upward sweep, and again hovered and fell. Of the two men it seemed to be unaware; lovely and self-sufficient it went on with its complex manoeuvres in the air. Anthony, after a few astonished minutes, took his eyes from it, and looked about him, first with a general gaze at all his surroundings, then more particularly at Mr. Tighe. The little man was pressed against the gate, his mouth slightly open, his eyes full of plenary adoration, his whole being concentrated on the perfect symbol of his daily concern. Anthony saw that it was no good speaking to him. He looked back at the marvel in time to see, from somewhere above his own head, another brilliancy—but much smaller—flash through the air, almost as if some ordinary butterfly had hurled itself towards its more gigantic image. And another followed it, and another, and as Anthony, now thoroughly roused, sprang up and aside, to see the better, he beheld the air full of them. Those of which he had caught sight were but the scattered first comers of a streaming host. Away across the fields they came, here in thick masses, there in thinner lines, white and yellow, green and red, purple and blue and dusky black. They were sweeping round, in great curving flights; mass following after mass, he saw them driving forward from far away, but not directly, taking wide distances in their sweep, now on one side, now on another, but always and all of them speeding forward towards the gate and the garden beyond. Even as a sudden new rush of aerial loveliness reached that border he turned his head, and saw a cloud of them hanging high above the butterfly of the garden, which rushed up towards them, and then, carrying a whirl of lesser iridescent fragilities with it, precipitated itself down its steep descent; and as it swept, and hovered, and again mounted, silent and unresting, it was alone. Alone it went soaring up, alone to meet another congregation of its hastening visitors, and then again multitudinously fell, and hovered; and again alone went upward to the tryst.

Bewildered and distracted, Anthony caught his companion's arm. Mr. Tighe was by now almost hanging to the gate, his hands clutching frenziedly to the topmost bar, his jaws working. Noises were coming from his mouth; the sweat stood in the creases of his face. He gobbled at the soft-glowing vision; he uttered little cries and pressed himself against the bars; his knees were wedged between them, and his feet drawn from the ground in the intensity of his apprehension. And over him faster and thicker the great incursion passed, and the air over the garden was filled with butterflies, streaming, rising, sinking, hovering, towards

ATHANASIAN PRINCIPLE IN WILLIAMS'S USE OF IMAGES 35

their centre, and faster now than Anthony's eyes could see the single host of all that visitation rose and fell, only whenever he saw it towards the ground, it turned upwards in a solitary magnificence and whenever, having risen, it dropped again, it went encircled by innumerable tiny bodies and wings.

Credulous, breathless, he gazed, until after times unreckoned had passed, there seemed to be a stay. Lesser grew the clouds above; smaller the flights that joined them. Now there were but a score and now but twelve or ten—now only three tardy dancers waited above for the flight of their vision; and as again it rose, but one—coming faster than all the rest, reaching its strange assignation as it were at the last permitted moment, joining its summoning lord as it rose for the last time, and falling with it; and then the great butterfly of the garden floated idly in the empty air, and the whole army of others had altogether vanished from sight, and from knowledge. It also after a short while rose, curvetting, passed upward towards the roof of the house, settled there for a moment, a glowing splendour upon the red tiles, swept beyond it, and disappeared.

Anthony moved and blinked, took a step or two away, looked round him, blinked again, and turned back to Mr. Tighe. He was about to speak, but, seeing the other man's face, he paused abruptly. The tears were running down it; as his hands released the bars Anthony saw that he was trembling all over; he stumbled and could not get his footing upon the road. Anthony caught and steadied him.

"O glory, glory," Mr. Tighe said. "O glory everlasting!" (*PL*, 52–56; ellipsis points in original)

The first movement begins with a positive contrast to the withering of the garden—"a sudden upward sweep of green and orange"—the colors, I take it, suggesting what has gone out of the grass and autumnal flowers—marigolds, probably. This glimpse is focused, intensified, and defined in something monstrous in size, intense in color, and moving definedly in "complex manoeuvres" between two points, in a ritual motion. Color and motion together make it "lovely and self-sufficient." The first movement ends with Mr. Tighe's adoration.

The next movement begins with the everyday equivalents of the monstrous thing, ordinary butterflies providing a visual equivalent for Mr. Tighe's adoration, as the withered garden had for his regret. These butterflies again are first seen in a flash, and again first color and then purposive movement follow the flash, but now in multitudes. Their movement unites itself with the top point of the ritual of "the butterfly of the garden," whose motion now takes on a fuller meaning—that is, drawing them in, for at the end of the downward movement "it was alone." The ritual is repeated, in a description that is more concise but that, unusually, marks its culmination with a word, "tryst," which draws attention to itself by its archaism. The second movement ends in Mr. Tighe's adoration again, now intensified into something grotesque, even comic.

The third movement repeats the ritual, its purposiveness now more fully recognized in such words as "centre," "dancers," and "assignation," until

36 STEPHEN MEDCALF

everything being done there is a third and culminating visual flash, shifted to the end of the movement as the single butterfly settles on the roof "a glowing splendour upon the red tiles." And we return to Mr. Tighe, recovering from and summing up his adoration, at once splendid and comic. The introduction, which showed Mr. Tighe as more receptive than we are, is balanced by an epilogue which suggests that he has understood more of what has happened in the interim than we have. "I always knew they were real, but to think I should see them," he says. "See the kingdom and the power and the glory" (*PL,* 57).

What then have we been reading? The analogy with Plato's myths, and Eliot's praise of Williams's capacity to put rare and elusive experience into words, suggest that the passage describes a vision which even as a vision need not have happened exactly like that, and which could be described in more literal and philosophical, although less adequate, words. The words I have in mind are Williams's own, when he describes, in his book *Witchcraft,* one of the experiences that, before the remotest suggestion of formulae, predispose toward the concept of magic. There, however, he speaks not of animals but of "the human body, and the movements of the human body. Even now, when, as a general rule, the human body is not supposed to mean anything, there are moments when it seems, in spite of ourselves, packed with significance. . . . Here, one is aware that a phenomenon, being wholly itself, is laden with universal meaning. A hand lighting a cigarette is the explanation of everything; a foot stepping from a train is the rock of all existence."[10]

What the vision of the butterfly describes is extended into sequences in time and multitudes in space, while the definition in *Witchcraft* is intense, single, and momentary. But they seem to be the same kind of experience, perhaps, too, the same kind as those which Plato has in mind in the *Symposium,* although Plato is not concerned with the phenomenon's "being wholly itself" but only with its being "laden with universal meaning." He connects the experience, in fact, with his theory of how we form concepts and universal class names, whereas Williams, more attractively to romantic and modern sensibility, tries to leave it as purely an experience as possible, while still trying to fit it into all our other experiences.

The attention to the phenomenon's "being wholly itself" is perhaps again remotely due to the influence of the idea of the incarnation. Williams's way of acknowledging that here, too, we should try to move our ideas in the direction of taking the manhood into God, is by fitting the experience into ritual. (He tried to do the same, it may be noted, with the complexities of

10. Williams, *Witchcraft* (London: Faber and Faber, 1941), 77–78.

ATHANASIAN PRINCIPLE IN WILLIAMS'S USE OF IMAGES 37

personal relation in which he found himself, as can be studied in *Letters to Lalage.*) He goes on in *Witchcraft:*

> But if the human body is capable of seeming so, so are the controlled movements of the human body—ritual movements, or rather movements that seem like ritual. A finger pointing is quite capable of seeming not only a significant finger, but a ritual finger; an evocative finger; not only a finger of meaning, but a finger of magic. Two light dancing steps by a girl may (if one is in that state) appear to be what all the Schoolmen were trying to express; they are (only one cannot quite catch it) an intellectual statement of beatitude. But two quiet steps by an old man may seem like the very speech of hell. Or the other way round.[11]

This sense of ritual is clearly what governs the style of the vision of the butterflies, although the deliberate unpretentiousness of the language preserves that passage from the danger of ritual, the danger of its substituting itself for what it conveys. It also governs the sense that what the butterflies are doing is itself a ritual, a dance. In *The Greater Trumps* Williams uses the image of dance as the pattern of the whole world as seen in the book, and, by using the given symbolism of the Tarot pack, takes a perilous but still successful step nearer the danger of ritual's substituting itself for meaning. In the most isolable visionary passage of the book, the phenomenon that carries meaning still remains wholly itself.

> A policeman's hand held them up. Henry gestured towards it. "Behold the Emperor," he said to Nancy.
> "You're making fun of me, my dear," she half protested.
> "Never less," he said seriously. "Look at him."
> She looked, and, whether the hours she had given to brooding over the Tarots during the last few days, partly to certify her courage to herself, had imposed their forms on her memory, or whether something in the policeman's shape and cloak under the lights of the dark street suggested it, or whether indeed something common to Emperor and Khalif, cadi and magistrate, praetor and alcalde, lictor and constable, shone before her in those lights—whichever was true, it was certainly true that for a moment she saw in that heavy official barring their way the Emperor of the Trumps, helmed, in a white cloak, stretching out one sceptred arm, as if Charlemagne, or one like him, stretched out his controlling sword over the tribes of Europe pouring from the forests and bade them pause or march as he would. The great roads ran below him, to Rome, to Paris, to Aix, to Byzantium, and the nations established themselves in cities upon them. The noise of all the pausing street came to her as the roar of many peoples; the white cloak held them by a gesture; order and law were there. It moved, it fell aside, the torrent of obedient movement rolled on, and they with it. They flashed past the helmed face, and she found that she had dropped her eyes lest she should see it. (*GT,* 67–68)

---

11. Williams, *Witchcraft,* 78.

Dangerously, the passage is introduced by simply juxtaposing the everyday reality and the given symbol with one word each, "policeman" and "Emperor." But the vague effect of light and dark that follows has a dislocating sensory effect like that of the flash of color which announces the butterfly. Nothing monstrous follows, nor the magical drawing of many into one: only the imaginative extensions of one into many, not in sequence like the one and many butterflies but simultaneously. The ritual details of costume and gesture enable a transfiguration of the thing put before us, first into the symbol of the Tarot, "helmed, in a white cloak," secondly to a semiarchetypal historic case, "stretching out one sceptred arm" like Charlemagne. There follows an accumulation of historic detail appropriate to Charlemagne; then the details of the present commonplace, the noise of the street and the costume and gesture of the policeman, are identified with those historic details. The ending is much more concise than in the vision of the butterflies: the principle behind the symbol is given at once—"order and law were there"—instead of being delayed like Mr. Tighe's "the kingdom and the power and the glory," and all the reactions of the observer who can see the vision are concentrated powerfully into the girl's dropping her eyes.

A hostile critic, Robert Conquest, has accused Williams of totalitarian instincts because he finds poetry in policemen.[12] But one is no more likely, after reading this passage, to reduce order and law to believing that a particular policeman is behaving correctly, than to worship a butterfly for embodying the kingdom, the power, and the glory, after reading the other. One is quite as likely to reflect how much particular policemen fall short of the expectations created by their rituals and costumes. The order suggested by the Athanasian Creed has been followed in the text, the particular representative of the Law has been seen as taken up into what he represents, and the Law has been preserved from being embodied in its particular representative. And the reader is little to be envied who will not enjoy butterflies and policemen the more for having read Williams, or who will not find the meaning of the world deepened.

We have, then, in both these passages and in many others in Williams's novels, the presentation of an object, wholly itself but laden with universal meaning—the tension of the one object with many others, of stillness with motion, of vague visual impressions with precise details, the use of ritual, of repeated and significant movement and costume—to hold these things together. Characteristically of Williams, the senses used are, overwhelmingly, sight and proprioception, the internal sense of structure and movement. Taste, smell, and touch are not used, and sound is subordinate to the other

12. Conquest, "The Art of the Enemy," *Essays in Criticism* 7 (1957): 55.

that the Clerk was removing; he turned, or sought to turn, words into mere vibrations" (*AHE,* 84–85). Magic thus is an attempt to convert sounds that have power because they have meaning, into sounds that retain power while deprived of meaning, which is a kind of reversal of the Athanasian formula—that is, it is like conversion of the Godhead into flesh.

The theme of the exaltation or reduction of language pervades the book in other ways. The magician, in a way akin to hypnotism, is said to speak over the daughter "those august words: 'peace, joy, love.' He used them for what he needed, and they meant to him—and to her—what he chose. . . . He wished her to be an instrument only; *peace, joy, love,* were but names for the passivity of the instrument" (*AHE,* 59–60). But, because she has in fact fallen in love, these words make, not her mind, but her body rise "against the incantation that all but appeased her" (59).

Again, one of the means of the development of a dead woman toward heaven is that a casual exclamation "Oh my God!" which had meant nothing to her in life, means something when it is used beyond death: "in this air every word meant something, meant itself; and this curious new exactitude of speech hung there like a strange language" (21). Conversely, the means by which a second dead person moves toward damnation is the use of language reductively to create a reductionist picture of the world: "she was keeping up a small continuous monologue. She did not talk of herself, but of others. The monologue was not (primarily) self-centred but mean. Men and women—all whom she had known—dwindled in it as she chattered. No-one was courteous; no-one was chaste; no-one was tender. The morning . . . grew darker and the street more sordid as she went on" (134).

It seems likely to be more than a coincidence that at the time when Williams was writing this novel, on Whitsunday 28 May 1944, C. S. Lewis, a close friend and at that time very much under his influence, preached a sermon connecting the relation of meaning to sound in speech with the maxim "not by conversion of the Godhead into flesh: but by taking of the manhood into God." Lewis called the relation, and the sermon after it, "Transposition."[14] The sermon is a remarkable piece of philosophical argument—in my own view, by far Lewis's best philosophical piece. Its starting point is the narrative in the Acts of the Apostles of speaking with tongues at Pentecost. Lewis points out that this phenomenon is evidently related to what is well known under the name *glossolalia,* which etymologically means precisely "speaking with tongues." But there is a difference in

---

14. Lewis, "Transposition," in *They Asked for a Paper* (London: G. Bles, 1962), 166–82; for date, see William Griffin, *C. S. Lewis: A Dramatic Life* (San Francisco: Harper and Row, 1986), 231.

42   STEPHEN MEDCALF

that the glossolalia at Pentecost is said to have been articulate and intelligible. Normally glossolalia is not intelligible; yet physically, and even to
some extent psychologically, it may be the same phenomenon.

Lewis draws an analogy with a passage in Samuel Pepys's *Diary* where
Pepys remarks that certain wind music has made him feel "really sick" as
he has been when in love with his wife, which makes him resolve to learn
wind music and make his wife do the same.[15] The same physical symptom, then, may signify, it appears, various responses—nausea, love,
aesthetic delight. More, the physical symptom itself becomes part of the
response: it not only signifies but is an aspect of the nausea or the delight.
It is, Lewis says, like the maxim of the Athanasian Creed because the lower
is taken into the higher. In general, he thinks, body can thus be said to be
taken up into mind. Williams has the same kind of thought in *All Hallows'
Eve,* but in a characteristically more paradoxical form: the physical action
of a certain way of throwing a hand, he says, "held something even greater
than the purpose which caused it. It was not only more than itself in its
exhibition of the mind behind it, but it was in itself more than the mind. So
killing, though it may express hate, is an utterly different thing from hate"
(*AHE,* 37). Lewis draws a further analogy with the representation, in a
plane, of three dimensions by perspective and of light by shading on white
paper. Just so, in *All Hallows' Eve,* a visionary painting of London is found
to be related to a real otherworldly London (113). Like Williams, too,
Lewis compares this transposition with the relation of value to a merely
mechanistic appetitive psychology. The sermon as a whole argues against
reductionism and for the recognition of spiritual reality.

The attack on reductionism is perhaps above all—apart from their religious feeling, of which it is an aspect—what united Lewis and Williams.
Williams in all his work is concerned that experience be taken seriously and
not be explained away—that Pauline's doppelgänger and Wentworth's auto-
erotism not be explained away by being absorbed in a causal psychological
explanation but that they be understood as genuine objects of justified fear
and hope, that the phenomenon that is wholly itself while expressing
universal meaning not be dismissed as subjective, merely aesthetic, an
epiphenomenon, but that it be understood in its own terms.

These insistences are part of Williams's belief in the Athanasian formula.
It follows for him that experiences of the transcendent must be taken as
leading us beyond the world of immediate experience. The picture of
London by Jonathan Drayton in *All Hallows' Eve,* a picture perhaps somewhat like those of Paul Nash, begins by seeming too bright, but it presently

15. Lewis, "Transposition," 169: Samuel Pepys, *Diary,* 27 February 1668.

enables Richard Furnival to see the actual London "illustrious with being" (*AH,* 113). Yet this is only the minor part of its work. In the whole book it is recognized as a gateway to the London that surrounds London, the London of the past and future of the city we know, the London of its dead; and that London, too, is recognized as only an aspect of the world of coinherence and of further transcendent things. In its last mention, the vision of the City of London is associated with the vision of the Grail; the blood of human history, the blood of London's history, is seen as the blood in the Grail, and the City beyond London is seen in the blood:

> As if she looked down a great distance she saw a small pool crimson in the light, and that too vanishing, till it was no more than the level of dark wine in a wine cup, and within it, before it vanished, she saw the whole City through which she had so often passed, vivid and real in that glowing richness. But she lost that sight as she realized that the City opened all ways about her and the hall in which she stood, in which also the daylight now visibly expanded. She heard the early noises of London outside the hall. (202)

The vision looks in both directions, to the London we see and to the heaven that vanishes out of sight. But it moves in only one direction: London is apprehended as an aspect of heaven, not heaven of London. This is the direction of all Williams's writing.

Language and Meaning
in the Novels of Charles Williams

Alice E. Davidson

Charles Williams's theory of language is central to his art. It leads him to be even more reverently respectful of language than are most serious novelists, and even more concerned with verbal precision. For he believed that language is no mere set of historically evolved signs related with varying degrees of arbitrariness to their accepted meanings. He believed language is intrinsically meaningful. Words—key words, at least—*are* what they mean. What they mean, moreover, is often more than material or psychological; it is spiritual, transcendent, and even divine. So language is, in a sense, sacramental. Verbal precision is a matter not just of aesthetics, but of morality and religion. Language is a sacred coinage, a medium for the exchange of meaning to which Dante, whom Williams greatly admired, pays tribute in *The Divine Comedy* (e.g., *Inferno,* 30.91–129). The relationship between a word and its meaning is not arbitrary but intrinsic. To emphasize this point, Williams not only slows his narrative to work for extreme verbal precision but also often focuses his narrative explicitly on the subject of verbal precision. It becomes at once his message and his medium. He also pushes language, at times, to acrobatic extremes wherein the brilliant and the merely precious sometimes jostle nervously side by side; but overall he achieves a rare degree of subtlety and accuracy.

All this, of course, has much to do with the special flavor of Williams's style. In his books we feel as if we had stepped into the spiritual milieu of *All Hallows' Eve:* "In this air every word meant something, meant itself; and this curious new exactitude of speech hung there like a strange language" (*AHE,* 21).

Readers unfamiliar with Williams can as a result easily miss his point—even, perhaps, when he tips his hand by conspicuously correcting and refining his own use of language. At one point in *War in Heaven* we are given this description of Gregory Persimmons's inner state: "By the afternoon, however, Gregory had recovered his balance, or, rather, his intention" (*WH,* 175). The distinction might seem in many a novel rather casual and minor. In this novel it is crucial and cosmic. "Balance" means for

Williams more than a simple state of coordinated physical or mental poise. It refers to a dynamic, multidimensional harmony of one's being that incorporates a transcendent, sustaining spiritual harmony. This is what we find in the always equable Archdeacon. He is poised at a center. In contrast, Gregory is manifestly *off*-balance, careening forward. "Intention" more accurately indicates an assertive momentum easily confused with steadiness of being.

Such degrees of precision make possible Williams's frequently delightful double entendre and irony as well as his remarkably exact rendering of states of mind and soul. In *Descent into Hell* he has the narrator make this nice distinction: "[Wentworth] found the thought of the Adela of past days a little disagreeable—no longer troublesome or joyous but merely disagreeable" (*DH,* 179). Williams conveys Wentworth's retreat into himself by means of this explicit definitional contrast. A genuine relationship may be—indeed must, at times, be—troublesome as well as joyous, because one is involved in it and lets it get inside where it can trouble one's inner world. But the actual Adela (in contrast to the convenient imaginary Adela he sleeps with) intrudes upon him now only from without. He keeps her at a distance; he cannot be inwardly troubled.

Naturally Williams, like other novelists, uses his characters' speech as a principal method of characterization. But again he goes a little further. His characters often revise their remarks just as he revises his own; and they, too, stop and examine their words, so that their medium becomes, for the moment, their main preoccupation. Moreover, language, as we have noted, is for Williams transcendent. Its reference is cosmic. So a character's relationship to language sometimes rises to the level of a major symbol revealing various stages of his spiritual career.

In *War in Heaven,* the Archdeacon's relationship to language is stable and balanced, just as he is. In contrast, Mr. Batesby reveals his intellectual poverty by missing the accuracy of language so necessary to the proper functioning of intellect and the achievement of truth—and of morality (cf. *WH,* 76).

For other characters the lack, or willful neglect, of verbal integrity is more crucial and ominous. Without a constant striving for verbal integrity, Williams seems to say, language drifts inevitably into increasing inaccuracy and eventual dissolution. It thus becomes both vehicle and symbol of damnation.

The scholar Wentworth, in *Descent into Hell,* moves swiftly from carelessness of meaning to deliberate lies and deceit to imbecility. A historian, he betrays his profession when he begins to manipulate words and meanings in his sources in order to refute his rival and further his own reputation. These first manipulations are so slight they could perhaps be rationalized as close, subtle analysis and individual interpretation. But they soon lead Wentworth to retreat altogether from troublesome fact to comfortable illusion—both humanly and professionally. Ultimately he is capable only of confused mumbling and can no longer even recognize his name (*DH,* 302). Wentworth's hell is in fact meaninglessness, know-nothingness. He arrives here by betraying that coinage of exchange, language, which is a God-given vehicle for meaning. He betrays the word.

When, in *All Hallows' Eve,* Evelyn wails, "I haven't done *anything,*" she condemns herself, for it is literally true that she has never accomplished anything worthwhile. The narrator says her "own justification was [her] only, and worst, accusation" (*AHE,* 20). She finds her only relief in babbling: she keeps up a petty, inane, complaining monologue by which she determines what the City will be for her: increasingly dark and sordid (134). So we all help to determine our own cities.

The preternaturally evil characters in the novels grossly falsify language and endure the inevitable results. After attaching to words like "comfort," "safety," and "happiness" the counterfeit meanings of dreams and the flight from fact into illusion (e.g., *DH,* 80-81), Lily Sammile is reduced to "meaningless gabble, such gabble as Dante, inspired, attributes to the guardian of all the circles of hell" (285).

Simon in *All Hallows' Eve* shows us the same progress toward imbecility. The Clerk distorts words for his own ends, most notably as he preaches a new gospel of "love" where the word *love* without its essential idea of interchange, of relation, has lost all meaning. He uses words like *peace, joy,* and *love* "for what he needed, and they meant to him . . . what he chose" (*AHE,* 59). Additionally, as an adept, Simon can manipulate the sounds that make language possible into mere vibrations devoid of meaning: his pronunciation, by "denying accents and stresses" that permit not only distinctions but communication, "was removing meaning itself from the words" (84). Williams then places the Clerk's efforts in a larger metaphysical context: the biblical idea of "the Word" as operative in creation and the redemption of creation. Simon thinks that if he can reverse that "final Jewish word of power," the Tetragrammaton (the four consonants making up God's unpronounceable name, *Yahweh*), he will reverse the order of creation, thus achieving absolute control in this world and beyond (85). The result is the destruction of meaning, and ultimately he can only contemplate his "creation," images of himself: "he stared at them, imbecile; imbecile, they stared back" (201). This is Williams's version of Dante's circle in hell for the falsifiers of words (*Inferno,* 30).

The alternative Williams offers to this ultimate imbecility is the heightened meaning actually present and discoverable in language. As we have already noted, the shadowy City of the dead calls a new, sometimes devastating precision down upon its inhabitants. So with Lester's "Oh my

LANGUAGE AND MEANING

God!" about which the narrator says:

> It was the kind of casual exclamation she and Richard had been in the habit of throwing about all over the place. . . . She had never thought it meant anything. But in this air every word meant something, meant itself; and this curious new exactitude of speech hung there like a strange language, as if she had sworn in Spanish or Pushtu, and the oath had echoed into an invocation. . . . Her mouth was uttering its own habits, but the meaning of those habits was not her own. . . . This was how they talked, and it was a great precise prehistoric language forming itself out of the noises their mouths made. She articulated the speech of Adam or Seth or Noah, and only dimly recognized the intelligibility of it. (*AHE,* 20–21)

Williams here points directly to his views as to the primal reality and power of language.

Again, Lester out of habit expresses her frustration by exclaiming, "Hell!"—and the narrator comments: "The word ran from her in all directions, as if a dozen small animals had been released and gone racing away" (*AHE,* 74). Whatever she consciously means, the word has its own true effect, its real force is unleashed.

Thus Williams insists that a word has power to call up the reality it names. When Lester utters the name of her husband, *Richard,* a word whose meaning she knows because she knows intimately the reality behind it, the physical and emotional being called Richard, she utters

> the only word common to her and the City in which she stood. As she spoke, she almost saw his face, himself saying something, and she thought she would have understood that meaning, for his face was part of the meaning, as it always had been, and she had lived with that meaning—loved, desired, denounced it. Something intelligible and great loomed and was gone. (*AHE,* 21)

Additionally, of course, a word gets real power for particular people through their associations and from their own intellectual perspective, distorted, limited as it may be. Furthermore, and more extraordinarily, the word not only *means* this individual referent, it *is* that referent in a way that *symbol* (merely representational) cannot be, but *image* can. For Williams the word is image. As the Clerk confirms that Evelyn can have Betty to talk to "always," "a hint of what he said was visible to them, a momentary sense of the infinite he named" (*AHE,* 137). Infinity for the Clerk appears spatially opening out; for Evelyn it closes down on a single room in which she talks to Betty eternally. "Infinity of far and near lived together, for he had uttered one of the names of the City, and at once (in the way they wished) the City was there" (137). Since "eternity" is one way of indicating the reality also called heaven or the City of God, again the word itself makes the reality present to the speaker, but in the speaker's categories, in whatever way it is reality for the speaker.

Similarly, Lester in bidding Betty goodbye says, "And if, by any chance, you should see Richard, give him my love," and the narrator points out: "The commonplace phrase was weighted with meaning as it left her lips; in that air, it signified no mere message but an actual deed—a rich gift of another's love to another, a third party transaction in which all parties were blessed even now in the foretaste" (*AHE,* 141). The gift of love and the sharing of responsibility, which, as Betty and Lester have come to realize, are part of the exchange or coinherence of the City, give the phrase its significance.

This wordplay sometimes goes so far as to seem at first sight comical, cute, or silly, and it can therefore be a major stumbling block to readers. Nevertheless, the most extreme examples occur predominantly in the last two novels, where Williams is most daring and most often successful. It is thus tied to both his key failures and his special successes. At first it is sometimes hard to tell which we are dealing with. Some of his clichés appear to be poor puns and yet are actually among his best images.

In *Descent into Hell* the narrator summarizes Wentworth's state after Adela's evening with Hugh: "cannibal of his heart" (*DH,* 67). The succinct phrase recalls the common phrase, "eating his heart out," a vivid—if trite—expression that is especially accurate in regard to self-destructive sexual jealousy.

Williams risks cheapening a major image from *Descent into Hell* when he makes it almost explicit. Both the workman, committing suicide, and Wentworth, committing a more thorough and culpable spiritual suicide, are descending a mysterious rope. After chronicling Wentworth's descent for most of the novel, Williams finally has him think he is nearing "the bottom of his rope" (*DH,* 275, 299). While Williams may have been trying to revitalize the expression "at the end of one's rope" by dramatizing its roots in experience, the cliché weakens the image, detracting from its previously accumulated mysteriousness and force.

Perhaps Williams's awareness of such unintended effects led him to greater discipline, for the sole late example of this use of cliché (in *All Hallows' Eve*) works well. Lester offers herself in substitution for Betty and finds herself leaning back on a frame in the shape of a cross: "Indeed she could have believed, but she was not sure, that her arms, flung out on each side held on to a part of the frame, as along a beam of wood" (*AHE,* 122–23). Here, if the image does begin in a literal rendering of the phrase, "to fall back on" or "to lean on," that source is obscured in the fact of experience literally represented: Lester's substitution is seen in the light of Christ's original vicarious sacrifice, and she literally falls back on the Cross as her "sole support." So had saints and martyrs before her, and "it sustained her" as it had them (123).

LANGUAGE AND MEANING

The reader of Williams learns gradually that in these novels even the most strange or precious wordplay may effectively serve a serious purpose. In *Descent into Hell* the one primary example conveys Pauline's distraught indecision over whether to risk going out in the night at her grandmother's odd request or to cling to the insulated security of home. Stanhope confronts Mrs. Sammile in Pauline's tortured mind as she wonders what is true peace:

> She would make a solitude round the dying woman and call it peace; the dying woman would die and never know, or dying know and call it well; the dying woman that would not die but see, or die and see; and dead, see and know—know the solitude that her granddaughter had called peace. (*DH*, 220)

The wordplay is based on Pauline's confusion of meaning in words: by calling solitude "peace" she mislabels, and this distortion of the reality carries over into further verbal confusion. Thus the words "die," "see," and "know" are interchanged in a sort of Shakespearean play on double meanings that recalls Wentworth's confusion of "eaves," "eves," and "Eves" (115). This verbal device represents her distress and her guilt in addition to the confusion that accompanies a serious consideration of Lily Sammile's invitation to comfortable illusion.

But the remainder of the same paragraph, which continues the wordplay, also points up a further function of this device:

> The edge of the other world was running up along the sky, the world where everyone carried themselves but everyone carried someone else's grief: Alice in Wonderland, sweet Alice, Alice sit by the fire, the fire burned: who sat by the fire that burned a man in another's blood on the grass of a poet's house . . . and a ghost in the fire was a ghost in the street, and the thing that had been was the thing that was to be and it was coming . . . she was coming, up the street and the wind; herself—a terrible good, terror and error, but the terror was error, and the error was in the terror, and now all were in him, for he had taken them into himself, and he was coming, down all the roads of Battle Hill, closing them in him, making them straight: make straight the highways before our God, and they were not for God took them, in the world that was running through this, its wheel turning within this world's air, rolling out of the air. No peace but peace, no joy but joy, no love but love. Behold, I come quickly. Amen, even so, come. . . .
> (*DH*, 221; final ellipsis points in original)

Here Williams uses a similar kind of verbal association to point to meanings lying beyond ordinary paraphrasable statement, beyond paradox and verbal contradiction, where language breaks down. Pauline's choice with its grave implications is made clear: she can sit by the fire in a wonderland of cozy make-believe, rejecting the coinherence of the City, or she can seek out the person who supposedly needs her and by so doing perform a Christlike act of substitution, bearing her ancestor's fear of the martyr's fire. Her error lies in being afraid; a "terrible good" is above all a *good,* and the undeniable cost is overbalanced by the reward, her citizenship in the City, her acceptance of love's law of exchange, and therefore of Love Himself ("Behold, I come quickly. Amen, even so, come"). Such wordplay may at times venture too far into the fond and precious, but it does not fall short of its main purpose. We should note with what restraint Williams uses it, and through it how much he attempts. Like Henry James, Williams can turn his compulsions into effective technique.

Williams's idiosyncratic style also leads him to evoke two or three levels of meaning in a single word, and at times even to force words into new meanings, new roles. He breaks and reshapes them in a manner analogous to the personal and idiosyncratic technique of Gerard Manley Hopkins. He thereby renders all his language more fluid and unstable, and full of sleeping potential. New slants of meaning in words can be evoked with minimum gesture. Any word may explode at any moment.

This technique is best exemplified in the word/concept *speed*. The term *speed* does not occur in any special way in the two earliest novels, which are Williams's most straightforward, especially in their diction. But in *Many Dimensions* we get a hint of what Williams will later do with it: develop it progressively from a mere measure of rate of movement or activity to various dimensions of mind, character, and spirit. For example, Frank is bewildered by what he sees in Chloe as she comes to reclaim the stone he has stolen: "There was rather in her face a largeness of comprehension, a softness of generosity and lovely haste to meet any approach" (*MD*, 292). But mere rapidity in itself is not a good, as Williams makes clear by often contrasting admirable speed with nervous, uncertain, directionless fret or hurry. The latter is one of those encumbrances Chloe must still clear away before she is fully "disposed to heaven" (294).

Similarly in *The Place of the Lion* Quentin's "fearful and lunatic haste" is explicitly contrasted with the lion's majestic, "inexorable speed" (*PL*, 94). In *All Hallows' Eve* Evelyn's compulsive, "infinite haste" in pursuit of her cravings (*AHE*, 103) is sharply different from Lester's controlled speed in a free response to someone else's needs. Her speed "depended now chiefly on her will" (141).

The clearest working out of this negative quality of haste comes in *Descent into Hell,* where Lily Sammile's restless, pattering footsteps, reechoing throughout Battle Hill, remind the reader of the endless and endlessly unsatisfying pursuit of a false security, the fretful, uneasy, nervous, insatiable quality of personal desire, of self-will, so clearly placed for us in *Many Dimensions* and in *Descent into Hell* (see *DH,* 77). Williams calls it "the haste of a search for or a flight from repose—perhaps both" (94).

Most often Williams uses "speed" in a positive sense to approximate an ordinarily undifferentiated quality of the total personality. The opposite of

LANGUAGE AND MEANING

sluggishness, dullness, tepidity, and sloth, it contains something of eagerness, alertness, unselfish and outgoing anticipation. Such speed is the appropriate response to the highest values in Williams's novels, just as for Dante speed up the purgatorial mountain is the only proper response to the offer of joy. The pilgrim must speed toward joy or deny it altogether, and thus in purgatory Dante sees the spirits of the slothful running and reciting examples of zeal or energy: "Haste, haste, lest time be lost for little love . . . that zeal in well-doing may make grace come green again."[1]

Here, I think, is the source of the concept in Williams and the key to his special use of it. In this world only certain things require speed in response, as Anthony discovers: there is no hurry for Dr. Rockbotham's practical considerations. "The things about which there was, if not hurry, at least a necessity for speed, were quite other" (*PL*, 161)—for example, the rescue of Damaris (169).

Williams's sense of speed has many affinities in the literature of religion. Compare the legendary recommendation of Ramakrishna that one must desire God in the same way a man with his head held under water desires air. Compare also St. Paul's image of the race: "Know ye not that they which run in a race run all, but one receiveth the prize? So run, that ye may obtain" (1 Cor. 9:24).

In *The Place of the Lion* "speed" becomes linked with what Williams is doing to our usual understanding of space and time. Speed (rate) as the quotient of distance divided by time ($r=d/t$) fascinates Williams much as it does Lewis Carroll in *Through the Looking-Glass,* where the Red Queen insists that Alice must run faster, even though "however fast they went, they never seemed to pass anything." As the Red Queen tells Alice: "Now, *here,* you see, it takes all the running *you* can do, to keep in the same place."[2] Williams refers almost explicitly to this passage in *The Place of the Lion,* where Anthony remembers his dream: "However fast he ran he couldn't catch up with the lion's much slower movement" (*PL*, 62).

Even in this very different context, speed still has implications for character, and the apparent outward movement represents the crucial interior movement. Compare, for instance, the Fool in the Tarot, whose motion is visible to Sybil alone (*GT*, 92–93), with T. S. Eliot's "still point of the turning world" ("Coriolan," I), or Yeats's dancer and the dance ("Among School Children," 8). To stand still, to lack proper speed, is to make no progress, or rather, to regress. On the other hand, we must in Eliot's words learn "to sit still" ("Ash-Wednesday," I), learn that the right kind of

---

1. *Purgatorio,* 18.103–105, in *The Divine Comedy of Dante Alighieri,* trans. John D. Sinclair, 3 vols. (1939-1946; reprint New York: Oxford University Press, 1961).

2. *Through the Looking Glass* (1871); reprinted in *Alice in Wonderland,* ed. Donald J. Gray (New York: W. W. Norton, 1971), 126, 127.

movement is not significantly in time and place at all, but interior: the movement Margaret makes in *Descent into Hell* along the face of her rock. Speed is a crucial index to character. The choice facing the dead workman in *Descent into Hell* is a matter of speed; he can hang back or press forward. "In the hastening or delaying of the end lies all distinction in the knowledge of the end when at last it comes" (*DH,* 209). Speed is an expression of will.

In *Descent into Hell* "speed" takes on special personal significance for Williams as few words do for any author. As one of the four virtues Stanhope feels necessary for the proper recitation of poetry (clarity, speed, humility, courage), "speed" seems to mean the rhythmic forward drive inherent in music, linked with energy, vigor, forthrightness, directness, and lack of the affectation associated with rhetoric and elocution. Pauline does not find Stanhope's style grandiloquent: "his verse was subdued almost to conversation, though . . . the rhythm of these conversations was a great deal more speedy and vital than any she could ever remember taking part in." Mrs. Parry's efforts toward "stateliness" and "slow realism" and "enigmatic meandering meditativeness" still "could not sufficiently delay the celerity of the lines" (*DH,* 124).

Here in the metaphor of speaking poetry (and playing one's role in the play) Williams is talking about the necessity for speed in living one's life. When Pauline hesitates to run out to help the man her grandmother says needs her, she is yielding to fear, doubt, distrust—the opposite of speed, of total unitive commitment. She must learn to assent to the urgency, the blessed speed of grace that Williams holds out as both the divine approach to men ("Behold, I come quickly"—Rev. 3:11; 22:7, 12; *DH,* 221) and the proper human response to God. Thus, both Pauline and the dead man learn to cooperate with the "swiftness of the Mercy" (160). After receiving grace from his encounter with Margaret, the suicide goes on "with more energy than he had ever known," thinking "that it was better to do at once what must be done" (209–10). For him "speed" is decisiveness, energy, and power; it brings him to grace. Likewise Pauline overcomes her fear, discovers her duty, and goes out in the night "quickly," with a "watchfulness" that "did not check her speed, nor either disturb the peace" (225)—i.e., without reckless haste or nervous hurry.

Williams is most explicit about the supernatural significance of "speed" when he has Pauline reflect on the meaning of the last act of the play, "the act in which physical sensation, which is the play of love, and pardon, which is the speed of love, and action, which is the fact of love, and almighty love itself, all danced together" (*DH,* 203). More than mere representation, the play conveys this power of grace to all who can receive it, and Williams objectifies this released power in the very atmosphere of Battle Hill: "The unusual brightness had been generally noticed. . . . It was an increase in

LANGUAGE AND MEANING 53

luminous power . . . a kind of swiftness moved in the air; all things hastened" (187). In all these examples Williams is not simply accumulating a large number of particular meanings; he is building an openness, a potential of meaning, a range of implication.

Williams's use of "speed" demonstrates for us his ability to unravel unexpected depths of meaning in a common word. He also, again like Hopkins, makes distinctive use of uncommon words, often odd but forceful words that enrich the narrative texture with their weight, allusiveness, and connotations. Some of these words are archaic or unlisted and possibly invented, and some are part of a consciously elevated and often religious diction.

Here we will look at only one successful example, the word *luxury* in *All Hallows' Eve*. As he comes under Simon's influence Richard begins to think of his relationship with Lester in a twisted, selfish way:

> Now she was gone, he could attend to himself. Luxuriating—more than he knew—in the thought, he turned. Luxury stole gently out within him, and in that warm air flowed about him; luxury, *luxuria,* the quiet distilled *luxuria* of his wishes and habits, the delicate sweet lechery of idleness, the tasting of unhallowed peace. (*AHE,* 78)

The repetition forces our attention to the word, and the presence of the Latin *luxuria*—meaning excess, luxuriance, and also connoting "vicious indulgence"—qualifies "luxury" beyond our bland modern usage to more of its former negative sense of lasciviousness or lust. When Williams adds the word "lechery," the archaic meaning of *luxury* (cf. Chaucer, among others), he has placed Richard's state of mind with consummate precision.

Finally, among those words distinctively used by Williams are many not in themselves uncommon, but not commonly found in realistic or semirealistic fiction. I have in mind all elevated and especially religious diction, a principal ingredient in Williams's curiously heightened style. Williams explicitly justifies this use of language in *The Place of the Lion,* where he has Anthony hesitate to explain his strange and rather mystical experience even to the sympathetic Richardson:

> Anthony found himself a little unwilling to speak, . . . because to recount his own experience would take them no farther. It was no use saying to another soul, "I did—I saw—I was—this, that, or the other," because what applied to him couldn't apply to anyone else, not to anyone else at all in the whole community of mankind. Some more general, some ceremonial utterance was needed. Now, if ever, he needed the ritual of words arranged and shaped for that end. (*PL,* 166)

This difficulty of overcoming the uniqueness and privacy of each individual's experience is of course Williams's primary problem in these novels, and allowing for his personal penchant for myth, poetry, and ritual, most of the time his use of "ceremonial utterance" seems justified.

54 ALICE E. DAVIDSON

Almost always in Williams's work, elevated style means not only biblical tone and cadence but also specifically religious diction. Usually, as in *War in Heaven,* it is appropriate to the character—the devout Archdeacon, the romantic Duke of the North Ridings, the mysterious Prester John—though it may at times seem a bit jarring, even startling, to the unsuspecting reader. The Archdeacon's thought and speeches are couched in the language of the Bible, and in fact he is frequently uttering a psalm under his breath ("Oh, give thanks to the God of all gods, . . . for his mercy endureth forever"—Ps. 136:2; *WH,* 47), giving a sermon (116), or praying (46). His prayer, especially, is in Williams's own favorite style, blending mystical literature (here, the *Revelations of Divine Love* of Julian of Norwich), Arthurian legend, and one of Williams's own odd mannerisms:

> "Ah, fair sweet Lord," he said half-aloud, "let me keep this Thy vessel, if it be Thy vessel. . . . And, if not, let me be courteous still to it for Thy sake, courteous Lord; since this might well have been that, and that was touched by Thee." (46)

The attitude and the epithets *fair, sweet,* and *courteous* are characteristic of the Lady Julian, with whom the Archdeacon shares more than the Christian name. Courtesy is the great value of medieval knighthood. And the slightly confusing use of demonstratives and pronouns to make the references a bit labored ("this might well have been that") is on many other occasions in the novels almost or actually ambiguous.

Likewise Williams permits Mornington the language of poetry and the Duke the high language of romance. As we should expect, it is to Prester John—the mysterious "priest-king," the only supernatural figure in *War in Heaven*—that Williams gives a highly formal, ceremonial language that frequently breaks out into absolute, prophetic pronouncements, either quoted from or couched in the language of the Bible: "I am John . . . and I am the prophecy of the things that are to be and are" (*WH,* 276). If we grant the need for such a character, such language is only fitting.

Like *War in Heaven,* most of the novels deal with something or someone supernatural (Graal, Stone, Tarot, "principles," etc.) thrust into the natural world, so we can expect extremes of elevated diction set off against realistic dialogue. The question is whether the juxtaposition works. In *War in Heaven,* where the elevated language creeps in from several sources, it is made to work reasonably well. In most of the other novels it is less noticeable (or obtrusive) and confined to description of the supernatural "intrusions" or to occasional phrases adopted from religious language and apparently favorites of Williams: for example, "under the Protection," (*MD,* 160), "under the Mercy" (*DH,* 245), "by high permission" (*AHE,* 106), which roughly mean in and through the grace of God, and are no worse than mannerisms.

LANGUAGE AND MEANING 55

The other extensive use of elevated language comes in *Descent into Hell* —perhaps surprisingly, at first glance, since this novel is less concerned with supernatural gimmickry, but its style seems more consistently heightened than that of the other novels.

There is first of all Stanhope's pastoral verse-drama written in his "most heightened, and most epigrammatic style" (*DH,* 13). We have no lines from the play itself apart from Adela's "I am only the perception in a flash of love" and the Woodcutter's answer, "A peremptory phenomenon of love" (125). But we know his "lucid exaltation of verse" (89) is yet "subdued almost to conversation" (124), an "entwined loveliness" (127). As in *The Place of the Lion,* Williams uses apparently fictitious quoted material, this time what he calls Foxe's account of Struther's martyrdom (*DH,* 74), which allows him to introduce archaic language and biblical quotations and then use them frequently. More important is the almost metaphysical discussion of the play, sometimes by the characters but especially by the narrator. In fact the narrator's prose is raised to a higher-than-usual formality throughout the novel, and this formal prose, coupled with Stanhope's and Margaret's mature and graceful speech (and, gradually, Pauline's also), gives the pervasive formal tone that raises this novel well above the sometimes playful and chatty tenor of much of Williams's fiction. In *Descent into Hell* Williams has something important to say, and he acknowledges it more straightforwardly. Consequently there are fewer problems in tone and inappropriate juxtaposition of levels of diction.

For example, the narrator describes the trumpet call at the opening of Stanhope's play: "It sounded, annunciatory of a new thing. It called its world together, and prepared union. It directed all attention forward, as, his blasts done, the Prologue, actors ready behind and audience expectant before, advanced slowly across the grass" (*DH,* 246). There are three typical features here. One is the unusual term *annunciatory* with its inevitable connotation, which is actually picked up earlier in the dialogue when the workman lifts his cap to Pauline "in an archangelic salute to the Mother of God" (228). The archetypal image is appropriate in both places, for in a sense Pauline is Mary, the Godbearer, to the workman, and the conclusion of the play heralds the reign of God in the life of Battle Hill. A second is the use of anaphora ("It sounded . . . It called . . . It directed") and the involved syntax in the last sentence with the modifying phrases breaking up the flow, possibly to convey simultaneity. Third, and perhaps the key to Williams's special manner, is the narrator's drawing back from the specific action to generalize on the significance of the trumpet blast—not just music, not just prologue or announcement in this play, but the very essence of a trumpet summons. He thus carries the reader beyond the immediate moment to consider this drama played out *sub specie aeternitatis.*

The style continues to heighten as Williams introduces a theory of aesthetics in which silence itself attains the quality of "speed" and becomes as important to poetry as is speech. The play becomes a vehicle for stillness even more than for speech.

> She recognized the awful space of separating stillness which all mighty art creates about itself, or, uncreating, makes clear to mortal apprehension. . . . That living stillness had gathered the girl into her communion with the dead; . . . and now again it rose at the sound of the trumpet—that which is before the trumpet and shall be after, which is between all sentences and all words, which is between and in all speech and all breath, which is itself the essential nature of all, for all come from it and return to it. (*DH,* 247–48)

Again Williams uses the repetition of syntactical patterns—"that which is before . . . which is between . . . which is between and in . . . which is itself"—to raise the narration to the ritual intensity his subject demands. It is effective.

The most obvious religious diction appears in the biblical quotations Williams sprinkles through his books. His characters often quote or mis-quote, but in *Descent into Hell* Williams injects the frequent quotation from Revelation, "Behold, I come quickly!" into the narration without identifying in whose mind or mouth it originates. In one particular instance, the narrator is speaking from Pauline's point of view, but he does not say, and we do not detect, that *she* thought of the connection between the end of the play and the end of the world (the second coming of Christ). The quotation might even be a line in the play.

> The dance of herself and all the others ceased, they drew aside, gathered up—O on how many rehearsals, and now gathered! "Behold, I come quickly! Amen, even so. . . ." They were in the groups of the last royal declamations, and swept aside, and the mighty stage was clear. (*DH,* 256; ellipsis points in original)

The narrator then makes explicit the connection with the trumpet: "It was the beginning of the end; the judgment of mortality was there. She was standing aside, and she heard the voice and knew it" (256). We now know the significance of the quotation, but not to whom to attribute it. The resulting slight sense of mysterious indefiniteness is effective here.

But often Williams's penchant for the indefinite leads to inexcusable obscurity, as with his use of unclear pronoun reference, often to multiple antecedents in a single paragraph (e.g., *PL,* 155–57; *AHE,* 52). Williams often allows his language to become to varying degrees vague and abstract when he deals with uncommon states of consciousness, such as Margaret's, and with supernatural happenings, such as the mysterious footsteps of the restless Lily Sammile, who is also the mythical Lilith (*DH,* 93–95). Frequently, however, the resulting lack of clarity defeats Williams's aim at

LANGUAGE AND MEANING

precision and can only be considered a lapse. No useful effect is sought or gained by such careless slippage.

Some of Williams's best effects, however, spring from his esoteric allusions. Their settings are carefully established. Here Pauline's musing on the incredible possibility that *all* things fulfill the law of exchange, the "doctrine of substituted love," goes to the heart of Williams's message, and he uses all his resources to shape the idea in suitable language:

> Perhaps everything was all at once, and interchanged devotion; perhaps even now he burned, and she and her friends danced, and her grandmother died and lived, and Peter Stanhope wrote his verse, and all the past of the Hill was one with its present. It lived; it intermingled; not among these living alone did the doctrine of substituted love bear rule. . . . About her the familiar and transfigured personages moved; this was the condition and this the air of supernatural life. *Ecce, omnia nova facio*. The incantation and adoration of the true substance of experience sounded. She fulfilled her part in a grave joy, aspiring to become part of that substance. (*DH,* 207)

To make the strange notion that Pauline can offer joy to her martyred ancestor an absolute condition of all existence, Williams quotes—in Latin, to heighten his effect—from Revelation 21:5, "Behold, I make all things new." These words attributed to God come immediately after the passage describing the vision of "a new heaven and a new earth" and "the holy city, new Jerusalem" (Rev. 21:1, 2). Williams is tapping the apocalyptic vision of a renewed creation to suggest a similar recreation of the new Jerusalem in the community of Battle Hill—or wherever anyone opens himself or herself to this "supernatural life." By setting his own image in this biblical context Williams enriches its meaning and gives—to some readers at least—a greater appreciation of what he is trying to do with a mere novel: describe life not so much as it is lived, but as it *may* be lived, the redeemed and transformed life to which the Bible, primarily, gives witness.

The worst idiosyncrasies of Williams's style are but the slight overreaching of a personal manner that is, at its best, brilliant. It is an eloquence of special precision, sometimes dense, sometimes elliptical, still highly personal, but in general thoroughly justified by its effects. Here is Peter Stanhope explaining the image of Gomorrah, the city of self-love that Wentworth has chosen:

> The Lord's glory fell on the cities of the plain, on Sodom and another. We know all about Sodom nowadays, but perhaps we know the other even better. Men can be in love with men, and women with women, and still be in love and make sounds and speeches, but don't you know how quiet the streets of Gomorrah are? haven't you seen the pools that everlastingly reflect the faces of those who walk with their own phantasms, but the phantasms aren't reflected, and can't be. The lovers of Gomorrah are quite contented, Periel; they don't have to put up with

ALICE E. DAVIDSON

our difficulties. They aren't bothered by alteration, at least till the rain of the fire of the Glory at the end, for they lose the capacity for change, except for the fear of hell. They're monogamous enough! and they've no children—no cherubim breaking into being or babies as tiresome as ours; there's no birth there, and only the second death. There's no distinction between lover and beloved; they beget themselves on their adoration of themselves, and they live and feed and starve on themselves, and by themselves too, for creation, as my predecessor said, is the mercy of God, and they won't have the facts of creation. No, we don't talk much of Gomorrah, and perhaps it's as well and perhaps not. (*DH,* 239–40)

And here are the narrator's reflections on Margaret Anstruther's approach to the knowledge of death:

The best maxim towards that knowledge was yet not the *Know thyself* of the Greek so much as the *Know Love* of the Christian, though both in the end were one. It was not possible for man to know himself and the world, except first after some mode of knowledge, some art of discovery. The most perfect, since the most intimate and intelligent, art was pure love. The approach by love was the approach to fact; to love anything but fact was not love. Love was even more mathematical than poetry; it was the pure mathematics of the spirit. It was applied also and active; it was the means as it was the end. The end lived everlastingly in the means; the means eternally in the end. (*DH,* 92–93)

Williams's style is most fluent, of course, when he writes of what he knows best: damnation and salvation. He can define with originality and precision these spiritual realities so that they exist concretely—not only in the novel but also in our own experience. The gently, sadly mocking tone of the first passage and the slightly heightened rhetoric of the second suit their subjects; without sentimentality or exhortation, in a matter-of-fact manner, Williams manages to convince us, and even to inspire in us a horror of Gomorrah and a desire for the "approach by love."

The Inner Lives of Characters and Readers: Affective Stylistics in Charles Williams's Fiction

Bernadette Lynn Bosky

Part of the genius and difficulty of Williams's novels lies in the author's approach of depicting subjective experiences—especially certain theological "facts"—so thoroughly and so well that they become universal and indisputable, not only as intellectual constructs but as affective response. As Gunnar Urang writes, "Williams' novels are not *about* the vision; they want to *be* the vision."[1] In his fiction, Williams conveys the inner lives of his characters in such a way as to affect the inner lives of his readers. Many critics have noted this dual accomplishment; this study explores some of the stylistic techniques that Williams employs to that end.

Both C. S. Lewis and T. S. Eliot noted that Williams's novels not only depict states of consciousness in the characters but also help awaken a sense of them in the reader. Eliot writes, "The capacity for recognizing the realities to which Williams was trying to draw our attention is numbed and atrophied in the world in which we live today. If this capacity is latent in you, Williams is the writer to bring it to consciousness." Geoffrey Parsons states that Williams's fiction "enacts" his theological concepts for the reader, and James Agee remarks that Williams "has a wonderful gift for conveying, and dramatizing, the 'borderline' states of mind or Being." In some cases, the main appeal of Williams's fiction is said to lie in this experiential dimension and the compelling way in which it is conveyed to the reader, whose "critical judgment is to be suspended temporarily in favor of participation."[2]

---

1. Urang, *Shadows of Heaven: Religion and Fantasy in the Writing of C. S. Lewis, Charles Williams, and J. R. R. Tolkien* (Philadelphia: Pilgrim Press, 1971), 80.

2. Lewis, "The Novels of Charles Williams," in *On Stories and Other Essays on Literature,* ed. Walter Hooper (New York: Harcourt Brace Jovanovich, 1982), 26; Eliot, "The Significance of Charles Williams," *Listener* 36 (19 December 1946): 895; Parsons, "The Spirit of Charles Williams," *Atlantic Monthly*, November 1949, 79; Agee, *Letters to Father Flye*

Many studies of this aspect of Williams's novels, such as that by George P. Winship, Jr., in *Shadows of Imagination,* refer merely to Williams's matter-of-fact use of supernatural elements.[3] Inherently, readers may more readily believe what they have seen depicted, even if the depiction is obviously fictional—in the same way a play can be more convincing than a lecture. However, Eliot and the others obviously refer to something more, something that distinguishes Williams's novels from other supernatural fiction.

Patricia Meyer Spacks comes closer, using Eliot's own critical term, when she writes that the supernatural element of Williams's novels sometimes "provides objective correlatives for modes of feeling." Yet it might be more exact to say that Williams's novels offer a *subjective* correlative, potentially as powerful a medium of experience as Eliot's approach—rooted, however, not in the objective depiction of associated situations or settings but rather in the discourse and perception of his characters. In this way, through the "spiritual crises" of Williams's characters, "the deep feeling of meditation and inquiry are conveyed to the reader."[4]

As Spacks points out, this affective engagement of the reader is a goal in which Williams failed at least as often as he succeeded.[5] In Williams's prose, the unifying mist of enlightenment does frequently thicken into obscurity and "clotted glory," as even Williams's friends readily admit.[6] Still, in both goal and method, Williams's novels are unique, and hence uniquely successful. Kathleen Spencer sums up these limitations and accomplishments: "In truth, the style is often difficult, but (where not simply the result of hasty writing), the difficulties seem to derive honestly from his subject. . . . Williams' style is further complicated by his desire not only to

---

(New York: George Braziller, 1962), 203; *experiential dimension:* Anne Ridler, introduction to *Image,* lv; James Roy King, "Christian Fantasy in the Novels of C. S. Lewis and Charles Williams," *Journal of Religious Thought* 11 (1953–54): 57; see also King, 52.

3. Winship, "The Novels of Charles Williams," in *Shadows of Imagination: The Fantasies of C. S. Lewis, J. R. R. Tolkien, and Charles Williams,* ed. Mark R. Hillegas, new ed. (Carbondale: Southern Illinois University Press, 1979), 113, 118; see also Agee, *Letters,* 203.

4. Spacks, "Charles Williams: The Fusions of Fiction," in Hillegas, *Shadows of Imagination,* 151; Eliot, "Hamlet," in *Selected Prose of T. S. Eliot,* ed. Frank Kermode (New York: Harcourt Brace Jovanovich/Farrar, Straus and Giroux, 1975), 48; W. R. Irwin, "Christian Doctrine and the Tactics of Romance: The Case of Charles Williams," in Hillegas, *Shadows of Imagination,* 145–46.

5. Spacks, "Fusions," 155–59; see also Urang, *Shadows of Heaven,* 92.

6. Humphrey Carpenter, *The Inklings* (New York: Ballantine, 1981), 124; see also Barbara McMichael, "Hell Is Oneself: An Examination of the Concept of Damnation in Charles Williams' *Descent into Hell,*" *Studies in the Literary Imagination* 1, no. 2 (1968): 59.

AFFECTIVE STYLISTICS

describe the . . . experience to us, but to do so in a language that will allow us to recreate the experience as we read."[7] This study explores *the means* by which Williams's novels touch the inner lives of his readers through the inner lives of his characters, when they do.[8]

Williams uses many stylistic techniques that, although not original to his novels, are combined by him to original effect. All of these promote Williams's basic vision of an inherently connected cosmos, in which the experience of the unity of all things (available in certain moments or states of being) grows naturally from, yet is more basic or important than, our usual forms of knowing ourself and others. "Williams," Irwin writes, "seems to have known that a desire to perceive unity, rather than fragmentation, is a strong motive to many minds and sensibilities."[9] Here we examine three major stylistic techniques that Williams uses to help present this experience of unity: choice of phrases and sentence structures that enact a paradoxical conjoining of opposites, conveying an understanding that transcends the apparent conflict; multivalent or shifting references, suggesting the interpenetration of and relationships among different levels of experience; and use of pronouns and other subject referents to convey transpersonal awareness and action.

The verbal union of opposites is one of the most basic ways in which an author can stylistically convey unity despite contrary appearances. This is one reason, perhaps, why paradox is basic to the language of mysticism, one variety of such experience.[10] This pattern of dualistic union (a self-referential term) is also a basic technique for writers who wish to convey unity in and by an artistic experience. Williams himself describes this process in *Shadows of Ecstasy,* when Roger Ingram meditates on the line by Milton,

---

7. Spencer, *Charles Williams* (Mercer Island, Wash.: Starmont House, 1986), 37.

8. This analysis obviously owes much to Stanley Fish's "affective stylistics"; see, for instance, "Literature in the Reader: Affective Stylistics," *New Literary History* 9 (1970): 121–62, and the book that later included that work, *Self-Consuming Artifacts: The Experience of Seventeenth-Century Literature* (Berkeley, Los Angeles, London: University of California Press, 1972). However, my work also includes assumptions beyond or even contrary to Fish's more careful kind of analysis, so my debt to this approach should not be construed as implying any responsibility for the uses to which it is put.

9. Irwin, "Christian Doctrine," 148.

10. See, for instance, Charles Morris, "Comments on Mysticism and Its Language," *ETC: A Review of General Semantics* 9 (1951–52): 3–8; also Keith Critchlow's neoplatonic study, *The Soul as Sphere and Androgyne* (Ipswich: Golgonooza Press, 1980), especially p. 7. For evocative commentary on the nature of paradox, which may be used to help explain its usefulness in these matters, see Rosalie L. Colie, *Paradoxia Epidemica* (Hamden, Conn.: Archon Books, 1972). My analysis here also owes much to the discussion of Sir Thomas Browne's similar use of this literary technique, in Frank L. Huntley's *Sir Thomas Browne: A Biographical and Critical Study* (Ann Arbor: University of Michigan Press, 1962).

"And thus the Filial Godhead answering spake": "The simple analysis, the union of opposites which so often existed in verse, was clear enough. There was the opposition of the Latin 'Filial' and the English 'God,' and of the ideas expressed in those words—Filial, implying subordination and obedience; Godhead—authority, finality" (*SE*, 99). Ingram's understanding of the line gives way to experience, an experience that has both rational and nonrational dimensions:

> And Roger Ingram was being left behind, even the Roger Ingram that loved the line, for the line was driving him down to answer it by dying and living. . . . Milton was but a name for a particular form of this immortal energy: the line was but an opportunity for knowing the everlasting delight, the ecstasy of all those elements that combined in its passionate joy, knowing it by being part of it. (100)

In this passage, Williams outlines an approach that he uses throughout his writings. He tells the reader about the process in *Shadows of Ecstasy,* but in other works he enacts it more and more effectively, climaxing in *Descent into Hell,* a tour de force of the technique.

Williams stresses that this experience may be beyond common categories of language, but it is not beyond our nature. In such moments, as when Sir Bernard encounters Isabel's reconciliation of pain and happiness through marital love, "the mind accepted a fact which was a contradiction in terms, and knew itself defeated by that triumphant contradiction" (*SE*, 210). As Glen Cavaliero notes, for Williams the ultimate example of this impossibility that must be accepted is the contradiction of the Incarnation.[11] When Williams presents the reader with meaningful phrases that encompass aspects usually found to be contradictory, he reinforces the "inclusiveness" and "universality" that, according to Gunnar Urang, characterize both theme and plot of his novels.[12] Moreover, when Williams's novels work to the same experiential ends on all levels—from the smallest unit of prose style to the widest thematic patterns of plot and imagery—that itself may help provoke feelings of fundamental unity despite multiplicity.

Williams's "arresting combinations of words," as Robert McAfee Brown calls them, abound. Brown notes three examples, all indicative of Williams's style and essential to his thought: "the excellent absurdity" of egalitarian hierarchy, "the obscenity of the Cross," and—in depiction of the paradoxical unity of Christ's dual nature—a reference to Messias as "the Divine Thing."[13] In Williams's novels, these paradoxical terms both present his

---

11. Cavaliero, "The Way of Affirmation: A Study of the Writings of Charles Williams," *Church Quarterly Review* 157 (1956): 24–25.

12. Urang, *Shadows of Heaven,* 75–77.

13. Brown, "Charles Williams, Lay Theologian," *Theology Today* 10 (1953): 216–17.

AFFECTIVE STYLISTICS

characters' developing awareness of unity and help the reader grasp those modes of understanding.

Most critical attention to Williams's use of this stylistic device concerns the use, in *Descent into Hell,* of the phrase *terrible good.* Certainly, that is the most extended use Williams has made of such a phrase; moreover, its thematic importance is indisputable. The motif of the "terrible good" is one way in which *Descent into Hell* works out, as Glen Cavaliero states, "that concern with the union of opposites which was haunting Williams so obsessively at the time he wrote it."[14] To Williams, the union of opposites in linguistic structures enacts specifically the kind of category transcendence necessary to encompass both the terror and the good of God and God's creation. Moreover, *Descent into Hell* uses the same stylistic device (as it were, microcosmically) at other points throughout the text. "She fulfilled her part in a grave joy," Williams writes (*DH,* 207), and elsewhere he refers to the "still violence of this last evening" (234).

Though it does so more clumsily and has received commensurately less attention, *Many Dimensions* also uses this technique to help convey the experience of an inclusive vision. In fact, just as *Descent into Hell* is defined by, and attempts to resolve, the tension between the terrible and the good, *Many Dimensions* explores the union of service and power that is expressed in the term "organic law." *Survey of Organic Law* is, of course, the book that Lord Arglay is writing, with the aid of his secretary, Chloe Burnett. But the phrase "organic law" also conveys the combination of living potential and unyielding necessity, which, Chloe learns, characterizes both the Stone of Solomon and the entire creation (under the Omnipotence) that it represents. Thus, Chloe is "The Pupil of Organic Law" (as chapter 2 is headed), and she and others enact "The Process of Organic Law" (as the final chapter is headed), both in a specific, literal sense and in a wider sense that furthers the theme of the novel.

Many Dimensions also provides a good example of the way in which Williams not only conveys the experience of paradoxical unity through such two-word phrases but also uses that basic principle to structure larger units of prose. Early in the novel, he subtly contrasts Chloe Burnett, who is just learning to submit herself to the Stone and what it represents, with Cecilia Sheldrake, who wants the Stone but has never learned to submit herself to much of anything. In the encounter, Chloe "experienced a sudden flicker of amused peace" (*MD,* 91). At first, "peace" comes as a slight shock: the adjective "amused" seems too frivolous for a term we have come to revere as much as we do "peace"; and most of us think of "peace" as a

---

14. Cavaliero, *Charles Williams: Poet of Theology* (Grand Rapids, Mich.: Eerdmans, 1983), 79.

64 BERNADETTE LYNN BOSKY

state—preferably enduringly, but at least temporarily, still—which contrasts with the activity and brevity of a "sudden flicker." The effect of the sentence, however, is to reshape our idea of peace into something less traditional and far more encompassing, in keeping with Chloe's growing understanding and acceptance of the nature of reality. Like Pauline's "grave joy," Chloe's "amused peace" implies a developing emotional maturity on the part of the character and demands it on the part of the reader. Our understanding of joy must broaden to include gravity as well as levity; our understanding of peace must enlarge to encompass dancing amusement as well as hushed repose.

In the same scene, when asked to take Chloe to London, "Cecilia with a cold grudge assented" (*MD*, 93). Again, Williams combines words that strike us emotionally as opposites, so that reading the sentence requires us to modify (however slightly or temporarily) our own outlook. The immediate conflict between "assent" and the "cold grudge" shows the way in which a positive act can be limited and lowered by selfishness, a limitation characteristic of Cecilia's perspective. Yet the overall movement of the sentence is optimistic. Just as Stanhope states that "The substantive, of course, governs the adjective; not the other way round," in the phrase "terrible good" (*DH*, 88), Williams ends this sentence on a note of active agreement, acknowledging the "cold grudge" but transcending it. This final perspective is offered to the reader, whether the character apprehends it or not.

In *The Forgiveness of Sins,* Williams writes that, because of the Fall, human beings know both good and evil by knowing good *as* evil—that is, by apprehending as evil that which, in unfallen (or redeemed) perception, is apprehended as good (*FS*, 19-21). This is one reason that, in Williams's novels, the conflict between good and evil "is not resolved by the simple defeat of evil but by some kind of transcendence of the terms, reaching beyond the conflict to a place where the old terms are meaningless."[15] To properly know God's love and the creation that reflects it, one must reconcile the "terror" (erroneously known as "evil") with the "good."

Some of Williams's sentences join contradictory sentiments grammatically, using parallel structures to imply an indisputable balance or unity. The best-known example of this is frequent in Williams's theology and basic to his novel *War in Heaven:* "This also is Thou; neither is this Thou." Such a sentence demands reconciliation of the apparent contradiction, but it leaves that reconciliation to the mind of the reader. Reading the sentence, and encompassing the two statements as factual, enacts a mental process basic

---

15. Spencer, *CW*, 25; see also Ridler, in *Image,* xxxiii, and Agnes Sibley, *Charles Williams* (Boston: Twayne, 1982), 42.

to Williams's Romantic theology: to fully keep in mind, at the same time, the ways in which mental or physical creations reveal God's nature and the ways in which they do not and cannot.

According to Winston Weathers, this balanced sentence structure characterizes what he calls "the rhetoric of certitude"—the style "in which an author writes if he intentionally wishes to communicate or unintentionally exposes his sureness, confidence, or even dogmatism" regarding the material under discussion.[16] Weathers finds many examples of "the rhetoric of certitude" in Williams's theology, especially in *He Came Down from Heaven* (220). Yet Weathers's approach, although valid and useful, does not go far enough. Certainly, for all of Williams's faith, his thought was based in a healthy skepticism as well.[17]

Especially in his novels, this combination results in prose that works in two ways. The facts of experience are stated with bald assurance—one must take them as given. However, Williams's novels are often less dogmatic about *why* reality works in certain ways, and the prose may convince the reader through affective technique rather than by argument or explanation. In *All Hallows' Eve,* Williams describes the geometry of the supernatural City, as it brings together characters with similar goals and natures:

> Each desired to breach the City; and either breach opened—directly and only—upon the other. Love to love, death to death, breach to breach; that was the ordering of the City, and its nature. It throve between Lester and Betty, between Richard and Jonathan, between Simon and Evelyn; that was its choice. How it throve was theirs. (*AHE,* 109)

This passage uses a number of techniques that Weathers identifies with "the rhetoric of certitude": simple and emphatic diction; "elaborate use of exact word repetition"; and use of "balanced" parallel structures, especially pairing (213–16). Yet the result of the passage is a strange combination of certitude and mystery. The passage does not argue (as Williams will elsewhere) in favor of the doctrine of coinherence. In fact, it does not try to explain the phenomenon at all. Rather, it conveys the feeling of order and the drawing together of similarity through the careful repetition and balance of the prose. The result is the subjective impression that the correspondences expressed here are real, aside from any explanations.

In *The Place of the Lion,* Anthony says to Damaris, "What you need very badly indeed is a thoroughly good Saracen invasion within the next fortnight" (*PL,* 27), again conjoining opposites in an unexpectedly meaningful whole. This line also demonstrates a second stylistic device, which Williams

16. Weathers, "The Rhetoric of Certitude," *Southern Humanities Review* 2 (1968): 213–14.

17. See Spencer, *CW,* 11–12; Ridler, in *Image,* xli.

66   BERNADETTE LYNN BOSKY

uses even more consistently in his novels: multivalent or shifting meaning, suggesting the interpenetration of and relationships among different levels of experience. In this case, Patricia Spacks points out, the "invasion of Forms" in *The Place of the Lion* is for Damaris "the equivalent . . . of the Saracen invasion . . . as fierce as any barbarians in their effects, yet working ultimately for good." Thus, the statement works in one way in the immediate scene, while holding another meaning that is revealed as the novel unfolds.[18]

This polysemy helps convey another aspect of the unitary experience that Williams's novels often present. Just as his use of dualistic unions challenges our usual categories of thought and judgment—presenting transcendence by the characters and inviting it in the readers—Williams's use of shifting or multivalent meaning challenges our usual categories of experience, including those of time and space and of nature versus the supernatural. As Robert McAfee Brown states, in Williams's theology "the point is that the whole cosmos is of a piece. It is one and it is God's, through all time and space, beyond all time and space." In fact, Brown points out, this unity is the necessary basis of Williams's most important specific doctrines, such as coinherence, the practices of substitution and exchange, and the way of affirmation of images. Williams believed that this unity could also be seen in the apparent diversity of nature, shown by "correspondence and the law of similitude," which he especially explored in his poetry.[19]

In *The Forgiveness of Sins,* Williams expresses both the impossibility and the necessity of using language to convey the reality of unity despite apparent barriers, including categories of time inherent in human perception: "Theology, like all sciences, has its own proper language, but even the theologians are always sliding back into a one-sided use of that language. Their terms ought to be ambiguous; they ought to carry meanings at once in time and outside time. It cannot be done" (*FS*, 17). Yet Williams did have some hope that artistic works could convey this kind of understanding, at least ideally; and this is certainly one of the goals of his novels. One thinks of Jonathan's painting in *All Hallows' Eve,* which both represents the artist's vision and awakens the same understanding in its viewer. Williams's description of the painting, like that of Roger Ingram's reverie on Milton, explicitly states a goal that he strove for as a novelist, especially as his career progressed: "The whole subject—that is, the whole unity; shape and

18. Spacks, "Charles Williams: A Novelist's Pilgrimage," *Religion in Life* 29 (1960): 286–87.

19. Brown, "CW, Lay Theologian," 220, 219–26; Valerie Pitt, "Conquest's 'The Art of the Enemy,'" *Essays in Criticism* 7 (1957): 330–35; R. J. Reilly, *Romantic Religion: A Study of Barfield, Lewis, Williams, and Tolkien* (Athens: University of Georgia Press, 1971), 152–54.

hue; rubble, houses, cathedral, sky, and hidden sun, all and the light that was all and held all—advanced on him. . . . There was distance in it, and yet it was all one. As a painting is" (*AHE,* 113). However, it is much more difficult to convey the unity of different levels of experience through the "linear medium" of prose, as Kathleen Spencer points out. Through play with multiple levels of meaning, Williams works at circumventing this limitation. As Mary Shideler notes, this also makes Williams's novels both difficult at first reading and richer with each rereading: "The later passages illuminate and fulfill the earlier ones, so that until one knows how the first statement of theme is resolved, he cannot apprehend it properly.[20]

Through polysemy, Williams conveys the feeling that the common life of his characters—and perhaps of his readers—simultaneously functions on many profound levels, whether the individual is aware of it or not. Many critics have noted Williams's insistence, in both his fiction and his theology, on "the supernatural at work *in* the natural."[21] Williams's work constantly presents a universe in which our actions have consequences that we cannot foresee rationally but that our spirit intuits. (See, for instance, "The Redeemed City," in his essay collection *The Image of the City.*) This is reinforced stylistically when, as in Anthony's remarks to Damaris, characters' casual speech says much more than they immediately intend. Sometimes these utterances mean more—to the readers' expanded awareness— than the characters themselves know. Often, Williams shows the characters slowly becoming aware of the "many dimensions" of speech; in the process, Williams schools the reader as well.

Descent into Hell's phrase *terrible good* is again an excellent example of this device; but other examples abound in that novel, and Williams develops the technique throughout his career. Anthony's remark about "the court of Damaris" in *The Place of the Lion* (27) makes it quite likely that Williams wants us to realize that she treats Plato and the other thinkers as her "subjects" in more than one sense. Elsewhere, this kind of play is made explicit. In *The Greater Trumps,* when Nancy drops the magical Tarot cards and Henry yells, "You fool!" (*GT,* 149), he is, as Thomas Howard writes, "as usual saying more than he knows"; the powers and insights of the Fool reverberate through the novel, and Nancy's education into that awareness provides the plot.[22]

---

20. Spencer, *CW,* 37; Shideler, *Charles Williams: A Critical Essay* (Grand Rapids, Mich.: Eerdmans, 1966), 9.

21. Urang, *Shadows of Heaven,* 154; see also Alice Mary Hadfield, "The Relationship of Charles Williams' Working Life to His Fiction," in Hillegas, *Shadows of Imagination,* 126.

22. Howard, *The Novels of Charles Williams* (New York: Oxford University Press, 1983), 141.

68   BERNADETTE LYNN BOSKY

In *Descent into Hell,* Stanhope clearly intends both common courtesy and implied theological doctrine when he tells Pauline, "*in exchange* tell me what's bothering you" (*DH,* 129; emphasis added). When the succubus speaks "in a breathless whisper" in the same novel (176), however, the reader is brought up short by an awareness which the viewpoint character, Wentworth, is trying to suppress: her speech is "breathless" both with feigned sexual excitement and because of her lack of true human substance; and worse yet, Wentworth is trapped because of the connection between those two, which he has accepted. Evelyn, in *All Hallows' Eve,* also reveals self-awareness even as she tries to hide it. She protests that her fate is unfair because she hasn't "done *anything*" (*AHE,* 20, 21). That lack of positive action is, of course, precisely the flawed choice that condemns her. Lester's reply, "Nor have I—much" (21), shows that she is willing to grapple with the issues Evelyn is trying to avoid—depicting in miniature the opposite directions their characters will take as the novel progresses.

Williams often appoints a character, already aware of more profound dimensions of experience, to draw attention to the implied multiple layers of meaning. In *Many Dimensions,* the Persian Prince serves that purpose at first: when Sir Giles innocently but ignorantly says he wants to know "all about" the Stone, the Prince replies, "I think you will know a great deal then" (*MD,* 11). The statement grows in significance as the reader learns more about the Stone, but it hints from the very beginning of hidden import. Later in the same novel, Chloe repeatedly uses the phrase *in a way* casually, discussing the powers and limitations of the Stone of Solomon, and Lord Arglay answers, "O la la! in a way— . . . But only in a way conformable to the Stone" (244). Thus, the reader is prepared for the resonance when Chloe is described as "persevering upon the Way" (265).[23] *The Greater Trumps* begins with Nancy Coningsby's attentive response to her father's term "perfect Babel" (*GT,* 7), showing an unconscious sensitivity that, in the course of the novel, will develop into conscious awareness. The strongest realization of this technique is the character Peter Stanhope, who in *Descent into Hell* instructs his fellow-character Pauline, and thereby the reader, in the multivalent impact of language.

Williams also strives for multilevel reference in and through complete

---

23. This can be compared and contrasted to Fish's examination of Bunyan's multivalenced use of "the way" in *Pilgrim's Progress* ("Affective Stylistics," 138–39; *Self-Consuming Artifacts,* 224–29). In part, Bunyan is more concerned with spiritual actions conveyed and hidden by spatial metaphors, while Williams is more concerned with experiences of the Logos conveyed and hidden in casual speech. In this entire discussion of polysemy, I also owe much to Judith Kollmann's study of vision and rhetoric in *Descent into Hell,* one version of which appears in this volume; an earlier version, heard at a conference, stimulated my thought on this topic in too many ways to acknowledge individually.

sentences; in this he is more ambitious, but sometimes less successful, than in the polysemy of individual words. At its best, this technique results in sentences that mean more than one thing, but each clearly, creating in the reader a feeling of startling excitement over fresh possibilities of meaning that the character is discovering. Feeling the exchange flow between Margaret Anstruther and the suicide's ghost, Pauline thinks, "This holy and happy thing was all that could be meant by God: it was love and power" (*DH*, 169). The reader does not ask whether "all that could be meant by God" refers to everything we use the word "God" to mean, or everything that God intends for us; clearly, it is both, as Pauline has reached a spiritual state in which all possibilities exist, and word and substance are seen as one.

Other times, however, Williams's syntax may be too unclear, as when Pauline, in an ecstasy, considers the difference between greed and exchange:

> Perjury, on her soul and in her blood, if now she slipped to buy sweets with money that was not hers; never, till it was hers in all love and princely good, by gift and gift and gift beyond excelling gift, in no secrecy of greed but all glory of public exchange, law of the universe and herself a child of the universe. (*DH*, 151–52)

Here connection is asserted, but at the cost of confusion. "Exchange," "the universe," and Pauline ("a child of the universe") are clearly united in one meaningful whole, but the exact relationships are obscure, grammatically and theologically. One is reminded of Winship's comments about the concluding chapters of *The Greater Trumps,* where syntax echoes the mist in which the characters find themselves, "cutting off the reader himself from anything like a clear knowledge of what is going on."[24]

In *All Hallows' Eve,* Williams uses entire paragraphs of description to refer to different levels of experience at once, conveying their unity and relationship. Of course, the City of the novel is at once postwar London and the City of the afterlife; moreover, as Gunnar Urang demonstrates, the opening paragraph of the novel describes Lester herself. Like postwar London or the City of God, Lester is done with her "crisis of agony," but there is still "much need for" her "labour, intelligence, patience"; for Lester in her postmortem education and in the physical and spiritual landscape she views, "much was to be done but could be." Similarly, when Lady Wallingford helps Simon prepare the sickroom for the spell against Betty, the closing is both mundanely physical and magically spiritual: the room is "shut off and shut in" in all senses.[25]

---

24. George P. Winship, Jr., "This Rough Magic: The Novels of Charles Williams," *Yale Review* 40 (1950): 288.

25. Urang, *Shadows of Heaven,* 84; *AHE,* 7, 118.

In all of these instances of polysemy, Williams makes the linear medium of prose point in many directions at once; he seeks to undermine many kinds of distinctions, to further an impression of unified experience. His protagonists realize and experience theological truths that transcend space and time, mingle natural and supernatural, and connect the most ordinary routine and the most profound dimension of meaning. As he conveys this through multivalent prose, Williams also helps induce this understanding and affect in his readers.

Among all of Williams's techniques of affective stylistics, the one least noted by critics is his use of pronouns and other subject referents to convey a sense of transpersonal awareness and action. Paradoxically, this may be less noted because it is most natural and graceful, occurring within passages that present a character's point of view but that generally are not remarked on within the text.

The transcendence of personal identity, subsumed into a greater identification with all humanity, is basic both to mystical experience and to Williams's theology. Specifically, the doctrines of coinherence and substitution must be based on a fundamental unity of all individuals, with and through the Incarnation of Christ. As Williams says in *The Forgiveness of Sins,* "It was to be a web of simultaneous interchange of good. 'In the sight of God,' said the Lady Julian, 'all man is one man and one man is all man'" (*FS,* 16). Note that Williams chooses a quotation that not only confirms unity, but also conveys it grammatically, through the use of the single rather than plural form. Similarly, Williams conveys the character's perspective—and shapes the reader's—through manipulation of grammar.

In his earlier novels, Williams does so more rarely, but the effect is still noteworthy. In a passage from Chloe's point of view in *Many Dimensions,* we read, "Dared she so, in action, deny the Stone? Thought was multitudinous but action single" (*MD,* 185). The lack of possessive pronouns in the second sentence has two major effects. First, it widens the implication of the statement beyond the immediate, so that it comments both on Chloe's situation and on a general human process. Beyond that, it may show Chloe's growing awareness of the way in which the Stone contains everything, bringing all people (including Chloe) together—her thought and other thoughts together becoming "thought," and separate actions becoming "action." The first effect provides an important abstraction, but the latter tries to engender a concrete experience.

Williams conveys the experience of transpersonal unity even more skillfully in *The Greater Trumps,* when he describes Nancy calming the storm:

> Everlasting destruction was near. Between that threat and its fulfilment stood the girl's slender figure, and the warm hands of humanity in hers met the invasion

AFFECTIVE STYLISTICS

and turned it. They moved gently over the storm; they moved as if in dancing ritual they answered the dancing monstrosities that opposed them. . . . The column of whirling shapes arose and struck, and were beaten abroad under the influence of those extended palms. (*GT,* 241–42)

The experience is archetypal, not specifically in Jung's sense, but in the Christian sense intended by Williams's quotation from Julian of Norwich. Nancy's ego-identity is unimportant, so Williams writes of "the girl's figure" and "it" instead of "Nancy" and "she." What do matter are the archetypal hands—"those palms" and "they," which grammatically may refer to Nancy's hands, or to "the warm hands of humanity in hers," or to both. The confusion is deliberate, since in the state of consciousness Williams wishes to depict as Nancy's point of view (and, if possible, help the reader to experience), all individual hands combine into the universal.

Like all of Williams's affective techniques, this use of pronouns and other subject referents flourishes in Williams's final two novels. Specifically, Williams uses it in the tour-de-force presentation of supernatural experience that forms the climax of each book. In *Descent into Hell,* for instance, once Pauline and her doppelgänger had been united, "she waited, and remembered only as a dream the division between herself and the glorious image by which the other was to be utterly ensouled" (*DH,* 262). Just as the experience challenged Pauline's usual understanding of identity, of self and not-self, this sentence must challenge the reader. When he or she gets to "the other," expected categories break down: it cannot grammatically refer to Pauline, to her double, or even to Pauline's martyred ancestor. Or, conversely, perhaps it refers to all three, brought together despite boundaries of space, time, and personality.

The conclusion of *All Hallows' Eve* presents a more extended, and even more careful, use of the technique. When actions grow numinous, characters are often referred to in this archetypal manner, as Betty's mother is identified merely as "the woman" and "she" during her final magical act (*AHE,* 183–87, 197–98). In fact, during the entire final chapter, names are used as rarely as possible: once identified, the Clerk becomes "he," and his acolytes are not even people, but "the diseased creatures" (197). As Williams writes, again with many levels of meaning at once, "they were now in a world of simple act. . . . They were in the City" (197).

Even more impressive is Williams's depiction of Lester's point of view as she finally crosses over from the borderland City to true eternity, approaching a unitary consciousness and receding from our world. At first she is concerned with her husband, identifying him by name and thinking, "Without him, what was immortality or glory worth?" However, as her awareness expands and her sense of our world diminishes, "Richard" becomes "Richard's figure," then referred to by the term "it" (*AHE,* 194).

At the same time, Lester becomes more aware of spiritual reality, symbolized by the river and the rain, which she "saw . . . with an admirable exactitude—each at the same time as she saw all" (194).

This paradoxical sense of combined separation and union is emphasized by Williams's use of the rising rose color (rain, baptismal water, wine, blood, dawn, unfolding rose-flower, fire) as a medium that both unifies and separates all the characters at the climax (*AHE,* 194-202). At the very end, Lester's personal awareness returns, and with it the awareness of Richard as a person. That may be an error on the author's part, but it is also necessary for the emotional impact—and polysemy—of Lester's farewell to Richard, "Good-bye, my blessing!" (203).

No quality of Williams's writing has been more mythologized than his presentation of internal states, especially religious experience. Since Lewis and Eliot, too many critics have remarked upon the experiential aspect of Williams's novels in tones of awe,[26] without examining the specific mechanisms by which Williams achieved it. Indeed, it is quite difficult to examine objectively the prose of subjective experience, and to analyze the separate devices that convey the impression of transcendence and unity. This study of three particular techniques is intended to begin a more concrete examination of the ways in which Williams depicts and enacts the "pattern of glory" in his novels.

26. See Chad Walsh, "Charles Williams' Novels and the Contemporary Mutation of Consciousness," in *Myth, Allegory, and Gospel,* ed. John Warwick Montgomery (Minneapolis: Bethany Fellowship, 1974), 56.

PART II

Fiction: Individual Works

Time in the Stone of Suleiman

Verlyn Flieger

Of all the ways to bring about change, the most risky, yet—or perhaps therefore—often the most effective, is by shock, by a violent dislocation of the perceiving sensibilities. Disjuncture, discordance, unexpectedness of presentation jolt the audience out of its complacency into a new state of awareness. Paradox blows the circuits and establishes new connections. Of no modern writer is this more true than of Charles Williams, who has been both praised and faulted for his use of discordance, for the striking and deliberately disparate features typical of his work. This is most apparent in his novels, with their hallmark combination of the esoteric and the mundane, of highly sensational, often shocking events taking place in the dullest and most ordinary of surroundings, all put in the service of presenting and promoting uncompromisingly Christian themes. Not for nothing have they been called "spiritual thrillers," though at first glance and if one does not take Williams seriously, the thrill may seem to undermine the spirituality. Herein resides the paradox. It is the risk Williams takes, and when he pulls it off (and he is not always successful) it works brilliantly.

The surface contrast in Williams's novels between the esoteric events and their everyday settings, the equally striking disparity between his avowed Christian impulse and his focus on the occult and the demonic, can either distract from or call attention to these elements' connection at a deeper level. His craft, then, must be more than simply a matter of arbitrarily bringing contradictory elements into conjunction so that their collision may generate some energy. The conjunction, the collision itself must have its own rationale, its own reason for being. In order truly to persuade, the surface contradictions must connect, not collide, at some deeper level.

Such deliberate contrast can either overshadow or highlight the daring of Williams's effort, the reach of his speculative thinking, and—more important—his ability to persuade his reader through the very disjunction of the elements with which he chooses to work. This looks easy, but it isn't. Neither the praise nor the blame he has been accorded does him full justice as a daring and speculative thinker able to weave apparently incoherent strands into a thematically and artistically coherent fabric.

76   VERLYN FLIEGER

That Williams was well aware of the poetic impact of disjunction and fully conscious in his own use of the technique is illustrated in the rhetoric of his own literary criticism, in the poets he selects to praise, and in the qualities he finds praiseworthy in their work. His essay on Wordsworth, "The Growth of a Poet's Mind," describes and analyzes the value of precisely this strategy of disjunctive creativity. It is the business of poets, Williams states, to work with discordant elements. Taking as his text Wordsworth's *Prelude,* Williams explores the poet's emphasis in that work on the power of poetry, wherein "darkness makes abode." In support of this he cites two episodes from the first book, episodes in which the poet becomes aware of the discordance between the natural and the supernatural worlds, aware of "unknown modes of being."

> Dust as we are, the immortal spirit grows
> Like harmony in music; there is a dark
> Inscrutable workmanship that reconciles
> Discordant elements, makes them cling together
> In one society.

This [writes Williams] is precisely the achievement of the great poets; in each of them discordant elements are united in one society by the inscrutable workmanship of their genius, and the society is the style.[1]

Not surprisingly, what Williams found valuable in Wordsworth is precisely what he used in his own work, for it is just this uniting of "discordant elements" into one society that is also Williams's achievement. Like Wordsworth's, Williams's own "inscrutable workmanship" unites the deliberately discordant elements he selects into the "one society" he wants to create. Furthermore, he states, "the society is the style." Here he is voicing a creative credo set out in different terms by J. R. R. Tolkien, who in his essay "On Fairy-Stories" made one of the essential goals of good fantasy that of creating "the inner consistency of reality."[2] When he wrote the essay Tolkien had in mind his own kind of fantasy, the creation of what he called a "secondary world," a wholly invented cosmos. Williams was attempting something in its own way bolder and more risky. In all his work, but especially in his novels, he was shooting for something much nearer to Wordsworth than to Tolkien, and that was to find a way to remain with the primary world but expand its "inner consistency" to include an apparently different, certainly a deeper, reality and to make both realities into one society.

1. Williams, "The Growth of a Poet's Mind," in *Selected Writings,* ed. Anne Ridler (London: Oxford University Press, 1961), 12–13.

2. Tolkien, "On Fairy-Stories," in *Essays Presented to Charles Williams,* ed. C. S. Lewis (London: Oxford University Press, 1947), 67.

Williams's own achievement, like that of the great poets he cites in his essay, is to make a virtue of disjunction, to seat the occult and the esoteric squarely in the middle of the everyday world, and to make these apparently discordant elements work in support of one another. For Williams it was exactly this operation, wherein "the society is the style," that was the crux of his work. For Williams the interface between the phenomenal and the noumenal was the point at which the collision and the connection happened; it was the place of the most concentrated power and experience. Like Wordsworth, he wanted to persuade his reader of the presence and potential of the extraordinary lying just under the surface of the ordinary, to show in the everyday material world the immanence of the spiritual one he saw as animating it.

One of his characteristic methods of persuasion was to place the most apparently discordant element at the very center of his story, to select a particular and usually mysterious *thing*—a magical object, a talisman, a supernatural manifestation of some kind—and make it the focus of both plot and theme. In *The Greater Trumps* it is the Tarot pack, in *War in Heaven* it is the Holy Grail, in *The Place of the Lion* it is the archetypal Platonic Forms, in *Many Dimensions* it is the mysterious Stone of Suleiman. Though this particular treatment is a recognized Williams trademark, the technique is not new with him but has been a staple, time out of mind, of some of the oldest literary forms, those of fairy tale and myth, as well as of their counterparts in modern fantasy. One has only to remember Aladdin's lamp, the Firebird's magical feather, the miraculous Sampo of the Finnish *Kalevala,* or—closer to Williams in time and place—the Silmarils, the holy jewels at the center of *The Silmarillion,* J. R. R. Tolkien's life work, his fantasy mythology of Valinor and Middle-earth.

Williams's treatment of such an item differs noticeably from the conventional method in one important respect, however. The central item in myth and fairy tale, whatever it may be, tends to be arbitrary in its magical capacities, following no law or principle but simply being what it is and doing what it does without any perceivable rationale. A close look at Williams's work will show that he usually contrives to invest his central item with some integrity, to have it operate in conformity to a principle. He gives it its own "inner consistency of reality," which, apparent or sub-merged, provides a solid basis for what seems to be most magical or supernatural and undergirds apparent collision and connection. The distinction between them, however, is often unclear, with the judgment as to which is which left largely to the reader, for the item in question is not just magic—always and however it operates, it is capable of apparent good and apparent evil. It is capable finally of wreaking supernatural havoc in the natural world if it is not contained or restored to its rightful place.

78 VERLYN FLIEGER

In a typical Williams novel the action arises from a situation in which the power inhering in the thing, whatever it may be, interacts explosively with human good and evil. It unleashes in the natural world supernatural forces beyond containment, and in so doing adds to the story a dimension greater than its deceptively simple *thingness*—for lack of a better term—in most cases appears to warrant. Each such item has its own characteristics and its own mode of operation, and it is this mode, consistent in itself, that contributes much of the persuasive power of his story. If the reader accepts the part, acceptance of the whole will follow. These characteristics and this mode of operation are not always overt. Williams tends to submerge his rationale under the surface shimmer of his plot. But just as the actor knows more than the audience about the motivations of a character, and that knowledge undergirds both the performance and the drama of which it is a part, Williams's own knowledge of his rationale and his creative security in relying on it, though these are seldom apparent, confer on his story a believability and a power to persuade that it otherwise would lack.

I propose to take a close look at the rationale behind one such artefact, the Stone of Suleiman at the center of *Many Dimensions,* and to show how its apparently supernatural properties have their own consistent principle of operation, whose integrity contributes substantially to the intellectual density of the story. Acknowledging—but for the moment setting aside—the obvious theological concerns implicit in the Stone's function in both theme and plot, I propose rather to focus on its more practical aspects and to address the issue of the mechanism, the means by which these are conveyed. I intend to do this, moreover, with reference to a particular source which I suggest that Williams used, and which supplied him with the operational principle on which to base the Stone.

At the beginning of the novel Williams goes to considerable length to give the Stone both a history and a pedigree. As the Hajji Ibrahim, the character most in touch with the Stone's historical and mystical import, recounts the story of the Stone to Lord Arglay,

> when the Merciful One made the worlds, first of all He created that Stone and gave it to the Divine One whom the Jews call Shekinah, and as she gazed upon it the universes arose and had being. But afterwards it passed from Iblis to Adam, and from Adam to Nimrod, and from Nimrod to Suleiman, and after Suleiman it came into the sceptre of Octavianus who was called Caesar and Augustus and was lord of Rome. But from Rome it came with Constantine to New Rome, and thence eastward—only in hiding—till our lord Muhammed (blessed be he!) arose to proclaim the Unity. (*MD,* 50)

From there, says the Hajji, it went to Spain, and from thence to a place in the hilt of Charlemagne's sword, and then, because "the world became very evil" (51), it went into hiding until the finding and merchandising of the Stone, which comprises the opening sequence of the novel. In spite of this impressive genealogy, however, Williams avoids defining the Stone, preferring to surround it with names and phrases that work impressionistically rather than definitively. Here the Stone's very unfamiliarity to the eyes of Western culture gives him an advantage. Unlike the Grail or the Tarot pack or the Platonic Forms, all of which have a known history and a context before and beyond his novels, the Stone of Suleiman is not an artefact immediately recognizable to most readers. Thus, not constrained by any known properties of the Stone, Williams is therefore more at liberty to work with it than he is to work with those others—freer to select his own rationale, his own consistent working principle. He is free also to bury that working principle below the manifest text, down where it will not distract from plot or theme. Thus, though the Stone is variously called *the Mystery, the End of Desire, the Unity, the First Matter,* and *the Center of the Derivations,* none of these is very useful in ascertaining what it is, what it does, or how it does it.

What it does, though that bears little apparent relation to what it is named, is almost immediately made clear and is the stuff of which the plot is made, the material that generates the surface shimmer. Of the Stone's various properties, the most manifest are its abilities to facilitate travel through space and time, to enable its user to look into another's mind or heart, to heal infirmity, and, finally, to multiply itself indefinitely without dividing its essence or losing any of its original substance. What it is also is soon told, but again, that explains little. The Stone is more than simply a magical object; it is the Holy of Holies, the I Am. It contains the Tetragrammaton, the name of God, but the name is in it, not on it—indeed, the name *is* it, if the Hajji Ibrahim is any authority. The Stone is the Name and the Name is the Stone.

This last has a direct bearing on how the Stone does what it does. The naked Name of God is too numinous, its presence too powerful, its implications too awesome for it to be used as a mere novelistic technique, however reverently handled. Its very power would overwhelm and diminish the believability of the story that attempted to contain it. It needs to be clothed in something lesser, to be given a mediating principle, a limit on capacity whereby the Stone it inhabits can be accepted as operating believably within the phenomenal world. The principle I would suggest is that of time, not ordinary everyday time, but time operating in a highly specific, clearly defined way. This is an element so obvious that it is apt to be overlooked. When Glen Cavaliero observes that "far from the Stone being in time, time is in the Stone,"[3] he is merely restating the perception of the novel's most

---

3. Cavaliero, *Charles Williams: Poet of Theology* (Grand Rapids, Mich.: Eerdmans, 1983), 71.

80 VERLYN FLIEGER

selfless character, Chloe Burnett. She inquires of Lord Arglay at the beginning of the action: "You mean that Time is in the Stone, not the Stone in Time?" (*MD,* 158). This seemingly innocent question, with its seemingly artless capitalization of the key words, offers a clear and important clue to the mechanism as well as the mystery that lies behind the story.

It is Williams's association of the Stone with time and space, or in the parlance of modern quantum physics, with space/time, in which I find the consistency of the novel to reside, and on which I propose to concentrate in this essay. This is not to dispute the host of Williams scholars, such as Glen Cavaliero or Agnes Sibley, whose studies have focused on Williams's treatment of the Stone in connection with Judaic and Islamic mysticism as well as with the mystical aspects of Christianity, and who find the Stone to be symbolic of Williams's espoused doctrine of coinherence. The implications of the Stone are vast, and Williams surely intends his reader to become aware of them all. The present study, however, will stake out and concentrate on a much smaller and more easily surveyed piece of turf—the technical and theoretical rather than the theological basis of the story, the *how* rather than the *what* or the *why.*

The book's title has been seen as an indication of the theological nature of its theme, but it may also supply a clue to the operative principle on which Williams builds his fantasy. Agnes Sibley associates the phrase "many dimensions" with "many mansions," as in the words of Christ in the fourteenth chapter of St. John: "In my Father's house are many mansions," and indeed the assonance and consonance of the root syllables foster such an association. In her view the theology of the title thus sets the tone for the entire book. "The whole tone of the book is one of opening to our sight wider possibilities; life is more mysterious than we have realized, and God is infinitely beyond our conceptions of space and time—He moves in other dimensions."[4]

This is a plausible association, especially given Williams's intense lifelong focus on the mysteries of Christianity. Nevertheless, it is not the only one available; there may be a theoretical one as well. Sibley derives her connecting premise from the weaker half of the phrase, the adjective rather than the noun; her following association of *mansions* with *dimensions,* while it is not invalid, somewhat exceeds St. John's frame of reference. That Williams intended more, and that his title conveys a deliberate reference to the physics and theory of space/time as well as to the Gospels, is plain from his choice of the noun *dimensions.* In the twentieth century the word *dimension,* both in sound and in meaning, has its own power, and—

4. Sibley, *Charles Williams* (Boston: Twayne, 1982), 56.

especially in the particular time in which Williams was writing—some very specific associations not with Christian mystery but with modern physics. Simply as a phrase, "many *dimensions*" cannot but suggest to the twentieth-century mind an increase beyond the conventionally accepted three dimensions and, thus, lead directly to the so-called "fourth dimension," that of time. The phrase in contemporary thought calls up all its associations with Einstein and relativity, and in imaginative fiction the speculative possibilities of space/time.

Thus there is more than one resonance to Williams's title, and its associative possibilities are multiplied. Though it addresses the content rather than the title, and though it does not take specific note of Einstein, Glen Cavaliero's critical study of Williams's work does associate the novel with two other contemporary books in the space/time mode, calling *Many Dimensions* "the kind of time-fantasy made popular by such books as J. W. Dunne's *An Experiment with Time* (1927) and P. D. Ouspensky's *A New Model of the Universe* (1931)."[5] Ouspensky's work, published in the same year as *Many Dimensions,* is not likely to have had a direct influence on Williams, though it addresses many of his interests, being occult, esoteric, and abstruse. Dunne's book, on the other hand, published four years before *Many Dimensions,* may well have had a direct bearing on Williams's particular treatment of time and on his characterization of the Stone itself.

Though it is rather out of fashion now, having been superseded by newer speculations in the realm of theoretical and quantum physics, *An Experiment with Time* found a wide audience when it first came out, perhaps because it was presented as neither scientific nor occult and was written by one who was neither a scientist nor a parapsychologist. Unlike Ouspensky, whose name and associations with Gurdjieff gave him and his books an exotic, Eastern—and to some a faintly suspect—flavor, Dunne was a thoroughly conventional member of the British establishment. According to J. B. Priestley, who in his own words was an "early and enthusiastic" reviewer of Dunne's book and who conducted his own experiments with time, Dunne was a regular army man who had served in the Boer War, an aeronautical engineer who designed and built the first British military aircraft, a clubman whose hobby was dry-fly fishing and whose first published book was on that unrarefied subject.[6]

Anyone less typical of the occult and esoteric, then, would be difficult to imagine. Dunne was to all appearances at several removes from anything hinting at the mystical or the parapsychological. Moreover, though he was

5. Cavaliero, *Poet of Theology,* 59.
6. Priestley, *Man and Time* (New York: Crescent Books, 1989), 244.

82   VERLYN FLIEGER

an engineer, he was nearly as far removed from theoretical physics as from the occult. Nevertheless, his work reached into realms of speculation traditionally the property of all those areas of interest. Dunne's *Experiment With Time* and its successor, *The Serial Universe,* set out a theory of time that, while it had no measurable effect on the physics of his day, nonetheless responded to it and that was immensely appealing to the unscientific but speculative mind.[7] *An Experiment with Time* found a surprisingly wide audience, and it exerted an influence not just on Priestley but on a whole generation of British writers, among them T. S. Eliot, James Hilton, E. R. Eddison, C. S. Lewis, and J. R. R. Tolkien.

What exactly was Dunne's theory, and how might it have affected Williams's treatment of the Stone of Suleiman? Let us look first at the theory. In brief, Dunne holds that time is not sequential but simultaneous; that it is not progressive but static; and that what are conventionally called past, present, and future are—like space—all equally present at any moment and equally available to the perceiving consciousness. This for Dunne is neither mystical nor scientific. It is simply a question of point of view. He first sets up what he calls Observer 1, that is, the conventional, everyday consciousness—aware of the clock, the round of the sun, the passage of linear, forward-moving time. Around Observer 1 he then wraps Observer 2, a wider consciousness that is always present but is most active in sleep and dream. For Dunne that consciousness, though largely unactivated in waking experience, can—and does in dreams—move more freely over the field of time and can observe events that to the waking consciousness (Observer 1) have not yet happened or are external to the dreamer's personal past. All that is necessary, then, to see into the future or the past is to widen the observer's field of attention, to awaken Observer 2. Dunne's theory goes on to postulate possible Observers 3, 4, 5, and so on, each succeeding observer with a field of attention surrounding the previous ones. But all that is really necessary to apply his theory to *Many Dimensions* is to accept the premise of the existence of the second observer.

Had Williams read Dunne's book? There is no hard evidence to demonstrate that he had, but given the popularity of the book with a particular stratum of the intellectual reading public, given also Williams's tastes and interests and the inquiring and speculative bent of his mind, it would be difficult to imagine that he had not. Moreover, two of the men with whom his literary name is most often associated, C. S. Lewis and J. R. R. Tolkien, *had* read *An Experiment with Time.* Lewis's copy is in the Wade Center at Wheaton College, Illinois, and Tolkien's in the possession of his

---

7. John William Dunne, *An Experiment with Time* (London: A. & C. Black, 1927); *The Serial Universe* (London: A. & C. Black, 1934).

TIME IN THE STONE OF SULEIMAN

son Christopher. Also worthy of note is the fact that, like Williams, each of these men tried his hand at stories of time travel. Lewis, indeed, specifically cites Dunne in an unfinished story of time-travel, his posthumously published *The Dark Tower*. And while Tolkien makes no specific reference to Dunne, both his unfinished time-travel story *The Lost Road* and his treatment of time in *The Lord of the Rings* owe a clear debt to Dunne's theory. Though at the time he wrote *Many Dimensions* Williams had not yet met either Lewis or Tolkien, I think we can safely assume that, like them (and it was undeniably likeness of mind and interest that drew Williams and Lewis together), he had read Dunne's book and that, also like them, he would be quick to see the possibilities it offered for imaginative speculation.

Now for the second question: how might *An Experiment with Time* have helped shape *Many Dimensions*? I suggest that Williams found in Dunne's theory a convenient and practical rationale for the operation of the Stone of Suleiman and that the Stone functions in Williams's novel in much the same way as does the field of time in Dunne's book. Thus, those of his characters who use the Stone to travel freely through time and space do so in the mode of Dunne's dreaming Observer 2, gaining physical access through the operation of the Stone to a wider field of attention than that available to those around them. The users' field of attention thus transcends the limited, waking attention field of those who witness with astonished eyes their apparent departures and arrivals. This is by no means the limit of the Stone's powers, which for Williams reach into theological profundities scarcely touched on by Dunne. Nevertheless, Dunne's theory offers a practical, operational rationale that can account for the Stone's otherwise inexplicable powers. It offers evidence that a more hard-edged principle is at work than simply the one Agnes Sibley calls "sheer wonder" and "magic as in a fairy story."[8]

What, in essence, does the Stone actually *do* in the novel? The answer is deceptively simple: it widens the field of attention. That is, through the action of the Stone the field of attention is so widened that the user has access to and can move in any direction across time and across the space that occupies time, whether that space is actual—locatable in actual geography—or mental—within the mind of another. If the movement is across actual space, the user of the Stone disappears to the perceptions of the surrounding "Observer 1's." If the movement is into mental space, as when Lord Arglay gains access to the mind of Sir Giles, the operation seems less one of physical transportation than of internalization of the Stone's process. Williams neatly avoids the practical problem of what would then appear to

8. Sibley, *CW*, 56.

the external observer: he situates Lord Arglay alone in his rooms. The narrative, and thus the reader, are *within* Arglay's experience. There is no external observer, therefore there is no external phenomenon to be observed.

The Stone's most immediate and obvious application, perceived variously as advantage or threat, is its ability physically to transport the body through space. But this simply makes it a kind of flying carpet, as Chloe Burnett observes. "Did you say it was the Crown of Suleiman, Mr. Montague? I thought he went on a carpet" (*MD*, 24). As such, whether Stone or carpet, it is simply a rapid-transit medium whose financial and economic implications appeal, for different reasons, to both the government and private industry.

Movement through terrestrial space (for Williams's vision is earthly, limited to the round world; nothing is said about "space travel," only travel through space) is a practical but not a particularly philosophical or theological consideration. The Stone's relationship to time is obviously the more complex and the more theological question. It is therefore no accident that the first question posed by Sir Giles Tumulty at the opening of the novel is "Does it work in time as well as space?" (*MD*, 12). It is in and through time that Williams will make most imaginative use of the Stone's possibilities. The Stone's most inexplicable property, its capacity to endlessly divide without surrendering its wholeness, is most readily explained if we can relate this aspect of the Stone to the comparable aspect of time, which, for all our arbitrary measurements, is itself seamless and indivisible. Like the Stone and its endlessly proliferatable Types, time is always entire; it is only our perception that seems to divide it, and it is our perception that must constantly be readjusted to bring time into conformity with our human expectations.

The Stone's most spectacular capacity, its ability to heal the sick, is likewise unexplained. The overtones of the episodes in which the news of its curative powers spreads and the villagers of Rich crowd around the Stone are intentionally and explicitly resonant of passages in the Gospels. As Agnes Sibley points out, "Williams describes, in a modern setting, a scene comparable to biblical accounts of the sick crowding around Christ."[9] There is, to be sure, no reason why the healings cannot be accepted as true miracles. However, if the Stone has a consistent principle of operation, that principle should be able to account for the Stone's capacity to heal infirmity, and that ability should be consistent with its ability in other areas.

I suggest that the Stone may heal by transposing the body back to a time when it was well. The paralyzed and bedridden Mrs. Ferguson is miracu-

9. Sibley, *CW*, 58.

TIME IN THE STONE OF SULEIMAN

lously healed when she travels back in memory to her girlhood and Sunday school days. "O," she says, "I do wish I could run now as well as I could then" (*MD*, 99). And suddenly, in the conflation of Now with Then that is the unique property of the Stone, she can. Oliver Doncaster's association of the Stone with the Urim and Thummim—those undefined, probably pebblelike objects used in ancient Israel to divine the will of God—is not to be overlooked, of course. Like the Urim and Thummim, the Stone is a Holy Thing, and like them it works with and for the will of God. But the mechanism by which Mrs. Ferguson's healing is brought about, I suggest, is the mechanism of time, and the theory behind that mechanism is J. W. Dunne's.

Avoiding the temptation yielded to by much science fiction, to devise and promote a particular system, and lest he become bogged down in mechanics and make his story hostage to its own operating principle, Williams wisely refrains from offering his reader any easy explanation of the Stone and its powers. In keeping with the rhetoric of Williams's strategy, this omission has the paradoxical effect of enhancing the story's persuasive effect on the reader. A variety of characters try to figure it out, and they come up with an equal variety of answers. Although the names used by the Hajji Ibrahim come closest to capturing for the reader the Stone's mystical significance, the most informed speculation about the Stone and at the same time the deepest questioning of its nature are put into the mouth of the rational, skeptical, ironic, and humane Chief Justice, Lord Arglay, arguably the most attractive character in the book. Musing on the Stone's capacity to transport its bearer through time, he considers the possibility that the past

> might, even materially, exist; only man was not aware of it, time being, whatever else it was, a necessity of his consciousness. "But because I can only be sequentially conscious," he argued, "must I hold that what is not communicated to consciousness does not exist? I think in a line—but there is the potentiality of the plane." This perhaps was what great art was—a momentary apprehension of the plane at a point in the line. The Demeter of Cnidos, the Praying Hands of Dürer, the *Ode to a Nightingale,* the Ninth Symphony—the sense of vastness in those small things was the vastness of all that had been felt in the present. Would one dare wish to *be* the Demeter? to be—what? Stone? yes, presumably stone. But stone of an intense significance—to others; but to itself? Agnosticism checked him; no one knew. (*MD*, 62–63)

Williams will commit neither his Chief Justice nor himself to an outright explanation of the Stone's operation. But the clues are there, the diagrammatic references to the line and the plane (Dunne went to great lengths to diagram his theory by means of lines and planes), the hint that there may be more than is "communicated to [Observer 1's] consciousness." The guiding principle is laid out—or rather, questioned out—for those who care to accept it.

86   VERLYN FLIEGER

Some pages further on, a less philosophically formulated but more explicit hint is given by a somewhat less persuasive source, Sir Giles Tumulty's associate, Palliser. Discussing the unfortunate lab assistant Pondon, who has been caught in a time loop by using the Stone to wish himself back into the past, Palliser remarks to Sir Giles, "As I understand it, all the past still exists and it's merely a matter of choosing your point of view" (*MD*, 156). His grasp of the concept is neither as speculative nor as imaginative as Lord Arglay's. Nevertheless, it conveys in more flat-footed language much the same idea. What Dunne describes as a widening of the field of attention by means of Observer 2, Palliser calls simply "choosing your point of view," but whatever the words, the operation under discussion is much the same. All time is accessible to the attention of the perceiving consciousness.

Perhaps the most vivid presentation of "choosing your point of view," of widening the experience of the field of time, is that which Williams assigns to Lord Arglay when he and Chloe attempt through the medium of the Stone to travel back in time to rescue Pondon.

> The room about him was the same and yet not the same. The table at his right hand seemed to be multiplied; a number of identical tables appeared beyond it in a long line stretching out to a vague infinity, and all around him the furniture multiplied itself so. Walls that were and yet were not transparent sometimes obscured it and sometimes dissolved and vanished. He saw himself in different positions, now here, now there, and seemed to recognize them. Whenever his mind paused on any one of these eidola of himself it seemed to be fixed, and all the rest to fade, and then his mind would relax and again the phantasmagoria would close in, shifting, vanishing, reappearing. (*MD*, 166)

Flickering across the field of time between the consciousness of Observer 1 and that of Observer 2, the attention of Lord Arglay perceives in multiple and overlapping images the appearances through time of the room he is in and of himself in it. The fact that he can see "himself in different positions, now here, now there," suggests that his Observer 2, occupying the plane, is conscious of a multiplicity of Observer 1's occupying points on a line. When his attention rests on any one of these points, "any one of these eidola of himself," the rest fade, and the one focusing his attention seems to be the only one, that moment in time the "present" and the others the unperceived "past" or "future." He finds that only by an act of will can he "prevent himself submitting to it and being conscious only of some precise moment" (167). In place of this submission to the moment, submission to the point rather than the plane, Williams has the scene culminate in Arglay's conscious "act of submission to the Stone; all times were here and equal—if the captive of the past could understand" (167), and with this acceptance Arglay's consciousness, and Chloe's as well, connect with that of the hapless

TIME IN THE STONE OF SULEIMAN

Pondon, who is freed thereby from his imprisonment in the loop and restored to the linear present.

It is only late in the story, after Pondon's rescue, after Sir Giles Tumulty's experiment with the hanged man and its horrendous outcome, that Williams ventures to offer his reader an explicit statement about what the Stone is. Characteristically, he places it in the mouth of his least reliable, least spiritually perceptive character, leaving readers to make of his explanation what they will. The Stone is, in the words of Sir Giles Tumulty, "a kind of rendezvous of the past and the future" (*MD,* 223). "But how does it work?" Palliser asks him, and again Sir Giles provides a characteristically superficial-seeming answer that yet has truth, a truth saying, in effect, that the Stone doesn't "work" in any conventional sense, that, rather, the user of the Stone "works" with and in the Stone. The Stone itself simply is. The parallel with Dunne's time theory is, though subtextual rather than explicit, plain to see. Time, like space, does not operate in us, but we in it. Time simply is. "Once you are in contact," Sir Giles explains, "and you choose and desire and will, you go into it and come out again where you have desired because everything is in it, anyhow" (225).

The theological issue of free will unwittingly raised by Sir Giles—"you choose and desire and will"—is intended, of course, to contrast with the "submission" to the Stone (and thus to the will of God) of Lord Arglay in the rescue of Pondon and, ultimately, of Chloe Burnett as she surrenders herself to become the path for the Stone's restoration. He is speaking, of course, in a purely scientific, purely materialistic sense, and Williams's clear and ironic point is that Sir Giles doesn't understand the true import of what he is saying. Nevertheless, he is on the right track. The Stone is, as he states unequivocally, the First Matter. But to call it the First Matter, even while this may to the mystical mind associate it with the Logos and the nature of God, does little to make its mode of being clear. To associate it with Time, however, and to apprehend Time in the terms described by Dunne, provides a practical context in which to understand the Stone's operations.

Nowhere is this more dramatically illustrated than in the terrifying final passage near the end of the book in the chapter entitled "The Discovery of Sir Giles Tumulty." The discovery in question is, of course, Sir Giles's final discovery of the true operation of the Stone, a discovery that comes in the moment of his death. His last attempt to use the Stone is made in utter frustration and rage at the most spiritually attuned character in the book, whom Sir Giles, typically, sees only in carnal terms as "that bitch of Arglay's," Chloe Burnett. Furious at what he imagines to be the "control" exerted by Arglay and Chloe, but especially by Chloe, over the powers of the Stone, he makes her the focus of all his hatred. "Damn you," he cries while holding the Stone, "I only wish I could get at you" (*MD,* 285–86).

The word *wish* is the operative one here, as it was, though with far different results, in the case of the crippled Mrs. Ferguson. In unwitting compliance with the terms of his own formula to "choose and desire and will," Sir Giles wishes himself into the Stone and then, in unwilling submission to his own desire, is inevitably drawn within its ineluctable operation. He cannot "get at" Chloe, for he is not equipped to understand what she truly is, but being given a clear vision of her asleep in her bed is moved to cry out at her, "O go to hell" (287). It is the annotation and gloss on his previous "Damn you," and he is given his wish. But since what he damns is not Chloe as she is but rather Chloe as he sees her—that is, as a type of himself—it is he who is condemned by his own words.

While it is not his last word on the Stone, or the Stone's last involvement with the phenomenal world (this is reserved for Chloe), Williams's final determination of the fate of Sir Giles—actually Sir Giles's unwitting but self-willed determination of his own fate—is a recapitulation of that essentially unpleasant character's whole self and activity played out within the Stone.

> He had willed to be in the future, and since that could not be, for the future as yet had lain only in the Mind to which it equally with the past was present, the Stone had revealed the future to him. He remembered; he knew what was to happen, for the merciful oblivion was withdrawn; he saw himself gathered, a living soul, into the centre of the Stone. . . . He was conscious also of a myriad other Giles Tumultys, of childhood and boyhood and youth and age, all that he had ever been, and all of them were screaming as that relentless and dividing light plunged into them and held them. He was doing, it seemed, innumerable things at once, all the things that he had ever done, and yet the whole time he was not doing, he was slipping, slipping down. . . . From the spirals of time and place he felt himself falling, and still he fell and fell. (*MD*, 288–89)

The scene is a kind of nightmare reprise of Lord Arglay's experience of perceiving at once the plane and the line and the point on the line. Yet with a powerful difference. Where Lord Arglay voluntarily submitted his will to the Stone, Giles Tumulty has tried to force the Stone to submit to his will. And as the attitude in each case is different, so will be the outcome. The Stone encompassed Christopher Arglay and yet left him free. It will encoil Giles Tumulty in "the spirals of time and place" and release him from those only into his death.

There is much more to this passage, of course. I have elided those portions (and they include some of the most powerful moments) in which Williams movingly and passionately invokes the presence and the action of God, characterized by him as the "light," or the "Mind," or the "Glory." I have omitted these portions not because they are unimportant—on the contrary, they are at the very heart of the episode—but because their import requires no explication. I intend not to draw attention to the meaning of the passage, which is immediately apparent, but rather to illustrate its working hypothesis, its technique; to use the episode to uncover and illustrate the submerged theoretical structure of the book, which is the persuasive underpinning of Williams's story.

Dunne's theory of time informs the concept behind the central image of the story, the image of the Stone of Suleiman. The theory provides the ground on which Williams's achievement is erected, the rhetorical strategy on which the story of the Stone and the integrity of its properties rest. Though it never obtrudes into the story, it is yet the ground whereon collision turns into connection, and the perceiving sensibility experiences a shift. The theory gives Williams's work that hallmark of paradox, and it reconciles the story's apparently discordant elements into "one society." What Williams himself found and praised in the *Prelude,* Wordsworth's "dark, inscrutable workmanship," is as typical of him as of Wordsworth. It is the test of true paradox that it can maintain opposites in creative tension. There can be no doubt that *Many Dimensions* passes that test. Its power resides precisely in such tension, a tension that gives to Williams's story and to his theme that "inner consistency of reality," which is the true measure not just of modern fantasy but of any creative endeavor that strives to give its reader a persuasive, convincing, but above all profound experience of change.

A Metaphysical Epiphany?
Charles Williams and
the Art of the Ghost Story

Glen Cavaliero

Charles Williams was eventually to achieve best-seller status at Christmas 1986, when "Et in Sempiternum Pereant" was included in *The Oxford Book of English Ghost Stories.*[1] Even in its present company it is something of an oddity; but for that very reason it all the more clearly illustrates, albeit on a miniature scale, the particular handling of supernatural themes which distinguishes Williams's novels from those of other writers in this field. It is a ghost story with a difference.

I

Any discussion of fiction of this kind is subject to the fact that the defining term is liable to misunderstanding and misuse. Theologically speaking, the word *supernatural* is to be understood in a teleological sense; that is, it denotes the natural in terms of its essential being and of its relation to its end or final purpose. The proper mode of apprehending the term is therefore not ratiocinative but contemplative. As an adjective, *supernatural* relates its several subjects not so much to the exceptional or the peculiar as to that dimension of being which constitutes the eternal relationship of life to its creative source, the dimension in which everything relates to everything else in what poets and mystics know as "the eternal present" or "the mysterium."

There are at least three attitudes towards any manifestation of the mysterium. It can be regarded or experienced as the preternatural or the weird; it can be treated as paranormal; and it can be accepted as the revelation of a spiritual order that provides the ambience and meaning of the

---

1. Ed. Michael Cox and R. A. Gilbert (Oxford: Oxford University Press, 1986), 421–29. Earlier, Williams's story was included in *Visions of Wonder: An Anthology of Christian Fantasy,* ed. Robert H. Beyer and Kenneth J. Zahorski (New York: Avon, 1981), 167–77. It was first published in *The London Mercury* 33 (1935): 151–55. My page references to this story are to the *Oxford Book* edition.

WILLIAMS AND THE ART OF THE GHOST STORY

material one. The fictive treatment of those subjects loosely referred to as "supernatural" tends to be influenced by one or other of these points of view.

The term *preternatural* signifies any kind of physical manifestation not attributable to the known laws of cause and effect. Writers whose understanding of the supernatural is limited to this perspective tend to describe the worlds of spirit and matter as being in collision: it is the difference between them, even their mutual antagonism, which they emphasize. The mysterium is presented as an enigma, threatening and dangerous. It is on these premises that the majority of ghost stories are written. Perhaps because of this, as treatments of supernatural themes they are dismissed by most literary critics as mere diversions. Virginia Woolf, for instance, reviewing Dorothy Scarborough's *The Supernatural in Modern English Fiction,* while she remarks on the "strange human craving for the pleasure of feeling afraid which is so much involved with our love of ghost stories" and speculates on the nature of this particular readerly response, largely ignores the moral or metaphysical capacities inherent in writing of this kind;[2] and indeed it is incontestable that the chief purpose of such well-known tales as Scott's "The Tapestried Chamber," E. Nesbit's "Man-Size in Marble," and the more sophisticated narratives of Montague Rhodes James is that the reader shall be frightened in as thorough and pleasurable a manner as possible.[3]

But there is a second literary tradition, one that treats the supernatural not as being abnormal but rather as *paranormal,* that is, as lying beyond the range of ordinary human knowledge not as a matter of kind but as a matter of degree. This approach to the mysterium is rational and scientific; its treatment of the hows and the whys of supernatural manifestations implies that there is no ontological distinction between material and spiritual qualities. The concept of mystery is diminished to the status of a puzzle calling for solution. A well-known nineteenth-century example of such a story is Edward Bulwer-Lytton's much anthologized "The Haunted and the Haunters," a tale whose alternative title "The House and the Brain" indicates

2. Woolf, "The Supernatural in Fiction," *Times Literary Supplement,* 31 January 1918; reprinted in *Granite and Rainbow,* ed. Leonard Woolf (London: Hogarth Press, 1958), 61–64 (quotation from p. 61).

3. M. R. James, a distinguished antiquary and biblical scholar, represents the preternatural tradition in its purest form. The ghosts and bogeys that infest the old churches, libraries, mazes, woods, and secluded homes he so evocatively describes serve as embodied threats to a comfortable, leisurely way of life that would otherwise seem to be immemorially assured. Indeed, in his fictional world the mysterium manifests itself not simply as preternatural but even as unnatural, as something obtrusive, disconcerting, alien; his spooks are invariably malevolent. (James, *The Collected Ghost Stories* [London: Edward Arnold, 1931].)

Unless noted separately, all stories mentioned are to be found in the Oxford anthology.

92 GLEN CAVALIERO

its quasi-scientific attitude to the workings of things magical and occult. This characteristically materialistic approach is more concerned with observation than with philosophical enquiry, though Lytton himself sought to combine the two in his alchemical romance *A Strange Story* (1862), a novel that can still command respect for its inner imaginative logic. But this quasi-scientific tradition is the least frequently practiced of the three literary approaches, its most popular manifestation being the time-warp or time-travel story.[4]

A third approach to the supernatural may be designated the *hermetic*. It is one in which material and spiritual realities are treated as aspects or dimensions of each other and as subject to the transcendence of the mysterium. This literary tradition views the supernatural as being the true province of the imagination and as the source of physical reality. It does not, as do the preternatural and paranormal traditions, regard the supernatural as an intrusion upon, or a mere extension of, reality; and it finds expression in two complementary literary genres, the occult and the visionary. The occult genre, while it takes spiritual categories as inseparable from material ones, does so in an essentially enquiring or manipulative spirit: it is a species of imaginative technology. In contrast, the visionary genre is essentially religious, and it issues in the form of parable, a tale that, being at once both simile and metaphor (a simile in relation to the spiritual dimension, a metaphor for the physical one), demonstrates the workings of the mysterium through spiritual and moral laws.

Charles Williams's tales of the supernatural draw mainly on this hermetic tradition, but they are more diverse in outlook and technique than may be apparent at a first reading. Two early novels, *War in Heaven* (1930) and *Many Dimensions* (1931), reflect his studies of the occult and his membership in the Fellowship of the Rosy Cross,[5] while *The Place of the Lion* (1931) and *The Greater Trumps* (1932) draw on neoplatonic and Cabalistic imagery. In all four of them the occult approach is complemented by the visionary one; they are in the fullest sense hermetic novels. Their controlling symbols are systematically deployed, containing the story rather than being themselves contained within it. *All Hallows' Eve* (1945), however, reveals a more purely theological understanding of the *supernatural*, a word which in Williams's vocabulary means what it says—that which is supremely or quintessentially natural. To such an outlook the kind of uncomfortable

---

4. Bulwer-Lytton, "The Haunted and the Haunters," *Blackwood's Magazine*, August 1859; reprinted in *Ghosts and Marvels*, ed. V. H. Collins, World's Classics (London: Oxford University Press, 1924), 71–125; *A Strange Story* (London: S. Low, 1862).

5. For Williams's membership in A. E. Waite's Rosicrucian order, see R. A. Gilbert, *The Golden Dawn: Twilight of the Magicians* (Wellingborough: Aquarian Press, 1983). Gilbert is also coeditor of *The Oxford Book of English Ghost Stories*.

WILLIAMS AND THE ART OF THE GHOST STORY

juxtapositions envisaged by M. R. James represent an imperfect aspect of the reality and are limited by a point of view that is, where matters of the spirit are concerned, by implication dualistic. For while James can at times turn the tables on his readers by satirizing, and thus subverting, the very tastes and preoccupations that lend substance to his adroit and eerie narratives, behind his stories lies an interpretation of life that conceives of the physical and the spiritual as contrasting categories, rather than as complementary or inseparable ones.

Like *Descent into Hell* (1937), "Et in Sempiternum Pereant" is a work that marks the passage of Williams's imagination from the occult understanding of the supernatural to the visionary. But whereas the occult elements in the novel, such as the figures of Lily Sammile and of Wentworth's phantom succubus, coalesce uneasily with the manifestation of an overriding spiritual order made apparent in the experiences of the leading characters, the short story, compressed as it is, fuses both these modes of awareness. To analyze its method and content is to appreciate the evolution of Williams's spiritual vision at a critical time in his theological development.

II

What is the story about? In the majority of ghostly tales the progress of events is clear: for example, in James's "Oh, Whistle, and I'll Come to You, My Lad," a university professor picks up an ancient whistle in the ruins of a church and, by blowing it, conjures up an elemental that proceeds to materialize in his bedroom. Or, in a well-known instance of the paranormal tradition, Algernon Blackwood's "The Empty House," an inquisitive old lady and her nephew spend the night in a haunted building and witness the reenactment of a crime committed many years before. Both tales begin with a slightly satirical account of "ordinary" experience and then proceed through mounting unease and dread (in James's case cleverly punctuated by mild farce) to a climax of overwhelming physical horror: the stories progress from curiosity through suspense and terror into shock, then through danger to deliverance—or escape. But it is less easy to break down Williams's story in this manner. It starts with a solitary walker (Lord Arglay from *Many Dimensions*) who sees something disquieting in a country lane—a house whose chimney appears to be on fire; he investigates the phenomenon, has an unnerving encounter with a spirit, and escapes back into the world of normality. Superficially the pattern resembles those of the James and Blackwood stories, but the details are imprecise. The opening, far from being satirical or prosaic, describes at some length Arglay's sense of taking an inordinate time to reach his proposed destination; the house itself is depicted only sketchily; and while the spirit-being has a good deal of

Jamesian unpleasantness about it (being flickery, hot, and tattered), the terror it arouses has less to do with its physical impact than with Arglay's own spiritual condition. And the latter's escape is willed; it is neither accidental, as in James's story, nor spontaneously induced as in Blackwood's. Realizing that here is a soul bound for hell, Arglay offers himself as a means to its salvation in the spirit, and in so doing is delivered from the edge of the pit to resume his interrupted journey.

From even this brief outline it may be seen that the story is multilayered. Taken merely on the surface level it would be a poor thing. It is not an exciting drama with an allegorical meaning dependent on it, for its interest is entirely allegorical. And throughout the story the allegorical pointings both draw attention to themselves and also point beyond themselves, so that not until the meaning is fully apprehended does the tale have the power to frighten.

The opening paragraph partakes of the dry, bantering style of *War in Heaven*. Having completed writing his *History of Organic Law,* Lord Arglay is about to visit a country house (a Jamesian motif here) to determine whether certain manuscripts—legal judgments reputedly made by Francis Bacon—are genuine. Arglay muses distressfully on a remark thrown out by their owner, "Everything that is smoked isn't Bacon" (421). It is the kind of facetious jest that Williams himself would seem to have particularly disliked, but the pun is to be endorsed by the events that follow—a characteristic instance of his ironic wit.

The next four paragraphs constitute a preparation for what is to happen inside the house. Arglay finds his progress becoming unaccountably slow: time seems to be gradually standing still. He toys with concepts of time and space (do certain roads cause people to go fast or slow?) and of time and consciousness (is he losing his sense of duration now that he is growing old?). These speculations seem to lead nowhere; yet they are relevant to what follows, for they are overtaken by a still more unsettling awareness.

> This was a new experience; it was lastingness—almost, he could have believed, everlastingness. The measure of it was but his breathing, and his breathing, as it grew slower and heavier, would become the measure of everlasting labour—the labour of Sisyphus, who pushed his own slow heart through each infinite moment, and relaxed but to let it beat back and so again begin. It was the first touch of something Arglay had never yet known, of simple and perfect despair. (423)

From outer solitude he comes to apprehend a totally solitary existence, the measure of all things being himself alone. Time has become movement without change.

The author having established a narrative consciousness that is itself descriptive of a basic alteration in perception, we are ready to proceed to the next stage in the story. What happens is itself conditioned by that alteration. It is the discovery of, and entry into, the smoking house. The latter is sensed as in a dream and is approached "tangentially" by a narrow path "hard and beaten as if by the passage of many feet" (423). Arglay, although "the last person in the world to look for responsibilities," feels impelled to seek entry in case the chimney should indeed be on fire (424). There is a double scriptural reference here: the smoke forms "a narrow and dense pillar of dusk . . . through which there glowed every now and then, a deeper undershade of crimson"; the allusion suggests the pillars of cloud and of fire from Exodus 13:21. But the image is qualified by the phrase "as if some trapped genius almost thrust itself out of the moving prison that held it" (423); then later, when Arglay goes outside again to take another look, "the smoke went up for ever and ever over those roads where men crawled infinitely through the smallest measurements of time" (425). One recalls "And the smoke of their torment goes up for ever and ever" from Revelation 14:11. Images of salvation and damnation are here being conflated—to what end, it is the purpose of the story to unfold.

The narrative next moves into the sphere of Arglay's moral consciousness: imagery gives way to specific comment. Not receiving any answer to his knocking, he begins to feel angry, and there comes into his mind "for no earthly reason" (424: a typical instance of Williams's serious way with a colloquialism) the image of his detested brother-in-law (Sir Giles Tumulty, one assumes), and he "wanted to have him merely to hate" (425). In this moment out of time we are at a point of judgment. Arglay pronounces his own judgment, in both senses of the term, by uttering the first of the two theological definitions that shape the story: "There is entire . . . clarity in the Omnipotence" (425). After which he proceeds to enter "a room empty of smoke as of fire, and of all as of both." "It was completely and utterly void"—one thinks of the room swept and garnished in Matthew 12:43-45. A door seems to open into a cellar, "a hinted unseen depth" (425), and stairs lead upward to, presumably, an attic. Arglay ruminates again. "There's no smoke without fire. . . . Only apparently there is. Thus one lives and learns. Unless indeed this is the place where one lives without learning" (425–26). The speculation affords a further gloss on the Sisyphus theme.

At this point comes the spectral manifestation. It has already been anticipated by a face half glimpsed by Arglay as he waits outside the house door. The description of that premonitory moment is a good instance of Williams's ability to achieve a surrealistic effect: "It had been only along the side of his glance that the face, if face it were, had appeared, a kind of sudden white scrawl against the blur, as if it were a mask hung by the window rather than any living person, or as if the glass of the window itself had looked sideways at him" (424). The hallucinatory impression is sharply

rendered. M. R. James himself could not have done it better.
The ghost is heralded by a "dank and deadly heat."

> The fantasy of life without knowledge materialized, inimical, in the air, life without knowledge, corrupting life without knowledge, jungle and less than jungle, and though still the walls of the bleak chamber met his eyes, a shell of existence, it seemed that life, withdrawn from all those normal habits of which the useless memory was still drearily sustained by the thin phenomenal fabric, was collecting and corrupting in the atmosphere behind the door he had so rashly passed—outside the other door which swung crookedly at the head of the darker hole within. (426)

The writing seems to be discovering, as much as reporting, the experience: the succession of clauses linked solely by commas induces a sense of breathlessness.

Arglay then hears "from without a soft approach" (426), and there enters the appearance of a man wearing nothing but an old black coat. Emaciated and bearing the scar of his own toothmarks in his flesh, he dances in a circle, gnawing at himself and repulsing Arglay's attempts to stop him. The latter finds himself once more obsessed with his hatred for his brother-in-law; in the process he becomes more and more like that which he has just seen. But, for the second time, right reason asserts itself and triumphs.

> The end here was not at the end, but in the beginning. There was no end to this smoke, to this fever and this chill, to crouching and rising and searching, unless the end was now. *Now—now* was the only possible other fact, chance, act. He cried out, defying infinity, "*Now!*" (428)

"Now" is the reality of God, the lucidity of the Omnipotence as against the futility of time that leads but to the pit. The meaning of Arglay's experience becomes clear in the following paragraph, which shows Williams writing at the height of his own lucid concentration and intensity.

> Before his voice the smoke of his prison yielded, and yielded two ways at once. From where he stood he could see in one place an alteration in that perpetual grey, an alternate darkening and lightening as if two ways, of descent and ascent, met. There was, he remembered, a way in, therefore a path out; he had only to walk along it. But also there was a way still farther in, and he could walk along that. Two doors had swung, to his outer senses, in that small room. From every gate of hell there was a way to heaven, yes, and in every way to heaven there was a gate to deeper hell. (428)

This is the vision embodied in Williams's two final novels; and in "Et in Sempiternum Pereant" salvation is likewise bound up with the idea of exchange. Arglay proffers an act of voluntary substitution that offsets the involuntary one whereby he has become the thing he has just witnessed. He wishes to be a ladder out of the pit for the lost spirit; he seeks his neighbor.

WILLIAMS AND THE ART OF THE GHOST STORY

But here the result is ambiguous. Something from behind him breaks through, and simultaneously he hears the weak wailing of the lost. Whether it is a wail of defeat or a wail of greeting is uncertain. But what is certain is Arglay's cry of "Now is God: now is Glory in God" (429). As he goes out he passes another spirit rushing in, "another of the hordes going so swiftly up that straight way, hard with everlasting time; each driven by his own hunger, and each alone." Arglay's last action is to repeat Dante's concluding line in the *Inferno,* "e quindi uscimmo a riveder le stelle" (429).

We emerge and behold the stars once more: "Et in Sempiternum Pereant" is a parable, a portrait of that particular state of self-absorbed hunger and resentment which Williams believed to be a manifestation of damnation. He had already depicted the state in certain poems in *Windows of Night* (1925) —"The Purchase," "A Dream," and "The Other Side of the Way" among them—and he was to refine the account in his portraits of Lawrence Wentworth and Evelyn Mercer in his last two novels. The parabolic nature of this tale is enriched by his choosing to have Lord Arglay, the symbolic embodiment of justice, himself become the subject of temptation: hatred and the desire to hate are part of the imprisonment in time which is another theme of the story. And the very ambiguity of the conclusion affirms the sovereignty of Divine Law. Whether his offer is accepted, Arglay's gesture of substitution is sufficient in itself. In Williams's interpretation of justice and redemption, the passwords for deliverance from hell are *lucidity* and *now.*

III

Elucidation, if not lucidity, is generally a required function of literary criticism. No text is worth much if it remains obscure, and no less than any other form of narrative art the ghost story consists of a message conveyed from writer to reader, using a code or system of reference that can be deciphered so as to make contact, the full meaning of which is realized in a particular context.[6] In a ghost story the message is the succession of recorded events, the code being the invasion and disturbance of normality by the abnormal. Contact is made through the registering of disturbance by the reader; and the nature and meaning of this response is dictated by the context, the general overview or attitude implicit in the author's manipulation of the imagery and narrative. And it is this context that determines the seriousness of the tale's pretensions. In the finest examples of the genre one finds a persuasive evocation of the mysterium.

---

6. I have adapted the terms *message, code, contact,* and *context* from Roman Jakobson, "Linguistics and Poetics," in *Style in Language,* ed. Thomas Sebeok (Bloomington: Indiana University Press, 1960), 350–77.

98   GLEN CAVALIERO

"Et in Sempiternum Pereant" is a story whose message is peculiarly dependent on code and context, and one (as in other of Williams's narratives) in which contact plays a reciprocal determining part. In James's and Blackwood's stories the message and the code are not logically inseparable. In "Oh, Whistle, and I'll Come to You, My Lad," hallucination and nightmare could account for the haunting on a naturalistic level: it would be possible to tell the story without entering the professor's consciousness. Again, in "The Empty House," the setting is realistically described and thus persuades the reader that it is objectively real; indeed, it is part of the author's intention, and certainly of his effects, that this should be the case. And in both stories what happens would still happen if, from the point of view of an outside observer, there were no ghost at all. But in Charles Williams's case the entire experience is subjective: code and message are at one.

Again, where contact and context are concerned, we find a similar fusion. The point of contact in a ghost story is the moment of fear, the manifestation of the Other, the unnatural posing as the supernatural: that point having been reached, the tale disperses. But in Williams's case the "point" is not the apparition as such but the manner in which Arglay reacts to it. His revulsion and fear are evidence of his identity with it, or of its identity with him; the resolution comes, first, with the acknowledgment of that relationship and, second, with the rejection of the terms proposed by it—he chooses *now* and *out* instead of *then* and *in*. The story effects its catharsis by denying the conditions under which the invasion constitutes a threat; it subverts itself. Hence the context controls the contact: the entire story happens not *to* Lord Arglay but *in* him.

"Et in Sempiternum Pereant" may indeed be read as a meditation on the ontology of metaphor. Its imagery being not so much sensuous as diagrammatic, one is the more aware that this story concerns a spiritual event. This is not to say that it is narrowly allegorical or a fable: in Williams's imaginative world the physical dimension does not illustrate the spiritual, it manifests it—just as in his theology the spiritual and the physical manifest each other. In Rilke's words, "The tree I look out at's growing in me."[7]

The recurring theme of duration that runs through "Et in Sempiternum Pereant" indicates the context in which it asks to be read. Williams was much preoccupied with the nature of time, and *Reason and Beauty in the Poetic Mind* (1933) provides a brief but suggestive discussion of what he calls "the specious present." The specious present is neither the fleeting moment nor the eternal now: it is "the present as at any particular time

---

7. Rainer Maria Rilke, "Everything beckons us to perceive it," in *Later Poems,* trans. J. B. Leishman (London: Hogarth Press, 1938), 128.

WILLIAMS AND THE ART OF THE GHOST STORY

considered in relation to the past and the future."[8] This is the present as necessarily understood in ordinary experience; and by its nature it is relative, provisional. The fleeting moment may exist, but it is unknowable. Indeed, it is not in human nature *to* know it; it is perhaps only animal nature that can. "The animal lives unhistorically; it hides nothing and coincides at all moments with that which it is; it is bound to be truthful at all times. unable to be anything else."[9] These words by Nietzsche serve to highlight the dilemma of self-conscious man, for whom the moment of eternity remains a special, deliberately realized experience or a grace-given one, the result of faith. And yet eternity would seem to be necessary as a philosophical referent. In Williams's words, "The nearest we can get to eternity is either all moments or one moment" (*Reason and Beauty*, 14). The two measurements are fused in Lord Arglay's "now."

As much as E. M. Forster or T. S. Eliot, Williams was concerned with the "eternal moment" in which one either steps out of time or gathers time within oneself—spatial metaphors, both of them. In "Et in Sempiternum Pereant" he presents judgment or choice as always being here and now—a fusion of space with time; but paradoxically he demonstrates this by a literary technique of dissolving "here" and "now." It is brilliantly deployed. Arglay's consciousness is physically actualized so that he walks into timelessness; at the tale's conclusion, one senses the same condition in his doubled movement in the smoking house. In both cases the physical movement corresponds to and enacts a movement of the spirit. The two are neither contrasted nor compared; they are the same event. Similarly, the theme of judgment and compassion, as embodied in the disconnection between fire and smoke, and thus between cause and effect, refers to the timelessness of the other dimension. In Williams's story the ghost does not invade this world; rather, the consciousness of the this-worldly protagonist expands into the world of spirit. It is the same reading of supernatural experience that we find in Williams's later novels, and it amounts, almost, to a metaphysical epiphany.

IV

It is in this connection that we find the real significance of fiction that treats of supernatural themes. Here is a literary genre with subject-matter for

---

8. Williams, *Reason and Beauty in the Poetic Mind* (Oxford: Oxford University Press, 1933), 11.

9. Friedrich Nietzsche, "On the Uses and Disadvantages of History for Life," in *Untimely Meditations* (1893), trans. R. J. Hollingdale (Cambridge: Cambridge University Press, 1983), 61.

100   GLEN CAVALIERO

which it is obvious that metaphor alone can be the expression; as such, it draws attention to the fact that language by its intrinsic nature is an arbitrary system of signs, and that no necessary or organic relationship exists between signifier and signified. It refutes the linguistic idolatries of naturalism, for the naturalistic techniques employed by the majority of novelists tend to disguise the necessarily provisional nature of fictive truth. In contrast, the ghost story emphasizes this provisional nature, since in the case of fiction portraying the fantastic or the preternatural the manipulative controlling nature of language becomes as inescapable as it does in poetry.

With regard to the latter, Williams is clear as to the relativity of poetic statements.

> Man cannot know things by any means but through his own nature, and it is that nature in its thousand different capacities, but still only man's, which the pattern of poetry makes ostentatious to us. . . . Therefore when the direct metre of verse appears in the midst of the indirect metre of prose, when a prose paragraph breaks into blank verse, we feel the intrusion undesirable, for we are violently reminded of what we have been encouraged to forget. (*Reason and Beauty,* 8)

A similar function is performed by the genre of the ghost story. The seeming outlandishness of its presuppositions alerts the reader to the fictional nature of the material; the reader is made aware of the relativity of fictive truth, of the fact that all forms of fiction, however persuasive, rely for their persuasiveness on the assumption that what is portrayed is an alternative view of reality, or at least a fantasy explicable in psychological or materialistic terms. And the ghost story exhibits this assumption undisguisedly in its most obvious form.

Williams's mature fiction, whatever its other limitations, does succeed in overcoming the disjunctions attendant on a materialistic understanding of the spirit; in reading it one is moved effortlessly from the one dimension of experience to the other. How this is accomplished can be seen in concentrated form in the literary technique employed in "Et in Sempiternum Pereant." The terms used in linguistic analysis—*message, code, contact, context*—arise out of a concentration on the nature of language itself, of human communication; and it is possible to construe them as secularizations of the fourfold levels of scriptural interpretation laid down by St. Thomas Aquinas. Aquinas posits that the text is to be read on two levels: "That first signification *whereby words signify things* belongs to the first sense, the historical or literal. That signification *whereby things signified by words have themselves also a signification* is called the spiritual sense, which is based on the literal and presupposes it."[10] This spiritual sense is the allegorical meaning. But

---

10. Aquinas, *Summa Theologica,* I, Q.I, Art. 10; trans. Fathers of the English Dominican Province, 2d ed., 22 vols. (London: Burns, Oates & Washbourne, 1920–24), 1:17; emphasis added.

St. Thomas goes on to lay down that this spiritual level, or meaning of the meaning, can itself be read in three senses: the allegorical sense; the moral sense; and the anagogical or mystical sense, which unites the other three (literal, allegorical, moral) as being themselves signs of the otherwise inexpressible transcendent order, the mysterium.

In relation to linguistic terminology, the literal sense is the message; the allegorical sense provides the code; the point of contact is the moral sense; the context is the mystical sense. And in Charles Williams's prose, as in his poetry, the four senses relate dynamically to each other. For if, as has been seen, code determines message and context contact, then for Williams the allegorical is the effective signification only to the extent that the recipient of the message is responding in the proper context. For Williams, that context was the spiritual dimension that in its temporal workings he called the City, and in its eschatological fulfillment Sarras.

That Williams expected his readers to intuit the meaning of his imaginative designations is what makes his work so baffling to contemporary sensibility: his habit of personifying into allegory, as in the above two terms, indicates a fusion of different kinds of discourse that, by its elliptical nature, can effectively obstruct response. But his own dictum, "This also is Thou; neither is this Thou," is the safeguard against too close a reliance on personal mythology: his emotional and intellectual balance was poised upon it. At the literal level, as a message, the phrase constitutes a paradox. Allegorically, through the capitalizations, it is coded into theological discourse. Its moral point of contact creates a blend of openness and skepticism that is the product of a context in which the transcendent, mystically apprehended reality is encompassing but never to be encompassed. The relativities revealed in linguistic studies, structuralist and poststructuralist alike, would not have surprised Charles Williams.[11]

Lucidity is in the Omnipotence alone, and now is the moment of its apprehension, all other time, as Arglay discovers in the smoking house, being the hour of death: this is the message of "Et in Sempiternum Pereant." Williams's close-packed prose and his interlacing of themes and imagery may seem at variance with the governing concept of lucidity, but the thrust of his story is clear enough. Justice and judgment are inseparably bound up with empathy and mercy; means and end are indissolubly at one, just as all time is one and now, even though the human condition is inseparable from awareness of before and after. The trap, the threat, the way down to hell is

---

11. Williams's dictum also applies to twentieth-century developments in literary criticism. As opposed to the idolatry of regarding the text as object-in-itself, implicit in Continental structuralism and the New Criticism alike, comes the proviso "Neither is this Thou"; on the other hand, as against the counteridolatry of dissolving the text in favor of the reader, which lies behind much poststructuralist thinking, "This also is Thou" remains a salutary and bracing contention that safeguards the standing and the significance of traditional literary studies.

102 GLEN CAVALIERO

to choose to live on the treadmill of grudging and resentment: the way out, however, the moment of salvation, is always here and now. "Ridiculous the waste sad time / Stretching before and after."[12]

Perplexing though it tends to be on a first reading, "Et in Sempiternum Pereant" remains a powerful instance of Williams's capacity for existential myth making. As a ghost story in the conventional sense it has the unusual quality of becoming more eerie with each reading, and this because its purport has to be teased out, so that through this necessary collaboration readers become so involved in the narrative that they are unable merely to sit back and be entertained by it. Moreover, through its interiorization of the structure of the traditional ghost story, "Et in Sempiternum Pereant" not only provides a haunting image of the theological and metaphysical nature of hatred and despair but also extends the possibilities of the preternatural as a subject for fiction in ways not attempted in Williams's novels, not even in *Descent into Hell.* By including it in their collection, the Oxford editors provided both a distinguished instance of a ghost story as such, and a comment on the genre as a whole.

12. T. S. Eliot, "Burnt Norton" (1935), in *Four Quartets* (London: Faber and Faber, 1944), 13.

Charles Williams,
a Prophet for Postmodernism:
Skepticism and Belief
in *The Place of the Lion*

Cath Filmer-Davies

In this poststructuralist era of literary criticism, the popular academic trend is toward skepticism and the concomitant debunking of any forms of absolutism, be they scientific, philosophical, or religious. We are told that literary texts are self-reflexive; and in the words of the most prominent philosopher of poststructuralist thought, Jacques Derrida, "Il n'y a pas de hors texte" (there is nothing outside the text).[1] Such literary and philosophical skepticism has been condemned by certain Christian critics, who find offensive any notion of doubt or questioning of what have traditionally been regarded as absolute verities. There has been something of a scramble to locate critics and writers in the absolutist tradition in order to rehabilitate "Christian" literary faith in authorial presence and the divinity of the text, and there are any number of papers reflecting the partial success of this endeavor.[2] The fact remains, however, that faith is conceived in and born out of doubts, questionings, and mysteries.

In Charles Williams's novel *The Place of the Lion,* skepticism is depicted as the nutrient agar of faith, while faith is supported and energized by the constant challenge it receives from skepticism. In the opening chapter, Williams sets up a textual dynamic between vision and faith, illusion and doubt. Readers, drawn into and confronted by this dynamic, are constantly urged to evaluate the truth or falsity of Williams's philosophical propositions. Where Williams departs from the frank nihilism of many poststructur-

---

1. Derrida, *Of Grammatology* (1967), trans. Gayatri Chakravarty Spivak (Baltimore: Johns Hopkins University Press, 1974), 158.

2. Including, alas, one of mine: "Of Lunacy and Laundry Trucks: Deconstruction and Mythopoesis," *Literature and Belief* (Center for the Study of Christian Values in Literature, Provo, Utah) 9 (1989): 55–64.

104 CATH FILMER-DAVIES

alists, however, is in the fact that the reader at no time has to privilege one or other option, but rather must see them in balance or perhaps in a dynamic interplay. For Williams's thesis appears to be something like Blake's aphorism from *The Marriage of Heaven and Hell*: "Without Contraries is no progression."[3] Certainly the plot of Williams's novel progresses through the tension between contraries, and this balance of skepticism and faith places Williams in a certain tradition of Christian writing, as well as in the vanguard of modern skeptical thought.

It is not surprising to find in Williams's work the proto-deconstructive turn. As John Heath-Stubbs points out, Williams's existentialism and "Christian sceptic[ism]" were major components of his transcendentalist philosophy.[4] Williams believed that skepticism is not antithetical to faith but in fact informs and constitutes it. According to Heath-Stubbs, this quality of disbelief means, for Williams, the human need—indeed, the human right and duty—to question. In his theological work *He Came Down from Heaven*, Williams "characteristically" emphasizes Mary's question to the annunciating angel, "How shall these things be?" As Heath-Stubbs explains, "This is a resumption, though on a new plane of experience, of Job's impassioned questioning of God in the Old Testament. 'Man was intended to argue with God, Humility has never consisted in not asking questions'" (14). In this context, Heath-Stubbs observes that Williams wrote approvingly of the skeptical views of Montaigne and Voltaire in his *The Descent of the Dove* (191–94, 201–3) and considered Kierkegaard important for contemporary Christian thought. So highly did Williams regard Kierkegaard that he is said to have been largely responsible for the decision of Oxford University Press to publish translations of Kierkegaard's work.[5]

But other influences on Williams also contributed to the visionary impact of *The Place of the Lion*—an impact that is compelling in its heterodoxical fusion of the experiences of the mystical, the transcendental, and the mundane. Humphrey Carpenter, biographer of the Inklings, believes that Williams's world view was shaped not only by a Christian upbringing but also by initiation into and membership in the Order of the Golden Dawn.[6] This complexity of influences on Williams seems to have given his novels a breadth of popular appeal, since his use of mysticism provides the supernaturalist frissons which readers of thrillers conventionally expect. Both

3. Blake, *The Complete Poetry and Prose,* ed. David V. Erdman, rev. ed. (Berkeley and Los Angeles: University of California Press, 1982), 34.

4. Heath-Stubbs, *Charles Williams,* Writers and Their Work, No. 63 (London: Longmans, Green, 1955), 15.

5. Heath-Stubbs, *CW,* 13–15; see also Diane T. Edwards, "Christian Existentialism in the Early Poetry of Charles Williams," *Seven* 8 (1987): 43–46.

6. Carpenter, *The Inklings* (London: Allen and Unwin, 1978), 77–81.

A PROPHET FOR POSTMODERNISM   105

Dorothy L. Sayers and Agatha Christie, contemporaries of Williams, have supernatural (and in Christie's case, occult) elements in their plots.[7]

That skepticism, existentialism, and mysticism all contribute to Williams's philosophy, and consequently to his novels, is evident in this account by his friend, critic, and twice-biographer Alice Mary Hadfield. For Williams, she writes, "everything is on the point of change; an enormous and hardly grasp-able threat or 'other' quality rises in every detail on which the mind turns; our very existence all but slips from us at times in the pressure of crisis and becoming—becoming what, we dare not say, but either something wildly different from ourselves, or sheer loss."[8] Although humans find themselves caught up in the "crisis" of "becoming," a kind of experiential deferral process, Williams allows for a resolution of human choices. One may choose either the Way of Affirmation or the Way of Negation—the latter a way of asceticism and denial, most suited to monasticism, the former a recognition of the immanence of God and the acceptance of all things as images of the divine. It is necessary to redress the emphasis placed by the monastic tradi-tion on the Negative Way by restoring to the pattern of life the balance of the Affirmative Way.

The first chapter of *The Place of the Lion,* which may be seen as a paradigm for the whole novel, foreshadows later developments in which the Affirmative and Negative Ways are balanced by the contrasting experiences of Anthony and Richardson. More importantly, it shows the potential for development through the crisis of change, from skepticism to belief, from illusion to vision, from intellectual debate (and the desire for self-sufficiency lying at its heart) to the full transcendent joy of life in life. This potential is seen initially in Anthony and Quentin and later in Damaris Tighe and her father. But the power of Williams's opening chapter is derived not only from its foreshadowing of later developments but also from the way it thrusts the reader in medias res, into the glaring actuality of what *is;* to read on is to choose the Way of Affirmation. And in the recognition of what is, the reader is admitted to the "crisis of change" presented in the sometimes turgid philosophical discourse between Anthony and Quentin, as well as in the frissons afforded by the sense of incalculability with which Williams is able to imbue the text.

In this novel, the sense of incalculability is close to the deconstructionist device of *aporia,* wherein readerly expectations are constantly displaced, subverted, or contradicted. Indeed the novel begins with an aporia, when readers are directed, by the textual collocation of the escaped lioness with

---

7. For example, Christie's *The Hound of Death* (1933) is a collection of stories of the macabre and the occult.

8. Hadfield, *An Introduction to Charles Williams* (London: Robert Hale, 1959), 77.

106 CATH FILMER-DAVIES

the men waiting for a bus, to expect the lioness to attack the two men or in some way to confront them physically. But this expectation is never fulfilled. Instead, the lioness is absorbed by a huge lion—in other words, the image of the lioness is replaced by an Image of *Lion-ness;* the physical image is subverted by a manifestation of the Platonic idea of lion-ness. But the action takes place at night, and fear has blurred the perceptions of the two men. Anthony is convinced, "There was a lion," but conviction is not absolutism, and Williams takes care to avoid textual certainties. There is, perhaps, a prototype of Derrida's own deconstructive prose in the following passage:

> [The tremendous lion] ceased to roar, and gathered itself back into itself. It was a lion such as the young men had never seen in any zoo or menagerie; it was gigantic and seemed to their dazed senses to be growing larger every moment. Of their presence it appeared unconscious; awful and solitary it stood, and did not at first so much as turn its head. Then, majestically, it moved. (*PL,* 15)

In this passage the statements about the lion are balanced by challenges to their validity: "It ceased . . . it was . . . it moved"; "It . . . seemed . . . it appeared." In the passage itself, excerpted from the main body of the text, there is an instance of aporia; the reader's acceptance of the appearance of the lion is immediately subverted by the verbs of perception, and the validity of perception (at least on this occasion) is in question, since this is a night on which "the moon was not high, and any movement under the trees was invisible" (13). Unlike Derrida, who has written that he does not believe anything like perception exists,[9] Williams does not undermine so utterly the validity of perception. Indeed, while the accuracy of perception on this occasion is doubtful, Williams widens the concept of "perception" into that of "vision," although the significance of vision is relative to the spiritual and psychological status of those who experience it. Though skeptical, Williams never approaches nihilism; rather, with his idiosyncratic uses of aporia, he pursues the progression, through contraries, to individuation and apotheosis.

Anthony effects, at the end of the novel, the redemption of Damaris Tighe through his apotheosis into a new Adamic figure (and consequently a disguised *figura Christi,* an image of the scriptural concept of the new Adam). Yet, in chapter 1, though it is obvious that Anthony is the protagonist, it is not possible to show, as some critics have attempted, that Anthony is morally the superior of Quentin.[10] Rather, both men exhibit humor, fear,

9. Derrida, "Structure, Sign and Play in the Discourse of the Human Sciences," in *The Structuralist Controversy: The Languages of Criticism and the Sciences of Man,* ed. Richard Macksey and Eugenio Donato (Baltimore: Johns Hopkins University Press, 1972), 272.

10. Cf. Agnes Sibley, *Charles Williams* (Boston: Twayne, 1982), 65; Thomas Howard, *The Novels of Charles Williams* (New York: Oxford University Press, 1983), 98–101.

selfishness, and indecision, albeit in varying proportions and with varying degrees of appropriateness.

At this early stage of character development, there is at work a deconstructive impetus that undermines certainties about the moral qualities of the two men. Thus, at the news from the search party about the escaped lioness, Quentin exclaims, "The devil there is!" while Anthony is "more polite" with his "I see—yes. That does seem a case for warning people" (*PL,* 9). On this evidence, Anthony is supposedly the more chivalric and courteous of the two. But a distinct discontinuity in Anthony's characterization appears almost immediately. Quentin asks, "Do you save me by luring it after you, or do I save you?" To which Anthony responds, "O you save me, thank you" (11). Anthony's response is clearly meant by the author to undermine the previous moment of chivalry by showing him as a human quite capable of fear and a desire for self-preservation.

Similarly, we perceive Quentin as somewhat cowardly, and Anthony as rather heroic—"What enormous fun!" he says of danger—yet this bravado is subverted a moment later as he confesses, "What I feel I should like to be in is an express train on a high viaduct" (*PL,* 12). Nor is Quentin portrayed merely as the impolite and craven coward; his cowardice is subverted by his refreshingly practical approach to the situation: to Anthony's question "What do we do if we see it?" Quentin replies, "Bolt. . . . Unless it's going in the other direction" (11). This careful attention to logicalities is also demonstrated in his response to Anthony's "It's more dangerous for you to hate than to kill, isn't it?" to which Quentin answers, "To me or to the other fellow?" (12)—a question designed to locate Anthony's argument in the concrete rather than in the general, in the world of experience rather than in mere intellectual philosophizing. Neither man, then, is simply heroic or craven, good or evil.

While it may seem contradictory to depict in both men character traits that seem so antithetical, and while the primary focus remains on Anthony, it seems that Williams is making some effort, not altogether unsatisfactorily, toward creating characters of some complexity, not merely stereotypes of moral good or evil. To have contrasted them too severely would be to show Anthony as a well-meaning fool for choosing such a friend as Quentin. For Anthony's regard and friendship to be valid, Quentin must have likable characteristics and a mind of some rigor. Thus, even in the apparent collocations of weaknesses and strengths, Williams endeavors to create a picture of friendship in which the reader can believe; that friendship is not *agape*—nonconditional—love at this stage but is instead perhaps a trace of the loyalty and the regard which lead Anthony into the role of a new Adam and which lead Quentin (and later also Damaris) to fulfill the role of the redeemed. Since redemption is impelled by agape, it is essential that love be

108   CATH FILMER-DAVIES

a reasonable response (although it will not be love of the full quality of agape) in the human context of the opening, scene-setting chapter. Anthony is a human savior, and his love for Quentin must in some sense be a love for something lovable, though Anthony progresses beyond that limited love as the plot develops until, later in the novel, he achieves self-sacrificial love.

This friendship between the two men and the seeming assurance of their mutual defense constructs a sense of security even after the lioness re-appears. Anthony and Quentin take shelter on a cottage porch; at this point all certainties are undermined, as the security suggested by the willingness of the men to protect each other and the availability of at least some shelter is shattered by the information that "this was something more than the ordinary cottage and was consequently more hostile to strangers" (*PL,* 13), information that provides a supernatural frisson. The reader is alerted to the fact that apparent shelter is very real danger.

Having provided this evidence of constant subversion of plot elements, I want to turn now to the issue of intertextuality. Those critics who have paid detailed attention to Williams's work have focused on the most obvious influences on his ontological approach to fiction. His approach is not as original as one might believe; indeed, there is a clear link with earlier spiritual "thrillers" which allows at least this novel, if not all of Williams's fictional oeuvre, to be placed in the context of a Christian novelistic tradition. If one considers the self-reflexivity of George MacDonald's *Phantastes* and *Lilith,* one becomes aware of a similar tension between belief and disbelief, between reality and illusion. Stephen Prickett has discussed, in a recent paper, the influence of the German writers, especially Goethe, on MacDonald in *Phantastes,*[11] and a reading of *Lilith* clearly reveals the same kinds of tension. Mr. Vane is "at home yet not at home"; he must "die" in order to live.[12] Near the conclusion of *Lilith,* Vane still ponders the nature of illusion and of reality (243). There is also a Berkeleian influence on MacDonald of the kind which prompts Lewis Carroll's Alice to argue in chapter 4 of *Through the Looking Glass* that she is not merely "a sort of thing" in the Red King's dream. Perhaps Carroll anticipates Christian absolutism in response to postmodernist arguments when he has Alice weep, only to have Tweedledee remark, "You won't make yourself a bit realer by crying. . . . There's nothing to cry about." MacDonald includes as an epigraph to the final chapter of *Phantastes* a quotation from Novalis: "Unser Leben ist kein Traum, aber es soll und wird vielleicht einer werden," which

---

11. Prickett, "Fictions and Metafictions: *Phantastes, Wilhelm Meister,* and the Idea of the *Bildungsroman,*" in *The Gold Thread: Essays on George MacDonald,* ed. William Raeper (Edinburgh: Edinburgh University Press, 1990), 109–25.

12. MacDonald, *Lilith: A Romance* (1895; reprint, Grand Rapids, Mich.: Eerdmans, 1981), 238–39.

A PROPHET FOR POSTMODERNISM 109

Macdonald translates, "Our life is no dream, but it ought to become one, and perhaps will." The same quotation, in English only, is the final sentence in *Lilith*.[13] A few paragraphs before, Mr. Vane muses, "Can it be that that last waking also was in the dream? that I am still in the chamber of death, asleep and dreaming, not yet ripe enough to wake? . . . If that waking was itself but a dream, surely it was a dream of a better waking yet to come" (251).

Illusion or reality? Such is the state of "Contraries" which pervades *The Place of the Lion,* particularly in the first chapter. But the parallels between MacDonald's work and Williams's extend to further tension between contraries—as expressed in the concepts of Life-in-Death and Death-in-Life.

It is difficult to say whether in 1931 MacDonald was a direct influence on Williams; the correspondences in their ideas might be because of shared interests in other writers. Both had read Coleridge and Blake; Williams's essay "Blake and Wordsworth" in the *Dublin Review* clearly indicates his familiarity with Blake's writings.[14] C. S. Lewis's experiences suggest that MacDonald's books were freely available early in this century, and certainly Williams would have had access to them.

Williams is close to MacDonald in his use of Coleridge's idea of Life-in-Death and Death-in-Life from *The Rime of the Ancient Mariner.* Using the literal meaning of the word *nightmare,* Coleridge's monster is female:

> Her lips were red, her looks were free,
> Her locks were yellow as gold:
> Her skin was as white as leprosy,
> The Night-mare LIFE-IN-DEATH was she. . . .[15]

MacDonald's nightmare is the character Lilith, a spiritual vampire, who belongs to the realm of the Undead. That she is a vampire is made clear by the attacks she makes on Mr. Vane, the spiritual pilgrim who seeks wholeness in the otherworld where Lilith abides. (But wholeness, as the Scriptures reiterate, is gained only by the voluntary laying down of one's life. One must, we are told, "lose one's life to gain it" [Matt. 10:39; 16:25; Mark 8:35; Luke 9:24].)

In one such attack, the sensual pleasure Vane enjoys from the experience is made clear; he experiences a delicious languor as Lilith bends over him, "her mouth [wearing] a look of satisfied passion [as] she wiped from it a

---

13. MacDonald, *Phantastes: A Faerie Romance* (1858; reprint, Grand Rapids, Mich.: Eerdmans, 1981), 182; *Lilith,* 252.

14. Williams, *Dublin Review* 208 (1941): 175–86; reprinted in *Image,* 59–67.

15. Coleridge, *Rime* (1798; here quoted in the revised version of 1834), lines 190–93; in *The Rime of the Ancient Mariner: A Handbook,* ed. Royal A. Gettmann (San Francisco: Wadsworth, 1961), 15. Cf. R. L. Breet and A. R. Jones, eds., *Lyrical Ballads,* by Coleridge and William Wordsworth (London: Methuen, 1963), 17n.

110   CATH FILMER-DAVIES

streak of red" (*Lilith*, 133). Lilith will not die to her Self, and to feed her Self she drains the life from others. Her existence in the Otherworld is that of the Living Dead—or of "Life-in-Death." She will not be "born again" into that good death which denies the self and lives for others, and in denying the self allows the soul to be spiritually individuated and whole.

Mr. Vane also refuses to dies to his "Self." His physical life is lived in a state of spiritual Death, or Death-in-Life, rather as the Ancient Mariner is doomed to live, exiled from humanity and trapped in his human existence, to repeat his "neverending story" to anyone who might take heed. Vane is physically alive but spiritually dead; Lilith is spiritually dead and physically undead. They are both aliens in this world where the willing "good death," that is, death to the self, results in spiritual life; in such a world one might expect to find a Raven. This one, like Poe's, cries "Nevermore!": "Once dying as we die here, all the dying is over. . . . Those who will not die, die many times, die constantly, keep dying deeper, never have done dying; here all is upwardness and love and gladness" (*Lilith*, 238–39).

The message is clear: to die to the self is to live spiritually. In the first chapter of *The Place of the Lion,* the same message is implied, providing at least an echo of both Coleridge and MacDonald. The victim of the Lion's attack is Mr. Berringer. Later in the narrative, the revelation is made that Berringer has been dabbling in the occult and experimenting with angelic forms as detailed in a four-hundred-year-old book of arcane knowledge (121). This book, we are told in an almost offhand way, contains several pages which are "mostly cursing" (124), and it is a kind of curse that causes Mr. Berringer to lie comatose after the visitation of the Lion. Mr. Berringer's quest for power focuses inward, on himself, rather as Mr. Vane's does in the early chapters of *Lilith.* While he is in the coma, Mr. Berringer, like Vane, is in the world of the Undead.

According to Williams's particular world view, true life relies on the surrender of the self. The critic Nancy Westerman summarizes the implications of "death-in-life" in Williams's lexicon:

> If one chooses to recognise what is, then one achieves life-in-life, energy and joy, and abundance of life [which] leads to death-in-death, surrender of the self in order to become love, the true self. If one denies what is, one becomes blind and destroys oneself by turning in on oneself. Death only achieves a continuation of the hell of life, a restless prolonged self-absorption.
>
> Refusal to die is the anti-form of the way of affirmation as suicide is the anti-form of the way of negation. Both are an impossible desire for self-sufficiency, a denial of what is. Part of what is, is the co-inherence in existence, each person a part of the whole order of being.[16]

---

16. Westerman, "A Response in Dialogue to Charles Williams," *The Ring Bearer: Journal of the Mythopoeic Literature Society of Australia* 1, no. 3 (1983): 11.

A PROPHET FOR POSTMODERNISM

111

There are echoes of both MacDonald and Coleridge here. The redeemed and individuated Mr. Vane exclaims: "I lived in everything; everything entered and lived in me. To be aware of a thing, was to know its life at once and mine, to know whence we came, and where we were at home—was to know that we are all what we are, because Another is what he is!" (*Lilith,* 243). And for Coleridge:

> He prayeth best, who loveth best
> All things both great and small;
> For the dear God who loveth us,
> He made and loveth all.
>
> (*Rime,* lines 614–17, ed. cit., 41)

Berringer, then, is in the coma as the result of his tampering with the unseen world of Universals, a tampering motivated by his thirst for knowledge. His death-in-life is commented upon ironically by one of the search party: "He *lives* here" (*PL,* 18, emphasis added). But he is hardly living at all, and death overshadows him, since he has refused to put the self to death. Of course, in this introductory chapter, the implications of Berringer's coma are merely hinted at and foreshadowed. What is clear, though, is that Williams invites, perhaps even compels, his readers to choose what *is*—sight, vision, recognition, and energy—so that they can experience life in spiritual wholeness.

The scriptural injunctions that in dying one lives and that in losing one finds fit Blake's notion of Contraries very well; by extension, they also fit the series of opposites in this first chapter of Williams's novel. Indeed, the Blakean influence on both MacDonald and Williams draws from older sources—possibly Swedenborg, and almost certainly Boehme. The importance of these influences is that they contextualize Williams and *The Place of the Lion* in the tradition of heterodoxical Christian thought. Orthodox Christians today, however, along with their nonbelieving contemporaries, are discovering the value of these contributions to literature and theology; indeed C. S. Lewis, commonly considered the arch-practitioner of orthodoxy, took up the concerns of MacDonald's novel *Lilith* in his final novel, *Till We Have Faces.* This novel, too, has some overtones of the skepticism of *The Place of the Lion*; similar questions are raised about the nature of perception and the validity of vision. Orual, Lewis's protagonist, resists the demands of the supernatural; her complaint against the gods is based on what she perceives as a cosmic riddle or joke, of which she is the victim. In this, Orual comes close in spiritual agonizing to MacDonald's Vane; but when Orual seeks to solve the riddle of the gods and to establish her own identity through learning, she exhibits traits similar to those of Williams's Damaris Tighe. Though Lewis's denouement is close enough to Christian absolutism to satisfy orthodox critics, it must be noted that Orual's "manuscript" trails off, unfinished. Like *The Place of the Lion* and *Lilith, Till We Have Faces* is self-reflexive to the last.

Williams's novel, then, at once strange, perplexing, and difficult, stands out not so much as the idiosyncratic work of arcane mysticism it has sometimes been deemed to be, but rather as a novel in that tradition of Christian heterodoxy that acknowledges the doubt, skepticism, and perplexity inherent in the human condition. Blake's Contraries become the impetus of spiritual growth and development in this tradition, and even in the first chapter of *The Place of the Lion* there is a progression achieved through the contraries of vision and mundanity expressed through the lioness and the Lion, the embodiment of lion-ness. The last lines of the chapter draw together these seemingly opposite binaries to conclude with quiet affirmation. The leader of the search party eyes Anthony suspiciously:

> "It wasn't a lion," he said. "There's been no lion in these parts that I ever heard of, and only one lioness. . . . What d'ye mean—lion?"
> "No," said Anthony, "quite. Of course, if there wasn't a lion—I mean— O well, I mean there wasn't if there wasn't, was there?" (*PL*, 20)

A few seconds later, resuming his journey with Quentin, Anthony speaks to himself: "But, damn it! . . . it *was* a lion" (21). Anthony has made an existential leap toward what Jung would call individuation. He has set foot upon the Way of Affirmation; he acknowledges, even in this moment of fear and of doubt, what "is," seen or unseen. The rest of the novel deals in essence with the respective journeys of Damaris Tighe and Quentin Sabot toward the same goal. Though Williams shares with MacDonald a dogged turgidity of style (as evidenced, for example, in the dialogue excerpted above), he also shares MacDonald's faith in the outcome of visionary experiences, of skepticism, and of doubt in continued tension with affirmation and faith.

The fact that writers of all kinds—from absolutist, relativist, orthodox, and heterodox backgrounds—have contributed to the literary renaissance of novels in this skeptical tradition (MacDonald in particular has recently become more widely read) indicates that there is in postmodernist thought an intrinsic value which compels recognition. If, as it has been said, the Devil can quote Scripture to his own ends, then it is more than probable that postmodernist skepticism can become, as it has for Williams, a way of faith. And that premise—that faith arises from doubt, that "without Contraries is no progression"—is at the heart of Williams's argument in *The Place of the Lion*.[17]

---

17. I wish to acknowledge my indebtedness to Hatfield College, Durham, for the research fellowship under which this article was begun.

Complex Rhetoric for a Simple Universe: *Descent into Hell*

Judith J. Kollmann

Four of Charles Williams's earlier novels (*WH, MD, PL, GT*) present the supernatural as an extraordinary intrusion into the natural world. The intrusion—in the form of a stone, a grail, angels, or Tarot cards—offers marvelous power, appears wonderful, and is, indeed, both good and beautiful. But the power the supernatural element offers is absolute, inevitably destined to be misused by an imperfect humanity. Consequently, the power threatens to destroy the material world. The action of these novels therefore tends to polarize between two groups of characters: on the one side are those who are possessed by the desire to control the supernatural; on the other are those who wish to restore the natural world, returning the supernatural element to its rightful place—namely, outside the natural dimension. Thus, the supernatural is perceived as something essentially alien to, and sharply distinct from, the material world.

By the time Williams wrote *The Greater Trumps,* however, he was questioning the line of demarcation between the dimensions, and in *Descent into Hell* the concept of a universe that is totally coinherent became the central vision. The basic premise of such a coinherent universe is that, while there is essential unity and interaction among all created things, both natural and supernatural, all things nevertheless maintain their individual identity and, therefore, their inherent diversity. As the concept is developed in the novel, the natural and the supernatural flow into and meld with one another so that what one normally considers opposite states become harmoniously coexistent. Space, time, and state of being are all affected: one place coincides with many places, perhaps all places of analogous structure or function. Time is coeval, the present coexisting with the past and future and possibly with eternity. The living and at least some of the dead either occupy the same space or are in close proximity with one another. Moreover, that which is normally considered external to humanity becomes internal, and the internal becomes external.

A corollary to this vision is the introduction of yet another dimension, one produced not by superimposing one dimension on the other but by fusing the natural and the supernatural. This dimension is the human person itself, that complex of body, intellect, emotions, and soul constituting the total human being. Because a basic tenet of Christian theology maintains that the person is formed by the fusion of the material and the spiritual (as in, for example, 1 Thess. 5:23), and because Williams was intimately familiar with Judeo-Christian texts and thought, in his work the human person can become the supreme manifestation of the coinherent universe. This concept reaches its most complete expression in *Descent into Hell* in two ways: through the struggle of the human for spiritual perfection (demonstrated most nearly by Margaret Anstruther) and through the perfection of art (demonstrated by the writing and production of a poetic drama, *A Pastoral*).

Charles Williams's concept is, therefore, of a universe in which all things are intended to coexist in a harmony that sustains and glories in diversity. For humankind· such coexistence is most fully realized in harmonious interaction at every level of human relations: friendship, marriage, family, societal structure, work. Salvation is achieved primarily by the refusal to place oneself ahead of either deity or neighbor. Williams's favored image for this concept of human coexistence was that of the "City," ultimately the City of God envisioned in the book of Revelation, but presently (if imperfectly) represented by London, Rome, New York, or any other city. Significantly, Battle Hill, the site of all the action in *Descent,* is described as "a suburb of the City" (*DH,* 11).

Separation from unity is possible in this universe, however, when a rational being chooses to put itself first. Such choice of self not only separates the individual from the rest of creation but—additional irony—also produces self-division. Thus, the election of self is seen to be so contrary to reason that, if it is continued, the individual inevitably degenerates into either idiocy or insanity—states that, it appears, Williams was convinced were the final circumstances of damnation. This process is exemplified by the military historian, Lawrence Wentworth.

Such, then, is the vision Williams offers his readers in *Descent into Hell*. Pauline Anstruther experiences this vision as "the hint of a new organization of all things: a shape, of incredible difficulty in the finding, of incredible simplicity found, an infinitely alien arrangement of infinitely familiar things" (*DH,* 206). This perception is directed toward both the exterior and the interior dimensions. It recognizes the coinherence of all things exterior to the human psyche, perceiving that the cosmos is without sharp lines of demarcation, not only between the natural and supernatural dimensions but also between infinite and finite and between eternal and temporal. Moreover, it rejects sharp distinctions between the human person and the universe as a whole.

Charles Williams's vision refuses to reduce the mysteries of the universe to the level of the human subconscious. Rather, everything in *Descent into Hell*—plot, characters, themes, language—exists to convince his reader of the validity of a cosmos that does indeed exist within the human psyche but simultaneously has an independent existence. For Williams, then, while the human mind is and must be the center of human perception, the mind is not the center of the universe or the source of the supernatural.

Instead, the psyche, in common with the rest of the universe, is part of the cosmic "sea" by which it is imbued. But more, it is a potent metonymy for either the Godhead or the satanic. For in this universe, sharp lines of demarcation do exist in one area: ethical choice. While there is great latitude in terms of when, where, and how such choices must be made, any being possessing reason must ultimately choose between salvation and damnation.

This choice may be made in a variety of ways, but in all the ethical choices made in the novel, language plays a significant role. In fact, linguistic choices at times become ethical choices in themselves. Thus, in this novel language is not only Williams's artistic medium, his means of communication and persuasion, but also one of his major themes. Therefore rhetoric is, first, the tool with which Williams cajoles us into accepting his vision of the universe as a reality as long as we are engaged in the act of reading the novel; the willing suspension of disbelief is particularly important in a tale of the fantastic that asks us not only to accept the existence of the supernatural but to accept a view of the supernatural that is probably very different from the reader's expectations. Second, the rhetoric is designed to persuade us of the logic of his version of the cosmos to such a degree that we will accept it as *reality*—or, at least, Williams hopes the rhetoric will so modify our thinking that we will concede the possibility that the real universe might be like the vision he offers us. And finally, the poet in Charles Williams, the man in love with language, wants his readers to reassess words as entities precious in themselves, to be neither used nor abused by the egocentric or the merely careless. Although never saying it explicitly, the novel as a whole is designed to remind us that Logos is a form of God and that the word has power. It can both create and destroy (the poetic play, *A Pastoral,* when performed with integrity, so weakens the demon Lily Sammile that she faints).

The present study can examine only a few of the rhetorical techniques with which Williams sought to achieve his goals, for the topic is vast. My examples range from smaller to larger syntactic units: first, Williams's use of the conditional conjunctive (usually, but not invariably, "as if"); second, a specific type of diction, words to which the text itself draws attention; third, his use of series of words or short phrases; and fourth, of the semicolon and its attendant syntactic structures.

The conditional conjunctive is one of Williams's primary means of slipping from the natural, mundane world into his version of the supernatural. It is clearly illustrated in the opening chapter of *Descent into Hell*. The novel begins placidly, as if it were simply a comedy of manners. There is a social gathering on Peter Stanhope's manor lawn. It is a sunny May afternoon, and the upper-class residents of suburban Battle Hill have gathered to hear Stanhope read a play that he has written and that he is offering to them in its initial production as their summer's cultural activity. In this quiet beginning, Williams accomplishes a good deal of the novelist's business of introducing characters, setting, and situation. Very little of the supernatural is permitted to intrude. The merest suggestion of a greater context slides in gently at the end of the first paragraph: "The grounds of the Manor House expanded beyond them; the universal sky sustained the whole. Peter Stanhope began to read his play" (*DH,* 9). But at this early stage, these sentences can be considered no more than a philosophical overview of an entirely normal situation.

Not until well into the first chapter, in describing the thoughts of a character (Pauline Anstruther), does Williams suggest the presence of the supernatural. Pauline is thinking of doppelgängers, and the reader becomes aware that she fears she is haunted by one. The narrator observes that it is "as if the Hill was fortunate and favourable to apparitions beyond men; a haunt of alien life. There had been nine in two years" (*DH,* 26). The first suggestion has been made that Battle Hill may be more than an ordinary suburb. The suggestion is initiated by means of the conditional conjunctive "as if," and the concept is not yet very radical; it is merely that the Hill *may* be haunted. The following phrase, "a haunt of alien life," appears at first a simple appositive, but because the next clause ("There had been") already accepts the existence of the apparitions so cautiously suggested, "a haunt of alien life" is seen to have been meant literally. Within two sentences the apparitions have been introduced and become fact. The reader has just been treated to a demonstration of sleight of syntax. The case for the existence of the supernatural phenomenon is strengthened as Williams, in the following paragraph, describes another incident with this "alien life" form when Pauline's doppelgänger appears as she walks homeward from the reading of the play. The succeeding paragraphs make a strong case for Pauline's sanity, and by the end of the first chapter the Hill is firmly established as, indeed, a haunt of alien life.

Every fantastic element of the novel is treated according to a similar pattern—that is, each element is introduced almost timidly, generally by means of a conditional conjunctive, but the unreal is immediately thereafter considered a fact, a reality. So, when Williams next deals with the Hill it is called a "Hill of skulls," which "seemed to become either weary or fastidious." It "lay like . . . a rounded headland of earth, thrust into an ocean

COMPLEX RHETORIC FOR A SIMPLE UNIVERSE 117

of death" (*DH,* 30–31). These sentences establish the second stage in the development of the Hill's supernatural potential: now not only is it accepted as a haunt of alien life but, shaped like the corona of a skull, it is rapidly being transformed by means of metonymy and allusion into a type of that sacrificial and suffering archetype, Golgotha. It may be noted that, by the use of another cautious introductory word, *seemed,* the Hill is being changed into a sentient place: it can become tired or choosy. The Hill now is not only a place of dying, not only haunted; it is itself haunting. Williams has created additional supernatural associations and has also begun the difficult process of establishing the identity of places by associating Battle Hill with Golgotha. This analogy is strengthened in its immediate context by the description of two martyrdoms that have taken place upon the Hill. Williams concludes this section with a passage (introduced by a conditional conjunctive) that paints a complete picture of the Hill as a place definitely haunted by primeval ghosts:

> But if the past still lives in its own present beside our present, then the momentary later inhabitants were surrounded by a greater universe. From other periods of its time other creatures could crawl out of death, and invisibly contemplate the house and people of the rise. The amphibia of the past dwelt about, and sometimes crawled out on, the slope of this world, awaiting the hour when they should either retire to their own mists or more fully invade the place of the living. (31–32)

Williams is nothing if not supremely efficient, and this passage serves several purposes. First, the coexistence of past with present has been introduced, and from this point on the text assumes the reality of aeviternity, although the concept needs, and receives, extensive development. Second, the passage prepares the reader for nearly every manifestation of the supernatural that will be made in the novel. Third, the essentially symbolic nature of this novel is being manifested in the equation of Battle Hill with "the slope of this world," a phrase that not only echoes the suggestion of a vaster landscape, the more encompassing perspective indicated in the opening paragraph of the novel, but also is the first step in preparing us for a subsequent view of Battle Hill as the initial foothill to alpine peaks. The rising mountains become a Dantean Purgatory that "carrie[s]" (96) the "real world" at its base.

In Williams's account of the laborer's death the conditional conjunctive serves to introduce an idea more complex than that of the coexistence of two dimensions:

> There had been, while the workmen had been creating the houses of the new estate, an incident which renewed the habit of the Hill, *as if* that magnetism of death was quick to touch first the more unfortunate of mortals. . . . [The laborer] longed to avoid them [his wife, coworkers, society as a whole], and *as if* the Hill

bade him a placable farewell there came to him as he left it behind him a quiet thought [of suicide]. (*DH,* 32, 33; emphasis added)

Now the Hill possesses a magnetism that affects not only the dead and the past but the living and the present as well; in addition, the Hill is capable of suggesting suicide to a living person's mind. When the laborer returns to a house that as yet is only a foundation and skeletal two-by-fours, he climbs a ladder, seeking a rope with which to hang himself:

He went up *as if* he mounted on the bones of his body built so carefully for this; he clambered through his skeleton to the place of his skull, and receded, *as if almost* in a corporeal ingression, to the place of propinquent death. (36; emphasis added)

In this important sentence Williams presents a vital element of the novel: the equation of the exterior world with the innermost elements of the human being—with the mind, soul, and organic interior of the body. The statement is the first step (perhaps the crucial step) in persuading his reader that the natural and supernatural dimensions meld, and meld completely, within the human being. The sentence proceeds by means of a series of verbs, each describing movement upward—"went up," "mounted," "built," "clambered" —and also through two visual images: "as if he mounted on the bones of his body," and "clambered through his skeleton to the place of his skull." The images describe the same impossible phenomenon in nearly synonymous terms. Even the simple repetition lends a poetic weight to the idea, making it seem more logical, but persuasiveness develops through the modulation from the conditional conjunctive—which establishes the first clause as a simile as well as a tentatively offered suggestion—to the implied metaphor and in so doing poses as emphatic an equation between the two elements of the figure as metaphoric language can achieve. Moreover, the phrase "the place of his skull" is evolving into metonymy as the reader is reminded of the earlier reference to Battle Hill as the place of skulls: thus, the reference of the sentence rapidly moves outward even as the images appear to close in on the body's organic structure and its symbols of death, the bones and skull. Then in the final clause, in contrast, "receded" suggests slow movement backward or away. All imagery is gone, and, except for the verb, the clause consists of two prepositional phrases whose most obvious features are multisyllabic, abstract, Latinate diction and a cautious, even timid, conditional conjunctive; however, here is the nuclear concept of the entire sentence: the place of propinquent death is found simultaneously open to the universe, affiliated with all suffering, yet also within a bodily ingression to the innermost self. This is an amazing sentence syntactically, structurally, and contextually. Its efficiency is characteristic of the prose in *Descent into Hell.*

COMPLEX RHETORIC FOR A SIMPLE UNIVERSE

As one might expect, on the next occasion that Williams uses the metaphor, the identification of the otherworld with the interior life of man has become a given. The conditional conjunctive is notable for its absence when Lawrence Wentworth goes for a walk to see whether Adela Hunt, in whom he is erotically interested, will return from London alone or accompanied by Hugh Prescott. Wentworth wants to feed his jealousy: "He would not go to spy; he would go for a walk. He went out of the room, down the soft swift stairs of his mind, into the streets of his mind, to find the phantoms of his mind" (*DH*, 66).

Another technique characteristic of this novel is the use of words or phrases that draw attention to themselves *as words*, either because there is something unusual about them (e.g., rare, unexpected, or obsolete diction: "hugger-mugger," "higgledy-piggledy," "propinquity") or because the reader's attention is deliberately drawn to them by the dialogue. These include the noun-adjective pairs: "terrible," "dreadful," or "fearful" modifying "good" or "joy." What all these words share is that they cease being simply the vehicles for the narrative and become a subject of the narrative. This can happen more or less explicitly and for greater or lesser thematic reasons. A notable example found in several places is *propinquity*, and its cognate *propinquent*. Four passages, distributed with care through the novel, are notable, and it is worth quoting them in full so as to see the emergent pattern.

A: He [the laborer] went up as if he mounted on the bones of his body built so carefully for this; he clambered through his skeleton to the place of his skull, and receded, as if almost in a corporeal ingression, to the place of propinquent death. (*DH*, 36)

B: But where superstition and religion failed, where cemeteries were no longer forbidden and no longer feared; where the convenient processes of cremation encouraged a pretence of swift passage, where easy sentimentality set up a pretence of friendship between the living and the dead—might not that new propinquity turn to a fearful friendship in the end? (91)

C: Time there had disappeared, and the dead man [the laborer] had been contemporaneous with the living [Wentworth]. As if simultaneity approached the Hill, the experiences of its inhabitants had there become co-eval; propinquity no longer depended upon sequence. (102)

D: One element co-ordinated original [Pauline] and translation [doppelgänger]; that element was joy. Joy had filled her that afternoon, and it was in the power of such joy that she had been brought to this closest propinquity to herself. (235)

The word attracts one's attention in each passage, not least because there is a careful development of sentence structure so that it comes at the end or

JUDITH J. KOLLMANN

climax each time. In *A* and *B* the word is also striking for its rarity, its length, and the alliteration in which it is found: "the *p*lace of *pro*pinquent death"; "*pro*pinqui*t*y *t*urn *t*o a *f*earful *f*riendship." It emphasizes, in *A,* that an anonymous laborer is about to commit suicide. Life and death here exist next to each other in conventional sequence. In *B* the word is again used to indicate proximity between life and death. The two states are still conventionally sequential, but now the propinquity has been extended to all the dead and all the living. In addition a strong argument is carried by the emphatic quality of the four adverbial clauses: namely, that boundaries between the states are in danger of breaking down because of this propinquity: the dead might invade the living. By *C,* only eleven pages farther, the transition has been made and the sequence between life and death is explicitly destroyed as the ramifications of coevalty are developed: now, two individuals, one dead, one alive, stand side by side, although unaware of each other. The invasion has not as yet gone so far as *B* has indicated; still, one-third of the way through the novel Williams has firmly established not only the coexistence of time and space but also of life and death and of the natural and the supernatural. All the boundaries that in daily life we assume to be real and fixed have here been shown to be illusory. Moreover, if the reader can accept the possibility of a dead man and a living one standing side by side, then the next step in propinquity, confrontation between the states, can be easily established; and the ultimate steps, intercourse (in both senses: communication and coitus) and exchange (between the dead and living but also between states), can follow readily and rapidly. We then can have Pauline and Margaret confronting dead men; the laborer returning to life; Wentworth having a succubus, presented to him by the demon of the dead, as his mistress; and Margaret dying into life. By the time Williams uses *propinquity* in passage *D* the novel is nearly finished. What is propinquent here may at first appear to be life and death, since doppelgängers traditionally presage death. However, this doppelgänger is not used conventionally. What the living Pauline meets is her own joyful other self, a "fear" that is, paradoxically, "joy" (234–35). The living Pauline, having existed without joy, has been more dead than her double. When the two become genuinely propinquent, they fuse together into Pauline's original personality and into a new life, a point Williams emphasizes by quoting from Dante's opening paragraph of *La Vita Nuova:* "Incipit vita nova" (*DH,* 292).

Propinquity, then, like *as if,* is at least in part a rhetorical strategy to draw the reader efficiently into a calm acceptance of Williams's supernatural dimensions. It is important that the acceptance be calm because, lurid though its title might be, *Descent into Hell* is not a gothic horror tale but a theological novel.

COMPLEX RHETORIC FOR A SIMPLE UNIVERSE

The adjectives "terrible," "dreadful," or "fearful," coupled with the nouns "good" or "joy," form pairs with more significant thematic purposes than that of propinquity, but Williams's technique of unobtrusively sliding in the fantastic or the important is manifest: the phrase is introduced in the midst of conventional social chit-chat by Myrtle Fox: "Nature's so terribly good. Don't you think so, Mr. Stanhope?" (*DH,* 19). Stanhope queries what she meant by the expression, "terribly good." She responds, "Terribly—dreadfully—very," and Stanhope gently corrects her: "You must forgive me; it comes from doing so much writing, but when I say 'terribly' I think I mean 'full of terror.' A dreadful goodness" (20). Miss Fox misses his point and the conversation becomes more general, attracting Pauline's attention. She connects it with her doppelgänger, wondering if the thing is a terrible good. The phrase subsequently recurs throughout the novel, generally when Pauline experiences a spiritual crisis, and therefore becomes a thematic refrain that clarifies the fundamental nature of the universe: for both the living and the dead, the cosmos as a whole is a terrible good because the paradox is integral to its creator. The concept was important to Williams, and he was still thinking of it six years later when he wrote that Dante "dreamed of Love, and saw in a cloud of the colour of flame the figure of a lord, 'of terrible aspect to whoever should look on him,' who seemed 'of such joy as to himself that it was a marvelous thing.' . . . A kind of dreadful perfection has appeared in the streets of Florence; something like the glory of God is walking down the street towards him."[1]

An even more complex device is the series: more complex first because it has potential for considerable stylistic variation, and second because the effects of the various types of series are more subjective. Fundamentally, a series is a group of successive coordinate elements in a sentence; such elements can be brief, consisting of single words or phrases, or lengthier, consisting of parallel dependent or independent clauses. Williams generally uses these two kinds of series to quite different effects and purposes. We will look first at the series of shorter syntactic units—rarely independent clauses unless they are short and so immediately successive that they have an emphatically serial effect (as in, for example, "It was midnight, the Hill was empty, she was alone" [*DH,* 222]).

The rhetorical effect of a series can be varied by, among other factors, the type and degree of its conjunctives and the length of the series. Only the last factor has received much scholarly attention, as for example in Winston Weathers's 1966 study, "The Rhetoric of the Series." By series length

---

1. Williams, *The Figure of Beatrice* (London: Faber and Faber, 1943), 20.

122 JUDITH J. KOLLMANN

Weathers means the number of elements, not the duration or the syntactic complexity of each element. Series length consists, for Weathers, of two, three, or four or more parts. He maintains that the two-part series has an "either-this-or-that" quality since only two choices or entities appear to exist. The two-part series, whether connected by commas, *and,* or *or,* is therefore authoritarian in tone. The three-part series is "the most frequently used," at least in nonfiction prose, for its effect "is normality and reasonableness, and it is distantly related to the syllogism."[2]

The four-or-more-part series, in contrast, gives the impression "of plethora, abundance, the unlimited. . . . At times the effect is extended to that of the diversity that is confusion. With this longer series, the writer moves from the certainty of the two-part, from the reasonableness of the three-part, to the more complicated emotional realism of the catalogue" (23).

This description offers a place from which to begin the discussion, although it immediately becomes evident that Williams used the series to more sophisticated effect than that provided by Weathers's compact definition. The major effect of most series (even Williams's), regardless of stylistic factors or of series length, is accretionary. If the elements are joined by commas or by *and,* the effect will be cumulative, as in: "politics, religion, art, science" (*DH,* 10) or "nearer and clearer and more frequent" (26). The series *adds,* normally with a driving, insistent force that increases its intensity when the series units are short, the syntax simple, the number of units large: "They seemed all . . . grotesque obtrusions into that place of rock and ice and thin air and growing sun" (97). Even when the list is couched in terms of negation the effect can be cumulative: "Never till he—not Pascal nor the Jesuits nor the old chattering pattering woman but he; not moonlight or mist or clouding dust but he; not any power in earth or heaven but he or the peace she had been made bold to bid him" (152). Only "either . . . or" establishes alternatives: "male or female . . . men or women" (22). However, Weathers's analysis does not take into account that the longer and more complex the syntax or the more interrupted the series, the less intense the driving effect will be and the more that effect will be overshadowed by other effects.

The example "Rising young men, and a few risen and retired old" (*DH,* 12) contains two two-part series in "young men, and . . . old [men]" and "risen and retired," but the reader might well have to look twice at this sentence to see that the two series are interlinked by "rising" and "risen." In the following passage the degree of syntactic complexity caused by

2. Weathers, "The Rhetoric of the Series," *College Composition and Communication* 17 (1966): 217–21; reprinted in *Contemporary Essays in Style: Rhetoric, Linguistics, and Criticism,* ed. Glen A. Love and Michael Payne (Atlanta: Scott, Foresman, 1969), 22–23.

interruptions of the nuclear series is even more elaborate:

> The convenience of all had determined this afternoon that he should be the first, and his neat mass of grey hair, his vivid glance, that rose sometimes from the manuscript, and floated down the rows, and sank again, his occasional friendly gesture that seemed about to deprecate, but always stopped short, received the concentration of his visitors, and of Mrs. Parry, the chief of his visitors. (13)

This sentence is made up of four series. The first, a noun series, is the nuclear one; it consists of three noun phrases that constitute the collective subject of the second independent clause in the sentence: "his neat mass of grey hair, his vivid glance, . . . his occasional friendly gesture." The elements of this series are tightly parallel in structure: a personal pronoun, an adjective, and a noun. But the clause as a whole is characterized by interruptions. One occurs between the second and third units, in a three-part dependent clause modifying "glance," and then the third unit of the initial series is similarly modified by a dependent clause consisting of a third series. Only then comes the main verb of the clause—completed, in turn, by a fourth series. Any potential abruptness in this concluding series has been smoothed by the graceful repetition of "of his visitors." The effect is one not of driving speed but of cadence, and despite the complexity of the sentence the primary objective is that of clarity and precision: a vivid picture of Stanhope reading his play is the result.

This passage also demonstrates Williams's use of his favorite connective: *and*. In any series, connectives may take any of three basic forms. First, there can be a mark of punctuation (normally the comma, but also the semicolon) between units, as in "naturally, efficiently, critically, solemnly, reverently" (*DH,* 9), or "He was approached, appeased, flattered, entreated" (174). Second, there can be commas between each pair of units except the last, which has a single articulating word, usually *and* (this, of course, is the norm of English usage). Third, there can be a connective word for every pair. As a rule, the simpler the connective, the faster the series appears to move. Williams was well aware of this effect and, as is clear from the examples quoted above, occasionally used simple series of single words connected by commas. He did not care much for the norm of English usage, the sequence joined by punctuation and a final connective word. Rather, he preferred clusters of two-part series, each connected by *and,* evidently because he liked the effect not only of multiple, interlinked series but also of multiple *and*s, an effect he frequently intensified by connecting other, nonserial syntactic structures within these passages by the same connective. The technique gives a majestic effect to the English language, and it dates at least to the King James Bible: "And ye shall rejoice before the Lord your God, ye, and your sons, and your daughters, and your menservants, and your maidservants, and the Levite that is within your gates" (Deut. 12:12).

124   JUDITH J. KOLLMANN

Among notable contemporary writers of fiction who have capitalized on this technique is Williams's fellow Inkling, J. R. R. Tolkien, who used it to elevate a narrative that began as children's fairy tale to its concluding elegiac mode:

> Then Elrond and Galadriel rode on; for the Third Age was over, and the Days of the Rings were passed, and an end was come of the story and song of those times. With them went many Elves of the High Kindred who would no longer stay in Middle-earth; and among them, filled with a sadness that was yet blessed and without bitterness, rode Sam, and Frodo, and Bilbo, and the Elves delighted to honour them.[3]

Williams used *and* for a similar effect—not for one of heroic elegy but rather for a sense of dignity in the measured cadences of a prose whose rhythm is neither fast nor slow but, above all, reasoned and serious:

> He stood in the fire; he saw around him the uniforms . . . the crowd, men and women of his village. The heat scorched and blinded and choked him. He looked up through the smoke and flame that closed upon him, and saw, after his manner, as she after hers, what might be monstrous shapes of cherubim and seraphim exchanging powers, and among them the face of his daughter's aeviternity. She only among all his children and descendants had run by a sacrifice of heart to ease and carry his agony. He blessed her, thinking her some angel, and in his blessing her aeviternity was released to her, and down his blessing beatitude ran to greet her, a terrible good. The ends of the world were on them. He dead and she living were made one with peace. (*DH*, 237–38)

There are twelve *and*s in this passage. They begin unobtrusively because they are used where they must be as a matter of course: to connect the simple, standard, conventional two-part series, "men and women." But then comes a three-part series of verbs, somewhat less conventional in phraseology as well as structure: "scorched and blinded and choked him." Here the *and*s serve to emphasize each verb of pain. Midway through the passage Williams introduces another variant on the three-part series: "cherubim and seraphim" seems like the normal series of two and, in content, merely an echo of numerous Old Testament passages citing heavenly beings, but Williams inserts a third element in a complex structure that does not at first glance even appear to be a part of the original series—yet, in terms of content, it is: "the face" of a human being's supernatural and unexpected aeviternity among the angelic hierarchies, it, too, exchanging powers—in this case, the power to bear the fear and misery of someone who lived four hundred years earlier. At the end of the passage the *and*s roll through a

---

3. Tolkien, *The Return of the King*, vol. 3 of *The Lord of the Rings* (London: Allen & Unwin, 1955), 309.

COMPLEX RHETORIC FOR A SIMPLE UNIVERSE 125

sentence that serializes the word *blessed/blessing* in a climactic apocalyptic vision whose style has risen to equal its content largely by means of a series in which *bless* is changed from verb to noun and the prepositions are changed to indicate the exact direction and movement of the blessing: "and in his blessing . . . and down his blessing." The blessing, the cherubim, seraphim, martyr, and girl become entwined by the several series until the whole passage comes to rest in the final sentence with its last series consisting of moderately inverted diction: "He dead and she living"; one expects "living" to precede "dead."

For Williams the series is a primary technique in persuading his reader that the impossible is logically acceptable. In one chapter (9, "The Tryst of the Worlds"), he employed 132 series of two parts, 30 of three parts, and 7 of four or more parts. Every chapter demonstrates a similar overwhelming frequency of usage. In "The Rhetoric of the Series," Weathers characterized two-part series as "authoritarian." Two years later, in "The Rhetoric of Certitude," he classified the two-part series as one of eight characteristics of the style of certitude, which he considered one of four contemporary styles; the remaining three are "judiciousness, involvement, and absurdity." Certitude is a rhetoric "in which an author writes as if he intentionally wishes to communicate or unintentionally exposes his sureness, confidence, or even dogmatism. The style of certitude is frequently to be found in discussions of religion, politics, and English grammar."[4] I find Weathers's description of the effect of two-part series somewhat unconvincing. Since Williams groups these series in clusters and often makes grammatical or structural variations (*blessed/blessing, rising/risen*), the effect is not simply dictatorial, not a "voice from on high," as Weathers suggests. Rather, the overall impression becomes one of balance and completeness—of a reasoned thought that is perceiving both sides of an issue, of all options, of all possibilities. The impression is of abundance, of rational completeness, of eminent reason, as well as of certitude.

Into this Williams slips something more: he pair-bonds some (but by no means most) of these two-part series so that one element of the series belongs in content to the natural dimension and the other to the supernatural.

---

4. Weathers, "The Rhetoric of Certitude," *Southern Humanities Review* 2 (1968): 213, 214. Weathers in this essay discusses Williams's prose as an example of this style and observes that "perhaps Charles Williams, in *He Came Down from Heaven,* manages, more than others, the style of certitude with a certain grace and ingenuity" (219). This essay is thought provoking; however, despite his disclaimer of bias against any type of rhetoric, it leaves one with the impression that Weathers is in fact prejudiced against those who write in this mode. This impression is due in part to a slight facetiousness that runs through his discussion (evident in the passages I have quoted) and in greater part to the fact that, having listed four styles, Weathers chose to discuss only one. Thus, the treatment of the subject is disproportionate.

He mates the literal with the figurative or the metaphysical, so that the reader, who is being conditioned by what almost amounts to subliminal manipulation, will accept both parts of the series as equally acceptable realities. An example occurs in Margaret's dream vision. Williams wants to equate topography with spiritual states:

> The earth itself seemed to lie in each of those mountains, and on each there was at first a populous region towards the summit, but the summit itself rose individual and solitary. *Mountains or modes of consciousness, peaks or perceptions,* they stood; on the slopes of each the world was carried; and the final height of each was a separate consummation of the whole. (*DH,* 95–96; emphasis added)

The first sentence appears to deal simply with topography, although the opening clause contains a somewhat illogical image (introduced cautiously with the verb *seemed*). The second clause lifts the reader's imagination from the base of the mountains toward the summit; the third lifts it to the peaks. This clause is finished by a literal two-part series. The second sentence is parallel in structure to the first, appearing to go over the same ground, but in fact it shifts the literal into the figurative. Maintaining the rhythm of the previous sentence, the second begins with two two-part series. However, these are connected not by *and* but by *or,* and the second element in each series is an aspect of human cognitive ability. The options have suddenly expanded: the mountains are no longer just topographical phenomena but can, if the reader chooses to let them (the choice is an effect of the connective *or*), possess metaphysical qualities. In the first clause of the second sentence Williams returns to the "illogical" image of the first sentence. But now, because of the figurative implications with which this sentence opened, it becomes clear that this clause is not at all illogical but is, rather, metaphysical, perhaps evoking the Valley in the Second Terrace of Dante's Mount Purgatory (Canto 7) and certainly implying that the mountains are symbolic of the supernatural dimension that cradles the natural world at its base. The third clause repeats the movement of the first sentence, sweeping the reader's imagination to the heights; the word "consummation" emphasizes the metamorphosed condition of these mountains into states of the human psyche.

As the novel develops, such passages come with increasing frequency. In the following paragraph, which occurs near the end of the novel, Williams grouped together, with an apparently casual disregard, various syntactic structures, expressing varying degrees of rational possibilities. But it is a casualness possible only because it has been developed over many pages with meticulous care:

> The stillness turned upon itself; the justice of the stillness drew all the flames and leaves, the dead and living, the actors and spectators, into its power—percipient

COMPLEX RHETORIC FOR A SIMPLE UNIVERSE

and impercipient, that was the only choice, and that was for their joy alone. (*DH,* 255–56)

If at this late stage, Williams has not persuaded his reader of the coinherence of the natural and supernatural dimensions, the argument is simply hopeless. So pairs normally found together—actors and spectators—are found in company with other pairs that normally are not possible. These sets are the impossibilities that have been brought into propinquity: the coexistence of flames and leaves in a state in which the leaves can exist without being consumed by the flames, and the dead can stand side by side with the living. The final two two-part series, first the adjectives "percipient and impercipient" and then the two parallel independent clauses, "that was the only choice, and that was for their joy alone," are extraordinary in their explicit stress on an authoritarian choice between two: now Williams has, indeed, stated what he had been trying to establish for 256 pages: namely, that the only choice a human being has is either to perceive or not to perceive the reality of the cosmic vision presented in the novel, and thereby, if one chooses perception, to accept joy in the beholding. At this point, Charles Williams's two-part series has indeed become very, very authoritarian.

He does not, however, use the series only to persuade us of the logic of his vision. The series is a versatile technique that can be used to portray the emotional or the illogical. In the examples I have given, the dominant impression is of clarity and balance in syntax and content. To create an impression of a mind out of control, Williams simply increases the number of units in the series, makes the comma the primary connective, and repeats words in associative verbal patterns that give a feverish or slightly delirious impression: "faint green light, light of a forest, faint mist in a forest, a river-mist creeping among the trees, moon in the mist" (*DH,* 115) is a five-part series that loops through repetitions of key words. When used in a lengthier passage, the effect is that of a disintegrating mind:

> *No, no; no canvassers, no beggars, no lovers*; and *away, away* from the City into *the wood and the mist,* by the path that runs *between past and present, between present and present,* that slides through each moment of all experience, *twisting and twining, plunging* from *the City and earth and Eve and all otherness,* into the green mist that rises among the trees; by the path up which *she* was coming, *the she of his longing, the she that was he, and all he in the she—patter-patter,* the *she* that went hurrying about *the Hill and the world,* of whom it was said that they whom she overtook were found *drained and strangled* in the morning, and a single hair tight about the neck, *so faint, so sure, so deathly, the clinging and twisting* path of the *strangling hair.* (120; emphasis added)

This excerpt contains thirteen series, of which six are three-part or longer, while several of the two-part series lose the usual impression of control because of the frequency of commas. Coupled as this is with the use of

128   JUDITH J. KOLLMANN

irregular syntax (such as the loose pronoun referents in "the she that was he" and the fact that the entire passage is a massive sentence fragment) the total impression is one of breathlessness and a near-hysterical state. While on one level the passage appears to be simply a stream-of-consciousness portrait of the abdication of reason, on the second level the passage is an accurate statement of what literally is the case: he *is* "she." "She," the succubus that seems to be Adela Hunt's double, is nothing other than Wentworth; "she" is his doppelgänger.

When Williams uses series to describe irrational states (there are several instances presenting Myrtle Fox's vacuous mind [*DH*, 19–21], Pauline Anstruther's fear and stress just before her theophany [220–21], and Lawrence Wentworth's tryst with Lily Sammile [112–21]) the text appears to be a portrait of a frenzied mind; but the subtext (carried, as in the passage just quoted, in devices such as word associations and allusions) demonstrates the unvarying logic present in the seeming unreason of the mind: the essential rationality of the cosmos continues to prevail, not despite the unreason, but by means of it.[5]

Williams's handling of longer series elements such as independent clauses can best be considered in connection with a fourth rhetorical technique, his use of the semicolon. Historically, British stylists have been very fond of this connective, but Williams is remarkable for his frequent and consistent employment of it and for the rhetorical purposes for which clauses are thus joined in *Descent into Hell*. In dialogue or internal discourse, particularly when Williams is portraying an irrational or emotionally overwrought character, the semicolon may connect syntactic units of any type: independent or dependent clauses, phrases, even single words. Elsewhere, however, Williams follows the norm of English punctuation and generally uses the semicolon to connect independent clauses. It is this seemingly conventional use that is highly idiosyncratic in Williams's style.

There are at least three reasons why Williams so liked the semicolon. First, there are the relative durations of pause that are psychologically imposed on the reader by marks of punctuation. The comma offers the briefest pause, the period the longest, and the semicolon one of intermediate duration.[6] The utility of all three variations is self-evident in the following example:

5. The point of *Descent into Hell* is not to reconcile opposites but to prove that all opposites are illusions created by mankind as a result of sin: man's mind, alone, divided the universe against itself, even in matters of rhetoric.

6. It should perhaps be noted that among the less common marks of pause—the exclamation, dash, parenthesis, and colon—Williams never, to my memory, uses the exclamation or parenthesis. The dash is used sparingly. The colon is more common, as it is a means of pointing. Williams typically uses it to indicate dialogue, and at times to indicate a significant conclusion, especially one of a theological nature. But while these are used for variety, they are not as distinctive as his passion for the semicolon.

COMPLEX RHETORIC FOR A SIMPLE UNIVERSE   129

Of the necessity of getting a living he did not think. Living, whether he liked it or not, was provided; he knew that he did like. He went carefully across the dim room and through the door; down the stairs, and reached the front door. It opened of itself before him, so he thought, and he peered out into the road. A great blackness was there; it changed as he peered. As if it fled from him, it retreated. He heard the wind again, but now blowing up the street. A shaft of light smote along with it. Before wind and light and himself he saw the night turn, but it was not the mere night; it was alive, it was made of moving and twisting shapes hurrying away of their own will. Light did not drive them; they revealed the light as they went. They rose and rushed; as they disappeared he saw the long drive before him, and at its end, in the street proper, the figure of a girl. (*DH,* 214)

A second reason for his preference is that, while the period tends to separate thoughts, the semicolon connects them. Williams almost invariably uses the semicolon to connect two clauses, the second of which is a development of the first. Third, the semicolon promotes the effect of a two-part series when two clauses parallel in structure are placed side by side, emphasizing the sense of balance, logic, or authority. Moreover, all three types of effect—pausal tempo, connection, two-part balance—encourage subtle shifts of argument or other developments within the passage. This is especially the case when, as is also characteristic of Williams, the semicolon is employed without an accompanying transitional word such as *however, nevertheless,* or *moreover.* In view of all this, it should not be surprising that semicolons tend to cluster in passages where Williams seeks to persuade us of a character's sanity, the validity of a metaphysical phenomenon, or the logic of a theological proposition. His mode of persuasion is not, as a rule, the argument of the philosopher or theologian; rather, it is that of the poet. He uses imagery, simile, metaphor, metonymy, and literary allusions. Williams develops concepts by means of images, placing them next to one another or pausing to develop one more completely, and connecting these by semicolons: "The grounds of the Manor House expanded beyond them; the universal sky sustained the whole" (9); "The house itself was dark; the ladder was white with a bony pallor against it, but it held no sun" (208); "He passed the finished houses; he came among those which, by the past or future, had been unbuilt" (210). The semicolons imply that each clause of the pair carries equal weight, equal significance; one does not supersede the other but exists in addition to the other, and, between them, they make one syntactic whole. In fact, the clauses are not equal. In each of these sentences Williams is doing something highly characteristic of him—one clause of a set is prosaic, factual; the other inserts a metaphysical implication. In the first example, the initial clause is a straightforward description of a landscape at ground level, merely suggesting some depth to the perspective, for "the grounds . . . expanded beyond [the audience]." The succeeding clause depicts the sky in this landscape, but, quite unexpectedly, it is a "universal sky" and, moreover, that sky "sustains the whole." The whole what? The reader has been teased into reconsidering the view. Normally one assumes the earth does the sustaining. But Williams, with maximum economy of words, has reminded us that in cold and sober fact, a vast nothing holds up the heavy planets; he has reminded us, too, that paradox is the essential nature of things. The second and third examples reflect the same technique but, occurring much later in the novel, do not worry so much about scientific fact; they simply incorporate metaphysical elements. The ladder is white against a black house, yet it reflects no light, so the source of its whiteness must be within itself; the dead man walks among houses eternally (i.e., either from the past or the future) unbuilt.

Williams does not limit his use of compound sentences to the development of concrete imagery; occasionally he uses them also to develop more abstract concepts. In these cases he tends to begin with a "nuclear" clause expressing the main observation and then to develop it by means of successive clauses: "He was the kind of figure who might be more profitable to his neighbourhood dead than alive; dead, he would have given it a shrine; alive, he deprecated worshippers" (*DH,* 10). Statements like this not only describe a character but also suggest that the mind that created such a balanced structure is observant, objective, and, above all, discriminating. In this particular sentence that effect is enhanced by its dispassionate amusement.

Another technique characteristic of Charles Williams is the deliberate return to a word or phrase in order to reexamine and reevaluate it. Not only is this another of those means by which the reader is kept aware of the value of language as an expression of moral integrity (or the lack of it), but it also becomes, on occasion, the poet's substitute for the philosopher's argument when the discussion of a completely abstract concept is necessary:

> The best maxim towards that knowledge was yet not the *Know thyself* of the Greek so much as the *Know Love* of the Christian, though both in the end were one. It was not possible for man to know himself and the world, except first after some mode of knowledge, some art of discovery. The most perfect, since the most intimate and intelligent, art was pure love. The approach by love was the approach to fact; to love anything but fact was not love. Love was even more mathematical than poetry; it was the pure mathematics of the spirit. It was applied also and active; it was the means as it was the end. The end lived everlastingly in the means; the means eternally in the end. (*DH,* 92–93)

Here Williams has attempted to argue what many of his readers would have assumed to be a contradiction in terms: namely, that love (an emotion) is as rational as not just mathematics but as pure mathematics, generally considered among the most dispassionate exercises of absolute logic. He therefore employed a format based on the classical syllogism, and the text seems at first glance to be a Socratic argument. But if one tries to sort out the major and minor propositions and the conclusion, one finds that the tripartite structure keeps falling back into a dyadic structure aided by the two-part compound sentences, and that it has a double conclusion as the sentence curves back upon itself: "The end lived everlastingly in the means; the means eternally in the end." The passage as a whole is deliberately circular, returning to the nuclear concept with which it began: the knowledge of oneself is an end, but knowing love is both the means and the end. So even this is only an apparent syllogism. It is actually dyad within dyad; and the duality is finally revealed to be, paradoxically, a unity. Only poetic language, it seems, is capable of expressing the paradoxic mystery of this universe.

What we see here, manifested on a small scale in both the structure and the content of this passage, is characteristic of *Descent into Hell* on every level. Although the novel gives the impression of being unbiased, objective, and open-ended, everything in it is in fact designed to establish Williams's vision of a universe that appears to be split in two but is, ultimately, one entity. In only one place is there a genuine choice between two elements. This, the novel stresses, is a choice that must, sooner or later, be made by every human being. That choice is, of course, between salvation and damnation, and the primary way of making the choice rests on whether the characters being put to the test will choose reality or an illusion of their own making. The constant reinforcement of this vision is pervasive in the novel; it is found in syntax, in sentence structure, in character development, and in thematic statements; every aspect of the writer's craft has been fused to express and sustain Charles Williams's vision of that unified cosmos, "of infinite difficulty in the finding, of incredible simplicity found."

All Hallows' Eve:
The Cessation of Rhetoric
and the Redemption of Language

George L. Scheper

Early in Charles Williams's last novel, *All Hallows' Eve,* Richard Furnival experiences a "vision," and in consequence, "rhetoric ceased" for him (*AHE,* 75–76). In the situation presented, the recently widowed Richard has just had, in the streets of London, a vision of his dead wife, Lester. The immediate effects of this vision are to impress upon him how precious and yet how unfulfilled their love had been ("Till that night he had not known how very nearly he had loved her") and to deepen his sense of the emptiness of his present life. He has, in the month since her sudden death, tried to fill this void with the normality of work and the renewal of male friendship, but the vision of Lester dramatizes the radical emptiness into which these other experiences now fall. Even when Lester was alive, the reliable "tide of masculine friendship," he now realizes, had defined its reality in relation to that other, centering, Beatrician presence: "But that tide had always swelled against the high cliff of another element, on which a burning beacon had once stood—and now suddenly had again stood." Richard now understands that he had, "for all his goodwill, so neglected her that he had been content to look at her so from his sea; he had never gone in and lived in that strange turret. He had admired, visited, used it. But not till this afternoon had he seen her as simply living. The noise of ocean faded; rhetoric ceased" (75–76).

With rich and poignant irony we are given to understand that only now, in her death, has Richard come to acknowledge Lester's being-in-herself, her *Dasein* or "real presence"—or, in terms of Williams's Dantean Romantic Theology, her reality as Beatrician God-bearing image or *theotokos.*[1] Upon

---

1. On the God-bearing image, see Williams, *The Figure of Beatrice* (London: Faber and Faber, 1943), chap. 2; *HCD,* chap. 5; and Williams, *Religion and Love in Dante* (1941), reprinted in his *Outlines of Romantic Theology,* ed. Alice Mary Hadfield (Grand Rapids, Mich.: Eerdmans, 1990), 96–99, 107–11. See also the following critical comments: Mary

THE CESSATION OF RHETORIC   133

that realization, the "noise of ocean," the "rhetoric" of his habitual manner of being-in-the-world, ceases for a moment. Moreover, this emptiness, this cessation of rhetoric, caused by Lester's unthinkable absence is, by divine Mercy, the occasion for the beginning of *"la vita nuova"* for Richard, just as the death of Beatrice was for Dante.[2] To explore the implications of this fictional moment is to enter upon some of the subtlest and most ambiguous areas of Williams's maturest thought as a lay theologian concerning language, imagery, and symbolism and upon his maturest technique as a narrative artist.

Part I of this essay attempts to identify some of Williams's key ideas about language, in particular the distinctions he draws among unfallen (prelapsarian), fallen, and redeemed speech and his sense of the approximation of the latter in the language of the Way of the Affirmation of Images, that is, in poetry and, especially, in the performative language of liturgy. Reference in this first section primarily will be to Williams's nonfictional prose writings and to his first five novels. Part II applies these concepts to a reading of *All Hallows' Eve* as a culminating example of Williams's sacramental vision of reality and liturgically inspired prose style.

McDermott Shideler, *The Theology of Romantic Love: A Study in the Writings of Charles Williams* (New York: Harper, 1962), chap. 2; R. J. Reilly, *Romantic Religion: A Study of Barfield, Lewis, Williams, and Tolkien* (Athens: University of Georgia Press, 1971), 171–72, 180; Gunnar Urang, *Shadows of Heaven: Religion and Fantasy in the Writing of C. S. Lewis, Charles Williams, and J. R. R. Tolkien* (Philadelphia: Pilgrim Press, 1971), 75, 86; Judith Kollmann, "The Figure of Beatrice in the Works of Charles Williams," *Mythlore* 48 [13.2] (1986): 3, 6; Ernest Beaumont, "Charles Williams and the Power of Eros," *Dublin Review* 479 (1951): 63–64; Nancy Enright, "Charles Williams and His Theology of Romantic Love: A Dantean Interpretation of the Christian Doctrines of the Incarnation and the Trinity," *Mythlore* 60 [16.2] (1989): 22–23, 25; Charles Moorman, *The Precincts of Felicity: The Augustinian City of the Oxford Christians* (Gainesville: University of Florida Press, 1966), 41; Dorothy L. Sayers, "The Poetry of the Image in Dante and Charles Williams," in *Further Papers on Dante* (New York: Harper, 1957), 187, 192; Angelee Sailer Anderson, "The Nature of the City: Visions of the Kingdom and Its Saints in Charles Williams' *All Hallows' Eve*," *Mythlore* 57 [15.3] (1989): 19; Charles A. Huttar, "Arms and the Man: the Place of Beatrice in Charles Williams's Romantic Theology" (1985), in *Studies in Medievalism* 3 (1991): 311–13, 321–24; Clinton W. Trowbridge, "The Beatricean Character in the Novels of Charles Williams," *Sewanee Review* 79 (1971): 335, 340.

2. On the death of Beatrice, see Williams, *Figure of Beatrice*, chap. 3; *HCD*, 101–2; Williams, *Religion and Love in Dante*, 96–97. On the analogy to the death of Lester, see Reilly, *Romantic Religion,* 177; Shideler, *Theology of Romantic Love,* 41–42; Marlene Marie McKinley, "'To Live From a New Root': The Uneasy Consolation of *All Hallows' Eve*," *Mythlore* 59 [16.1] (1989): 15; Sayers, "Poetry of the Image," 194–95; Trowbridge, "Beatricean Character," 342–43.

I. The Redemption of Language

It is remarkable that a writer as notably rhetorical in his own manner as Charles Williams is, by common consent, acknowledged to be[3] should in his imaginative writings so consistently use the term *rhetoric* primarily with its pejorative or negative connotation of abuse of language. For example, in Williams's earliest novel, *Shadows of Ecstasy* (written c. 1925; published 1933), reference is made to Nigel Considine's Spenglerian "Proclamation" to Western civilization, which the admiring Roger Ingram admits is couched in an "extremely rhetorical style" (*SE,* 53) and about which the more skeptical Sir Bernard cautions that "this magniloquent kind of rhetoric can never be trusted" (113). Later, even the poetically minded Roger, who is drawn to Considine's challenge to Western rationalism, concedes that his teachings are "a mad mixture, purple rhetoric and precise realism" (244)—thus putting into antithetic conjunction two modes of using language.

Parallel to Considine in Williams's first novel is the figure of Simon the Clerk in his last novel, *All Hallows' Eve,* in which Lady Wallingford, Simon's own consort, reflects that "that world was his for the taking. Rhetoric and hypnotic spells and healing powers would loose idolatry" and heresy on the world (*AHE,* 89). Here again *rhetoric* is contrasted with grace, this time by a more explicitly pejorative association with the operations of magic and heresy. It is interesting to note that in *Terror of Light,* a religious

---

3. For sympathetic assessments of Williams's rhetorical style, see Winston Weathers, "The Rhetoric of Certitude," *Southern Humanities Review* 2 (1968): 213–22 passim, esp. 214–16, 220; C. N. Manlove, "The Liturgical Novels of Charles Williams," *Mosaic* 12 (1979): 161-81 passim, esp. 180 (on liturgical rhetoric); W. R. Irwin, "Christian Doctrine and the Tactics of Romance: The Case of Charles Williams," in *Shadows of Imagination: The Fantasies of C. S. Lewis, J. R. R. Tolkien, and Charles Williams,* 2d ed., ed. Mark R. Hillegas (Carbondale and Edwardsville: Southern Illinois University Press; London and Amsterdam: Feffer & Simons, 1979), 139, 147–48 (the rhetoric of faith). Among critics who argue that Williams must "tell" what he cannot "show" are Glen Cavaliero, *Charles Williams: Poet of Theology* (Grand Rapids, Mich.: Eerdmans, 1983), 158–77; Patricia Meyer Spacks, "Charles Williams: The Fusions of Fiction," in Hillegas, *Shadows of Imagination,* 152–53, 156–60; and Edward Croft, "Where Words Fall Short: Limitations of Language in *All Hallows' Eve,*" *Mythlore* 50 [13.4] (1987): 18–19. Less sympathetic are Urang, *Shadows of Heaven,* 76–80 (dogmatic rhetoric); George Winship, "This Rough Magic: The Novels of Charles Williams," *The Yale Review* n.s. 40 (1951): 288 ("murky rhetoric"); Don D. Elgin, *The Comedy of the Fantastic: Ecological Perspectives on the Fantasy Novel* (Westport, Conn.: Greenwood Press, 1985), 97 ("abstract rhetoric"), 112 ("rhetorical, not actual"); and Roger Sale, "England's Parnassus: C. S. Lewis, Charles Williams and J. R. R. Tolkien," *Hudson Review* 17 (1964): 212–15 ("totalitarian" rhetoric). T. S. Eliot maintained that Williams had no "palpable design" upon his reader (introduction to *All Hallows' Eve* [New York: Pellegrini & Cudahy, 1948], xiv), although in a recent symposium Bernadette Bosky has argued that he precisely had ("Centennial Retrospective on Charles Williams," *Mythlore* 48 [13.2] [1986]: 13, 15).

THE CESSATION OF RHETORIC

drama written at the same time Williams was composing *All Hallows' Eve* and sharing many of the same interests (it was revised shortly before Williams's death, although a first version was acted as early as 1940[4]), Simon Magus, the historical prototype of Simon the Clerk, is denounced by Saul as "a rhetorical necromancer from the East."[5] Moreover, in *The House of the Octopus,* Williams's last play—published in 1945, the same year as *All Hallows' Eve* and also the year Williams died—the thought occurs yet again, as the heavenly Flame corrects the missionary Anthony for having "talked much . . . in a grand rhetorical Christianity" (*CP,* 309).

Williams consistently purveys this negative connotation of rhetoric in his most serious theological writings. In his 1943 essay "What the Cross Means to Me," speaking of "the sorrow and the obscenity" of the Cross as stamped upon the human condition, Williams says, in an aside, "I do not wish to seem here to become rhetorical; I do not underrate the great and pure beauties which are presented and revealed to us" (*Image,* 134), thus syntactically paralleling rhetoric and inaccuracy. Similarly, Williams begins *The Forgiveness of Sins* (1942) with a critique of the unconvincing rhetoric of much theological writing (4) and ends with a postscript on the impossibility of passing final moral judgments, adducing Churchill's reference to Hitler as "that bad man":

> One must distinguish [Williams argues] between the rhetorical force of the phrase and its literal meaning. The rhetorical force is of the greatest value to us at the present time, and may, of course, be entirely justified. It comes to us with a sense of the greatest sincerity, but that is only to say that Mr. Churchill is a superb rhetorician. In view of human history one can hardly believe that rhetoric necessarily implies sincerity. (*FS,* 110)

In short, rhetoric—though of great value "at the present time" (i.e., in the postlapsarian world and in time of war)—does not belong to the primordial or to the final and sempiternal use of language. This implication is more explicit in *He Came Down from Heaven* (1938), when Williams says in speaking of Cain's crime, "He not only killed his brother; he also made an effort to carry on the intellectual falsity which his parents had experienced when they fled from facts in their new shame. He became rhetorical—it is, so early, the first appearance of a false style of words: 'Am I my brother's keeper?'" (*HCD,* 116).

Calling attention to these passages is not to imply that rhetoric, the art of using language to please, instruct, or persuade, is for Williams an inherently suspect activity, for in Williams's incarnational, sacramental theology, every

---

4. Alice Mary Hadfield, *Charles Williams: An Exploration of His Life and Work* (New York and Oxford: Oxford University Press, 1983), 191.

5. *Terror of Light,* in *CP,* 342.

136   GEORGE L. SCHEPER

being or thing is understood to be an original good. At the same time, however, every good thing can, by choice, be "known as evil" (as Williams explains in his analyses of the myth of the Fall [see *HCD,* 14–19; *FS,* 20]); that is, it can be put to inappropriate, perverted, or infamous abuse, and this would apply to rhetoric as to any other art. Thus, Roger Ingram's ironically titled book *Persuasive Serpents: Studies in English Criticism* serves as an epigrammatic caveat against the rhetorical excesses of gnostic tendencies in literary criticism (*SE,* 8). Similarly, in a moment of "dreaming luxury" Richard deserts his admiration for his friend Jonathan's spiritually powerful paintings, momentarily preferring instead the "exquisite" carved hand on Simon's front door because "art, he thought, should be persuasive" (*AHE,* 78)—Richard is momentarily lulled, that is, into preferring visual rhetoric to the power of art after its own manner.

Still, we might well ask, with Wayne Booth in *The Rhetoric of Fiction,* what else can literature be but rhetorical? What might *non*rhetorical language be like, and how would we recognize it?[6] The first point would simply be to recognize the limitations of language itself. T. S. Eliot, in a widely quoted comment in his introduction to *All Hallows' Eve,* sees as characteristic of Williams's work as a whole that "what it is, essentially, that he had to say comes near to defying definition" and resists satisfactory expression in conventional literary forms. In a recent article on this subject, Edward Croft comments, after citing Eliot, that Williams's "apprehension of what he attempts to render is rooted in a realm of experience inaccessible to conventional perception."[7]

So to begin with, account must be taken of the ultimate inadequacy of language. For Williams, the "one law of literary criticism," in counteraction to the postlapsarian tendency toward rhetoric—and in dramatic contrast to most contemporary literary theory—is "the law of emptying the words": "clear[ing] the mind of our own second-hand attribution of meanings to words" and allowing the art or literary work's "own stillness" to prevail (*HCD,* 10–11).[8] Isabel Ingram, trying to define her love for Roger, how she

---

6. Booth, *The Rhetoric of Fiction* (Chicago and London: University of Chicago Press, 1961), 99, 109, and passim.

7. Eliot, introduction to *All Hallows' Eve,* xiii; Croft, "Where Words Fall Short," 18.

8. Cf. *DH,* 247. See comments in John Sheehan, "Liver as Well as Heart: The Theology of Charles Williams," *Renascence* 37 (1984): 35–36. An interesting analogue in contemporary fiction is the emptying of language sequence in Margaret Atwood's *Surfacing,* in which the narrator shamanistically recovers unitive contact with the natural world through the abandonment of rationalizing and dichotomizing discourse ([New York: Fawcett, 1972], 210–13); cf. Ursula Le Guin's short story "She Unnames Them," in which Eve undoes the Adamic imposition of names (*New Yorker,* 21 January 1985, 27). For a brilliant recent study of *apophasis* ("unsaying" or "speaking-away") as specific mode of discourse in mystical theology, see

THE CESSATION OF RHETORIC 137

wanted for him what he wanted "even more than he did, since I hadn't myself to think of and he had," must finally forgo language: "I don't call it anything. . . . There isn't anything to call it. It's the way things happen, if you love anyone" (*SE,* 209). At any ultimate point of knowing, Williams knew, language must fail; the great paradigm in literature for Williams was Dante in the final Canto of the *Paradiso*: "Da quinci innanzi il mio veder fu maggio / che il parlar nostro ch'a tal vista cede" (Thenceforward was my vision mightier than our discourse, which faileth at such sight).[9] Williams's own comment is that at this point, "the Knower begins to know after a quite other manner, about which nothing can be said," adding that it is "astonishing (but blessed) that this great poet should have said so little in the ordinary speech of Christians; he omits so much that any small Christian versifier would have put in" (*Figure of Beatrice,* 231—in contrast, for instance, to the "grand rhetorical Christianity" of the missionary Anthony in *The House of the Octopus*).

In effect, what Williams, and Dante, take us back to is the great Nominalist/Realist controversy of the Middle Ages.[10] Williams, a convinced Realist, argues acerbicly that "the concentration of the ingenious mind is always on the symbol and never on the fullness of symbol and symbolized—this concentration brings its own reward. The reward is the gradual death of all living meaning"; or, again, that "the poet who, in his own mind, mistakes his own word for the thing imagined is lost."[11] But can language ever reflect the "fullness of symbol and symbolized"?

Perhaps nowhere in imaginative literature has the attempt to deal with such questions been presented so boldly or dramatically as in Williams's fourth novel, *The Place of the Lion* (1931). Here the narcissistic young scholar Damaris Tighe represents the Nominalist attitude that, as it happens, is excoriated in a fictional medieval text quoted in the narrative, according to which "certain heretics" declared that "strength or beauty, or humility . . . were no more than words used for many like things and had in themselves

---

Michael A. Sells, *Mystical Languages of Unsaying* (Chicago: University of Chicago Press, 1994); in terms of Sells's analysis, Williams (whom he does not discuss) would be an instance not merely of apophatic theory but of apophatic discourse, or "performative apophasis" (3–5).

9. 33.55–56; trans. P. H. Wicksteed, Temple Classics (1899; reprint, London: J. M. Dent, 1958), 402–3.

10. Cf. Clifford Davidson, "Williams' *All Hallows' Eve:* The Way of Perversity," *Renascence* 20 (Winter 1968): 89; George Winship, "The Novels of Charles Williams," in Hillegas, *Shadows of Imagination,* 113.

11. Williams, *Outlines of Romantic Theology,* 49; *Image,* 183.

138   GEORGE L. SCHEPER

no meaning" (*PL,* 167). The Realist rejoinder, as it were, comes in the form of an actual invasion of the world by the Archetype Beasts.

The Realist position for Williams is, in essence, that words have properly an indissoluble connection to realities-in-themselves, so that the purest and even highest aim of language is none other than "accuracy," as the "pig-headed precisian" Anthony reflects (*PL,* 63), and as the precisian Williams himself exclaims in one of his essays, with regard to certain comfortable dishonesties common in theological writing: "Accuracy, accuracy, and again accuracy! accuracy of mind and accuracy of emotion. If the Church is to look forward to a wholesome mental life her members must discipline themselves to honesty" (*Image,* 157). More succinctly, as the Flame in *The House of the Octopus* declares, "heaven is always exact" (*CP,* 298). Conversely, as Williams famously says in an essay on Milton, "Hell is always inaccurate" (*Image,* 30).[12]

Thus, in prelapsarian and redeemed speech, words "fulfill" their Image; as the Chorus in *The House of the Octopus* says, "Ours is a world without opinions; here / everything is what it is, and nothing else" (*CP,* 299). By contrast, fallen speech veers away from the Image and toward inaccuracy: "It is one of the intellectual results of the Fall that our language has always to speak in terms of the Fall; and that we cannot help our language does not make it any more true" (*Image,* 82; cf. *FS,* 17). For Williams, it is not shared or collective intellectual life but individualistic isolation that most breeds this inaccuracy. It is, for example, the solipsistic "seclusion" of Damaris Tighe and the "habitual disposition towards unrighteousness which it involved" that leads her into scholarly inaccuracies (*PL,* 140–41); and the same principle is operative, more decisively, in the case of the more committed solipsism of Lawrence Wentworth in *Descent into Hell:* Wentworth's inaccuracy, beginning in the fudging of scholarship, culminates in the tour-de-force portrayal of incoherence and imbecility with which that narrative concludes. The incoherence that inundates Wentworth is the extreme negative instance of the failure of language (although it is a pattern common to all of Williams's self-damning characters, notably, as we shall see, Simon the Clerk and Evelyn in *All Hallows' Eve*). It is crucial to the meaning of Williams's novel that the emptying of meaning experienced by Wentworth be recognized as antithetical in significance to the spiritual

---

12. On the theme of accuracy see Anderson, "The Nature of the City," 20; Manlove, "Liturgical Novels of Charles Williams," 173; Elizabeth Wright, "Theology in the Novels of Charles Williams," *Stanford Honors Essays in Humanities* 5 and 6 (1962): 26; and Alice Mary Hadfield, "The Relationship of Charles Williams' Working Life to His Fiction," in Hillegas, *Shadows of Imagination,* 132–33.

THE CESSATION OF RHETORIC 139

"emptying" that preludes redeemed speech, although it can be seen as parodying that *kenosis.*

The linguistic means to accuracy, to adherence to the "fullness" of the Image, to the communication of any deep personal truth, as Anthony perceives in *The Place of the Lion,* is "some more general, some ceremonial utterance. . . . Now, if ever, he needed the ritual of words arranged and shaped for that end" (*PL,* 166). The "ritual of words" that Anthony discovers, the primal and true use of language, is, precisely and simply, *naming.* Drawing upon the "million-year[-]old memory" deep "in his brain" and "the nature of Adam" that lives in him (265), Anthony in the role of a second Adam performs the mythic action that sends the Archetype Beasts back out of the world: he names them (282). Returning to the Edenic situation in which "the Adam" was divided in two and the man performed the work of naming the creatures,[13] Anthony utters "an incomprehensible call . . . a sound as of a single word" in the prelapsarian "language in which our father Adam named the beasts of the garden" (277). Strictly speaking, "naming" could be construed as an act of coercive power, but Williams's sense seems to be closer to the idea of "calling the name," as if in acknowledgment of the proper being of the one called—as we see in the subsequent application of the motif to human situations in the novel.

Analogous to the mythic Adamic naming is, in the human situation, simply the calling of a person's name. Most dramatically, in the midst of a hellish vision in which Damaris is tormented by a vile and foul-smelling pterodactyl croaking Latin jargon at her—the projection of her own academic narcissism—she begins to be saved by the feeble and broken effort of simply calling Anthony's name: "An . . . An . . . A . . . A . . . A . . ." —thereby to a degree at last acknowledging her interdependence with another.[14] Later, emerged from her near-fatal self-preoccupation, Damaris calls out Quentin's name in an effort to come to *his* aid (*PL,* 243, 245). The paradigm for this sacramental name calling is biblical, and not only Adamic but covenantal and redeemed: God or angel calling patriarch or prophet to service, or the encounter of Mary Magdalene and the risen Jesus in John's Gospel when "Jesus said to her, 'Mary' [and] she turned and said to him in Hebrew, '*Rabboni!*'" (John 20:16). The latter encounter is reimagined by Williams in *Terror of Light* as the redemptive encounter of Mary Magdalene with the consort of Simon the Magus, Luna—who is freed thereby of her bondage to Simon (*CP,* 357).

---

13. *PL,* 266. Anthony's Edenic action is precisely the antithesis of Wentworth's regressive, solipsistic "Return to Eden" in chapter 5 of *DH.*

14. *PL,* 183; cf. Moorman, *Precincts of Felicity,* 53.

140 GEORGE L. SCHEPER

Not only the calling of a name but the utterance of a simple reply, such as Damaris's response of "Yes, yes" to Anthony's call (*PL,* 284; cf. Matt. 5:37) or Lester's answer of "I'm here" to Betty's call (*AHE,* 120), is, for Williams, redemptive speech, analogous to Abraham's or Moses's "Here I am" (Gen. 22:1–2; Exod. 3:4), or the Virgin Mary's "Behold the handmaid of the Lord" (Luke 1:38). Similarly Adamic, or redeemed, is the utterance of simple, unpremeditated exclamations, such as Damaris's father's response to the archetypal Butterfly: "O glory, glory" (*PL,* 56), or the cartman's reaction to the transformation of his horse: "My God! O my God!" (172), or the hanged workman's response to the saintly gaze of Margaret Anstruther: "He wanted to speak; he could not find words to utter or control. He broke into a cry, a little wail, such as many legends have recorded and many jokes mocked. He said: 'Ah! ah!' and did not think it could be heard" (*DH,* 165).

Implicit in the foregoing discussion is that a threefold pattern concerning the nature of language is premised in Williams's writings: (1) a primordial, prelapsarian Adamic speech of "naming"; (2) our present fallen language, prone to "rhetoric"; and (3) a movement toward the recovery of unfallen language, that is, toward redeemed speech.[15] To this we need to add two observations: first, that there is a natural resemblance between stages one and three, between prelapsarian and redeemed language, in that both convey in their simplicity and purity the "fullness" of the Image; and, second, that the purifying "emptying" of coinherent redeemed speech can be mimicked or parodied by the meaningless "emptying" of incoherent fallen speech, as experienced by Wentworth in *Descent into Hell.* Similarly, in Williams's imaging of human experience, poetry and liturgy—the prime purveyors of redeemed language in our culture—are always being parodied by rhetoric and magic, their respective antitheses.

We have already seen what Williams might mean by "redeemed speech" in his comment about "emptying" words and in the namings, callings, and exclamations instanced in *The Place of the Lion* and other fictions, but nowhere does he express his idea of it more succinctly than in his comment that "the epigrams of saints, doctors, and poets, are the nearest we can go to the recovery of that ancient validity, our unfallen speech" (*Image,* 82). We have a good notion of what Williams must have meant by these "epigrams" in his frequent citation, in both his fictional and his nonfictional writings, of such favorite sayings as: "This also is Thou; neither is this Thou"; "He saved others; himself he cannot save"; "Your life and your death are with your neighbor"; "My Eros is crucified": dicta that for Williams

15. On the matter of vision and "redeemed speech" see Reilly, *Romantic Religion,* 168–73; Moorman, *Precincts of Felicity,* 41; Wright, "Theology in the Novels of CW," 191.

THE CESSATION OF RHETORIC   141

resonate with self-evident truth, that represent not opinions of this or that person but simple conformity to the facts of experience.[16] Moreover, in his fictions Williams frequently attempts to recreate redeemed speech in the dialogues or "spiritual colloqu[ies]" (*AHE*, 120) taking place between his more saintly characters, such as Sir Bernard and Isabel Ingram in *Shadows of Ecstasy*, or Anthony and Richardson in *The Place of the Lion*, or Sybil and Nancy in *The Greater Trumps*, or the defenders of the Graal in *War in Heaven*, or Peter Stanhope (a verse playwright of a "most epigrammatic style" [*DH*, 13]) and Pauline and Margaret Anstruther in *Descent into Hell*, or Lester and Betty and Jonathan and Richard in *All Hallows' Eve*—dialogues now sonorous with Book of Common Prayer prose and now studded with pithy epigrams such as "Go with God," "Give him my love," and "Under the Permission."

Such colloquies have occasionally elicited negative criticism, both from Williams's detractors and from many of his admirers, for their alleged artistic naiveté: their combination of frontal directness and (ironically) rhetorical "plumminess," for their dogmatic earnestness and sprightly whimsy, their seemingly inauthentic speech rhythms, and their two-dimensionality of characterization.[17] But the frequent charge of two-dimensionality, at any rate, might in fact lead to a more appropriate reading of Williams's prose style as analogous to the style of the Byzantine icon. (Cavaliero has already suggested such an analogy for Williams's poetry as being "kindred in spirit" to the stylized approach of Byzantine art, with its carefulness in conveying the incarnational humanity of Christ but without the "misleading naturalistic humanism" of three-dimensional or perspectival art.)[18]

More directly relevant analogs to Williams's style in his fictional colloquies between saintly characters or in his heightened narrational moments are the language of poetry and the language of liturgy. For Williams, poetry is a supreme expression of the Affirmative Way of spirituality, the Way of the Images epitomized in Dante.[19] As Williams

---

16. See Cavaliero, *Poet of Theology*, 164.

17. On the character of Williams's fictional dialogue, especially the "spiritual colloquies" of his saintly characters, and the issue of two-dimensionality of characterization, see Cavaliero, *Poet of Theology*, 162 ("plumminess"); Urang, *Shadows of Heaven*, 77–78, 82 ("banality"); Irwin, "Christian Doctrine and the Tactics of Romance," 142–43 ("monistic" vision); Winship, "This Rough Magic," 290–91 (dualistic characterization); Weathers, "Rhetoric of Certitude," 214–16; Spacks, "Charles Williams," 156–57; and Agnes Sibley, *Charles Williams* (Boston: Twayne, 1982), 144.

18. Cavaliero, *Poet of Theology*, 169.

19. Williams, *Figure of Beatrice*, 9-11. On the Affirmative Way of Images, see especially

142   GEORGE L. SCHEPER

says in *The Descent of the Dove,* "Poetry can do something that philosophy can not, for poetry . . . has already turned the formulae of belief into an operation of faith" (123). The supreme exponent of poetry within Williams's fiction is, of course Peter Stanhope in *Descent into Hell,* whose poetic masque is described as "the powerful exploration of power after his own manner" (*DH,* 89); its rhetorical antithesis is defined by Myrtle Fox: "Art ought to be beautiful, don't you think? Beautiful words in beautiful voices. I do think elocution is so important" (84).

The language of liturgy, however, even more than that of poetry, is for Williams the accessible prototype of redeemed speech. Liturgy is, said Williams, "the voice of Christ in the Church," just as for the great Anglican divines of the seventeenth century it was "their natural and holy speech" (*Image,* 123, 122). The modern reader must realize that, for Williams, liturgical language is properly a rich and sensuous language—expressive rather than persuasive or rhetorical—a supreme exemplar of what he calls the Way of the Affirmation of Images, closer, in fact, to the language of D. H. Lawrence than to the docetic, "devotionalized" style resulting from the modern Church's "unofficial Manicheism" (*Image,* 69). For example, Sybil Coningsby, one of Williams's saintliest characters, speaks in a moment of crisis with "eternal peace in her voice," in richly symbolic phraseology: "I know the dance. . . . I saw the gold in the snow . . . and your father was in it and safe. . . . [T]he Fool is here to hold them . . . and there's no figure anywhere in heaven or earth that can slip from that partner. They are all his for ever." Williams's narrator explains: "She was not very clear what language she was using; as from the apostles on Pentecost, the single gospel flowed from her in accents she had not practised and syllables she had never learned" (*GT,* 171–72)—i.e., she has practiced the "emptying of words." As if to underscore the point, the chapter ends with Nancy, Sybil's disciple, saying, with liturgical cadence that could come from the Book of Common Prayer, "The dance is in my ears and the light's in my eyes, and this is why I was born, and there was glory in the beginning and is now and ever shall be, and let's run, . . . for the world's going quickly and we must be in front of it to-night" (182).

The case for the analogy between Williams's prose style and the style of liturgy has been well put in a persuasive critical essay by C. N. Manlove,

---

Dove, 57–58, and the essays "Sensuality and Substance" and "The Way of Affirmation" (*Image,* 68–75 and 154–58); also the following critical comments: Wright, "Theology in the Novels of CW," 128–41; Sayers, "Poetry of the Image," 185–88; Robert McAfee Brown, "Charles Williams: Lay Theologian," *Theology Today* 10 (1953): 225–26; Dennis F. Kinlaw, "Charles Williams' Concept of Imaging Applied to 'The Song of Songs,'" *Wesleyan Theological Journal* 16 (1981): 89; Anderson, "Nature of the City," 19–20; Reilly, *Romantic Religion,* 158–59.

THE CESSATION OF RHETORIC 143

who argues that "'Liturgy' . . . could be said to capture the essence of Charles Williams' novels. . . . It is these aspects—ceremony and adoration in a public context—that his novels express." The view of the universe implicit in orthodox liturgy and that implicit in Williams's fiction, Manlove argues, are the same: "ordered, hierarchical, ceremonial, intercorrespondent, a joyous cosmic dance in which all things participated, a 'web of diagrammatized glory, of honourable beauty, of changing and interchanging adoration'"; the object, he continues, "of all Williams's novels is to reveal the co-inherent, patterned glory of the universe. The accent, therefore, is on adoration." Manlove argues that Williams's novels manifest such liturgical characteristics as a ritual pattern centered on emulation of Christ's self-sacrifice, motifs of transfiguration (e.g., a traffic policeman seen as the Emperor of Trumps of the Tarot [*GT,* 67]), a recurrent or cyclical structure, and a formal, ceremonial style marked by shifting viewpoints, alternations of dialectic with "intrusive" narrational "spiritual commentaries," and he concludes that if "we can see Charles Williams as a liturgical writer . . . then some of the criticisms to which his work has often been subject may have less force," although "it must be said that appreciation of Charles Williams' novels involves at least some prior sympathy on the part of the reader in the same way that no one can enter into the Liturgy of the Church without previous disposition to do so."[20]

Many readers have noticed the unusual prominence in Williams's novels of descriptions and, indeed, re-creations of actual liturgical services; few novelists have so centered their plot action on liturgical moments.[21] At the Mass in Lambeth, in *Shadows of Ecstasy,* the African king Inkamasi is, as Wright puts it, "given grace to choose death over renunciation of his faith"[22] and, as the Mass is presented through the viewpoint consciousness of another character, Philip, we are told that "the Rite ordered his mind. He forgot to try and reconcile; he was moved by reconciliation" (*SE,* 129). At the Christmas service in *The Greater Trumps,* Nancy Coningsby—who had been told by her aunt Sybil that she didn't love anyone—is swept up in the "dim floods of power and adoration . . . these songs and flights of dancing words which wheeled in her mind," and under the power of psalms and hymns bidding worshipers "rise to adore the mystery of love" and of the Athanasian Creed's definition of the Incarnation as the "taking of the manhood into God," she achieves a transformed awareness of the glorious-

20. Manlove, "Liturgical Novels of CW," 161 (citing, for "web of . . . glory," *FS,* 18), 177, 180.

21. See Wright, "Theology in the Novels of CW," 35; Charles A. Huttar, "Seeing Williams' Work as a Whole: Church Year and Creed as Structural Principles," *Mythlore* 51 [14.1] (1987): 14–18, 56.

22. Wright, "Theology in the Novels of CW," 35.

144   GEORGE L. SCHEPER

ness of the people around her (*GT,* 132–35). Similarly, in *The Place of the Lion,* a plain Breaking of Bread service in a rather dowdy evangelical church is transfigured in the eyes of the casual visitor Richardson—himself a follower of the *via negativa* and one who holds himself rather above liturgical expressions—into a gloriously mythic Liturgy of the Divine Unicorn (*PL,* 197–99). And *War in Heaven* ends, after the terrible sufferings endured by the Christlike Archdeacon of Fardles, with the re-creation of a liturgy in the village church, at which the Archdeacon is able to recollect his heart, take the sacrament, and die peacefully, "in the presence" (*WH,* 285–88).

What is distinctive about each of the liturgical sequences above is that first, they not only are described in some detail but are in effect *re-created* so that to a degree the reader encounters the language and imagery of liturgy itself; and second, they are not merely "lyrical" interludes but have a decisive impact on the action. For if history is what has happened, liturgy is what *is* happening; it is, as Williams says, "more a thing done than a thing said" (*Image,* 122). Williams understood liturgical language to be what philosopher J. L. Austin has termed "performative language," in which "the ritual word is itself the critical act rather than a report of, or stimulus to, action."[23] Thus Manlove comments aptly that the words of the antiphonally sung Creed in *The Greater Trumps* is really "exchange in operation, and its statements are in a sense acts";[24] just as the Archdeacon of Fardles, approaching the Mysteries in his final liturgy, "distinguished no longer word from act" but "was part of the Act" (*WH,* 285; cf. *AHE,* 141). The precise antithesis of liturgy as performative language is, as we shall see in analyzing *All Hallows' Eve,* the attempted compulsory language of magic.

II. Language, Liturgy, and Magic in *All Hallows' Eve*

The recognition of ritual language as performative is central to a cogent reading of *All Hallows' Eve.* One of the frequently criticized plot elements in this novel is the efficacy of Betty's infant baptism, performed by her nursemaid, in protecting her from the magical operations of Simon the Clerk. As her fiancé Jonathan reflects when the story is told, "so this child of magic had been after birth saved from magic by a mystery beyond magic" (*AHE,* 158). Some readers have seen this as a literal-minded pitting of one form of magic against another,[25] but Williams is precise: magic is

---

23. Cited by Herbert Fingarette, *Confucius—the Secular as Sacred* (New York: Harper Torchbooks, 1972), 11.

24. Manlove, "Liturgical Novels of CW," 169.

25. "Ex opere operato"—Urang, *Shadows of Heaven,* 90; cf. Beaumont, "CW and the Power of Eros," 66.

THE CESSATION OF RHETORIC   145

overcome by *mystery*. It is the "natural affection" of the nursemaid and her ritual language ("There, dearie, no-one can undo that; bless God for it" [104]) that are operative, first by an act of substitution in the web of coinherence—for Williams, simply a fact of the universe—and second, on a "naturalistic" basis, as a vague dream-memory Betty carries in her mind like a pearl of great price.

The magic-versus-mystery dichotomy is central to the meaning of *All Hallows' Eve*, for the operative binary polarity for Williams is not the Eliadean sacred versus profane, but rather the sacred versus the perverse, the "inscape" of nature and grace versus the Infamy of denial and exclusion (*Image*, 105). If for Williams liturgy and performative liturgical language represent the epitome of approximation to redeemed action and speech, then their opposite is not secular, profane, or banal action and speech but rather the operations and pseudo-performative incantations of magic. The sacred/profane polarity does not work in explicating Williams because, as a Christian committed to an incarnational theology, Williams constantly reiterated his repudiation of Manicheism and reaffirmed everywhere in his writings, whether in poetry, drama, essay, or fiction, his Athanasian faith in the goodness of matter and the body, indeed of all creation and all eventuality as "holy fact."[26]

Strictly speaking, it is therefore inappropriate to speak of binary oppositions at all with regard to Charles Williams, for—as a metaphysical monist—he recognized the ultimate reality only of the good.[27] Existentially, to be sure, he fully acknowledged the presence of evil (indeed, Williams was quite impatient with theodicies that would attempt to "explain away" the problem of evil),[28] yet not its existence as a separate "principle" but rather only as a perverse way of relating to the good. According to Williams's analysis of the myth of the Fall, Adam and Eve chose to introduce "contradiction" into the good, to, as it were, know good as evil—just as the redeemed mentality

---

26. See *Image*, 66, 110; *DH*, 279, 283; also the following critical comments: Chad Walsh, "Charles Williams' Novels and the Contemporary Mutation of Consciousness," in *Myth, Allegory and Gospel: An Interpretation of J. R. R. Tolkien, C. S. Lewis, G. K. Chesterton, Charles Williams*, ed. John Warwick Montgomery (Minneapolis: Bethany Fellowship, 1974), 73; Anne Ridler, introduction to *Image*, xlix; Robert C. Holder, "Art and the Artist in the Fiction of Charles Williams," *Renascence* 27 (1975): 85–86; Hadfield, "Relationship," 133–34; Shideler, *Theology of Romantic Love*, 72.

27. Irwin, "Christian Doctrine and the Tactics of Romance," 142–43 (Williams's metaphysical "monism"); cf. Winship, "This Rough Magic," 290–91 (Williams's dualistic morality). Metaphysical monism and practical moral dualism do not, in fact, seem an unlikely configuration.

28. C. S. Lewis, ed., *Essays Presented to Charles Williams* (1945; reprint, Grand Rapids: Eerdmans, 1966), xiii.

146 GEORGE L. SCHEPER

is to know even evil as good (*HCD,* 18; *FS,* 20). So it is very misleading, if we are to follow Williams's own metaphysics, to speak of opposites or dichotomies at all; concerning "spirit" and "matter," the saintly Lester, we are told, "did not dichotomize" (*AHE,* 171; cf. *Image,* 113). But it is hard to overcome the habit of dualistic thinking and speaking, as Williams well understood, lamenting that this "is our first intellectual descent from heaven; we are compelled to use terms which we know are inaccurate" (*FS,* 17).

At any rate, in the present moral world as we know it experientially, magic is for Williams the exact antithesis of liturgy, precisely as the magician is the antithesis of Christ—is, that is, an Antichrist.[29] Just as the Antichrist of the Apocalypse is a "false Christ," so Williams's Antichrist figure is one who resembles but ultimately is antithetical to Christ.[30] The resemblance may be virtually a caricature and impossible to mistake as such, as in the "paralleling" of Simon and Christ in *All Hallows' Eve,* or misleading and ambiguous, as in the case of Considine in *Shadows of Ecstasy.* So, too, the operations and language of magic "resemble" the language and performance of liturgy, but in ways that are finally antithetical. Magic, in short, *parodies* liturgy, just as the magician parodies Christ.

The concept of parody of the sacred is enormously helpful in finding a useful critical stance for reading Charles Williams, and it serves virtually as a genre-concept.[31] Moralistic literary tradition is inextricably bound up with dualities, and thus with the Manichean tendency, whereas the mode of parody of the sacred is more consonant with Charles Williams's monistic metaphysics: things either are good or are misapprehensions and caricatures of the good. The moral choice of the Way of Perversity, therefore, finds its apt and natural literary image in parody.

It is interesting that Williams's first and last novels, *Shadows of Ecstasy* and *All Hallows' Eve,* should both focus on the image of a magus and the question of power. Both Nigel Considine and Simon the Clerk seek ultimate

---

29. It should be noted that the Greek prefix *anti-* here implies correspondence or resemblance rather than opposition, as in the pairing of type and antitype in typological exegesis: see Charles A. Huttar, "Charles Williams, Novelist and Prophet," *Gordon Review* 10 (1967): 60. Sibley (*CW,* 147) cites Williams's reference to Satan as "God's shadow" in his early play *The Rite of the Passion* (*Three Plays* [London: Oxford University Press, 1931], 142), and the Skeleton in *Thomas Cranmer* calls himself "Christ's back" (*CP,* 54). On the figure of the Antichrist, see *Image,* 117–21; also Davidson, "Way of Perversity," 87; Bernadette Bosky, "Grace and Goetia: Magic as Forced Compensation in *All Hallows' Eve,*" *Mythlore* 45 [12.2] (1986): 20; Huttar, "CW, Novelist and Prophet," 60–61, 73.

30. Kollmann suggests instead the term *Apostate* figure: "Figure of Beatrice in the Works of CW," 4–5.

31. See Davidson, "Way of Perversity," 86–87; Bosky, "Grace and Goetia," 20–21; Wright, "Theology in the Novels of CW," 35; Urang, *Shadows of Heaven,* 73.

THE CESSATION OF RHETORIC

power over life and death; both have achieved an unnatural longevity; each seeks to be a Messiah and create followers; and each practices what looks like a personal asceticism, teaches either universal ecstasy or universal love, performs healings or other "signs," and, in general, seems to emulate Christ. Summing up the formal parallels between Considine and Christ, for instance, Huttar concludes that there is about Nigel Considine, as with Milton's Satan, "a genuine greatness and a breath-taking attractiveness," such that "only ultimate[ly]" is he antithetical to Christ.[32] But Williams explicitly identifies the essence of the Antichrist figure as lying in his "consciousness of a kind of *otherness* from men" (*Image,* 121); by contrast, the essence of the truly Christlike life is to know that we live "for" and "from" others (*Image,* 148–49). Thus, Considine's gnostic ideal of putting away every desire but the conquest of death (*SE,* 265–66—analogous to the false asceticism of Klingsor in Wagner's *Parsifal*) and his teaching that every shadow of ecstasy, whether love or art, should be abandoned for what is higher (102) are only parodies of the genuine *via negativa* and are wholly at variance with the affirmation of the sacramental goodness of creation, which was for Williams a first principle of theology. Moreover, in the ultimate matter of self-emptying love, Considine is wholly antithetical (and not just "only ultimately" antithetical) to Christ. Considine confesses that, unlike "the poor wretch who died" (i.e., Christ), in "the choice between defeat and victory . . . I've chosen victory" (247, 222); this is in contrast with the saintly Isabel and King Inkamasi, who both understand that victory cannot come until one has been "wholly defeated," nor plenitude be found until one has known "utter despair" (233; cf. 168–69).

In the case of Simon the Clerk and his magical operations in *All Hallows' Eve,* Williams's technique of sacred parody achieves an effective culmination.[33] Like Considine, Simon enjoys a preternatural longevity and has positioned himself to become a Master of the world as he believes he has become Master of life and death. He has founded a kind of church, and he practices healing and preaches to followers who call him "our Father" (*AHE,* 32) a message that is "mostly Love, with a hint of some secret" (31). But Simon has entered further into Antichristhood. He has cloned two images of

---

32. Huttar, "CW, Novelist and Prophet," 63, 60. Huttar refines his views in a later article proposing that the ambiguity of the figure of Considine derives from a period when Williams's views of Milton's Satan were undergoing radical transformation: "Williams's Changing Views of Milton and the Problem of *Shadows of Ecstasy,* " *Inklings-Jarhbuch* 5 (1987): 226. (The critical controversy over Considine is in fact a microcosm of the longstanding critical debate over Milton's Satan.) Also see Judith Kollmann, "Charles Williams and Second-Hand Paganism," *Mythlore* 40 [11.2] (1984): 7.

33. Davidson, "Way of Perversity"; Huttar, "CW, Novelist and Prophet," 73; Bosky, "Grace and Goetia," 20; Anderson, "Nature of the City," 17.

148 GEORGE L. SCHEPER

himself to work in the world, thus parodying the Trinity itself in a hideous "triplicity," and he has practiced intercourse just once, "and that for a rational purpose," in order to beget a child to be the instrument of his magic, to send forth into the world of the dead—thereby creating a parody of the Holy Family.[34] Actually, Simon's awareness of the divine prototype is presented as being merely of a "tale" about another Jewish "sorcerer," named Joseph, whose "attempt at domination had been made and failed. . . . The living thing that had been born of his feminine counterpart had perished miserably" (53). The passage brilliantly transposes the terms of Luke's story into the understanding of a man who can understand not mystery but only power and magic. A few pages later we are given a further insight into Simon's views on "that other" one who had "perished miserably": Simon had studied the means of continual regeneration,

> but so doing, he had refused all possibilities in death. He would not go to it, as that other child of a Jewish girl had done. That other had refused safeguard and miracle; he had refused the achievement of security. He had gone into death—and the Clerk supposed it his failure—as the rest of mankind go—ignorant and in pain. The Clerk had set himself to decline pain and ignorance.[35]

But power, as Williams once said, "is not something that one has; it is something one is." Christ's self-emptying dereliction of power utterly confounds the gnostic magician.[36]

The character of Simon the Clerk is based, of course, largely on the biblical figure of Simon Magus (Acts 8:9–24), whose character and role were elaborated in various early Christian documents, which Williams draws on for his account of Simon in *Witchcraft* (1941), written just a few years prior to *All Hallows' Eve*. In this work Williams brings in a number of details interesting in relation to the novel, particularly that of Simon Magus making an image to contain the soul of a slain child for purposes of necromancy and divination.[37] Williams also uses Simon the Magus as a

34. *AHE,* 87–89, 52; cf. Charles Williams, *Witchcraft* (1941; reprint, New York: Meridian/New American Library, 1959), 31–34.

35. *AHE,* 93; cf. *SE,* 108, 168, 233.

36. Williams, "The Figure of Arthur," in *Arthurian Torso,* ed. C. S. Lewis (London: Oxford University Press, 1948), 89. On the theme of true power as dereliction of power in Williams, see Shideler, *Theology of Romantic Love,* 132–34; Spacks, "CW: The Fusions of Fiction," 151; Bosky, "Grace and Goetia," 21; Irwin, "Christian Doctrine and the Tactics of Romance," 140–41; Sibley, *CW,* 146. In contrast, Urang argues that Williams's vision of a universe of love ultimately resolves itself into a vision of power (*Shadows of Heaven,* 90–92).

37. Williams, *Witchcraft,* 34. Williams also speaks of the futile desire of evil spirits to unite with matter (155)—futile because they reject its fundamental goodness—offering the testimony of a witch about the experience of intercourse with the Devil: "his nature cold within me as spring-well-water" (162), which is echoed in Lady Wallingford's recollection of how the birth

THE CESSATION OF RHETORIC

character in *Terror of Light,* "a rhetorical necromancer from the East" (*CP,* 342) who seeks an exchange of knowledge with the Christians. When Peter tells him that the heart of the Christian mystery is "Others he saved; himself he could not save," Simon scoffs, "That is not magic; that is pulpit stuff" (354)—which, one knows, is precisely Williams's point. One detail in the play of particular interest in relation to the novel is that Saul sees Simon's followers as being "like the insect worshippers in the prophet Ezekiel" (341)—just as the painter Jonathan depicts Simon the Clerk and his followers as an assembly of beetles.

In fact, Williams's portrayal of Simon the Clerk as Antichrist in *All Hallows' Eve* is succinctly epitomized in the iconographic language of that very painting, in which Simon is limned hideously but accurately (even by Simon's own testimony) as a kind of blank imbecile, or rather as "an orating beetle" preaching to a bowed mass looking like "a ranked mass of beetles" and seeming to lead them into a cleft in a dull grey rock (*AHE,* 33, 35). Semiotically, the painting reads as an inversion of the familiar Byzantine and medieval images of the Harrowing of Hell, in which Christ heroically leads the massed, waiting souls out of limbo.[38] Jonathan's other painting, of postwar London massively flooded with light, is "like a modern Creation of the World, or at least a Creation of London" (27). As the painting of Simon captures with dreadful accuracy the inaccuracy of Hell, so the painting of the City captures the sacramental quality of everyday reality, as apprehended by what Sir Joshua Reynolds called "common observation and plain understanding," adopted by Jonathan as his own anti-Gnostic motto. As a pair, the paintings are emblematic of Zion and Gomorrah, the Way of Coinherence and the Way of Perversity, of Simon's empty rhetorical hell as the antithesis of the inscape of the City of Light.[39]

As for Simon's actual activities, they bear only the most superficially literal resemblance to the ministry of Christ: he preaches "Love, with a hint of some secret"—a nice allusion to some sort of Gnostic illuminism—but as the narrator tells us when Simon misunderstands Lester's willingness to accompany Evelyn to Holborn, seeing it as submission, "He who babbled of love knew nothing of love" (*AHE,* 145; although that does not discredit the truth: "the maxim was greater than the speaker"—151). The "peace" and

---

of Simon's child felt to her "as cold as spring-water" (*AHE,* 86; cf. Davidson, "Way of Perversity," 90; indeed, all of chapter 7 of *Witchcraft,* "The Goetic Life," is full of interest in relation to *All Hallows' Eve*).

38. See Gertrud Schiller, *Ikonographie der Christlichen Kunst,* 3 vols. (Gutersloh: Gerd Mohn, 1971), 3.41–65, figs. 99–176.

39. Holder, "Art and the Artist," 81–87; Davidson, "Way of Perversity," 91; Moorman, *Precincts of Felicity,* 48–49.

150   GEORGE L. SCHEPER

healing he offers his followers are narcotic and illusory. As for his magical operations, their power over nature is only, as Marlowe's Mephistophilis would put it, "per accidens" (*Doctor Faustus* 1.3.50), and as the narrative proceeds Simon's malice grows in inverse proportion to the progressive futility of his actions, as he resorts to lesser and lesser (i.e., more and more mechanical) means.[40] As in his love-homilies Simon progressively resorted to language without meaning, seeking to turn "words into mere vibrations" (85), in his magic he sought to turn language back upon itself, culminating in the reversal of the Tetragrammaton.[41]

Here, through the technique of parody of the sacred, Williams offers us a structurally neat antithetical parallel to the "law of emptying the words" (*HCD*, 10–11), which we have seen was for Williams a way to redeem

---

40. *AHE*, 136; cf. *Witchcraft*, 107.

41. On the magical reversal of language, see Davidson, "Way of Perversity," 89–90; Anderson, "Nature of the City," 18; Shideler, *Theology of Romantic Love*, 135–37; Wright, "Theology in the Novels of CW," 35. Williams's portrayal of Simon has understandably raised the question of anti-Semitism. Simon's Jewishness is an integral component, in his own mind, of the magus role he has elected to play. It positions him, he thinks, to reverse the "great pronouncements [that] had established creation in its order; the reversal of those pronouncements could reverse the order. . . . He would come presently to the greatest—to the reversal of the final Jewish word of power, to the reversed Tetragrammaton itself " (*AHE*, 85). And at the beginning of the long passage concluding chapter 3 of the novel, which establishes Simon as one of the viewpoint characters, we are given a lengthy reflection on Simon's Jewishness and on the role of Jewry in sacred history. But it becomes immediately apparent that this reflection cannot actually represent Simon's viewpoint and must be that of the narrator or implied author who speaks of the "august" role that had been proposed for the Jews but of how "when that End had been born, they were not aware of that End," and, taken by "deception . . . they had, bidding a scaffold for the blasphemer, destroyed their predestined conclusion, and the race which had been set for the salvation of the world became a judgment and even a curse to the world and to themselves. . . . They remained alien—to It and to all, and all to them and—too much!—to It" (50–51). Despite the theological nuances, and Williams's clear repudiation of prejudice and injustice against Jews (see *Image*, 161–63; *FS*, chap. 8), the rhetoric of the passage clearly warrants the questions that Nancy-Lou Patterson has raised about anti-Semitism in Williams's writings ("The Jewels of Messias: Images of Judaism and Antisemitism in the Novels of Charles Williams," *Mythlore* 20 [6.2] (1979): 27–31) and that have been pursued in detail in the recent polemical monograph by Andrea Freud Loewenstein, *Loathsome Jews and Engulfing Women: Metaphors of Projection in the Works of Wyndham Lewis, Charles Williams, and Graham Greene* (New York and London: New York University Press, 1993)–see chap. 5, "Charles Williams's Extrusion Machine," esp. 231–40. Not only is the viewpoint presented in the *AHE* passage unyieldingly and stonily dogmatic but, especially for a work written in the 1940s, references to the Jews being an "alien" Other and a "curse" to the world and to themselves are incredibly insensitive. It is almost as though we were being presented with a case in point in Williams's own work about the danger of idolatry he says inheres in the Way of the Affirmation of Images (in this case, the "diagrammatized" scheme of salvation history itself becomes the idol), as well as about the dangers of being carried away by theological rhetoric.

THE CESSATION OF RHETORIC 151

fallen language. Thus, while there is an outward superficial resemblance between the prelapsarian "Adamic" speech of Anthony in *The Place of the Lion* or Sybil's mystic "pentecostal" language in *The Greater Trumps* and the mere imbecility of Simon or the incoherence that engulfs Wentworth in *Descent into Hell*, the relation is only that of parody.

Comparable to Simon's systematic draining of meaning from language is the speech of Evelyn, at first a ceaseless stream of self-indulgent and self-referential gabbling or yammering (*AHE*, 16–17) and finally mere whining, complaining, and meaningless rejoinders: her words, "instead of gaining significance, had lost it; they emerged almost imbecilely" (142). Thus, ensconced in the dwarf-body Simon has made for her and Lester, she is content to croak "a mass of comments and complaints: 'But you would think, wouldn't you?' or 'It's not as if I were asking much' or 'I did think you'd understand' or 'He needn't' or 'They could at least' . . . and so on and on through all the sinful and silly imbecilities by which the miserable soul protects itself against fact" (167; ellipsis points in original).

Antithetic to this essence of fallen language in Simon and Evelyn is the "speech of pure joy," the mutual "blessing" (*AHE*, 177) exchanged among the friends—the living Richard, Jonathan, and Betty and the dead Lester in Jonathan's flat on All Hallows' Eve. Unlike the ineffectual incantations of magic, the progressively redeemed speech among this group of people is truly performative language. Lester asks Betty, when she sees Richard, to "give him my love," and we are told that "the commonplace phrase was weighted with meaning as it left her lips; in that air, it signified no mere message but an actual deed—a rich gift of another's love to another, a third-party transaction in which all parties were blessed even now in the foretaste" (141).

Lester, who becomes the initiator of this redeemed language, does not begin the story as an enlightened person. She had been, in her life, far from saintly; true, she had not been, as the narrator says, particularly sinful in the flesh—but that had been largely "mere fastidiousness" (*AHE*, 175). The truth is, she had mainly been interested in "the apparatus of mortal life; not people . . . only the things they used and lived in." And yet "the sincerity of her interest"—like Damaris's dedication to honesty of scholarship in *The Place of the Lion*—has provided at least a starting point for her postmortem spiritual journey (*AHE*, 13, 69–70). That journey begins in the void, in "the landscape of death," where "all meaning had been left behind" (22, 18). This image of emptiness runs as a leitmotif through the entire first chapter of *All Hallows' Eve*, but it is a neutral emptiness, a limbo,[42] which may prove to

---

42. Cf. Dante's Ante-Purgatory—see George Reynolds, "Dante and Williams: Pilgrims in Purgatory," *Mythlore* 47 [13.1] (1986): 4.

152   GEORGE L. SCHEPER

be the beginning either of a progressively more meaningless incoherence, as it does for Evelyn, or of a mind- and soul-clearing *kenosis,* or self-emptying, as it does for Lester, which marks the inception of a "New Life"—the Dantean title of the chapter, in fact.[43]

In any case, as Williams was never a metaphysical dualist, only a moral one—"There is but one dichotomy: that between those who acknowledge that they live from the life of others, including their 'enemies,' and those who do not" (*Image,* 113)—the fundamental fact of the situation is to be understood as good, and what Lester and the reader discover is that in this void, emptied of the inaccuracies of postlapsarian language, words mean exactly what they say, however mindful or unmindful a given speaker may be of that fact. Thus, when Evelyn complains, "I haven't done anything," or Lester exclaims, "Oh my God," these exclamations, which in ordinary life may have "meant nothing" in particular, are no longer without meaning for "in this air every word meant something, meant itself; and this curious new exactitude of speech hung there like a strange language. . . . 'I haven't done anything . . . Oh my God!' This was how they talked, and it was a great precise prehistoric language forming itself out of the noises their mouths made. She articulated the speech of Adam or Seth or Noah, and only dimly recognized the intelligibility of it" (*AHE,* 20-21; cf. 151).

As in *The Place of the Lion,* the simple act of calling upon a person out of need or love—Lester calling the name of Betty or Richard, or Betty calling the name of Jonathan or Lester (*AHE,* 68–71, 120)—is the root and essence of redeemed speech. "'Lester!' [Betty called.] As the word left her lips, it was changed. It became—hardly the Name, but at least a tender mortal approximation to the Name" (125). It "hung in the air, singing itself," a single note that effectively counterbalances and cancels Simon's incantations, for it is the perfect antithesis to the magical nonword, the reversed Tetragrammaton.

Hence the simplicity, the deceptively innocuous quality of the dialogical exchanges between these "companions of the coinherence" in some of the key moments of the narrative: the moment when Lester asks Betty's forgiveness, the moment when Lester puts herself at Betty's disposal, the dialogue among the two couples in Jonathan's flat when Lester and Evelyn appear in the dwarf body. But in their simplicity, the exchanges are sacramental. When Betty, seeing Lester in need but not yet knowing of what, asks, "What's the matter? Can I do anything?" (*AHE,* 100), she has, in fact, asked the simple question that Percival should have asked the Fisher

---

43. See Wright, "Theology in the Novels of CW," 39, on emptiness, John of the Cross, and the *via negativa.* See Sells, *Mystical Languages,* esp. the introduction (1–13) and chap. 2, "The Nothingness of God in John the Scot Eriugena" (34–62).

THE CESSATION OF RHETORIC 153

King and that would have delivered the Waste Land.[44] It is analogous to the simple expression of empathy Margaret extends to the suicide in *Descent into Hell*: "My dear, how tired you look!" (*DH*, 166). For Lester, Betty's words are, precisely, sacramental; they occasion the two women's "real presence" to each other. They become God-bearers for one another, and so Lester sees Betty in her glorified form, Betty as God sees her: "Betty gay, Betty joyous, Betty revitalized, but still Betty" (*AHE*, 100—exactly as Pauline sees her own glorified self that bore her ancestor John Struther's fear [*DH*, 234–35]). Thus Lester and Betty beheld each other "and the charity between them doubled and redoubled, so that they became almost unbearable to each other, so shy and humble was each and each so mighty and glorious" (*AHE*, 139). The two women are Beatrices for one another.[45]

We have noted how in several of Williams's earlier novels the redemption of language and of time is often represented, and re-created, through a liturgical sequence. Unlike these earlier novels, neither *Descent into Hell* nor *All Hallows' Eve* incorporates an extended liturgical description, other than, in the latter, the story of Betty's baptism. Moreover, both focus on human interactions as such, rather than on human interactions in relation to a symbolic artefact such as the Grail, the Stone, the Tarot, or the Archetypes. Nevertheless, at the structural and symbolic center of each of these final novels (as at the heart of each of his two last plays, *The House of the Octopus* and *Terror of Light*) Williams places an act of compassionate "substitution," which is presented explicitly as an imitation of and participation in Christ's eternally contemporaneous and efficacious act of substitution on the Cross. As Hadfield says with reference to Williams's poetry, "The moment of substitution when Christ's body was broken for man . . . underwrote all Williams' use of time."[46] In effect, then, both *Descent into Hell* and *All Hallows' Eve* are given a fundamentally liturgical structure as a whole, constructed around that central sacramental action. As both novels also deal with the intersection or interpenetration of the two worlds of the living and the dead, the moment of substitution is experienced in synchronicity across those worlds and across time in the web of coinherence—one of

44. See Williams, "Figure of Arthur," 64.

45. See Huttar, "Arms and the Man," 312. Cf. Trowbridge, "Beatricean Character," 340–42; Nancy Hanger, "The Excellent Absurdity: Substitution and Coinherence in C. S. Lewis and Charles Williams," *Mythlore* 34 [9.4] (1983): 16; and George Lee, "And the Darkness Grasped It Not: The Struggle of Good and Evil in Charles Williams," *Mythlore* 19 [6.1] (1979): 19–20, who compares Betty's subordination of will to that of the Virgin Mary.

46. Alice Mary Hadfield, "Coinherence, Substitution and Exchange in Charles Williams' Poetry and Poetry-Making," in *Imagination and the Spirit*, ed. Charles A. Huttar (Grand Rapids, Mich.: Eerdmans, 1971), 243.

154   GEORGE L. SCHEPER

Williams's most distinctive and reiterated themes; as the Flame says in *The House of the Octopus*: "The young shall save the old and the old the young / the dead the living, and the other living the dead" (*CP,* 310).[47]

At the moment of Margaret's expression of compassion for the suicide in *Descent into Hell,* the dead man, we noted, cries out "Ah! ah!" and moans. But in the silence there is an answering groan, and a tremor is felt that causes china to tinkle, papers to shift, and ornaments to fall. The slight tremor felt on Battle Hill at that moment is, of course, none other than the reverberation of that tremor, eternally present throughout history, emanating from the hill of Golgotha, and "the groan was at once dereliction of power and creation of power. In it, far off, beyond vision in the depths of all the worlds, a god, unamenable to death, awhile endured and died" (*DH,* 171). As Williams expressed it in his 1943 essay on the Cross: "By that central substitution . . . He became everywhere the centre of, and everywhere He energized and reaffirmed, all our substitutions and exchanges" (*Image,* 137; cf. "Taliessin at Lancelot's Mass," *TTL,* 89–91). In a comparable vision, contemporary poet Galway Kinnell in "To Christ Our Lord" calls the cross "the pattern and mirror of the acts of earth."

It is fascinating to compare this moment in *Descent into Hell* with the parallel moment in *All Hallows' Eve,* when Lester puts herself at Betty's disposal and suffers Simon's magical operations in her place. "Lester said, 'Betty, if you want me I'm here,' and meant it with all her heart. . . . She was now incapable of any action except an unformulated putting of herself at Betty's disposal" (*AHE,* 121)—a perfect embodiment of the Boddhisattva prayer of Mahayana Buddhism or, more relevantly, the Christian ideal of "being Christ for one another" (as in Tom Conroy's hymn "Anthem").[48] And indeed, during that act of compassionate substitution, Lester feels herself "leaning back on something, some frame which from her buttocks to her head supported her; indeed she could have believed, but she was not sure, that her arms, flung out on each side held on to a part of the frame, as along a beam of wood" (122–23). Simultaneously, in Jonathan's flat—and here the language and imagery are closely reminiscent of that earlier passage in *Descent into Hell*—Richard hears "a small tinkle. Something had fallen. . . . He felt the floor beneath him quiver, and the tinkle was followed by a faint echo in different parts of the room. Things shook and touched and settled. The earth had felt the slightest tremor, and all its inhabitants felt it"

---

47. Cf. *HCD,* 130; *Image,* 101–2; but see critique by Urang, *Shadows of Heaven,* 89.

48. E. A. Burtt, ed., *The Teachings of the Compassionate Buddha* (1955; reprint, New York: Mentor, 1982), 130–40; Conroy, in *Glory & Praise: Songs for Christian Assembly,* 3 vols. (Phoenix, Ariz.: North American Liturgy Resources, 1980), 2.8.

THE CESSATION OF RHETORIC

(114). It is, in narrative time, midafternoon of 31 October, All Hallows' Eve, and in mythic time, it is "the ninth hour" (Matt. 27:46-51).[49]

Twenty years earlier Williams had set forth as a principle of romantic theology that "the lover knows himself also to be the cross upon which the Beloved is to be stretched, and so she also of her lover [and so here of her friend] . . . —the annihilation of the selfhood which the saints have sought" (*Outlines*, 124). Williams was fond of quoting as "perhaps the greatest epigram of all" Ignatius of Antioch's ambiguous "My Eros is crucified" (*Dove*, 46), and the image of the lover on the cross of his or her love would no doubt have been familiar to Williams from Shakespeare's sonnet 42 ("both for my sake lay on me this cross") and more pertinently from St. John of the Cross's "Madrigal *a lo divino*" in which Christ the shepherd/lover dies on a tree from the wound of love in his heart (an image reflected also in late medieval stained-glass windows depicting Christ crucified not by Roman soldiers but by his own spouse).[50]

Thus the earth-tremor of Christ's self-emptying act of substituted love is felt at the center of each of Williams's two last novels. But whereas the sacramental moment of exchange is surrounded in *Descent into Hell* by mythic and allegorical elements—from a return to Eden to the Harrowing of Hell and the Last Judgment—and by a corresponding mythopoeic language, the moment in *All Hallows' Eve* is surrounded by liturgical elements and liturgical language and is parodied by their magical antitheses. *All Hallows' Eve* reflects, in fact, the structure of the Mass itself.[51] One reminder of this specific liturgical framework is the sederlike All Hallows' Eve meal in Jonathan's flat: "a rough meal of bread and cheese and cold

---

49. The central action of Betty's forgiveness and Lester's substitution, which J. J. Boies has called "as fine a scene of spiritual discovery as any in English" ("Existential Exchange in the Novels of Charles Williams," *Renascence* 26 [1974]: 228), has called forth a great deal of commentary as the most intense expression of the Coinherence (along with the substitutions in *Descent into Hell*) in all of Williams's writings; see, for example: Anderson, "Nature of the City," 18–19; Bosky, "Grace and Goetia," 20; Beaumont, "CW and the Power of Eros," 2; Charles Moorman, "Sacramentalism in Charles Williams," *Chesterton Review* 8 (1982): 46–48; Urang, *Shadows of Heaven*, 70; Wright, "Theology in the Novels of CW," 49–50; Ridler, in *Image*, xlvii; Huttar, "CW, Novelist and Prophet," 74–75.

50. See *The Poems of St. John of the Cross*, ed. with English translation by John Frederick Nims (New York: Grove Press, 1959), 40–41; Schiller, *Ikonographie*, 2: 447, 452, 453. That the crucifier participates in the exchange of love is reflected in Williams's image of Judas as having done for Christ what one cannot do for oneself (*Terror of Light*, in *CP*, 369–70)—an idea developed at length in Kazantzakis's *Last Temptation of Christ* and, returning the image to Williams's starting point of marriage as crucifixion, in Alan Dugan's "Love Song: I and Thou" ("I can nail my left palm / to the left-hand cross-piece but / I can't do everything myself. / I need a hand to nail the right, / a help, a love, a you, a wife").

51. Cf. Williams, *Outlines*, chap. 5, "The Mass in Romantic Theology."

scraps and wine. There was not much, but there was enough, and they ate and drank standing, as Israel did while the angels of the Omnipotence were at their work in Egypt" (*AHE,* 174). Moreover, the tremor at the moment of Lester's sacramental substitution, accompanied by a tinkling as of a bell, is reminiscent of the ringing of the Mass-bell at the moment of consecration, and at that moment ("suddenly certain of Lester—not for himself, but in herself. . . . She lived—that was all; and so, by God's mercy, he") Richard's "heart lifted": *sursum corda* (114). The communion lies in the exchange itself: Lester "had suffered instead of Betty, as Betty had once suffered through her," and the consequence, in Lester's mind, is as simple as, "'Well, that's saved her getting up.'" But in these words what she is put in mind of is not her own act on behalf of Betty, but

> only how once or twice, when she had been thirsty in the night, Richard had brought her a glass of water and saved her getting up; and in her drowsiness a kind of vista of innumerable someones doing such things for innumerable someones stretched before her, . . . [and each such act] was a deed of such excelling merit . . . that all the choirs of heaven and birds of earth could never properly sing its praise; though there was a word in her mind which would do it rightly, . . . the word was like a name, and the name was something like *Richard,* and something like *Betty* and even not unlike her own. (125–26)

Even the "rhetoric" of heaven, then, must cease and defer to the act of love, which can be "named" only by either its own signifier, *love,* or, perhaps even better, by the names of the lovers themselves.

Thus, acts of love (what Wordsworth in "Tintern Abbey" called "that best portion of a good man's life, / His little, nameless, unremembered acts / Of kindness and of love"), the word *love* itself, the names of lovers and "the Name which is the City" form a continuous chain of communion in the Coinherence. This is indeed the communion of saints (see *Dove,* 163), a component of the Creed which is renewed at every Mass but most especially on the Vigil and Feast of All Saints (31 October and 1 November, respectively). The title of the novel refers, of course, specifically to the Vigil, while one passage alludes to the doctrine itself, calling Betty's admiration of Lester "one mode of the communion of saints" (*AHE,* 160).

Some of the imagery in the novel is, in fact, specific to the services for the feast of All Saints. The Epistle for All Saints in the Book of Common Prayer, from the seventh chapter of Revelation, describes the spiritual marriage of the Lamb to the one hundred and forty-four thousand who are "sealed" in the heavenly City (the scene portrayed in Van Eyck's famous Ghent altarpiece), and Williams alludes several times to the image: "What had looked at Lester from Evelyn's eyes, what now showed in her own, was pure immortality. This was *the seal of the City,* its first gift to the dead who entered it. They had what they were, and they had it (as it seemed) for ever"

THE CESSATION OF RHETORIC   157

(*AHE*, 107, emphasis added; 151, 163). The Gospel reading is the Beatitudes, and the Collect refers to the "unspeakable joys" of the communion of saints. The Breviary surrounds these readings for the day with a more complex orchestration of the same themes, including an excerpt from a homily by St. Bernard on the yearning to share in the communion of saints. The use of psalms and hymns that celebrate the breaking forth of "a yet more glorious day," especially Psalm 147, with its vivid images of the word of God showering down like rain and hail, may have suggested the imagery of drenching rain throughout the novel's final chapter, "The Acts of the City": "On the vigil of the hallows, it was gloomily and steadily raining . . . October closing in a deluge. The vigil of the saints was innumerably active in the City, and all London lay awake under it" (182, 187).

The tremendous imagery at the close of the novel of the deluging rain in the night and the irresistibly emerging "roseal glow" of the dawning of the feast day parallels the great mythic concluding visions of Dante's *Purgatorio* and Part II of Goethe's *Faust*.[52] The rain and roseal glow, which are as a stench of blood and burning flesh and a torment to Simon, are to Betty— "still fresh from the lake of power, the wise waters of creation"—a scent of rose garden and a vision as of "dark wine in a wine cup" (*AHE*, 201–2). For Lester, it is the moment of separation,

> the most exquisite and pure joy of death. . . . She saw each of them with an admirable exactitude. . . . But she was not very conscious of herself as herself; she no longer thought of herself as bearing or enjoying; the bitterness, the joy and the inscape of those great waters were all she knew. . . . The approach of all the hallows possessed her, and she too, into the separations and unions which are indeed its approach, and into the end to which it is itself an approach, was wholly gone. (194, 203–4)

Lester's unsentimental Beatrician acceptance of separation here may indeed be off-putting to some contemporary sensibilities (McKinley, in the subtitle of her article, calls it "the uneasy consolation of *All Hallows' Eve*"), but it is a dramatically apt rendering of the theme of "holy indifference" of medieval spirituality, as conveyed, in fact, in Williams's earlier portrait of Mary in the Nativity play *Seed of Adam* (*CP*, 155–59). This experience of kenosis, which is Lester's final entry into the Coinherence,[53] is parodied by Simon's "reunion" with his clone-images, which is the moment of *his*

---

52. I am persuaded by Reynolds that the imagery of the novel's concluding vision reflects not the final cantos of Dante's *Paradiso*, but of the *Purgatorio*: see his "Dante and Williams," 6, and cf. Thomas Howard, *The Novels of Charles Williams* (New York and Oxford: Oxford University Press, 1983), 152, 180; Cavaliero, *Poet of Theology*, 93.

53. On Lester's "Ascension" and the parallel with Christ's departure from the apostles, see Reilly, *Romantic Religion*, 177; Sibley, *CW*, 88; Trowbridge, "Beatricean Character," 342.

158   GEORGE L. SCHEPER

dissolution; instead of loss of self, however, he has *only* himself, as he wanted, and incoherence.

But the dominant note is restoration of wholeness and the redemption of speech, which had been abused by the rhetoric of magic, through the performative language of blessing. Like the liturgy itself, the novel ends with blessing and sending forth: even Lady Wallingford is blessed with an emptying of her mind, which for her is an opportunity for a second birth through a kind of *via negativa* (*AHE*, 204–5); Simon's followers are released from their illusion; and even his hall and its furnishings, despite the perverse uses to which they have been put, are restored to innocence: "The morning of the feast imperceptibly began. . . . More than humanity was holy and more than humanity was strange. The round hall itself, and its spare furnishings, and the air in it were of earth, and nothing could alter that nature. The blessedness of earth was in them and now began to spread out of them" (195–96). This goodness and sacredness of all created beings (excepting only the free and deliberate choice of refusal of the good) is the overwhelmingly dominant note whose sound is increasingly heard as the novel achieves its climactic vision of the Hallows, "the visible proofs of [Christ's] love for mankind."[54]

The calculated rhetoric of Simon is undone by the spontaneous utterances of love; the appeal to arcane and esoteric gnosis undermined by "common observation and plain understanding"; the illusory powers of magic dissipated by the genuine impact of liturgical acts and liturgical language—Betty's baptism; Lester's act of substituted love; the sederlike meal at Jonathan's flat; the "spiritual colloquies" expressive of simple relational truths and commitments; small acts of exchange, such as the coins for a phone call an elderly gentleman bestows on Lester in her dwarf-body (*AHE*, 171) or the patient answer of a train station porter to an inattentive passenger—all of which express "the deep confluence of the City," and because of which there "was no smallest point in all the place that was not redeemed into beauty and good" (65). These are, in short, the acts of the City, and the corresponding speech acts are analogous to the performative language of liturgy.

The paradigm of this performative language is blessing, the antithesis of the compulsions of magic or even of the persuasiveness of rhetoric: unlike magic, which seeks absolute control, or rhetoric, which seeks to bring about change, blessing is a linguistic expression of an actual love or faith relationship, a spontaneous expression of delight and praise for the goodness of things or persons as they are and of commitment to the furtherance of

---

54. Alice Mary Hadfield, *An Introduction to Charles Williams* (London: Robert Hale, 1959), 143 (with reference to the Arthurian poetry).

THE CESSATION OF RHETORIC 159

their well-being.[55] In the biblical tradition, the primal blessing is God's pronunciation of creation as *tov,* "good" (Gen. 1:10, 18, 21, 25), indeed "very good" (1:31).

This blessing mode is represented in the novel not only by the nurse's baptism of Betty or the saintly colloquies among Lester, Betty, Richard, and Jonathan, but also by Lester's sacramental vision of the city of London, "as if from the height of the cross" (*AHE,* 167); for now, on this All Hallows' Eve, the time of her last, decisive engagement with her living friends, Lester's vision, as she focuses on the Thames in all its sacred ordinariness, is intensely sacramental:

> The Thames was dirty and messy. Twigs, bits of paper and wood, cords, old boxes drifted on it. Yet to the new-eyed Lester it was not a depressing sight. The dirtiness of the water was, at that particular point, what it should be, and therefore pleasant enough. The evacuations of the City had their place in the City; how else could the City be the City? Corruption (so to call it) was tolerable, even adequate and proper, even glorious. These things also were facts.[56]

She blesses the evacuations of London, precisely as Julian of Norwich, one of Williams's favorite spiritual authorities, blesses human evacuation, for God "comes down to us in our humblest needs. For he does not despise what he has made."[57] How much Williams took to heart Julian's "creation-centered spirituality," as Matthew Fox calls it,[58] can be seen with particular force and frankness in his essay "The Index of the Body," apropos of his comments on the Sacred Body (*Image,* 84–85).[59] This incarnational vision

---

55. See Thomas G. Simons, *Blessings: A Reappraisal of Their Nature, Purpose, and Celebration* (Saratoga, Calif.: Resource Publications, 1981), 6, 35.

56. *AHE,* 168; see McKinley, "'To Live from a New Root,'" 14; Manlove, "Liturgical Novels of CW," 178; Cavaliero, *Poet of Theology,* 95.

57. Julian of Norwich, *Showings,* trans. Edmund Colledge and James Walsh (New York: Paulist Press, 1978), 186. Williams's regard for Julian is evident in *FS,* 23, 99; *Image,* 68, 87.

58. Fox, *Original Blessing: A Primer in Creation Spirituality* (Santa Fe, N.M.: Bear & Co., 1983), 63–64.

59. See also Williams's approving citation of a second- or third-century early Christian canon declaring that "if any bishop or priest or deacon, or any cleric whatsoever, shall refrain from marriage and from meat and from wine, not for the sake of discipline but with contempt, and forgetful that all things are very good and that God made man male and female, blasphemously inveighs against the creation (*blasphemans accusaverit creationem*), let him be either corrected or deposed and turned out of the Church (*atque ex Ecclesia ejiciatur*). And so with a layman" (*Dove,* 57). On this point Kollmann cites the Talmudic injunction that "man shall be called to account for every permitted pleasure he did not take" ("Figure of Beatrice in the Works of CW," 4). On Williams's anti-Manichean spirituality, see Sayers, "Poetry of the Image," 185–87; W. H. Auden, "Charles Williams: A Review Article," *Christian Century* 73 (1956): 553; Reilly, *Romantic Religion,* 165–66; Kinlaw, "Concept of

160   GEORGE L. SCHEPER

is, in turn, the basis of what can be called Williams's erotic spirituality, as in the scene where the "dissolving nothingness" of Simon's anti-Tetragrammaton flows up Lester's body, until it approaches "that in her which her fastidious pride had kept secluded from all but Richard," when a sudden sign of life from Betty breaks the spell and it subsides (*AHE,* 123). As Williams argues in *The Descent of the Dove,* the assault on Eros has always been central to the "obscenity" of the cross: "depth below depth of meaning lies in that phrase [of Ignatius]—'My Eros is crucified.'"[60] It is precisely appropriate that the high symbol of magic's stance of hostility and compulsion toward nature, the anticreative word, the reversed Tetragrammaton, should oppose itself, futilely, to the center of Lester's erotic creatureliness.

That Williams's concern with magic and the occult has little of the sensational or "gothic" about it has always been obvious; rather, it is for him the effective literary symbol for that complex of attitudes—Docetic, Gnostic, Manichean, Nominalist—opposing themselves to the acknowledgment of "holy fact," the sacramental reality and goodness of the world as given. Far from an irrelevant or exotic theme, Williams's choice of the symbolism of magic and what he calls the goetic life speaks with uncanny directness to the human situation at the turn of the twenty-first century, as the overriding social and political issue resolves itself into the ecological question of the fate of the earth.[61] On the one hand are the Faustian symbols of the goetic

---

Imaging," 89; Anderson, "Nature of the City," 19; Winship, "Novels of CW," 123. Urang, however, wonders whether Williams was not, in fact, "tempted" by the Manicheism he so deplored: "If Docetism involves relaxing the hold on the reality of the image in itself in order to examine that to which the image refers, Charles Williams may well be suspected of the literary manifestation of this ancient deviation" (*Shadows of Heaven,* 87). Urang in fact goes on to define Williams's spiritual vision as "magic sacramentalism" (89-90), as Beaumont charges Williams with "illuminism" ("CW and the Power of Eros," 74), but these are distinctly minority perspectives.

60. *Dove,* 76; cf. 46. On Williams's "erotic spirituality" see his *Outlines,* 44, and the following critical comments: R. J. Davies, "Charles Williams and the Romantic Experience," *Études Anglaises* 8 (1955): 298; Evgeny Lampert, *The Divine Realm* (London: Faber and Faber, 1944), 93; and Beaumont, "CW and the Power of Eros," 71–72, who sees "a suggestion of Swedenborgianism"; other critics rightly stress the orthodox incarnational basis: Reilly, *Romantic Religion,* 164–65; Huttar, "Arms and the Man," 330–31; Sister Mary Anthony Weinig, "Exchange, Complementarity, Co-inherence: Aspects of Community in Charles Williams," *Mythlore* 24 [7.2] (1980): 28; Nancy Enright, "CW and His Theology" (above, note 1), 22–23.

61. On the question of the "relevance" of Williams's concern with the imagery of magic as a meaningful vehicle for exploring the problem of evil, critics are divided. Urang sees the integrity of everyday reality swamped in Williams's writing by the dominance of "allegorical idea over image" and of the sempiternal over the mundane (*Shadows of Heaven,* 89–90); Geoffrey Parsons comments that "magic seizes the book [i.e., *AHE*] midway and the result

THE CESSATION OF RHETORIC 161

life—compulsion and control, and their linguistic expression, command and rhetoric; on the other are the symbols of the web of coinherence—exchange, liturgy, and sacrament, and *their* linguistic expression, affirmation and blessing. Williams raises and dramatizes the fundamental question of whether the possible human future lies with power or with the dereliction of power, with the way of compulsion or the way of blessing.

---

is both incredulity and horror" ("The Spirit of Charles Williams," *Atlantic,* November 1949, 79); and Cavaliero argues that until the triumph of Divine Love at the close, in *All Hallows' Eve,* "the world of magic and the world of love are pitted against each other almost as though the difference between them were less of kind than of degree" (*Poet of Theology,* 95). In contrast, Shideler sees Simon's attempt to dominate Betty with a word as an apt symbol, "not, perhaps, very remote from sins that are committed around, and by, ourselves" (*Theology of Romantic Love,* 137); Sayers sees the relevance of Williams's concern with Gnosticism and magic in the "sinister parallelism between the aims of magic and the aims of what nowadays we are accustomed to call 'science.'" Sayers adds that with contemporary coercive psychologies of "conditioning" and politics of raw power, "between the aims of the exploiters of power to-day and the aims of the magician there is no difference; the only difference is one of method. Of the license given to unreason and the exploitation of power, the magical element in Charles Williams's work stands as the image and symbol" ("Poetry of the Image," 202–3).

PART III

Poetry

The Occult as Rhetoric
in the Poetry of Charles Williams

Roma A. King, Jr.

The word *occult* is generally associated with the esoteric and bizarre. Its presence in Charles Williams's work may stand between him and some potential readers. That Williams's interest in the occult was no more than a brief youthful enthusiasm, as is sometimes thought, can no longer be supported. It was continuing, actually more pervasive (although better integrated) in his last volume of poetry than in his first. By the time he came to write *Taliessin through Logres* and *The Region of the Summer Stars,* he had learned better how to integrate all his materials into an organic whole.[1]

Much of his knowledge of the occult came through A. E. Waite and the mystical order which he founded and of which Williams was an active member. Although Anne Ridler reports that Williams always spoke of having belonged to The Golden Dawn, the order into which he was initiated in 1917 was officially called "The Fellowship of the Rosy Cross." Founded by Waite in 1915, it was related to The Golden Dawn in that both shared common roots in Theosophical, Rosicrucian, and Masonic traditions, and in that Waite had himself been a member of both The Golden Dawn and the Masonic Lodge. It differed, however, from that branch in which MacGregor Mathers, Aleister Crowley, and William Butler Yeats were active. Waite's order was mystical rather than magical; its membership was open to those desiring "knowledge of Divine Things and union with God in Christ."[2] And although the symbolism derived primarily from the Jewish Cabala, its mode of interpretation of that medieval tradition was Christian.

---

1. My earlier treatment of Williams's use of the occult, in *The Pattern in the Web: The Mythical Poetry of Charles Williams* (Kent, Ohio: Kent State University Press, 1990), was of necessity brief. In this essay I develop the theme more fully, emphasizing especially how he built upon but went beyond the occult to discover in it a rich source of imagery that comes to consummation in the Christian revelation, and how he used the occult as a rhetorical device to communicate his own ideas.

2. R. A. Gilbert, *A. E. Waite: Magician of Many Parts* (Wellingborough, Northants: Crucible, 1987), 183.

166   ROMA A. KING, JR.

R. A. Gilbert's recently published biography of Waite provides indisputable information that permits us at last to speak confidently about an aspect of Williams's life and art about which up to now we could only surmise. In 1914, Williams read Waite's book *The Hidden Church of the Holy Graal,* and its impact on him was immediate and lasting. He wrote Waite praising the book, enclosing a copy of his first volume of poems, *The Silver Stair,* and in return received an invitation to visit Waite at his home in Ealing. Thus began an association that was to last for years.

Williams became an active member of the order in 1917, for ten years participating regularly in the meetings and serving almost continually as an officer, becoming inactive only in 1927. In September 1928, Waite called on Williams in his office at Amen House. We do not know what happened at that meeting, but as far as the record reveals it was the last between the two men. Williams at that time apparently severed his formal relation with the mystical order. He perhaps felt he had received from it all that it had to offer. The parting must have been amicable, however, since correspondence continued between the two until 1931.[3]

We do not know how deeply Williams was involved in occult studies before he met Waite, but we do know that Waite's writings, particularly *The Hidden Church of the Holy Graal* (1909) and *The Secret Doctrine in Israel* (1913), and Williams's experiences in the order provided him with a wide range of material that was to prove continually useful.

By 1928, Williams was on the threshold of his most fruitful literary period. He had already published four volumes of verse and perhaps had written another, *Heroes and Kings,* which was published in 1930. In the same year his first novel, *War in Heaven,* appeared. It was followed rapidly by *Many Dimensions* (1931), *The Place of the Lion* (1931), and *The Greater Trumps* (1932). *Shadows of Ecstasy,* although written even before *War in Heaven,* was not published until 1933. In all these and, indeed, the two others that followed, the occult is a recurring theme. In many respects, the novels may be considered preparatory work for his great poetry that was to come.

My purpose in this essay is not to record all references to the occult in Williams's poetry, but rather to determine the nature of his interest in the subject and, by examination of selected passages, to discuss how he used occult knowledge to communicate his own poetic vision. Moreover, I will confine my references primarily to the two volumes that compose his most mature work, *Taliessin through Logres* and *The Region of the Summer Stars.*

Williams was drawn to the occult, no doubt, by a feeling that magic and mystery, even Christian mystery, share common roots. Occultists, in general,

3. Gilbert, *A. E. Waite,* 149.

THE OCCULT AS RHETORIC

agreed that all things, corporeal and spiritual, derive from a common first matter, and that despite the diverse forms in nature, all are of and in the One. They perceive a relationship between the part and the whole, and they acknowledge the possibility of concourse between what is below and what above. These recurring ideas must have been a powerful stimulus to Williams's imagination, leading him to find not identities but analogies between the occult and his own Christian beliefs. Williams was by temperament inclusive, and although he regarded the Incarnation as the consummate revelation, he considered it a fulfillment, not a rejection, of all other insights. He has Lord Arglay in *Many Dimensions* say, for example, that "amid all this mess of myths and tangle of traditions and . . . and . . . febrifuge of fables, there is something extreme and terrible" (*MD,* 151; ellipsis points in original). Williams himself saw in the mess and tangle and "febrifuge" something common and continuing in the human spirit that was simply part of being human. This openness of mind and spirit gives his poetry scope and universality.

In a significant essay, "The Index of the Body," published in 1942, Williams explains his interest in the occult and states how he proposes to use it in his poetry. Coming fifteen years after he left the mystical order, four years after the appearance of *Taliessin through Logres,* and only three years before his death, this statement can safely be said to represent his mature thought. Here he speaks about astrology, but what he says applies equally to other branches of the arcane: "The word 'occult' has come into general use, and is convenient, if no moral sense is given it simply as itself. It deals with hidden things, and their investigation." This broad definition serves his purpose well. He continues: "We are concerned not so much with the pretended operations of those . . . schools as with a certain imagination of relation in the universe, and that only to pass beyond it" (*Image,* 83).

In this essay, I shall show how Williams turns to rhetorical rather than substantive or operational ends five recurring themes in occult literature:

1. The entire cosmos is a structured meaningful whole in which all parts are interrelated and interdependent.

2. All things terrestrial and spiritual derive from a common first matter and the two terms *matter* and *spirit* are in fact only two ways of speaking of the same substance.

3. All terrestrial things owe their powers to a corresponding celestial power, and by understanding the relation between them, one can use the earthly type to invoke the heavenly archetype.

4. The invocation may be either white or black magic. (I shall say more later about the difference between the two and between both and Christian grace.)

5. Through occult means, personal and social transformation is possible.

168   ROMA A. KING, JR.

In developing the last of these themes, I shall explore in some detail Williams's use of two important images—the pentagram and the Sephirotic Tree—in which all the themes are brought into an organic wholeness.

The concept of cosmic interrelatedness and interdependence (theme 1) is expressed in Williams's poetry less as an abstract idea than as an imaginative vision that, through imagery, embodies simultaneously the intellectual, emotional, and sensuous. Many of the images are astrological. In "Taliessin in the Rose-Garden" (*Region,* 23–28) Williams writes:

> The Acts of Identity [created things] issued from the Throne; there
> twelve images were shown in a mystery, twelve
> zodiacal houses; the sun of the operative Emperor
> wended through them, attended by the spiritual planets,
> attributing to the themes [the divisions of the Empire] their
>   qualities of cause and permanence:
> in each the generation of creation, in each the consummation.
>
> (lines 80–85)

The houses are the lunar months that describe the annual path of the sun around the planets. In the circular and cyclical course, images of eternity, the sun both measures the temporal limits within which the planets operate and impregnates them with life. In the precision of their movement, the planets, each in rhythmic harmony and interrelatedness with all others, become a paradigm of what Williams calls the Coinherence, and in their interdependence, an image of exchange, the heavenly law of the life in Christ. They are images in movement, the cosmic dance, of which Williams speaks so vividly in *The Greater Trumps.* This ceaseless dance, this intricate interplay, though precise and repetitive is always lively and fresh, seemingly spontaneous.

The moon was an especially attractive astrological image for Williams, because he saw it as representing movement in stillness, changelessness in change. Next to the sun the moon is the most important of the heavenly bodies since it moves through all the signs of the zodiac and was thought to influence everyone's horoscope. It represents mystery and the supernatural. It reflects received light, and it became for Williams an image of regenerative grace, a reconciling element between seemingly opposing forces, terrestrial and celestial. Moreover, the moon was especially useful because it could be at once an image of constant change and of eternal changelessness. It enters a new sign of the zodiac approximately every two and a half days, and yet, in spite of all these changes, it is part of a stable and recurring cycle that replicates the eternal order.

In "The Prelude" to *Taliessin through Logres* (1–2), Williams uses an image that brings this vision of cosmic coinherence into brilliant focus. He speaks of "geography breathing geometry" (line 9). Geography, the study of

THE OCCULT AS RHETORIC

the physical surface of the earth, maps in realistic detail the concrete and specific. Geometry, concerned with the abstract and universal, discovers and depicts diagrammatically relationships that reveal the pattern by which objects may be related on the basis of corresponding structures. Geometry unveils the previously "hidden" within the visible. The most important word in the statement is *breathing*. The relationship is not mechanical but organic and living, revealing the common derivation and "hidden" unity of all things.

The images expressing interrelatedness, therefore, are not always exclusively astrological. Some involve the human body. The astrological zodiac, Williams says, was thought to depict a relation between the planets and certain parts of the body (*Image,* 80–87). This concept became the source of a different group of images. He gives as examples the house of the Water Carrier, Aquarius, which is related to the eyes; the Twins, Gemini, to the arms and hands; Scorpion, Scorpio, to the genitals; the Balance, Libra, to the buttocks. Moreover, the human body as a whole forms a microcosm that is to the macrocosm as an index is to a book: the word in the index is less than the subject to which it refers, but it rightly names it, suggests something of its content, and points to where it may be found in its fullness. It may be, he admits, that the idea that the houses exert special influence upon the spatial universe is a fable—but if so, he maintains, it is a worthy fable. Nor can it be argued that they, sun and moon, for example, exercise no influence at all. Although many of the attributes claimed by the astrologers may be indeed arbitrary, they must be allowed "a kind of authentic poetic vision" (*Image,* 83).

Williams pictures the Empire, the kingdom on earth, and its Emperor, not God but "God-in-operation," as a female body. A major source for this image is undoubtedly the Jewish Cabala, in which prominence is given to the Sephirotic Tree as a diagrammatic depiction of man's spiritual journey in search of reunion with God.[4] The tenth and last of the Sephiroth, or Stations, Malkuth, lying at the base of the Tree, represents the earth, or the Kingdom. It is feminine, the estranged Bride of Kether, the first Sephira, the Male God, with whom she awaits reunion. In "Taliessin in the Rose-Garden," Williams speaks of bringing "to a flash of seeing the women in the world's base" (*Region,* 28; line 195). In the same poem, he writes, "Women's travel / holds in the natural the image of the supernatural" (lines 170–71). In "The Son of Lancelot," he discovers "the pattern in heaven of Nimue" (*TTL,* 56; line 56). And at least three times in "The Calling of Taliessin" (*Region,* 10–22), he refers to the shadow of Brisen as the pattern

_____

4. A. E. Waite, *The Holy Kabbalah* (1929; reprint, with an introduction by Kenneth Rexroth, New Hyde Park, N.Y.: University Books, 1960), 191–213.

170 ROMA A. KING, JR.

by which the yet unmade Logres will be formed. (A fuller description of the Tree and of Williams's use of it follows later in this essay.)

On the map prepared as end papers for *Taliessin through Logres,* Logres is depicted as the head of the body; Gaul as the breasts; Italy as the hands; Jerusalem as the hollow or genitals; Caucasia as the buttocks; and Ispahan as the place of ejection. In "Taliessin in the School of the Poets" (*TTL,* 27–30) occurs a passage reminiscent of the human figure sometimes superimposed on the zodiac and the Sephirotic Tree:

> Skeined be the creamed-with-crimson sphere
>   on a guessed and given line,
> skeined and swirled on the head-to-heel,
> or the radial arms' point-to-point;
> reckoned the rondures of the base
>   by the straight absolute spine.

(lines 31–36)

The consummate image of the cosmos as a self-sustaining organism is the Holy Trinity, subtly but brilliantly expressed in "The Founding of the Company" (*Region,* 34–38). He writes:

> beyond Broceliande he had seen afar
> a deep, strange island of granite growth,
> thrice charged with massive light in change,
> clear and golden-cream and rose tinctured,
> each in turn the Holder and the Held—as the eyes
> of the watcher altered and faltered and again saw
> the primal Nature revealed as a law to the creature;
> beyond Carbonek, beyond Broceliande,
> in the land of the Trinity, the land of the perichoresis,
> of separateness without separation, reality without rift,
> where the Basis is in the Image, and the Image in the Gift,
> the Gift is in the Image and the Image in the Basis,
> and Basis and Gift alike in Gift and Basis.

(lines 98–110)

To see the Trinity as granite may seem incongruous. Although it suggests the strength and durability of God, granite is, nevertheless, lifeless and inert. This granite, however, is a living "growth." "Thrice charged with massive light," it moves in a continuous pattern of change, "of separateness without separation, reality without rift," each part both Holder and Held. Not surprisingly, the eyes of the watcher "alter and falter," unable to follow the rapid changes or to discern details in the pattern. The watcher, however, by a feat of imagination and a gift of grace grasps, within human limits, a saving notion of the living substance from which all things visible and invisible derive. The last three lines of the passage summarize the *perichor-*

THE OCCULT AS RHETORIC

esis, an esoteric word that literally means "going around" (suggested in the convoluted syntax of the lines) and that was first used by John of Damascus, seventh-century theologian, to explicate the biblical passage "the Father is in me, and I in the Father" (John 10:38). In later times, according to the *Oxford English Dictionary,* the word *circumincession* was used instead, as being more expressive—i.e., "an insitting or indwelling in rotation or reciprocally." In summary, a variety of images found in occult literature serve Williams's purpose by pointing beyond themselves to the Christian doctrine of the Trinity, a Unity hinted at but never fully grasped by the occultists.

Maintaining that all things terrestrial and spiritual derive from a common first matter, Williams rejected dualism, the belief that there are two opposite and irreconcilable creative forces. He held instead that matter and spirit were only two modes within the Absolute Unity of Being (theme 2). He saw the occult as an instinctive expression of man's elemental need for ultimate unity, a unity consummately expressed in the Christian revelation. For the poet, and for our primary purpose, it also provided a rich source of expressive imagery: "The visionary forms of the occult schools are but dreams of the Divine Body" (*Image,* 84). Christians, however, may push the analogy further and "ask whether the body is not indeed a living epigram of virtue." He uses *virtue* in its fullest sense, meaning power and strength as well as goodness. Such virtues, he argues, are at once physical and spiritual. The human body as microcosm reflects in itself the singleness and unity of the macrocosm, the Holy Trinity. To the head he attributed intelligence; to the breasts, doctrine and creeds; to the hands, grace and mystery (the hands of invocation at the altar in Lateran); to the genitals, generation; to the buttocks, the "holy flesh" (a term he borrowed from Dante), balance and foundation; to the alley, rejection, ejection. Together they compose an organic unity in which all the virtues, physical and material, coexist. In his map, each represents a province and together they constitute the Empire.

Underlying all these images—the cosmos, the human body, the living granite—is Williams's doctrine of coinherence, which is never an image but always the imaged reality, the ultimate mystery whose archetype is the Holy Trinity.

Williams's living universe, in which matter is interpenetrated by spirit and spirit is incarnate in matter, is the scene of continuous communication (theme 3) between heaven and earth:

> the logothetes [messengers] run down the porphyry stair
> bearing the missives through the area of empire.
> ("The Vision of the Empire," *TTL,* 6–13; lines 10–11)

Williams was familiar with the hermetic doctrine of "correspondence"— the belief that all terrestrial things owe their power to a corresponding celestial pattern and that by understanding the relation between the two, one could

172   ROMA A. KING, JR.

use the earthly type to invoke the powers of the heavenly. He was aware
also of the many forms of divination that had been used by magicians, often
for nefarious operations. He also acknowledged that both magic and
Christian mystery have something in common, and he found in the
magician's rod and Merlin's cut hazel an analogy to the Pope's hands lifted
in invocation at the altar in Lateran.

He distinguished, however, between white (theurgic) and black (goetic)
magic and between both and Christian sacrament (theme 4). Black magic is
performed perversely in order to grasp powers and to control them. Its
consummate evil is that it violates the Coinherence. In *The Secret Doctrine
in Israel,* A. E. Waite had written that the *Zohar* "always recognized the
claims of magic as the art of secret power, but . . . condemned [it] in all its
branches and modes."[5] Williams's villains are most often black magicians:
in his novels, Gregory Persimmons, Sir Giles Tumulty, Nigel Considine,
Simon LeClerc; in his poetry, the "headless Emperor" of P'o-lu, the
"brainless form," who resides in "antipodean Byzantium" (*TTL,* 12).

The ancient magicians wielded wands and rods and performed black
magic. Merlin's instrument, on the other hand, was the cut hazel. He is,
Williams said, "apart from the whole question of sin and grace. He is rather
as if time itself became conscious of the future and prepared for it" (*Image,*
191). The cut hazel Williams defined as a kind of "natural grace."[6] Merlin
was a white magician, as Virgil was said to have been, superior to the pagan
black magician but less than the Christian sacramentalist.

When the old magic gives way to its antitype, it is the hands of the
Christian priest—not the ancient Roman magician Vibenna's rod nor
Merlin's hazel—that become the channels of mediating grace (*TTL,* 9; lines
93–97), or what Williams frequently called "largesse," meaning something
freely given with neither consideration for desert nor expectation of return.
Calvary is the supreme example. Williams, in "The Calling of Taliessin,"
could write:

> Poor, goetic or theurgic, the former spells
> seemed beside the promise of greater formulae;
> poor—control or compact—the personal mastery,
> the act of magic, or the strain of ancient verse
> beside the thickening dreams [intuited vision becoming concrete reality]
>   of the impersonal Empire

5. Waite, *Secret Doctrine* (London: William Rider and Sons, 1913), 113.

6. Williams, Notes on *Taliessin through Logres* prepared in response to questions from C.
S. Lewis (unpublished; copy provided to author by Thelma Shuttleworth; hereafter cited in
the text as Notes).

THE OCCULT AS RHETORIC

and the moulded themes of the Empire.[7]

The beginning stanza of "Taliessin at Lancelot's Mass" (*TTL*, 89) shows the transition from old magic to new mystic reality:

> The altar was an ancient stone laid upon stones;
> Carbonek's arch, Camelot's wall, frame of Bors' bones.

Lancelot's altar was anticipated by the home of the Grail king ("Carbonek"), Merlin's effective magic in erecting "Camelot's wall," and the diagrammatic pattern in the human body of the heavenly archetype. But even beyond these, Lateran itself rests on the spot where the Lupercalia was celebrated, where "rods of divination between Lupercal and Lateran" (*TTL*, 54; "The Son of Lancelot," line 8) link the old with the new, Christian with Pagan Rome. Beyond the Empire lies Broceliande, then Carbonek, and eventually Sarras, the land of the Coinherent Trinity.

Williams found in occult lore also a treasure of transformation images (theme 5) which, when interpreted in light of Christian grace, become the culminating motif of his poetry. Two are especially suggestive: the pentagram and the Sephirotic Tree. The pentagram is a recurring image in Western magic. Its lower four points represent the four elements, earth, air, water, fire, and the upper point signifies the surrounding spirit. When the points are all connected so as to present an enclosed area and when the fifth point is directed upward, the figure becomes a means of invoking blessings and, particularly in Williams, of signifying integration, coinherence. I have noted that in "The Calling of Taliessin," the pentagram with Brisen at its topmost point becomes the channel through which grace flows, providing both the pattern and the empowerment for the founding of Logres.

In "The Coming of Galahad" (*TTL*, 69–74), it symbolizes integration on both personal and communal levels. In lines 97 through 99, a serving maid of the castle says,

> This morning when the Saracen prince was christened
> dimly the lord Percivale's pentagram glistened
> in the rain-dark stones of his [Palomides'] eyes . . . .

Palomides, the hesitant Muslim convert, has just accepted baptism, the first step in a spiritual journey the end of which he cannot foresee. Percival, seemingly at first an intrusion in the poem, is nevertheless throughout the volume the symbol of coinherence. Williams calls him the imagination of the other world in contrast to Taliessin, who is the imagination of this one

---

7. *Region*, 12; lines 81–86. For further amplification of treatment of the poetry of ancient magic and Williams's indebtedness to the *Mabinogion* poet, see King, *The Pattern in the Web*, chap. 5, "Behold a Radiant Brow," especially pp. 128–29.

174 ROMA A. KING, JR.

(Notes). At this point, the consummation remains a dimly glimpsed vision. The pentagram is not fully realized. I shall have something to say directly about where that journey leads.

In the concluding lines of the poem (lines 146–64), the same image is used with broader implications for the Empire as one Body. Taliessin speaks enigmatically in the passage beginning: "Proofs were; roofs were: I / what more? creeds were; songs were." In context it is clear that he refers to the possible recovery in the Empire of that pattern which provides the key to all meaning. "Proofs . . . creeds . . . songs" are means to that end. But what of roofs? He continues, referring to the planets Mercury, Venus, Jupiter, Saturn, and the "Earth between." Reintroducing the astrological imagery here provides a cosmic context for the transformation theme. Together the planets compose five "undimensioned points" (line 104)—that is, disconnected and therefore composing no coinherent pattern. What is the desired connection and how in the process do roofs function? In line 149 he refers to roofs "slanted to each cleft in each wall, with planets planted," and in lines 100 to 108 to the undimensioned points that if joined would form a pentagram. Here we have five undimensioned points, with two lines slanting outward from each. If the clefts between all the lines were joined, they would form a pentagram, the image of coinherence. That pentagram glimpsed only dimly by Palomides is seen clearly, if only momentarily, by Taliessin in an apocalyptical foreview of the coming cosmic victory of coinherence over division.

In "Taliessin in the Rose-Garden," Williams says of Cain, "at a blow he split the zodiac" (*Region,* 27; line 143), the image being that of a failed pentagram, a fragmented Empire. And Taliessin, the poet, the imagination of this world, sees himself in a vision:

> And I there climbing in the night's distance
> till the clear light shone on the height's edge:
> out of the pit and the split zodiac I came
> to the level above the magnanimous stair, and saw
> the Empire dark with the incoherence of the houses.
>
> (lines 151–55)

These lines describe the sad split state of Logres as it presently is on the point of becoming mere Britain.

The five houses introduced into "The Coming of Galahad" are here further developed in a manner that places them indisputably in context of the Christian tradition by giving Jupiter a new significance, a theme implied but not fully developed in "The Coming of Galahad" in line 153, where he refers to Jupiter as having a "moon of irony and of defeated irony." Women, who "share with the Sacrifice the victimization of blood" ("Taliessin in the Rose-Garden," line 162); Pelles, the Grail King with his bleeding wound

THE OCCULT AS RHETORIC   175

inflicted by the Dolorous Blow (the Fall); and Blanchefleur, who died from giving a cup of blood to save another—are all in some way involved in the restoration, but, clearly, in themselves they are incapable of completing it. They find their fulfillment in Jupiter, the heavenly planet with the deep red scar, the bleeding wound, which becomes the archetype of all sacrifices brought to fulfillment on Calvary. Jupiter provided the fifth and topmost point, the surrounding spirit that brings the undimensioned points into coinherence and gives the image specific Christian significance in that Christ becomes the integrating power.

The Sephirotic Tree, supreme image of transformation, is borrowed from the Jewish Cabala with modifications by later Christian hermeticists.[8] The Tree depicts diagrammatically the path humans must follow in the spiritual quest for reunion with God. At the top of the diagram abides the incomprehensible God, the Zero, as he was sometimes called, because he is without measurement; the Nothing, because he is no-thing but everything. At the foot of the tree lies Malkuth, the last and most remote of the ten sephiroth, the channels through which the creative power flowed at creation. They are also the stages through which one must pass in the effort to close the breach between oneself and God. Malkuth is the material earth, counterpart of the masculine God, the Bride lying in exile awaiting reunion with her heavenly Spouse. The nine Sephiroth above Malkuth form a triad of triads arranged within a triad of pillars or columns. The column on the right is masculine; that on the left is feminine. Together they represent the opposing forces inherent in creation, the love that creates and the wrath that destroys. The middle column, asexual (God contains all that is, both masculine and feminine), is the reconciling and balancing force. The triad immediately above Malkuth, the unconscious or spiritually unawakened, represents humankind in the early stages of transformation; the second, the conscious, humanity awakened and in the process of striving. Its attainment represents the highest level of awareness possible in the natural state. The third, the superconscious, is separated from the second by an abyss establishing the demarcation between the Ideal and the present reality, between man and the Ineffable Imageless God.

No detailed discussion of all ten Sephiroth is required, but some knowledge of the first four is helpful: *Malkuth,* feminine, earth; *Ysod,* masculine, air; *Hod,* feminine, water; *Netzach,* masculine, fire. Malkuth is sometimes called Zion or Jerusalem, the place of beginnings. (In the map of the World as Body, published in the first edition of *Taliessin through Logres,* the genitals are called Jerusalem.) Ysod, located just above Malkuth,

---

8. Two basic sources of information on the Sephirotic Tree are Waite, *Holy Kabbalah,* and David Sheinkin, *Path of the Kabbalah* (New York: Paragon House, 1986). I am especially indebted to these writers, among others.

is named the funnel or, sometimes, "the sacred organ of intercourse." He is the channel through which energy flows downward from God impregnating and enlivening the feminine earth. Hod lies on the left of the tree; Netzach on the right. They represent opposing elements operating in dialectical union. Achieving the state of Netzach signals victory over the natural elements and admission to a plane of higher humankind's consciousness and spiritual awareness. The Sephira immediately above Netzach is Tipereth, or beauty. Beyond the abyss lies the ultimate goal, reunion with God.

Williams uses the Sephirotic Tree and the Porphyry Stair almost interchangeably. In "Taliessin in the Rose-Garden," the two become so intertwined that they compose one complex image. An important difference, however, is that Williams regards the Tree as having fulfillment within context of the Stair. The Stair introduces the element of sacrifice, as Williams understood it, the shedding of blood, the Old Covenant that found its fulfillment on Calvary in the New Covenant. The Porphyry Stair, mounting upward between the newels, is so called because the porphyry stair in the Emperor's Palace led from the hall to the throne room.

In "The Death of Palomides" (*TTL,* 78–80), the Tree image provides the structuring principle on which the poem develops. The poem serves as a summarizing illustration of how the Sephirotic Tree becomes a transformation image with specifically Christian implications. Palomides, the Persian dualist, for whom the material world and the human body were anathema, initially rejected the Incarnation. Now, on the point of death, at an unspecified interval following his baptism when Percivale's pentagram glistened only dimly in "the rain-dark stones of his eyes," he looks back and sees that the paths that once seemed "interminable" (line 29) were really stations along the way toward spiritual enlightenment. He recalls especially one incident, an encounter with two old Jews whom at the time he scornfully rejected but who in retrospect seem the beginning of a process he could not then have understood, nor would have accepted if he had. "Sea-grey was one and sea-wrinkled, / one burned sun-black, with clawed hands" (lines 9–10). They sit around a fire in an act of worship incomprehensible to the young rationalist:

> their chant
> dropped into pauses, poured into channelled names.

> The first mathematics of Ispahan trembled
> before the intoned formulae; . . .
> . . . .
> . . . they pronounced *Netzach.*
> . . . .
> *What is Netzach? . . .*
> *Netzach is the name of the Victory in the Blessing:*

THE OCCULT AS RHETORIC

For the Lord created all things by means of his Blessing.
(lines 11–14, 20, 22–24)

To know the name of someone or something, it was thought, was to penetrate its power. The two old men invoked the Power by calling on the various sacred names by which the one God was known. The channels are the Sephiroth, the stages through which the creative force flows downward. The first old man represents the state of Hod, water, and the second, that of Netzach, fire. To achieve Netzach is to bring the opposing powers together in a dialectical balance. That victory is grounded in the blessing—something the young dualist could not grasp. The "mathematics" of Persia, the dualist separation of soul from body, "trembled," we are told, before the "intoned" Jewish affirmation that all creation, terrestrial and celestial, was good and that matter and spirit were two ways of perceiving the one substance. The two old men speak by inference of the mystic belief that the world was created through the help of the Hebrew alphabet. When God created heaven and earth, he did so through the instrumentality of the second letter *Beth*. This was not because that letter was the initial of the word *bara* 'to create' or *bereshith* 'in the beginning,' but because it was the initial letter of *barach* 'to bless.'[9] In short, God created everything and gave it his blessing by pronouncing it good. Such a view makes possible the union between so-called matter and spirit and, incidentally, prepares for the Incarnation, the Word made Flesh. A. E. Waite, in *The Secret Doctrine in Israel,* puts it this way: "He unfolds Himself in the voice of blessing and passes continually from the Unknown into the range of apprehension by means of this voice, uttering the speech of wisdom" (61).

Looking back to his leaving the prophet, his disillusionment with Iseult, his pursuit of the Blatant Beast (raw sex), his compromise of honor when he cheated at the Tournament, and his eventual reluctant and painful conversion and baptism, Palomides sees it all as a sequel to that trembling excitement he felt but sublimated as he listened to the two old men chanting, "The Lord created all things by means of his Blessing."

Having achieved Netzach and looking now toward Tipereth, Palomides is aware of a "scintillation of points" (a hint of the undimensioned points in process of forming a pentagram) emanating from a fire (Netzach) that typifies the Fire of Pentecost. It is falling all about him, the rays of light from above intermingling with the "points of the eagle's plumes, plumes that are paths." They sweep upward from the symbols of fire and plumes to the "unbelievable symbol"—unbelievable in that it transcends rational thought. At the top of the Tree/Porphyry Stair lies the Inexpressible God. In

---

9. Waite, *Secret Doctrine,* 55–56.

"Taliessin in the School of the Poets" (*TTL,* 27–30) we have a parallel passage descriptive of the Victory:

> between right and left newel
> floats the magnanimous path of the stair
> to a tangle of compensations,
> every joint a centre,
>   and every centre a jewel.
>
> Each moment there is the midmost
>   of the whole massive load;
> impulse a grace and wonder a will,
> love desert, and sight direction,
> whence the Acts of Identity issue
>   in the Pandects and the Code.
>
> (lines 50–60)

In "The Death of Palomides," written against a background of Jewish and Christian understanding of the Unity, Williams brings the whole to culmination in a passage that implicitly embraces the Christian doctrine of Incarnation:

> If this is the kingdom, the power, the glory, my heart
> formally offers the kingdom, endures the power,
> joins to itself the aerial scream of the eagle . . .
> That Thou only canst be Thou only art.
>
> (lines 57–60; ellipsis points in original)

We may conclude that Williams did indeed find in the literature of the occult a variety of ideas that were, so far as they went, compatible with his own thinking. He denied, however, that the occult has any inherent "moral sense," and he dissociated himself from its "pretended operations," declaring that he was interested in the subject only as "a kind of authentic poetic vision" and "only to pass beyond it" (*Image,* 83, quoted more fully above). He placed the whole within the larger Christian framework in which, he maintained, it found fulfillment. The considerable contribution of the occult to Williams's poetry, therefore, was largely psychological and rhetorical. It stimulated his imagination, enriched his language, and provided a vivid, suggestive imagery that gave scope and universality to his work. The way in which he was able to merge images, the Sephirotic Tree and the Porphyry Stair, for example, permitted him to express through rhetorical means a sense of the coinherence in its totality—intellectually, emotionally, sensuously—that no amount of mere statement ever could. All this brought freshness and excitement to a kind of poetry—that dealing with religious experience—which today often seems dogmatic, trite, and anemic.

Coinherent Rhetoric
in *Taliessin through Logres*

Angelika Schneider

> Great literature is simply language charged with meaning to the utmost possible degree.
>
> > (Ezra Pound)

> All poets whose apprehension of the world is peculiarly complex or passionate are likely to employ an unusual vocabulary or an uncommon syntax, or both, to convey with the utmost exactitude the unique quality of their vision.
>
> > (John Press)

> I always mean to be lucid, I always mean to be elementary, . . . but some twist of language puts me off.
>
> > (CW)[1]

Of all twentieth-century revolutions, the most far-reaching and fundamental is taking place largely unheeded by the public eye. Scientists, expanding the frontiers of knowledge, have become increasingly aware of the interconnectedness of everything that exists and the partiality and ultimate invalidity of our deeply rooted belief in a mechanistic, one-cause-one-effect world. The endeavor to understand phenomena by analysis into ever smaller elements is being replaced by the examination of wholes and processes—molecules, cells, bodies, social and ecological systems. Even in the physical sciences, scientists now recognize the dependence of "objective" experimental results on the "subjective" situation of the examiner; no longer can they see themselves as totally separate from the matter under examination. The perception that every element can be understood only as part of a larger pattern that develops according to discernible principles has found entry into all branches of modern science and has opened new fields such as cybernetics and ecology. Modern thinking, however, is still largely based on the

---

1. Pound, as quoted by Craig La Drière, "Structure, Sound and Meaning," in *Sound and Poetry,* ed. Northrop Frye, English Institute Essays, 1956 (New York: Columbia University Press, 1957), 107; Press, *The Chequer'd Shade: Reflections on Obscurity in Poetry* (London: Oxford University Press, 1958), 23; Williams, letter to Phyllis Potter, 15 January 1945 (Marion E. Wade Center, Wheaton College, Wheaton, Ill.).

"optical illusion" that we as individual beings are separate from existence as a whole, on the illusory differentiation of subject and object, on the mechanistic view of eighteenth- and nineteenth-century science.

Ever since the Enlightenment, the vision of oneness that underlies the word *universe* has been relegated more and more to the irrational, to the scope of the mystic and the artist. Poets of every period before the present century have sought to give expression to their intuition of a unity underlying the fragmentation of sensory perception. In the perception of classical art this basic oneness is seen as an overriding system of order apprehensible by reason, to which all man-made systems must strive to conform. The romantic artist experiences or intuits unity through sublime imagination or profound emotion and seeks to communicate these through his or her art. With the dissemination of Newtonian and evolutionary science in the nineteenth century, such perspectives were increasingly discounted. The symbolist, aware that symbols can arouse and communicate emotion, could still postulate the relation between symbol and communicated reality as a reflection of some greater whole. The modern artist, however, totally despairing of the existence of an aesthetically satisfying, unified reality, can at best create islands of meaning true within themselves but without valid reference to reality as a whole.

Charles Williams was and was not a modern in this sense. He shared on a profound level the experience of fragmentation and meaninglessness pervasive in his generation. Unlike his brother Inklings Lewis and Tolkien, he was unable to see this as an aberration in contemporary thought and to align himself and his art with the world view of an earlier time. Yet he was committed to a Christian belief in a meaningful whole, fallen and redeemed creation, and experienced vividly the artistic vision of the oneness of all things.

Because it affirms the reality of both the separateness and the givenness of the material world we experience and the validity of our search for unity and meaning, Williams's world view still seems prophetic in a period of growing polarization between, on the one hand, economic well-being as the only value in a coincidental cosmos void of meaning and, on the other, religious fundamentalism as the attempt to deny reason in order to force a pattern on chaos. Between the two, visionary scientists, theologians, and the more important "new age" philosophers are saying just what Charles Williams's works, particularly the Arthurian poems, expressed in a different and highly individual idiom fifty years ago.

Williams's unique interpretation of orthodox Christian theology is an attempt to reconcile his conflicting intuitions of reality as one and whole, although experienced in fragmentation and contradiction. The basis of this interpretation is the concept of *coinherence,* the fundamental interrelatedness

COINHERENT RHETORIC IN *TALIESSIN* 181

of all elements and aspects of existence. God is for Williams the center and source of this coinherent reality; human beings, endowed with free will, can affirm their mutual interdependence, freely engaging in exchange with one another, or they can deny it and see it as evil—in Williams's words "gaze . . . on the Acts [of God in creation] in contention" (*TTL*, 10). Since every subordinate element can fulfill its nature only in relation to the whole of which it is a part and in its interaction with other elements, however, no one can place himself or herself outside this network and view the rest "objectively"; the refusal to participate in exchange with all other elements is detrimental both to the individual entity and to the whole of which it forms a part, that is, to human society. This is the insight expressed by Dante in the words Williams prefixes to the Arthurian poetry: "Unde est, quod non operatio propria propter essentiam, sed haec propter illam habet ut sit."[2]

The Arthurian cycle is Williams's prime attempt to embody in artistically satisfying form the full extent of his vision of the coinherence and its consequences for the conduct of human life. It is my contention that, while using the Arthurian myth as a vehicle to express his view of the development of the individual and his or her role in society, and of that which tends to the ultimate good of both, the poet sought to exhibit in his rhetoric, in the images and the language that constitute the very fabric of his verse, his own apprehension of the coinherence—that is, of reality—itself. A close examination of the kind of imagery Williams employs for this purpose, and of the language (its syntax, lexis, and phonology) in which the imagery is embodied, will show how the verse is informed by this intention.

I

Imagery—the participation of an image in, and its communication of, the reality it represents—is for Williams one of our chief means of apprehending the coinherent unity of all things. Poetry, therefore, being made up of images, is both formed by and expressive of the interrelatedness of all things, all elements, aspects, and levels of existence. Every individual image in the Arthurian poems—person, place, event or object, metaphor or simile —by the very fact of being an image shows forth the existence of relationship among disparate elements. The bard Taliessin is the center and protagonist of the poems, not only or primarily because he is Williams's alter ego, but because poetry is the chief image of coinherence and he is its source.

2. *TTL*, [viii]; Williams cites the *De Monarchia* 1.3. Elsewhere he translates: "The essence is created for the sake of the function and not the function for the essence" (*Dove*, 132). The "function" of any particular "essence" (i.e., being) is its participation in the life of the whole of which it forms a part.

Beyond this, the images that occur in these poems exemplify the nature of reality by the way in which the poet weaves them together. Images already fraught with meaning from a wide range of literary, mythic, and experiential sources occur in a variety of contexts in different poems; each context adds further shades of meaning, and the various images are linked together to form a dense network of interrelationship, a mirror of the coinherent nature of existence.

This technique of enriching the significance of a single image, making it more complex and meaningful, may be illustrated by Williams's use of the human arm. As a part of the human body, the arm shares in the body's role as an image of organic relationship and as a means of awakening and communicating love. Love, being the very essence of relationship, communicates most fully the nature of the coinherence. The arm as an image of the body as a whole and as a channel of love is explicated in "Bors to Elayne: the Fish of Broceliande," where the fish of Bors's love enters Elayne's body through hand and arm (*TTL,* 24-25). In "The Coming of Palomides," Iseult's arm awakens Palomides' adoration and reveals to him the truth of the union of spiritual and physical nature, a truth denied by his Islamic faith (35). Taliessin's arm and hand, the instruments whereby his poetry is written, also give the signal for the charge that decides the battle of Mount Badon in Arthur's favor (17); they thus open the way for the establishment of Logres as the union of political order and religious truth. In "The Star of Percivale" the joined arms of Taliessin and the enslaved girl are "bands of glory" imaging spiritual union in mutual love (46). The arm of an enslaved person serves as a central image in the two succeeding poems as well. It conveys the signal of ascent from rebellious bondage to the freedom of voluntary acceptance in "The Ascent of the Spear" (49) and forms a channel of revelation to Taliessin in the complex imagery of "The Sister of Percivale." Here the figures of an enslaved girl and Blanchefleur are superimposed, breath of trumpet blast and muscle of water-bearing arm are blended in an encompassing and profound insight into the nature of all being (51). This—by no means complete—catalog of the multifarious uses of a single image in the Arthurian poems may suffice to show how its significance is developed and enriched in the course of the work, making of one simple element a many-faceted network of meaning, a subordinate pattern within the larger pattern of the whole, in itself a representation of coinherence.

Williams employs three different types of image to express the nature of reality as relationship: "metaimages," which express the function of imagery itself as a means of understanding coinherence, the chief of these being poetry; images envisaging the network of relationship of which existence is composed, the primary one of which is the human body; and the individual actions of the figures in the Arthuriad, participating in or rejecting that exchange which is the activity of coinherence. These three types of image I now examine in turn, beginning with the last.

Arthurian Myth

This is, of course, the narrative matter, the "stuff" of the poems. Arthur's love of self (his choice to see "the kingdom made for the king" [*TTL*, 21]; also his incestuous and basically narcissistic relationship with his sister, Morgause), Lancelot's love for Guinevere, and Balin's fatal venting of his anger in the infliction of the Dolorous Blow point to the nature of exchange by showing the consequences of its rejection. Taliessin's free renunciation of Dindrane, her sacrificial giving of her life's blood for the healing of another, a slave's free choice of continued servitude, Bors's and Elayne's wholehearted performance of their appointed tasks, equally demonstrate the nature of exchange by showing the consequences of participation. But it is not always that simple. Palomides rejects the vision of coinherence that is briefly disclosed to him by Iseult and is left cut off from all relationship; yet by acquiescing in his loss, and by being baptized, he becomes part of the community. In contrast, Lamorack, although accepting the impossibility of his love for Morgause, remains in bondage to it and is ultimately destroyed.

It is the irony of existence that the way of exchange, though the only way of salvation and therefore the source of good, is "rich in sorrow, rich in heart's heaviness," as the pope realizes in his final prayer, adding the plea, "send not the rich empty away" (*Region,* 47). Through his prayer, through his embracing of loss—as each person must finally embrace it, for only thus can the irony of existence be defeated—the roots of life-giving Broceliande grasp and hold immobile the tentacles of hell, and evil is for a time defeated, as "the roses of the world bloom . . . from Burma to Logres" (54).

The Human Body

The image, or network of images, that most completely expresses Williams's vision of the coinherence as a unity encompassing the whole of life is the human body and its geographic counterpart, the empire centered at Byzantium. The discovery of cell metabolism, intracellular communication, and the genetic code gives the metaphor of organic unity on which this image is based an even greater aptness than the poet knew. Obvious to him were, of course, the body's material nature, the differentiation and cooperation of the various organs, its sensibly evident wholeness. In his superimposition of body physical and body politic, drawn in words in "The Vision of the Empire" and in lines on the endpapers of the first edition of *Taliessin through Logres,* Williams makes of Paul's metaphor for the church as the body of Christ a complex, many-leveled representation of reality.

From the Emperor, the indwelling unity of the whole, "operative Providence" ("Preface," *Region,* 6), "God as known in Church and State, God as ruling men" (*Image,* 181), emanates the "identity" of the "categories"—the correspondence of images—which conveys his truth to all parts of the empire. All human faculties, represented by provinces or "themes" of the empire, participate in the life of the whole by fulfilling each its own function. Beyond that, each faculty contributes to the individual human being's fulfillment and to the perfection of society by enhancing knowledge of the coinherence. It is this understanding that empowers the individual to engage purposefully in exchange, even to its uttermost height, to the point of complete substitution; this alone can reverse evil and bring healing of the ruptures caused by those who have refused relationship.

Central to Williams's body image is his emphasis on its physicalness; this is aptly symbolized by the buttocks. They form the base of the spine, giving the body straightness, balance, and stability, and are also a symbol of erotic love—particularly in its more playful vein. By choosing this part—and the corresponding province, Caucasia—to represent the physical aspect of human life, associating it with images of natural beauty, laughter, dance, and physical prowess, Williams truly gives "greater honor to those parts we deem lesser" (1 Cor. 12:23) and confirms the inherent goodness of our physical and sexual natures.

With our physical nature, however, no matter how good in itself, we also inherit our participation in humankind's propensity to "gaze . . . on the Acts [of the Emperor] in contention" (*TTL,* 10)—to deny interdependence, refuse relationship, and, thus, bring about evil. Sin is real and, although not caused by sex, is yet propagated through it, since this tendency is passed on from one generation to another. For this reason the myth of the origin of evil is enacted at Jerusalem, place of the organs of generation, birthplace of three world religions, and the site of gravest contention among them.

The evil that humans have brought about by refusing their own true natures is more than an inherent psychological tendency; it is also historical fact, and part of the way we are. This is imaged in "the feet of creation walk[ing] backward" (*TTL,* 11), away from the creature's own good. The antiemperor in P'o-Lu has turned away from all participation in society and is totally self-absorbed among fetid marshes devoid of life, a vivid image of hell.

By superimposing these two sets of images, the organically integrated parts of the body and the politically and economically integrated provinces of the empire, the poet provides himself with a kind of shorthand imagery. By alluding to any part of either system, Williams is often able to suggest a whole complex of images with but a single word, thus creating a tapestry of peculiar richness and density.

Metaimages

Poets' unique understanding of the imaging function of poetry is Williams's prime metaphor for an understanding of reality that motivates those who hold it to engage actively and voluntarily in exchange. It is the bard Taliessin who (in "The Vision of Empire") dreams of the establishment of the kingdom of Logres, the achievement of the ideal human society. It is his poetical insight that perceives the empire-as-body, that complex image of human society and of the individual's role therein. He contributes the decisive stroke for the establishment of Arthur's kingdom in the battle of Mount Badon. He is the lover of Dindrane (or Blanchefleur, the sister of Percivale, one who in Malory "bled a dish full of blood for to heal a lady" [2.348])—and to love is for Williams always to see the true nature both of the beloved and of Love itself. Dindrane serves in the Arthurian poetry as the one image of the Negative Way to divine knowledge—the search for the wholly Other beyond all images. This is the necessary complement of the Affirmative Way, the experience of God in creation. Taliessin's love for her shows his deep understanding of her way, although it is contrary to the one he himself has chosen. He also teaches in the school of the poets, where those who aspire to knowledge and to the means of communicating it "stud[y] precision" while "Taliessin remember[s] the soul" (*TTL,* 30). And it is he who gathers about him a company of people who, living in awareness of the Coinherence, carry this knowledge from the failure of Logres into the history of Britain.

Magic and myth, in both of which symbols play a central role, are another important source of metaimages in the cycle of poems. Logres is ritually founded by Merlin's rites of magic, and he is given power to oversee its development. His magic enables him to protect the birth of Galahad and to provide for his nurture among the nuns, thereby making possible Galahad's achievement of the Grail. This, the apotheosis of the work, signifies the possibility of individual salvation through exchange and substitution in spite of Logres's failure to achieve the reign of God in human society. Merlin's magic thus makes possible the full realization of the individual's potential through total participation in the coinherence. Since magic can control the power inhering in images by virtue of their relationship to external reality, it also serves as a fitting symbol of wisdom: King Solomon is "grand master . . . in sublime necromancy" (*TTL,* 84). The magic pentagram is the blazon of Percivale, who represents "the contemplation of the images" (*Region,* 52), the "spiritual intellect"[3]—love coupled with rational insight, which alone leads to divine vision. In thus making

---

3. Williams, "Notes on the Arthurian Myth," in *Image,* 177.

186   ANGELIKA SCHNEIDER

magic a means to salvation, Williams confirms the validity of every form of search for deeper knowledge, so long as this knowledge does not serve personal power. The power of magic can, however, be perverted; its perverted use is exemplified by Arthur's choice to exploit "the kingdom . . . for the king" (*TTL*, 21) and by his dream "of a red Grail in an ivory Logres / set for wonder, and himself Byzantium's rival" (55). Arthur's nemesis, Mordred, shows where the self-centered instrumentalization of supernatural power leads. He has nothing but small-minded contempt for "such fairy mechanism" and can envisage the Grail only as a "cauldron of Ceridwen" that "my cooks would be glad of" (*Region*, 44).

A wide range of pagan and Christian, astrological and literary sources of myth are drawn upon by the poet as well. Persons or objects already imbued with high symbolic value in Western tradition—dragon and unicorn, Midas's gold, Wordsworth's stone and shell, and many others—are interwoven with the Arthurian myth and add to the poems' peculiar density of meaning. The evocative and insight-giving power of images displayed by magic ritual and mythic symbol is thus both demonstrated and affirmed.

Another means expressing the idea of coinherence in imagery is fusing in a single image, and thus in the reader's perception, very different, even contradictory, aspects of reality. The most pervasive of such multivalent images is the hazel, both the cut branch—incised wand of magic, rod of discipline and measurement—and the uncut, the budding shoot and fruitful bush. In numerous poems the hazel image points to the paradoxical unity of wildness and order, of prolific life and mathematical precision, of nature and supernature. The pervasive use of color symbolism has a similar effect; the color red, for example, brings together the concepts of sacrifice, erotic love, and divine vision, as well as of their total perversion in the hell of P'o-Lu.

A final, ubiquitous type of image is to be found in metaphors that contract time and space and, by merging them in a single metaphor, overcome our normal perceptions of things as separate in space and consecutive in time.[4] Frequently, these two dimensions are simply made equivalent in expressions like "through town and time" (*TTL*, 20) or "these cover the years and the miles" (44). Speed is an image of intensity of longing—particularly of longing for the divine—that unites space and time by seeking to transcend both: "the mere speed of adoration" (46), "by three ways of exchange the City sped to the City" (85). In the repeated phrase "accumulated distance," space is unimaginably compacted; and the closing words of *Taliessin through Logres*, "let the Company pray for it still" (91), project the time of the Arthuriad into the present of the reader.

It is evident that the multitude of complex images contained in the

---

4. This metaphor for a totally different perception of existence is treated in far greater depth in Williams's novel *Descent into Hell*.

COINHERENT RHETORIC IN *TALIESSIN* 187

Arthurian poems forms a closely interwoven web whose intricacy is yet enhanced by associations from the reader's own experience, by allusions to other works of literature, or by the accretion of meanings from poem to poem of the cycle. The network thereby created in itself images the nature of reality as seen by Williams—and as postulated by most present-day scientists.

II

We turn now to an examination of the language of the verse, to the syntax, lexis, and phonology of the words and sentences employed. It will be seen that the poet, by a plethora of unusual and sometimes eccentric usages, gives the individual words a high degree of semantic weight while at the same time closely interconnecting them into a fabric of extraordinary density that emulates the effect we have seen in the imagery.

On the syntactic level the poet's most prominent cohesive device is the asyntactic conjoining of linguistic elements—from single words to complete sentences—into larger units. The clear separation of the individual elements by means of punctuation marks short of a full stop—semicolons, colons, question marks, and occasional dashes, often accentuated or further subdivided by line endings—sets each element into high relief, while at the same time piling them one on top of the other: "Arthur ran; the people marched; in the snow / King Cradlemas died in his litter; a screaming few / fled; Merlin came; Camelot grew" (*TTL,* 15). The reader receives a welter of vivid impressions almost simultaneously, creating a sense of rapid activity and dynamic development as well as a feeling of time compacted or transcended.

The appositional linkage of nominal phrases is another means of joining ideas or images in such a way as to minimize the distance between them. By not specifying the precise relationship existing between individual concepts or images, the poet can suggest a variety of meaningful associations simultaneously: "[Arthur] came to a carved tavern, / a wine-wide cell, an open grave" (*TTL,* 40); "the king's friend kneeled, / the king's organic motion, the king's mind's blood, / the lion in the blood roaring through the mouth of creation" (21).

In Williams's poetic diction a number of different devices intensify the ordinary semantic and syntactic linkage of ideas and images. One such device is the often original, sometimes almost too obtrusively alliterative, compound, such as *flesh-fire-coloured* (*TTL,* 66) or *jewel-joint-justiced throne* (28). Such compounds frequently yoke semantically incompatible elements—*sun-black* (78), *sea-bone* (7), *grace-pricked*(28). The poet is past master in the use of all the rhetorical devices that by repetition reinforce semantic relationships, such as "kinds and kindreds" (6), "that cuts the

Obedience from the Obeyed" (33), "Patient, the king constrained patience" (57). Particularly prominent is the use of words with negative prefixes in a way that suggests their opposites, whether stated or not—"unmathematic," "visible, invisible," "dishallowing," "unangelic." As in classical oxymoron (in which the poems also abound), two contradictory meanings are almost fused, yet without obliterating the tension between them.

Williams skillfully augments the common range of a single word's connotations by repeating the word or its cognate in such unusual contexts that, even though they occur in different poems, the sense of the earlier context "echoes" in the later use. "The pedlars of wealth" that "stand plausibly by" in "The Calling of Arthur" (*TTL,* 14) resonate in the phrase "Tristram's plausible skill" in "The Coming of Palomides" (37). The "trigonometrical milk" of "The Vision of the Empire" (8) is echoed both in "Gospels trigonometrical" in "The Coming of Palomides" (33) and in "mystical milk" in "Taleissin at Lancelot's Mass" (89). Even phrases as simple yet unexpected as "dangerous eyes" (36), "long eyes" (39), and "easy eyes" (48) serve to link the contexts in which they occur. Such echoes— numerous examples of which could be given from almost every one of the poems—increase the semantic weight of the expressions involved, by adding to them the connotations of the other occurrences.

The poet also closely juxtaposes words with very different semantic properties. This not only laces the poems with original and vivid metaphors but also communicates a sense of interconnectedness of different aspects of experience, facets of existence normally seen as dichotomous or incompatible. Abstract is everywhere joined to concrete—"shapes and names" (*TTL,* 26), "fame and frame" (7), "ridged space" (44), "magnanimous thumb" (45)—and the organic to the inorganic—"the world's brows" (7), "your hand's pool" (24). Words lifted out of their common contexts are fraught with new meaning and enrich the verse with a wealth of striking metaphors, like "manacled by the web" (91) or "the harp on my back / syllabled the signal word" (5).

Finally, there are the phonological properties, the sound effects of Williams's language, to be considered. Each of these, too—the rhythm and verse forms employed as well as the ubiquitous use of alliteration, assonance, and rhyme—makes its own contribution to the meaning structure, augmenting both the wealth of imagery and the intricate links formed by the syntactic and semantic devices described.

The use of alliteration is, of course, a deliberate reminiscence of the Old English strong-stress meter well suited to the time of the narrative; in the same way end-rhyme and verse forms in some of the poems are used to suggest a particular poetic style pertinent to the content, arousing deliberate associations in the reader's mind. It would be a mistake to see the multifarious rhyme schemes and stress patterns as primarily ornamental and to reject

COINHERENT RHETORIC IN *TALIESSIN* 189

the poet's style as overadorned. An examination of the pervasive alliterations, assonances, and internal rhymes reveals that almost invariably such effects either suggest additional relationships beyond those inherent in syntax and lexis or emphasize the existing ones. Examples could be given from almost every line of the verse, so I will confine myself to two from the beginning and the end of *Taliessin through Logres:* "Carbonek, Camelot, Caucasia" from the opening of the "Prelude" (*TTL,* 1) and the closing lines of the final poem, "to the barrows of Wales / up the vales of the Wye; if skill be of work or of will" (91). In the first example, by the alliterative naming of the three places, the poet suggests the inner connection between the concepts for which they stand—Carbonek is the Grail or Kingdom of God, Camelot the society built to prepare its coming, and Caucasia the simple, physical nature of humankind, less spoilt by the Fall than our minds and therefore readier for the Kingdom, able even now to "shadow" the "beyond-sea meadows" (*Region,* 40). In the second example, the rhyme and consonance of the first part carry eye and voice along smoothly and quickly, attaching these qualities to Taliessin's ride. In the second part the same devices add to the straight semantic content, the desirability of skill in work and will, giving a sense of the necessity of all three together for the achievement of the task.

Similar results are achieved by rhythmic effects. Usually the verse measure reinforces the ordinary prose rhythm of speech, thereby giving it particular emphasis. In the few poems in which the rhythm of the verse occasionally does differ from that of ordinary speech, the effect of poetic heightening is all the more marked. Thus, in "The Coming of Palomides" the shorter, regular, end-rhymed, four-stress lines create an atmosphere of ritualistic, almost pedantic, formalism expressive of the Persian knight's frame of mind, while in "Talessin at Lancelot's Mass" the regular rhyme and flowing rhythm endow the verse with a ritual grace.

Where the rhythm is less obtrusive it nevertheless often adds subtle shades of meaning. As has been noted, line endings, like punctuation marks, serve to highlight individual elements without interrupting the flow of speech: at the battle of Mount Badon, Taliessin "rode over the ridge; his force / sat hidden behind" (*TTL,* 16); Merlin first appears to Arthur "black with hair, bleak with hunger, defiled / from a bed in the dung of cattle" (14). A change in rhythm has a similar effect, as, for example, the sudden intrusion of a regular pentameter into a rough five-stress meter with feet of varying length:

> Her hand discharged catastrophe; I was thrown
> before it; I saw the source of all stone,
> the rigid tornado, the schism and first strife
> of primeval rock with itself, Morgause Lot's wife.

(38)

190 ANGELIKA SCHNEIDER

A more subtle example is the stanza in which the three places are named:

> Carbonek, Camelot, Caucasia,
> were gates and containers, intermediations of light;
> geography breathing geometry, the double-fledged Logos.

(1)

Here the increasing line length augments the growing complexity of thought: both break off suddenly after "intermediations" to throw the monosyllable "light" into relief, giving it its full range of literal and metaphoric meaning: weightlessness as well as brightness, the clarity and simplicity of wisdom contrasting with the complexity of knowledge developed in the last line of the strophe. There the chain of polysyllables culminating in "double-fledged" breaks off, giving the final "Logos" a quality similar to "light" in the previous line.[5]

Thus everywhere the poet employs the sound quality of words to create new links between them, revealing connections beyond those given by syntax and lexis. Ultimately everything is connected to everything else, and Williams almost succeeds in making his language express this truth in spite of the inherent limitations both of language and of our apprehension of reality.

III

In concluding, the question must be raised as to the success of these poems, seen not as an extraordinary tour-de-force by a master manipulator of language but as poetry. Note must be taken in this regard of the difference between the style of most of the poems of *Taliessin through Logres* and those of *The Region of the Summer Stars*. Evidently, Williams himself became aware that in the end less is more, that his attempt to communicate his vision in the very fabric of his rhetoric almost overstrained the resources of the language while loading the poems with a weight of potential meaning at least occasionally more likely to obscure than to reveal the basic message. Too often, the poems can be more fully appreciated by an avid solver of crossword puzzles, someone who enjoys uncovering every last linguistic twist, than by the straightforward, sympathetic reader. And Williams himself wrote that he was "glad to think that the SUMMER STARS are more lucid. They ought to be."[6] The later poems are far more uniform in style—all but

---

5. For further examples of Charles Williams's use of rhythmic and sound effects, see Angelika Schneider, "A Mesh of Chords: Language and Style in the Arthurian Poems of Charles Williams," in *Arthurian Literature* 5, ed. Richard Barber (Woodbridge, Suffolk: D. S. Brewer; Totowa, N.J.: Rowman and Littlefield, 1985), 107–14.

6. Williams, letter to Phyllis Potter, 15 January 1945.

one are composed in a flexible, unrhymed meter of five stresses divided only into large paragraphs, similar to the longer poems of *Taliessin through Logres*. Alliteration and internal rhyme are more rarely and subtly employed. The language is reminiscent of Williams's unmistakable "high" prose style, full of characteristic capitalizations, elisions, inverted word order, and the use of a vocabulary freighted with theological, ritual, scientific, and archaic expressions. Yet, while all the rhetorical devices present in the earlier cycle are still to be found, they are used far more sparingly and less obtrusively. The verse flows more smoothly; the language—given the poet's heightened style—is almost natural.

This is not, however, to say that the earlier cycle is a failure. The wealth and density of image and metaphor, linked and intertwined by all the devices of diction, syntax, and sound that the poet's rhetoric commands, frequently imbue these poems with the intricate brilliance and variegated color of a masterfully cut diamond. They have been compared in grandeur of design and complexity of detail to a Gothic cathedral.[7] For the reader who has become accustomed to the poet's world, close and repeated reading is rewarded by the delight of discovering ever new depths, shades, and layers of meaning. Vistas are opened which transcend the limits both of the senses and of logical thought, yet without ever leaving the realm of sight, sound, and intellect. Rather than transporting us into a mystical realm of pure intuition, the poet furnishes the intellect with a new capacity to interpret the evidence of the senses; to see into, beyond, and between the elements of our experience. Each element is revealed as that which it truly is: *both* a complex whole in itself *and* a part of a larger and still more complex structure in a hierarchy ultimately involving everything. To gain this perspective is strenuous; much like mountain climbing, it requires a certain cast of mind. But those willing to make the effort may succeed in gaining an apprehension of reality as an ever-changing network of infinitely intricate patterns, an apprehension truer to its actual nature than our mind and senses are normally capable of perceiving.

7. John Heath-Stubbs, "The Poetic Achievement of Charles Williams," *Poetry* (London) 4, no. 11 (1947): 44–45.

Continuity and Change in the Development of Charles Williams's Poetic Style

David Llewellyn Dodds

No critic of Charles Williams's poetry has failed to note the extraordinary change in his style between the appearance of *Three Plays* in 1931 and *Thomas Cranmer of Canterbury* in 1936. Some critics have written more perceptively about one aspect of this change than another. For example, John Heath-Stubbs notes that Williams's "early poetry follows a variety of styles. . . . There are verses Pre-Raphaelite, Chestertonian, Kiplingesque, Macaulay-ish. He had also a great facility—an all but fatal facility—for pastiche of earlier styles." It is, therefore, not simply a matter of change from one single style. Charles Moorman complements this by pointing out that it is not simply a change to a single "late style," either, for the two Arthurian volumes, *Taliessin through Logres* (1938) and *The Region of the Summer Stars* (1944), may "be viewed as structural entities, each having its own characteristic style."[1]

The changes have not, however, been given sufficient consideration in terms of continuity and development. The complex web of Williams's late style interweaves many early and enduring strands. And, with much of Williams's manuscript material now accessible, we are able to study this development, and its history, in a degree of detail never before possible.[2]

---

1. Heath-Stubbs, introduction to *CP*, v; Moorman, "The Structures of Charles Williams' Arthurian Poetry," *Studies in the Literary Imagination* 14, no. 2 (1982): 101. I am grateful to Dr. Moorman for giving me a corrected copy of this essay.

2. My thanks to Dr. and Mrs. R. J. N. Pellow for their kindness in letting me examine the Williams papers in their possession and for their great hospitality, and to Dr. Pellow especially for magnanimously on his own initiative searching the diaries of his father, J. D. C. Pellow, for references to Williams to aid my researches and for allowing me to quote from them. Dr. Pellow has kindly deposited photocopies of all of the relevant references he discovered, in the collections of the Bodleian Library (MS. Facs. c. 134), the Wade Center, the Charles Williams Society, and the Inklings Gesellschaft. I am pleased to thank Anne Ridler for her kindness in allowing me to see, and in permitting me here to quote from, Williams's letters to her and other papers relating to his Arthurian poetry. I am very grateful to the Estate of Charles

DEVELOPMENT OF WILLIAMS'S POETIC STYLE

Historical research suggests various other corrections as well.

For instance, Heath-Stubbs describes all of Williams's early styles as "really a little outdated at the time when he wrote," contrasting them with a later style that "is wholly his own," though "not a 'modern' style, in the sense of owing very much" to the work of "Eliot and others in the twenties and thirties." And Moorman calls Williams's early style "conventional and uninteresting in form and diction, though not in theme."[3] Both speak with the advantages—and dangers—of hindsight.

Did Williams's poetry seem outdated, unoriginal, or merely conventional, when he wrote as a contemporary of Chesterton and Kipling? The criticism of that period suggests it did not.

Theodore Maynard, in the introduction to *Our Best Poets: English and American,* ranked Williams third among "the twelve best contemporary English" poets—after Chesterton and Alice Meynell, and ahead of Yeats.[4] Maynard's chapter on Williams is a revised version of an essay published in 1919, in which he not only calls Williams "a major poet" but says "his poetry has a greatness to which few of the moderns have attained, and promises a greatness which none of the moderns can hope to surpass."[5]

Williams for kindly permitting me to quote from Charles Williams's unpublished writings; quotations from previously unpublished writings © The Estate of Charles Williams 1995: *All Rights Reserved*. It is my pleasure to thank the staff and especially Mrs. Marjorie Lamp Mead, of the Marion E. Wade Center, Wheaton College, Wheaton, Illinois, for all their kind help with my researches and for their hospitality. It should be noted that the papers of Charles Williams, Margaret Douglas, and Raymond Hunt in the collection of the Wade Center have not been assigned catalog numbers and have not yet been fully or finally cataloged in every instance: consequently, in the notes in this essay, papers in the collection of the Wade Center are usually designated by the word *Wade* in parentheses, with or without further detail. I also acknowledge with gratitude the assistance of the staff of the Bodleian Library (and, in the case of note 6, the Taylorian Library), Oxford, and I especially thank Dr. Judith Priestman for giving me the Bodleian Library's permission to quote here from Williams manuscripts in its collection.

3. Heath-Stubbs, in *CP*, v–vi; Moorman, "Structures," 103.

4. (London: Brentano's, 1924), ix–x. In a letter to J. D. C. Pellow of 5 September [1924], Williams comments on Edward Shanks's review of the book in the September issue of *The London Mercury* (10: 545–47); Williams says, "I think he only means that in putting G. K. C., A. M., and Me above Yeats Maynard shows very little critical instinct. Prostrate before Her, kneeling before G. K., and with my foot on my own head—I tend to agree." (Here and elsewhere, I expand the + sign to "and.")

5. Maynard, "The Poetry of Charles Williams," *North American Review* 210 (1919): 402. In refusing to maintain his ranking of "best poets" too strenuously, Maynard notes "the strong originality and individuality of each" and says, "Nobody who had the least literary sense could possibly mistake the work of any one of these poets for the work of any other" (*Best Poets,* xi).

194   DAVID LLEWELLYN DODDS

If the degree of Maynard's praise for Williams's early poetry is unusual, the fact of it is not. Between 1912 and 1931 Williams published seven volumes of poetry and verse drama. They were reviewed—always favorably in the *Times Literary Supplement,* for example. Williams even enjoyed a degree of international recognition, including the award of a Diploma and Bronze Medal by the Olympic Games in 1924.[6] Major poets and critics acclaimed him. As late as 1935, Chesterton himself wrote to Williams expressing "the profound admiration" he had always had for Williams's "extremely individual poetry."[7]

By 1931, at age forty-four, Williams had enjoyed no insignificant poetic career—and success. He was recognized as a real and original poet, one with a definite, distinctive voice of his own, a modern poet, perhaps a major poet. And he had begun to realize an aspiration of long standing. Since at least 1912, he had wanted to write an Arthurian epic. Now, at last, he found himself able to begin, writing his Grail poem in the form of a cycle. He had published two installments of it in his last two books of poetry, *Heroes and Kings* (December 1930 or January 1931) and *Three Plays* (1931). They were well received. Kenneth Sisam called those in *Heroes and Kings* "a great achievement" and even predicted the kind of wider success Williams had not yet enjoyed: "You will have to go on with the Arthurian legend which will one day make a popular volume at 5/-." Lascelles Abercrombie also praised them, saying they made him "wish very vehemently to see" Williams's "transvaluation" of the Arthurian story completed, and in October of that year he helped the process along, by publishing two more component lyrics in the anthology *New English Poems.*[8]

---

6. Maynard's book first appeared in New York (1922). Williams was mentioned in P. Selver's review of "A Miscellany of Poetry 1920–22," ed. W. Kean Seymour, in *Das Literarische Echo* 25 (October 1922–October 1923), col. 734: Williams comments in a letter to J. D. C. Pellow of 7 September 1923, "But O my dear Pellow! . . . O admire me! I am indeed, indeed IT. . . . Isn't this glory?" (Ellipsis points following "Pellow!" are in the original.) J. D. C. Pellow notes in his diary entry of 21 August 1924 that Williams "has been awarded a Diploma and Bronze Medal by the Olympic Games but is uneasy as to what it means, how many others received awards, so is not boasting at present." Professor Lewis Chase included Williams in a course of lectures, "Contemporary Poets, Chiefly British," given at Duke University in 1931 (see the vault folder "Correspondence between C. W. and Professor Lewis Chase" in the Marion E. Wade Center).

7. Chesterton to CW, letter of 12 November 1935 (location of original unknown; transcription by Raymond Hunt in binder of "Miscellaneous Correspondence," Wade Center). At least one great critic who was acquainted with both preferred Williams's early poetry to his later: Dame Helen Gardner told me she thought his early poetry better, in good part on account of its being more memorable (cf. Maynard, "Poetry of CW," 402).

8. Sisam to CW, undated carbon copy of letter of late 1930 or early 1931; Abercrombie to CW, letter of 15 February 1931 (both in the Wade Center).

DEVELOPMENT OF WILLIAMS'S POETIC STYLE 195

Williams's poetic career would seem to be crowned by success as an Arthurian epic poet. But this very same Arthurian cycle is the focus of the radical change in his style. By the date of Chesterton's admiring comment, November 1935, this change was well under way.

The whole matter of Williams's change of style is mysterious. This is due, in part, to the paucity of evidence from the period 1931 to 1938. In particular, almost nothing has yet come to light to inform us about the period from October 1931, when *New English Poems* appeared, until late 1934, leaving this quite a dark age. Different versions of the Arthurian poems from this period testify that Williams revised them, but we do not know exactly when he did so. On 24 October 1929, Williams had told Thelma Shuttleworth that he had "been toying with the Arthurian legends in a dozen poems."[9] Writing to Humphrey Milford on 28 February 1930, he said he had "raised the number to nearly forty. I should think another twenty or thirty would see it through. And then for revision."[10] Though Williams began revision, he did not write another twenty or thirty poems in this style: forty-nine survive, three apparently fragmentary.

Some evidence suggests that the change was not thoroughly conscious or intentional from the start. A list of nineteen poems survives, headed "The poems of Taliessin." Williams gave it to Anne Ridler, who assigns it to late 1934. This list combines poems written by 1931 with others written after that time: in fact, it combines poems in what had become Williams's old style with poems in the new. Because of the forms of the titles used, it is not always possible to tell whether a poem is old or new, but four poems are certainly new: "The return of Taliessin," "The School of the Poets," "Taliessin's Meditation," and "The Last Voyage." "Taliessin's Meditation" is unfamiliar; Anne Ridler thinks it is what later became "The Coming of Galahad." The others seem clearly to name versions of poems published in *Taliessin through Logres:* "Taliessin's Return to Logres," "Taliessin in the School of the Poets," and "The Last Voyage." Drafts of the latter three also survive, independently. This list shows that *Taliessin through Logres* did not simply succeed an earlier abandoned cycle, but grew out of it.[11] By the time Williams prepared the list and consulted with his young friend and fellow poet Anne Ridler, he must have begun to suspect that his style had changed and had developed too much to allow any easy accommodation of old and new. She expressed her doubts about including some of the early poems listed, mentioning others for consideration instead.

9. Bodleian Library MS. Eng. lett. e. 136, f. 49.

10. Letter entitled "King Arthur" (Wade).

11. See Ridler, introduction to *Image,* lxiii.

However, a letter of 15 February 1935 to Anne Ridler suggests that Williams still, at that date, planned to combine old and new poems in the volume which he there, for the first time, entitles *Taliessin through Logres.* He quotes from a poem he began writing the night before—what would become "Percivale at Carbonek"—but says it occurred to him while meditating on "The Riding of Galahad"—presumably the poem published in *Heroes and Kings.* And he speaks of revising another early poem, "The Passing of Merlin," by removing its refrain.

Some time thereafter—when, exactly, is uncertain—Williams became convinced that the poems meant to fill out and finish his *The Advent of Galahad*[12] cycle had in fact quite outgrown it. For by the time *Taliessin through Logres* was finally published in 1938, it included only three poems corresponding to single earlier poems: "The Departure of Merlin," which has replaced "Taliessin's Song of the Passing of Merlin"; the "Prelude"; and "Taliessin at Lancelot's Mass." Of these, the last is closest to, and incorporates most from, its original, "Taliessin's Song of Lancelot's Mass"; even so, it is a very different poem, the product of a thorough remaking. Surviving drafts, and earlier versions published in *Christendom,*[13] show that careful revision emphasized characteristic features of the new style after the change itself had taken place.

What motivated this great change? Not simply a lack of success, in achieving a distinctive voice, getting things published, or gaining a real degree of critical recognition. Various likely factors may be suggested, though no conclusive account seems possible.

Anne Ridler writes with characteristic modesty of her role, saying, "I provided—within the limits of my capacity—a useful testing-ground for the new versions." But her willingness to combine, in detailed comments, interest and encouragement with the observations of a perceptive critic and practicing poet must have made a substantial contribution. She admits that, after reading the opening speeches Williams had drafted for *Cranmer,* she "had urged him to abandon the blank verse of *Three Plays* in favour of the new *Taliessin* rhythms." He did, with the result that his new style made its first public appearance in that play. Even here, however, and throughout her remarks, she suggests that her contribution took the form of supporting and

12. Williams gave the cycle this title retrospectively in 1940, but it is convenient to use it (see *AP,* 151–52).

13. Williams, "Taliessin through Logres," *Christendom* 8 (No. 29), March 1938, 19–30: the selection includes "Prelude," "Taliessin's Return to Logres," "The Calling of Arthur," "Taliessin's Vision of the Empire," and "The Crowning of Arthur." In each instance, the poem has been further revised for publication in book form.

DEVELOPMENT OF WILLIAMS'S POETIC STYLE 197

confirming something Williams had already initiated himself.[14]

We have noted John Heath-Stubbs's precise suggestion that Williams's later style "is not a 'modern' style, in the sense of owing *very much*" to the Modernism of Eliot and others (*CP,* v; emphasis added). But there may be a crucial debt, in helping to motivate the change. As suggested above, during Williams's early poetic career, 1912 to 1931, the range of what was considered "modern poetry" was much wider than literary Modernism. Nevertheless, some things seemed more "modern" than others. In *War in Heaven,* Kenneth Mornington, discussing poetry with the Duke, produces, as "something modern," sample lines that parody Modernism: "And that impotent contextual meaning stinks In all our manuscripts, of no matter what coloured inks." But he follows this with the remark "Better be modern than minor," to which the Duke replies, "I agree" (*WH,* 106). "So Williams himself came to think," Anne Ridler says, "and he began experimenting with new versions of some" of his Arthurian poems (*Image,* lx). This seems to receive confirmation from the words with which Williams begins a lecture on *Taliessin through Logres:* "If not the best, at least the most modern."[15] There is even the suggestion of a specific debt in a letter in which Williams quotes from and discusses a draft of what ultimately becomes "The Vision of the Empire": "Taliessin, rather like Mr. T. S. Eliot (not unintentionally), remarks that he is a 'being of Logres, in and out of the image.'"[16] Whatever his specific debts to Eliot or literary Modernism more generally, Williams may well have turned away from a style that seemed insufficiently

---

14. Ridler, in *Image,* lxi, lxiii.

15. Williams, undated lecture notes entitled "Taliessin" (Wade).

16. Williams to Anne Bradby [later, Mrs. Ridler], letter of 24 April 1935. C. S. Lewis apparently suggested to Williams that "Palomides before His Christening" sounded like Eliot (cf. Lewis, "Williams and the Arthuriad," in *Arthurian Torso,* ed. C. S. Lewis [London: Oxford University Press, 1948], 163), for in his written notes answering Lewis's questions and comments Williams says, "Only when T. S. E. talks like the New Test[ament]" (Charles Williams, "*Taliessin through Logres.* Notes for C. S. Lewis," p. 6). The full history of these notes is far from clear: on 25 January 1942, Margaret Douglas wrote to Raymond Hunt enclosing "the answers to a list of questions which C. S. Lewis asked Charles about the Taliessin book"; on 2 March 1942 Hunt, writing to Douglas, refers to "ANSWERS TO C. S. LEWIS--20 sheets, numbered," saying Williams had told him "all about this on Friday, 9th December '38. . . . He spoke of it as a thing done the other day" (Wade). Details given in their letters make clear that the twenty sheets correspond to the eight-page typescript "*Taliessin through Logres.* Notes for C. S. Lewis" which survives: it is not clear whether the twenty-sheet version survives, and no collation of the extant typescripts and carbons has been made: I quote from Anne Ridler's copy. We may note, in passing, how "The Star of Percivale" answers, playfully but seriously, the image of "the damp souls of housemaids / Sprouting despondently at area gates" from Eliot's "Morning at the Window," which Williams comments upon in *Poetry at Present* (Oxford: Clarendon Press, 1930), 167.

198   DAVID LLEWELLYN DODDS

"modern," and his growing dissatisfaction with his own poetry in this respect may be the chief explanation for his change of style.

Williams's sudden illness and close brush with death in the summer of 1933[17] may have made their own substantial contribution to the change, confronting him in his work as a poet with a new sense of urgency and seriousness at what was perhaps already, for other reasons, a crucial time.[18]

Another factor, one that has received much comment, is the influence of that poet long treated as a proleptic "modern," Gerard Manley Hopkins. Here we encounter a good example of the way in which, though we cannot certainly establish a cause, we seem able to observe the development itself and the contexts in which it occurs. Anne Ridler has called Hopkins's influence on Williams both "fruitful" and "elusive," saying, "I do not mean to suggest more than that Hopkins gave him a key to unlock resources which he already had." Charles Moorman has responded by suggesting "that all of the characteristics of Hopkins' verse appear in Williams'," while interestingly undertaking to show their substantial differences, not least, perhaps, how Williams adapted what he used to the service of different forms of poetry.[19]

Anne Ridler also notes the delay of Hopkins's influence. She reprints, and draws attention to, Williams's remarks on his enjoyment of Hopkins's poems in an early appearance, and she says that "there is a quotation from 'The Habit of Perfection' copied into the Commonplace Book, but they had no influence on his own writing at the time" (*Image,* lxi). Williams writes of the admiration he felt for Hopkins's poetry at "round about twenty," when he first met it (in volume 7 of the 1906–07 edition of Alfred Miles's *Poets and Poetry of the Nineteenth Century*). He also says that "one even wished one could write like it—in a general way. But one did not try to" (*Image,* 48–49). The quotation from "The Habit of Perfection" in the Arthurian Commonplace Book concludes a note about the effect of the Grail, at its appearance, on the "meats on the table." Williams quotes stanza 4—clearly from memory, since his four slight variants occur in no published text.[20] Thus, Williams admired the poetry of Hopkins and knew some by heart, quoting it from memory a decade after first encountering it. Yet he did not, until some twenty-seven years had passed since first reading it, try to write like it.

---

17. Alice Mary Hadfield, *Charles Williams: An Exploration of His Life and Work* (Oxford: Oxford University Press, 1983), 90.

18. Mrs. Thelma Shuttleworth and Mr. Richard Jeffery have each, independently, suggested this to me; while I have not encountered any evidence to substantiate it, I find it likely.

19. Ridler, in *Image,* lxi–lxii; Moorman, "Structures," 108–13.

20. Ridler, in *Image,* lxi; Williams, *Image,* 48–49; Williams, Arthurian Commonplace Book (Bodleian MS. Eng. e. 2012: described as *The Holy Grail,* from the inscription on the spine of the volume), 163: my critical edition of this book is forthcoming.

DEVELOPMENT OF WILLIAMS'S POETIC STYLE   199

Referring to Williams's preparation of the second edition of Hopkins's *Poems* in 1930, Anne Ridler says that "he had re-read Hopkins at the right moment" (*Image,* lxi). But here is a further, and apparently characteristic, instance of delayed effect. Williams's editorial work on Hopkins generally corresponded with the composition of *The Advent of Galahad.*[21] Yet the *Advent* poems show no evidence, before or after revision, of the influence of Hopkins. Williams's extraordinarily vigorous poetic activity and his thorough rereading of Hopkins coincided—with no immediate effect.

Within a few years, however, the effect came, as a component of Williams's new style. We cannot assign an exact date to some of the most striking early examples of Hopkins's influence, but one instance can be confidently dated relative to *Taliessin through Logres:* a pair of occasional, private sonnets that, dextrously transformed, become "Taliessin's Song of the Unicorn."[22] This provides an opportunity to study continuity and change in Williams's poetic practice. One continuing feature is the interrelation between private and public poetry. The apparently private and occasional may become public in one form or another. Williams's first major work, *The Silver Stair,* seems to be the first great example of this process, as well.[23] The unicorn sonnets also suggest that Williams's late style was not simply worked out in public Arthurian poetry. There is a vital interchange between private and public practice. But there also seems to be a new dimension to this, beginning around 1928 and continuing until Williams's death. During this period, Williams's poetry—private and public, non-Arthurian and Arthurian—often exhibits a common, developed vocabulary of images. And during this period Williams develops an Arthurian "Myth" that, with its common imagery, characters, and setting,

---

21. Williams says that he did the editing because Bridges was "preoccupied with *The Testament of Beauty*" (published 24 October 1929) and Bridges "had given general approval, and the text was with the Printer" when he died on 21 April 1930 (introduction [dated "*July* 1930"] to *Poems of Gerard Manley Hopkins* [London: Oxford University Press, May 1937, "Oxford Bookshelf" reprint of November 1930, ed. 2], [ix]). Williams wrote to Bridges on 11 January 1930 that as soon as the *Life* of Hopkins "is a little nearer publication, I shall put the Poems in hand" (Bodleian: Dep. Bridges 13, f. 92). *The Advent of Galahad* grew from "a dozen poems" in October 1929 to "nearly forty" by 28 February 1930 (see nn. 9 and 10 of this article).

22. I have worked from Margaret Douglas's typed transcription of these sonnets, in the Wade Center.

23. Williams's wife took it to be occasional private poetry—about her (see *Image,* xvii); so does Mrs. Hadfield (see *An Introduction to Charles Williams* [London: Robert Hale, 1959], 31–35; *Exploration,* 16–19); but note how Williams in his lecture "Me," referring to "the first love sonnet" of *The Silver Stair* (London: Herbert and Daniel, 1912), 11 (sonnet 9), speaks of "the young lover there (not I, I have always declared)" (TS., superscribed in an unidentified hand "Balham Institute June 1926" [Wade]).

200 DAVID LLEWELLYN DODDS

interrelates public and private poetry, correspondence, and other aspects of daily life.[24]

The integration of the unicorn sonnets into *Taliessin through Logres* shows distinctive features of Williams's late style. Sonnets become Song (*TTL,* 22–23) with the addition of a total of eight lines (lines 1–4, 18a, 19a, 20, 33b–34a, and 35). The debt to Hopkins that the sonnets reveal—most strikingly in the line "(O twy-fount, crystal within crimson, of the Word's side)"—is enhanced in revision. Here Williams alters "within" to "in," and he adds line 35: "horn-sharp, blood-deep, ocean and lightning wide." Verbal repetition is used in line 1 ("Shouldering shapes of the skies of Broceliande") to link "Taliessin's Song of the Unicorn" with "The Crowning of Arthur" by echoing line 41 of that poem ("Shouldering shapes through the skies rise and run" [*TTL,* 20]). This is further varied in lines 33b–34a, "the sound of enskied / shouldering shapes." This is also an example of repeated imagery: the unicorn is gathered into the pattern of "the beasts of Broceliande" imagery introduced in "The Crowning of Arthur." The use of repeated images to unify a long poetic work is characteristic of Williams. Once again, we can turn to *The Silver Stair* for good examples, in its use of chivalric imagery, of the Mass, and most notably of gold and silver. However, Williams's use of repeated words, phrases, and images in the late poetry exhibits a difference of degree—in thoroughness, clarity, and complexity—that yields an unprecedented poetic richness.

Williams's late style is also characterized by something more than patterns of imagery: his use of complex, comprehensive images. The "beasts of Broceliande" are in fact an example of this, as well. So are the references to "Caucasia" in lines added to the sonnets (2, 20). For "Caucasia" is a component of the image that, to use Williams's words, identifies "the Empire of Byzantium (in one significance) with the human organism" (*Image,* 181). And "the beasts of Broceliande" are linked, through heraldic beasts, with the knights of the Round Table, as part of a complex image. *Taliessin through Logres* may be sharply contrasted with *The Advent of Galahad* in this respect. In the earlier cycle, there are many references to Byzantium and the Emperor, and the integration of Arthurian "Logres" into the Empire and its subordination there are already accomplished. In "Taliessin's Letter to a Princess of Byzantium," her "body is made one with Arthur's hall" (*AP,* 184–90). Similarly, in the earliest of the *Advent* poems,

---

24. For published examples, see *Letters to Lalage: The Letters of Charles Williams to Lois Lang-Sims,* ed. with commentary by Lois Lang-Sims (Kent, Ohio: Kent State University Press, 1989), 53, 65; see also *AP,* 157–59, 267. In his "sketch of an *autobiography*" in a letter to Raymond Hunt of 1 March 1940 Williams says, "In those days there was no (as it were) Household . . . 'In those days'—meaning 1926–8 or so" (Wade).

DEVELOPMENT OF WILLIAMS'S POETIC STYLE

"Percivale's Song to Blanchefleur," he identifies parts of her body with people of Logres (*AP*, 205–8). Here are clear forerunners of the identification of the Empire with the human organism in the later poetry. But in neither case is the image taken up outside of the poem in which it occurs: neither is developed as a complex, integrating image in the cycle.

The unifying function of the character Taliessin is as much a part of *The Advent* as of *Taliessin through Logres*. And Williams's exposition, contemporary with the *Advent* poems, of what he had accomplished—or intended—in his retelling, reveals a further development. In his final summary, he says that "all this history Taliessin has seen (1) in the cycle of the Table; and (2) in the spiritual life of the Princess of Byzantium, who recurs constantly throughout as the image of all that a mistress is to her lover, and the Blessed Virgin is to the Church, and every elect soul is to the world" (*Image*, 178). Here is not only the unifying function of Taliessin as one who has seen all, but the idea of an image recurring constantly throughout the cycle, and one that further integrates by the implied correspondence between the events of her spiritual life and those of the main action, the history of the Table. The intention of a comprehensive unifying image is clearly stated here, but no such thing is realized in that part of the *Advent* cycle that was written. Nor was it realized until *The Advent* had given way to *Taliessin through Logres*—at least, not in poetry.

For here we encounter not only another sort of delayed effect, but an instance of a perhaps equally characteristic advancement by detour. It is presumably no coincidence that the two of Williams's novels that feature complex, comprehensive images, *The Place of the Lion* and *The Greater Trumps*, were written in 1931 and 1932:[25] that is, between the writing of the bulk of *The Advent* (by 28 February 1930) and its eclipse by the new poetry. One of the most significant differences between Williams's later and earlier Arthurian poetry thus follows a detour into prose, where Williams worked out the use of a unifying, integrating, comprehensive image. There seems to be a delay of a couple of years before this bears fruit in the late poetry. But it does bear fruit.[26]

There also seem to be some particular fruits. The complex image involving "the beasts of Broceliande" surely reflects the master image of *The Place of the Lion*. And, to return to our starting point, Williams intends, by his additions to the sonnets, to gather the unicorn into the comprehensive

---

25. See Stephen Medcalf's discussion of these novels above, pp. 33–39.

26. A similar detour and delay preceded Williams's at last finding himself able to begin his Grail epic: J. D. C. Pellow's diary entry for 5 January 1926 notes that Williams "is writing another novel—about the Holy Graal and Black Magic and an Archdeacon"—later published as *War in Heaven*.

202 DAVID LLEWELLYN DODDS

"beasts of Broceliande" image, even as the unicorn is integrated into the complex image of the Angelicals in the novel (chaps. 10, 12).[27]

To study another of the outstanding characteristics of Williams's late style conveniently, we must turn to different examples. A good description of this feature is that given by Brian Horne with references to an example in Williams's prose. Discussing *Descent into Hell,* he says of the end of chapter 3 that Williams gives "the scene a sudden surrealistic twist" by describing Wentworth going "out of the room, down the soft swift stairs of his mind" (*DH,* 66).[28] Once again, we are encountering a feature of long standing in Williams's poetry which is present in a heightened degree in his late style. *The Silver Stair* provides an excellent early example. Sonnet 13 is headed "He appoints Time and Place for Meeting with his Lady." It begins, "The threshold of my house thou shalt not cross," and lines 7 to 14 read

> And come not even when with three or four
> I pace the gardens or by wall or fosse
> Look in upon the town. But rather thou
>   Turn as I turn at sunset and pass through
> Thy inner chambers toward those balconies
>   Of prayer that God hath built for us. Things due
> Shall there be paid and rendered, time allow
> Content beyond all labour and all ease.[29]

From the title through line 11, there is no suggestion that we are concerned with anything but movement and meeting in the external world. Nothing has prepared us for the "sudden surrealistic twist" of "those balconies / Of prayer." But the effect is inherently startling, even when it is not sprung upon us in this way. "Palomides before His Christening" provides a similar "surrealistic twist" when Palomides seems to be climbing a trail in the external world, actually passed by Dinadan, and then, suddenly, is apparently climbing up a body (*TTL,* 65).

---

27. Note *The Chaste Wanton* where "this phoenix, this / vigilant unicorn of the wilderness / ramping by a Red Sea of blood" and "complex heraldic splendour of mankind" appear together (*Three Plays* [London: Oxford University Press, 1931], 84), and "Taliessin's Song of the King's Crowning" (*Three Plays,* 135–37; reprinted in *AP,* 177–78). Interestingly, in one of the undated fragments about "the golden creatures" of Carbonek and Merlin's "emblazonment of Logres" the speaker, presumably Taliessin, says "But me no arms he found; I, I alone, / ride dully" an exile alike in Camelot and Carbonek (Williams holograph [Wade]). See also *AP,* 9–11, on the symbolic relations between the Round Table, Arthur, Pelles, and Carbonek/Broceliande.

28. Horne, "The Systematic Theology of Charles Williams," Ph.D. diss., University of London, 1970, 159: my thanks to Dr. Horne for lending me a copy of his thesis.

29. *The Silver Stair,* 15. For another early example, see my "*The Chapel of the Thorn:* An Unknown Dramatic Poem by Charles Williams," *Inklings-Jahrbuch* 5 (1987): 146.

DEVELOPMENT OF WILLIAMS'S POETIC STYLE 203

C. S. Lewis seems to be attending to the same feature when he discusses what he sees as Williams's "characteristic use of the senses," a use "difficult to define." He takes one example from "The Sister of Percivale," in which a slave is reaching for a bucket of water drawn for a well when

> A trumpet's sound from the gate leapt level with the arm,
> round with breath as that with flesh. . . .

(TTL, 52)

In describing this use, Lewis says, "We have the impression that we have seen a picture, though on analysis it turns out that the thing is not really picturable. . . . The esemplastic power fuses together images from different senses."[30]

The four examples bring together different particulars. In the last, "images from different senses": visible (perhaps even tangible) qualities are attributed to a sound.[31] In "Palomides before His Christening," one vivid, physical thing with another, body with mountain. In the first two, something external and spatial with something internal, or spiritual—something intangible or abstract, though very real. But all seem different examples of the same kind of effect, the "sudden surrealistic twist."

The effect is, in its different forms, a common feature of Williams's late style, often combined with the other characteristics we have noted. Indeed, the image identifying the Empire with the human organism is an example of it. Interestingly, while it is a characteristic of his early poetry as well, it is not very common in *The Advent of Galahad.* Bors's visionary experience in "Bors' Song of Galahad" (*AP,* 214–17) is a sustained example of the "sudden surrealistic twist" but is an unusual occurrence as well. The feature returns in a novel degree of force, after a hiatus, in *Taliessin through Logres.*

We are so fortunate as to be able to watch Williams deliberately heightening the effect in one instance, through possessing two partial drafts of "Percivale at Carbonek." An undated holograph[32] includes:

> At the threshold of Carbonek the High Prince doubted.
> Was eternity worthy the doubled anguish of time?

In Williams's letter of 15 February 1935 to Anne Ridler, the corresponding lines read:

---

30. Lewis, *Arthurian Torso,* 197.

31. For an early example of this type, see Joachim's "vision of sound" in *The Chapel of the Thorn,* quoted in Dodds, "*Chapel,*" 148.

32. In the vault folder "Charles Williams: Poems (Unpublished)" (Wade).

On the threshold of Carbonek the High Prince doubted,
his fibre torn by the infelicities of time[.]

Williams comments that "even Galahad doubts if even eternity is quite worth it." But the presumably earlier version of the line, which says this almost as prosaically, has been vividly revised. In "Percivale at Carbonek" as published (*TTL*, 81–83) the process has been taken further still (stanza 3):

Doubtfully stood the celestial myrmidons, scions
of unremitted beauty; bright feet paused.
Aching with the fibrous infelicity of time,
pierced his implacability, Galahad kneeled.

This final form shows evidence of other revision as well as the "sudden surrealistic twist" of "the fibrous infelicity of time." For in the letter Williams quotes a stanza:

Angelic were they or faery; all myrmidons
of unremitted beauty; astonished they stood.
The High Prince fell on his knees in the gate of Carbonek,
pierced the implacability, crying *Lancelot, forgive me.*

Such comparisons enable us to see Williams refining his style in various particulars. Though we cannot say certainly, since the letter includes only selections, Williams seems to have expanded one stanza to two. The swift and obvious drama of Galahad falling on his knees, crying out, has been replaced (and, to a certain extent, transferred to the passionate Lancelot). Stanza 2 reads:

Joy remembered joylessness; joy kneeled
under the arch where Lancelot ran in frenzy.
The astonished angels of the spirit heard him moan:
Pardon, lord; pardon and bless me, father.

In the letter, Williams speaks of "the Joyous Prince" and of "Joy having to be forgiven for the necessity of its own birth." The final version multiplies the surrealistic twists by moving from Galahad and Lancelot in stanza 1 to the abstract or impersonal "joy" and "joylessness" in stanza 2, but with "joy" very humanly remembering and kneeling. Stanzas 2 and 3 mirror each other: "joy kneeled. . . . The astonished angels . . . heard": "Doubtfully stood the celestial myrmidons. . . . Galahad kneeled."

The "Angelic" and "astonished" of the draft have been transferred and altered. "Astonished they stood" seems the sort of half-line one would expect in the late poetry,[33] yet its removal is clearly an improvement. Not only is

33. Compare, for example, "Bold stood Arthur; the snow beat; Merlin spoke" ("The Calling of Arthur," *TTL*, 14).

DEVELOPMENT OF WILLIAMS'S POETIC STYLE

the vivid detail of "bright feet" introduced, but the section is ambiguously elaborated. Does the second of the mirroring stanzas simply repeat the first, from a different angle, or is there a development? "Galahad kneeled" could describe the same act of going down onto his knees as "joy kneeled" does, or it could mean "Galahad continued to kneel." In either case, developing the sequence "heard," "stood," "paused" increases the effectiveness of the description, as does the progression of stanzas 2 and 3 culminating in "Galahad kneeled." Similarly, replacing both "crying" with "moan" and the simplicity of "Lancelot, forgive me" with "Pardon, lord; pardon and bless me, father" gives a far more vivid and convincing impression of Galahad's grief.

We have seen how features characteristic of Williams's early poetry are continued and given further development in his late poetry. One of the things that most distinguish this later poetry from what precedes it is the extent to which the different parts of it are integrated by the proliferation of the surrealistic twist, by the repetition of words and images, and by the use of patterns of images and great complex unifying images. Now we may consider how the poetry is interwoven and enriched in this way, by tracing, at some length, one sequence of images in which verbal repetition plays an important part. Its imagery also involves it with the Empire–human organism image, though it is not a part of that complex image. And it begins with another example of the surrealistic twist being heightened by revision. It is also a sequence that is, in various ways, related to the central imagery of Williams's Arthurian cycle, that of the Holy Grail.

Drafts survive of what eventually became "Taliessin's Return to Logres." In one, as revised, occur the lines:

> the young god Nimue's arm
> waved, naked and bright,
> through Merlin's distances
> shaken and assuaged
> I saw the Emperor's star
> flash seven times down the arm
> of a Druid maid.

(One revision worth noting here is the alteration of "the sevenfold star" to "the Emperor's star.") At the bottom of the page, however, with an apparent indication to insert them after "waved, naked and bright," occur the following lines:

> By whose wizard art
> I saw the seven stars
> shoot down a naked arm
> to a naked heart.[34]

---

34. Williams, holograph on the back of a carbon copy of "Percivale's Last Song" with his

206   DAVID LLEWELLYN DODDS

In another draft, these lines are deleted:

> Down the naked arm
> into a naked breast,
> fell the sevenfold star[.]

But further down the page, these lines occur:

> the sevenfold stars fell fast
> down a naked arm
> into a naked breast—
> the stars that the Emperor cast.[35]

(In the second of the deleted lines, "heart" has been altered to "breast.") As published in *Christendom,* the corresponding lines of "Taliessin's Return to Logres" read:

> The sevenfold stars fell fast
> caught by the outstretched hand
> of the Logrian horizon's arm—
> the stars the Emperor cast.

There is, interestingly, some resemblance here to lines from the *Advent* "Prelude" (*AP,* 165–66), "so have I caught in a dying tale / a word and a word of the great Sangrail." Lines 45 to 48 of "Taliessin's Return to Logres" as revised for the book publication (*TTL,* 4) make this resemblance all the more interesting:

> Beyond the farms and the fallows
> the sickle of a golden arm
> that gathered fate in the forest
> in a stretched palm caught the hallows.

What is seen in each version is a wonder. If the imagery of the drafts had remained, it would be part of a different sequence of arm and hand imagery in the late poetry, of which other notable examples occur in "The Coming of Palomides" (section 6: *TTL,* 36–37), "Lamorack and the Queen Morgause of Orkney" (st. 3: *TTL,* 38), and "Taliessin in the Rose-Garden." But instead, in the *Christendom* version, the middle two lines of the last draft quoted have been replaced by lines introducing a mysterious geographical-

---

MS. alterations (Wade); note that Anne Ridler identifies "Taliessin's Return" as the first of the new poems she "can date definitely" and says it was begun in September 1934 (*Image,* lxiii).

35. Williams, holograph on the back of a carbon of "Taliessin's Song of the Passing of Merlin" with Williams's MS. alterations (Wade).

DEVELOPMENT OF WILLIAMS'S POETIC STYLE 207

anatomical element: what does the catching is the "hand / of the Logrian horizon's arm." Here is a stranger and more wonderful image than that which it replaces, but also a rather awkward-sounding second line. Williams was clearly willing to submit this version for publication, yet just as clearly he continued to work on the poem—and produced something far better. "The sickle of a golden arm" not only sounds better but is also a more mysterious image. It sounds as if something is both a sickle and an arm. The "either the golden sickle / flashed, or a signalling hand" of the preceding stanza seem no longer alternative possibilities but something that is both. The sickle flashing in a Druid wood (lines 15–16: *TTL*, 3) suggests the cutting of the sacred mistletoe. But here, "the sickle of a golden arm" gathers "fate" and seems both to cut and to catch. Revision has created a wonderfully strange image—all the more so for the consideration that "The Sickle" is the name of a constellation in Leo.[36] Revision has also introduced "fate" and "the hallows." "The hallows" do not necessarily exclude the "seven golden stars" (line 12: *TTL*, 3), but they replace the "sevenfold stars . . . the stars the Emperor cast" with something ambiguous and far richer. For the expression "the hallows" inescapably suggests, without specifying, that this is the first appearance of the Grail in the cycle. Where the poet-speaker of the *Advent* "Prelude" has "caught in a dying tale / a word and a word of the great Sangrail," here the mysterious "sickle of a golden arm" may have caught the thing itself.[37]

The replacement of "caught by the outstretched hand" with "in a stretched palm caught" is clearly another improvement. The syntax and assonance produce a tauter, more dramatic effect, as do the slight oddness and the ambiguity of "a stretched palm" in comparison to the more prosaic "the outstretched hand." However, either version would serve to initiate the sequence under consideration. In "Mount Badon" word and image are echoed when Taliessin is brought to see "the place for the law of grace to strike": "he stretched his hand; / he fetched the pen of his spear from its bearer" (*TTL*, 17). And Palomides, in "The Coming of Palomides," says, "I too from Portius Iccus forth / sailing came to the Logrian land: / there I saw an outstretched hand" (34). Lamorack, in "Lamorack and the Queen

---

36. J. R. R. Tolkien identifies The Sickle as "the Hobbits' name for the Plough or Great Bear" in *The Lord of the Rings*, rev. ed. (London: Unwin, 1966), 1:187—with what, if any, precedent outside his own *legendarium* I have yet to discover. If this constellation is indicated, still other names offer further potential enrichment of the poem: "Arthur's Plough," "Charles's Wain," "the Big Dipper."

37. Williams may be indebted to Tennyson's *Idyll* "The Holy Grail," where Bors sees the Grail "in colour like the fingers of a hand / Before a burning taper" glide across the "seven clear stars of Arthur's Table Round" (lines 657–95). Tennyson identifies the constellation as "The Great Bear" (*Poems*, ed. C. Ricks, 2d ed., 3 vols. [Harlow: Longman, 1987], 3:483–84).

Morgause of Orkney," in telling of her incestuous encounter with Arthur, says that "her arm was stretched to embrace / his own stretched arm" (40). In the mural of Solomon in "The Last Voyage,"

> Rigid his left arm stretched to the queen Balkis;
> where her mouth on his hand tasted effectual magic,
> intellectual art arm-fasted to the sensuous.
>
> (84)

In these examples, the word "stretched" or "outstretched" is repeated as part of the image, though the word evoking the image—"palm," "hand," "arm"—varies.

But the repetition of "stretched" is not a necessary feature. "Bors to Elayne: on the King's Coins" presents words of related meaning: "the small spread organisms of your hands; O Fair, / there are the altars of Christ the City extended" (*TTL*, 43) and "Christ the City spread in the extensor muscles of your thumbs" (45). In "The Star of Percivale," "The king's poet leaned, catching the outspread hands" (46). Similarly, the arm of the slave drawing water in "The Sister of Percivale" "reached for the gain" (52). In "The Coming of Galahad" Taliessin watches Guinevere's "hand / lying on her heart" while she looks at Galahad: "The bone of the fingers showed through the flesh; they were claws / wherewith the queen's grace gripped" (73–74); in "Taliessin in the School of the Poets," he tells how the dying "Virgil clutched at clumps of song" (30). In "The Son of Lancelot," the rhyme word from "Mount Badon" recurs, without "stretched": Merlin scries "with the hazel of ceremony, fetched to his hand" (54). Recalling this are these lines from "The Last Voyage," which occur in the context of those already quoted about Solomon and Balkis:

> in a laureate ceremony,
> Virgil to Taliessin stretched a shoot
> of hazel—the hexameter, the decasyllabic line—
> fetched from Homer beyond him. . . .
>
> (84)

In these last two examples, we see the pattern of imagery intertwining with another repeated image, that of the hazel. In his *Poetry Review* article about *Taliessin through Logres,* Williams notes having developed this image and, in fact, cites these as two examples of its use (*Image,* 182). This image, brought together with the stretched hand in such places, is also first introduced in "Taliessin's Return to Logres"—as a result of revision for book publication. The *Christendom* reading (st. 8)—"in a song struck hard to the singing"—is replaced by "into the camp by the hazels" (*TTL*, 5).

One of the most important effects of integrating different poems by such a sequence of repeated word and image is to provoke the mind to consider

DEVELOPMENT OF WILLIAMS'S POETIC STYLE

together the incidents and objects of perception so united. Are there significant interrelations beyond the verbal? In this respect, the comparatively restrained imagery of the stretched arm seems more successful in stimulating a fruitful play of the imagination than does the hazel. For the hazel is sometimes explicated within a poem in a way that seems imposed and external, as perhaps in "The Son of Lancelot": "the implacable hazel / (a scar on a slave, a verse in Virgil, the reach / of an arm to a sickle, love's means to love)" (*TTL*, 55).

The interrelations of the sequence are especially illuminated by "the hallows" that form part of the first appearance of the stretched-hand image. They suggest the traditional Hallows of Christ's Passion, and so preeminently the Grail, yet their reference does not specify, and is not limited to, these alone. "Hallows" are things—and not only things, but places and people as well—which are hallowed or holy, which are, to quote the "Prelude," "gates and containers, intermediations of light" (*TTL*, 1) or which are, to quote again "The Son of Lancelot," "love's means to love." "Hallows" are theophanic.

The relation to this is explicit in the examples from "Bors to Elayne: on the King's Coins": Elayne's hands are, or contain, "the altars of Christ" and indeed "Christ the City" spread in her thumbs (*TTL*, 43, 45). It is evident, too, in images of hands catching or receiving that are clearly related to this sequence. For example, "Bors to Elayne: The Fish of Broceliande" includes "shall I drop the fish in your hand?" and "Will you open your hand now to catch your own / *nova creatura*? . . . *accipe*, take the fish" (*TTL*, 24, 25).[38] And "The Son of Lancelot" has this description of the birth of Galahad, the Achiever of the Grail:

> The child slid into space, into Brisen's hands.
> Polished brown as hazel-nuts his eyes
> opened on his foster-mother; he smiled at space.
>
> (58)

Interestingly, the last line quoted is followed, in a draft, by "having (seemed it) the gain already of the Grail."[39]

No explicit reference to Christ, or any suggestion of the Eucharist or obvious allusion to the Grail, is associated with Iseult's "outstretched hand,"

---

38. Here, this sequence and the other sequence of hand and arm imagery noted earlier (e.g., in "The Coming of Palomides" and "Taliessin in the Rose-Garden") converge and illuminate each other most clearly.

39. Williams holograph, "The Son of Lancelot" (Bodleian: among the papers placed in the Library by Mrs. Hadfield in 1983). Note also that in "Percivale's Last Song" Galahad *becomes* the Grail (*AP*, 243–45).

210   DAVID LLEWELLYN DODDS

yet Palomides' vision of it is presented as theophanic. And this seems
further reinforced by a delicate link with Grail imagery, in itself quite subtly
and delicately presented, elsewhere. Palomides' description, "Her arm
exposed on the board, between / Mark and Tristram sat the queen" (*TTL,*
34), has verbal echoes of "The Crowning of Arthur" where "spirit, burning
to sweetness of body, / exposed in the midst of its bloom the young queen
Guinevere" (21). There, those lines are followed by

> Guinevere's chalice flew red on an argent field.

> So, in Lancelot's hand, she came through the glow,
> into the king's mind. . . .

Thus, Guinevere is heraldically associated with the Grail by means of
traditional color imagery.[40] She is a type of the Grail. So, by poetic association with her, is Iseult, whose theophanic character is in this way focused
and underscored. In consequence of these Grail associations, the improper
responses of Arthur and Palomides are further illuminated. Thus, Arthur's
response here to all that is presented to him, "his city," "the kingdom," and
Guinevere, prepares us for his later "dreaming of a red Grail in an ivory
Logres," of "the Grail cooped for gustation and God for his glory, / the
aesthetic climax of Logres" (55, 58). Our consideration of Arthur's and
Morgause's incest (40) is sharpened by its inclusion in this sequence. In
turn, a line in "The Star of Percivale," "the king in the elevation beheld and
loved himself crowned" (47), adds to this complex of references that
illuminate each other. In the same poem, "Lancelot's gaze at the Host found
only a ghost of the Queen"—which contrasts with his proper service in
bringing her "in [his] hand," in "The Crowning of Arthur" (21). Guinevere
herself is absent from "The Star of Percivale," but its relation to the
sequence enriches the picture of her response to the Grail Knight in "The
Coming of Galahad" (73–74). That relation may help to suggest that her
agony, though part of an improper response, yet bears promise of something
better. In "The Star of Percivale," Taliessin "catching the outspread hands"
of the maid, who, having received a theophany, has become herself
theophanic, comments upon and reinforces the correct response, from which
Arthur and Lancelot have departed: "*More than the voice is the vision, the
kingdom than the king*" (46). The way is pointed toward the proper
reversals, which come at last in "Taliessin at Lancelot's Mass," all the more
forcibly for the sequence and its connections with Grail and eucharistic
imagery: "the mystical milk rose in" Guinevere, "the mother of Logres'

---

40. And, in particular, by an allusion to Tennyson's *Idyll* "The Holy Grail," lines 115–23,
149–55 (ed. cit., 3:467–68).

DEVELOPMENT OF WILLIAMS'S POETIC STYLE

child," and Arthur "entered into salvation to serve the holy Thing" in the Mass whose celebrant is Lancelot (89). The Grail and eucharistic connections relate this sequence of imagery to the Empire-body image with its identification of hands and Rome, most notably in "The Vision of the Empire" (9).[41]

We could follow further the exploration of *operatio propria* (*TTL*, epigraph) and the theophanic that the sequence encourages, whether with respect to a slave reaching "for the gain" (52) of a bucket of water (an unexpected but true type of the Achievement of the Grail?) or to the poetry of Virgil and Taliessin. But enough has been said to demonstrate the fruitfulness of Williams's use of repeated words and images and interrelation of patterns of imagery in the late poetry. It would be foolish to suggest that this integration of the Arthurian poetry was all the effect of deliberate, conscious effort. On the other hand, the evidence of Williams's revisions suggests that much of it must have been.

All of the examples just given were drawn from *Taliessin through Logres.* But this sequence of imagery is continued in later poems published in periodicals, revised, and included in *The Region of the Summer Stars.* In "The Queen's Servant," first published in *Poetry London* in 1943, Taliessin "named a blessing from Merlin, / and she stretched her open hands to the air; there / they were full at once of roses" (*Region,* 40). And in "Taliessin in the Rose-Garden," first published in the January 1941 issue of *The Dublin Review,* Taliessin describes

> rays shaken out towards the queen's hand stretched
> to welcome the king's friend, or a slave's to trim
> the rose or pluck a nut from the uncut hazel,
> or the princess Dindrane's to the fair conclusion of prayer.

The text is that of *The Region* (26), where the revisions include the tightening of "when the queen's hand is stretched" and the addition of the last line quoted.

But at the beginning of this essay, it was suggested that Williams does not simply have a single "late style." And Charles Moorman was commended for suggesting that each of the two volumes, *Taliessin through Logres* and *The Region of the Summer Stars,* has "its own characteristic style."[42] We

---

41. See *AP,* 155–56, for the continuity and development of this image. Here also in "The Vision of the Empire" is a reference to other Hallows of the Passion, the "iron nails," which may, even more readily than the Grail, alert us to the possibility that implicit attention to suffering is a regular element of the sequence we have been considering—from the beginning, with the "stretched palm," among other things, recalling Christ's in the crucifixion.

42. Moorman, "Structures," 101.

212   DAVID LLEWELLYN DODDS

may conclude by giving some attention to the continuity and further development of Williams's style, once the great change had taken place.

Charles Moorman is surely right when he suggests that the outstanding formal differences between the two late volumes are part of a difference in style.[43] *Taliessin through Logres* is characterized by immense formal and metrical variety: for example, fourteen of the twenty-four poems are stanzaic, and half of these have regular schemes of end-rhymes (as do two other poems), yet with only one rhyme scheme repeated among all of them. By contrast, only one poem in *The Region of the Summer Stars* is stanzaic, and it has no rhyme scheme. Also, a greater proportion of the poems in *The Region* are long: five of the eight have between 99 and 200 lines, one has 331 lines, and another has 436; whereas in *Taliessin* sixteen have between 27 and 80 lines, seven have between 100 and 185, and only one is longer, with 257 lines. Hindsight reveals certain nonstanzaic, long, and narrative poems in *Taliessin*—"The Son of Lancelot," "The Coming of Galahad," and "The Last Voyage"—as vanguards of Williams's last style.

The direction of this development was quite deliberate. In his lecture on *Taliessin through Logres* Williams says, "I hope in another year I shall have lost taste for this first group, and only read them by accident."[44] More precise intentions become emphatically clear later. By the end of November 1941 we find Williams, having finished "The Departure of Blanchfleur,"[45] lamenting, "I shall never manage the longer *narrative* poems I want till I can get down to them steadily." And Margaret Douglas noted, as Williams prepared the poems for the volume which would eventually be called *The Region of the Summer Stars,* that "he wants to go on to longer ones." After having sent the book off to the publisher, Williams confirmed this, expressing his wish to "work on a new and longer Taliessin series." For, as he had written to his wife a few days earlier, he had a new-felt conviction: "One cannot know poetry by reading or writing lyrics."[46]

In his article on *Taliessin through Logres* published in the March-April 1941 issue of *The Poetry Review,* Williams discussed his use of interior rhymes, concluding, "I do not find I altogether wish to continue using them;

---

43. Moorman, "Structures," 99–100.

44. Williams, undated lecture notes entitled "Taliessin" (Wade).

45. Eventually published in *The Wind and the Rain* 1 (1942): 210–14, and in revised form as "The Departure of Dindrane" in *Region.*

46. Williams to Raymond Hunt, letter of 29 November 1941 (Wade); Douglas to Raymond Hunt, letter of 21 April 1943 (Wade); Williams to Anne Renwick [later, Mrs. Scott], letter of 19 May 1943 (Bodleian MS. Eng. lett. d. 452, f. 68v); Williams to Florence ["Michal"] Conway Williams, letter of 7 May 1943 (Wade).

DEVELOPMENT OF WILLIAMS'S POETIC STYLE 213

the verse of future poems may, I hope, be more sparing, and even here one poem, *The Son of Lancelot,* is very nearly free from them" (*Image,* 183). He chose the longest Arthurian poem he had yet published as pointing the way forward, but his future practice quite failed to fulfill the hope expressed here. Longer, nonstanzaic poems followed, but they were as profoundly marked by the use of interior rhymes as are the other seven nonstanzaic poems in *Taliessin through Logres.*[47] Interestingly, even such poems as had been published by early 1941—"Divites Dimisit" (December 1939) and "Taliessin in the Rose-Garden" (January 1941)—exhibit the characteristic high frequency of interior rhymes.

Williams groups together "certain stanzaic poems" with "other non-stanzaic poems" in his consideration of interior rhymes. But in *Taliessin through Logres,* fourteen of the twenty-four poems are visibly stanzaic, and two more are end-rhymed regularly. Of the fourteen, seven have regular end-rhyme schemes—with "Taliessin's Song of the Unicorn" notable as the only end-rhymed poem that also shows pronounced interior rhyme. Of the remaining seven, only three are marked by interior rhymes; of these, only "The Star of Percivale" corresponds to Williams's description, "the interior rhymes are exactly repeated in each stanza" (*Image,* 183).

Thus, although we might talk in detail about the various styles of Williams's later poetry, we might also plausibly distinguish two major styles and say that in Williams's late development, stanzaic end-rhymed poems give way to long, nonstanzaic interior-rhymed poems.

Though Williams had developed good means for integrating formally diverse poems, and so, more importantly, for accommodating additions to his Grail cycle, he might ultimately have found this change problematical to his intentions of completing that cycle. Here, we may note some comments which Williams made to his wife, in a letter of 23 August 1944, with respect to what proved his last completed work in verse, the play *The House of the Octopus.* When all allowances have been made for the differences between a play and a series of long, nondramatic poems, it seems quite appropriate to think that these remarks, revealing both Williams's aspirations and his awareness of the difficulties involved, apply to all of his last verse. Williams writes of the "need" he recognizes "for a style which is as much beyond my more recent style as that beyond my earlier. I can be content with nothing but a manner of writing which is almost the thing itself happening: purity, charity, pain, joy . . . there remains but the facts of existence . . . as I see them." In seeking such a style, he says, "I am at an

---

47. This applies not only to seven of the eight poems in *Region* but, for example, to the late fragmentary drafts "The Calling of Galahad," "The Daughter of King Brandegoris," "The Taking of Camelot," and the poem about the Throne and Councils of Arthur, included in *AP.*

214   DAVID LLEWELLYN DODDS

almost impossible thing."[48] But this is not the place for a detailed evaluation, comparative or otherwise, of these two late styles, or for a consideration of any of the possible difficulties which Williams's Arthurian poetry presents.[49] Instead, we may end with some slightly earlier remarks, Charles Williams's own evaluation of the late Arthurian poetry *in medias res,* from a 1943 letter to his wife:

> I worked at verse for a couple of hours last night—only to know it must all be done over again, and yet again. My last style is my best, no doubt, but is it the most deceitful! and (unless one is careful) the most monotonous. I grow more and more inclined to think that all lies (as you said) in the Holy Spirit—the roseal light in *Taliessin* and the soil of the rose-gardens. There are no poems in English, so far as I know, about the Trinity like these![50]

48. In "Letters from Charles Williams," with an introduction by Anne Ridler, *Charles Williams Society Newsletter,* no. 75 (Autumn 1994): 15. I am very grateful to Mr. Christopher W. Mitchell, the Director, and Mr. Adrian Esselström, of the Marion E. Wade Center, for the most kind labor of determining, from the context of letters preceding and following this in Williams's correspondence with his wife, that he is here referring specifically to *The House of the Octopus,* and for confirming that there are ellipsis points in the original of the passage quoted.

49. For suggestions of some difficulties, see *AP,* 10, 13, 156–61, and my "Magic in the Myths of J. R. R. Tolkien and Charles Williams," *Inklings-Jahrbuch* 10 (1992): 51–55.

50. Charles Williams to Florence ["Michal"] Conway Williams, letter of 30 March 1943 (Wade). We may note that a more thorough, less impressionistic account of the development of Williams's poetic style must be preceded by the extension to his earlier poetry of the kind of study conducted by Angelika Schneider in *A Mesh of Chords: Sprache und Stil in der Artusdichtung Charles Williams* (Ph.D. diss., University of Cologne, 1984); see also her substantial English digest, "A Mesh of Chords: Language and Style in the Arthurian Poems of Charles Williams," *Arthurian Literature* 5 (1985): 92–148, which, however, does not include the data presented in her Ph.D. dissertation. There have been critical comparisons of published *Advent* poems with *Taliessin* poems and of different published versions of late poems: Vernon L. Ingraham, "The Verse Drama of Charles Williams" (Ph.D. diss., University of Pennsylvania, 1965) provides the most notable examples of both.

PART IV

Drama

An Audience in Search of Charles Williams

George Ralph

Charles Williams's dramas in general presuppose a faith commitment on the part of the audience.[1] The plays tend to demand, moreover, considerable awareness of church teaching. More than his novels and poetry, Mary McDermott Shideler points out, Williams's "plays force the readers' attention upon Christian doctrine and tradition with an urgency that is matched only in certain of the essays."[2] A prime case in point is *Thomas Cranmer of Canterbury,* which presumes knowledge of the religious and political history of England and specifically of Canterbury as its ecclesiastical center, acquaintance with the Book of Common Prayer, and experience with the Anglican liturgy. As Alice Mary Hadfield suggests, "a member of the audience . . . must become a person living within the social and political framework of Cranmer's time."[3] E. Martin Browne claims that the play "sometimes takes too much knowledge in the audience for granted."[4] Kenneth Pickering reports audience confusion at the original production in 1936, summarizing press reviews in such terms as "a sense of bewilderment" and "demands on its audience to which few were equal."[5]

---

1. This feature of the dramatic works is one of many shared with Williams's medieval theatrical predecessors. While the assumption of identification with a particular faith may well be justified by the respective occasions for which the plays were originally commissioned, their publication and subsequent production at least opens the question of their effectiveness for a more general contemporary audience.

2. Shideler, *Charles Williams: A Critical Essay* (Grand Rapids, Mich.: Eerdmans, 1966), 40.

3. Hadfield, *Charles Williams: An Exploration of His Life and Work* (New York and Oxford: Oxford University Press, 1983), 137.

4. Browne, ed., *Four Modern Verse Plays* (Harmondsworth: Penguin, 1957), 12.

5. Pickering, *Drama in the Cathedral: The Canterbury Festival Plays 1928–1948* (Worthing: Churchman Publishing, 1985), 20. As a cast member of a production of *Cranmer* directed by E. Martin Browne at New York's Union Theological Seminary in 1960, the present author found the response of a relatively sophisticated audience a mixture of awed respect and puzzlement.

218   GEORGE RALPH

Pickering further observes that the Eucharistic question in the sixteenth century "is an extremely complex historical issue to convey in dramatic terms."[6] Nevertheless, more than a superficial understanding of the debate over the Eucharist is required to follow such lines (leaping suddenly out of the scene in which King Henry appoints Cranmer archbishop in order to facilitate his divorce) as the Skeleton's

> Has not much adoration quenched communion?
> Must not Christ intend to restore communion?[7]

This compression of theological argument into a few cryptic lines, with little context, extends to the treatment of historical incident throughout the play. Indeed, in order to keep the reader abreast of events, Williams has supplied marginal notations indicating year and circumstance. Since this device is of no aid to the audience member, in the original performance the information was conveyed by a child who turned the pages of a large book.[8]

Gerald Weales states: "Any definition of Williams's thought . . . is difficult because he seems always to be communicating intuitions rather than exhibiting dogma."[9] Further, according to Weales, Williams characteristically "illuminates [his] material by personal vision. It is impossible that that vision should be shared exactly by anyone else."[10] In any case, Williams demands an intellectual engagement in what is a bodily (i.e., theatrical) form. Charles Williams himself reports having responded with positive enthusiasm to the suggestion that Milton, in his masque *Comus,* "for the actual dance substituted a philosophical."[11] A certain theological sophistication is required frequently to follow the "action" not only in *Thomas Cranmer of Canterbury* but in the later dramas as well. Even in the one prose play, *Terror of Light,* for which Williams had been criticized for

---

6. Pickering, *Drama in the Cathedral,* 203

7. Williams, *Thomas Cranmer of Canterbury,* in *CP,* 9.

8. Agnes Sibley, *Charles Williams* (Boston: Twayne, 1982), 11; Pickering, *Drama in the Cathedral,* 207. An excellent analysis of the compressed structure of *Cranmer* in terms of its scriptural, prayer-book, and historical content—and of an audience's difficulty with all of this—is presented in Pickering's study.

9. Weales, *Religion in Modern English Drama* (Philadelphia: University of Pennsylvania Press, 1961), 142.

10. Weales, *Religion in Modern English Drama,* 147. On 142–43 Weales quotes T. S. Eliot as proposing that Williams wishes essentially to communicate a sense of his own experience.

11. *FS,* 25, n. 2. The footnote concludes: "The physical nature of the dance passes into the intellectual measure and there maintains itself in the sound of the verse." An interesting gloss on this statement of Williams is provided by Peter Walker in his essay "*Horae Canonicae:* Auden's Vision of a Rood—a Study in Coherence," in *Images of Belief in Literature,* ed. David Jasper (New York: St. Martin's, 1984), 73.

AN AUDIENCE IN SEARCH OF CHARLES WILLIAMS 219

making his biblical characters too earthy, the characters themselves engage in philosophical discourse. At the opening of the play, Thomas and Peter and John discuss different meanings in "waiting," followed by Mary's brief pronouncement on church order. A moment later, John and Saul, who turn out to have been long-time friends, enter into a disputation on the Law. Near the play's conclusion Mary gives utterance to a kind of theological-liturgical rumination on the work of the Spirit:

> It was that which lay first on the waters and moved, and there was light; and lay entwined in my body and moved, and there was my son; and lay about you, the Companions, and moved and there was the Church. Joyful and sorrowful and glorious are the children of His love. Light on the waters, light in the body, light in the Church.[12]

To cite but one further example of compressed theological doctrine, from one of the verse plays, Lorna in *The House of the Octopus* answers the question "what *is* sin?":

> What, unless one is careful, one forgets,
> because, if one does not forget it, it is unbearable.[13]

In considering Williams's intent in *Thomas Cranmer of Canterbury* "to make clear the relevance of his ideas to plain men," Hadfield stresses his belief in the simultaneity of time, and asks: "Could intellect, wisdom, feeling, also be the triangle poetry, theology, body?" (*Exploration,* 136). Possibly so, but it is rather heady stuff for an audience to absorb, even subliminally.

Williams's penchant for liturgical drama will, of course, increase its appeal for some and lessen it for others. *Cranmer* owes much of its structure to the Book of Common Prayer of the Anglican Church.[14] Many of the plays end with a chorus, or a character, or several characters, giving voice to a formal liturgical recitation or song.[15] Examples would include the hymn of salutation of *The Rite of the Passion,* the choral Gloria Patri of *Cranmer,* the litany of *Seed of Adam,* the dismissals of *The Death of Good Fortune* and *The House by the Stable,* the Te Deum of *Judgement at*

---

12. Williams, *Terror of Light,* in *CP,* 373. What Williams cut from the script after the play's initial performance suggests that he may have become aware of the difficulty of some of his images. See, e.g., 370 nn. 1, 2.

13. Williams, *Octopus,* in *CP,* 270. The remainder of Lorna's response is fairly lucid.

14. Pickering makes the point that the Singers, in their use of collects and offices, "invite the audience to worship and pray during the performance itself" (206).

15. Among modern religious dramatists, the French Catholic Paul Claudel made earlier use of this device. His *L'Annonce faite à Marie* concludes with a company of men and angels singing the Angelus. Claudel's play has been translated into English by Wallace Fowlie as *The Tidings Brought to Mary* (Chicago: Henry Regnery, 1960).

220   GEORGE RALPH

Chelmsford, the canticle of *Terror of Light,* and the benediction of *The House of the Octopus.*

In addition to the intellectual demands and the presupposition of faith allegiance, Williams's dramaturgical medievalism can be a stumbling block for some audiences. His inspirations, besides perhaps the early liturgical drama, were the mystery play dealing with biblical events and the somewhat later morality play. These two influences can be seen in an early nativity play, *Scene from a Mystery,* first published in 1919. The characters—all of whom enter at the outset—include Mary, Joseph, Gabriel, Satan, the shepherds, the kings, Herod, Caiaphas, and "our Lord Love." As in the mystery play, much of the address is formal and presentational, with characters generally moving forward to present their respective speeches. The three shepherds, like those of the Towneley *Second Shepherds' Play,* complain of socioeconomic conditions. Stage directions are minimal, and they tend to disappear altogether as the play progresses. There are no transitions between the "scenes" within the *Scene.* At the same time, as in the morality, all of the characters function as embodiments of principles; they are symbols.[16] The 1931 *The Rite of the Passion* demonstrates a similar admixture of mystery and morality elements. The characters enter in procession. Christ appears again as the character "Love." Characters make expository pronouncements concerning who they are and what they are about. As in *Scene from a Mystery,* persons are paired in a kind of symmetry of opposites. Stage directions are few, and essentially unnecessary. Speeches are didactic. There is intellectual progression, but no real dramatic action: in this sense the piece is static, an expository pageant. Although Williams will subsequently move away from certain features of his medieval models, notably in abandoning archaic diction and rhymed couplets, he will retain his interest in exploiting the possibilities of the mystery and morality genres.

The embodiment of ideas, of precepts, in theatrical form remains for Williams paramount. Of *Seed of Adam* Williams writes:

> This Nativity is not so much a presentation of the historic facts as of their spiritual value. The persons of the play, besides being dramatic characters, stand for some capacity or activity of man.[17]

William V. Spanos considers this play "more a dramatization of the concept

---

16. Williams, *Scene from a Mystery,* in *Charles Williams Society Newsletter,* no. 71 (1993): 10–22. Exemplifying how an idea could stay with Williams until it grew to full fruition, Satan at one point exclaims: "O Gabriel, what dost thou in man's house?" (12). This will become Man's house as the setting for the 1939 *The House by the Stable,* with the archangel Gabriel in residence, much to the annoyance of Hell.

17. Williams, program note to *Seed of Adam,* in *CP,* 173.

AN AUDIENCE IN SEARCH OF CHARLES WILLIAMS

of sacramentalism than it is a sacramental drama."[18] Of *Cranmer* he argues that the play's unity is conceptual rather than genuinely dramatic (120–21). Glen Cavaliero speaks of Williams's tendency, in *Seed of Adam,* "to make his idea bring forth the verse rather than to let the verse carry the idea."[19] Gerald Weales, it is worth noting, defends what many critics feel to be excessively cerebral in Williams's drama, on the grounds that "for him, ideas have emotional meaning; the mind and the heart, for Williams, are not . . . separate."[20] Nor, indeed, is it the case that Williams never succeeds in making ideational conflicts dramatic. In *Cranmer,* for instance, the Priest and the Preacher, who at the beginning of the play hurl imprecations at each other, are a clear and effective device. Their contrast with Thomas in his speech upon entering is nicely ironic, and efficient in revealing something of the archbishop's temperament.

As a result of the primacy for Williams of ideas, the plays tend to lack what could be considered Aristotelian structure or development. Cavaliero refers to *The Rite of the Passion* as a "non-musical oratorio," with the dramatic "action" achieved through what is said rather than what is done (40). The sense of a pageant (Williams subtitles the work "A Pageant Play") rather than a drama emerges again most clearly in *Judgement at Chelmsford*—albeit an intellectually sophisticated pageant of the truths, the possibilities, and the reaches of faith in history and in one's life. Moreover, some scenes of fairly sprightly dramatic interchange do occur, as in the girls' by-play and the attempt to perform Nicholas Udall's religious interlude in episode 4. Basically, however, Williams's theatrical experimentations remain within "the tradition of the morality play with its overt symbolism."[21] Because Williams is concerned with working a single theme, that of the nature of God, Sibley avers, "one cannot say that there is 'development' in the mature plays" (*CW,* 7).

A major problem for those accustomed to Aristotelian dramatic action, even when events may occur in historically chronological sequence, is the apparent non-passage of time. John Heath-Stubbs regards *Seed of Adam* as "the most original in technique of all his plays. In it, the ordinary categories of time and space are abolished, and the Nativity is depicted as an eternal,

---

18. Spanos, *The Christian Tradition in Modern British Verse Drama: The Poetics of Sacramental Time* (New Brunswick, N.J.: Rutgers University Press, 1967), 165.

19. Cavaliero, *Charles Williams: Poet of Theology* (Grand Rapids, Mich.: Eerdmans, 1983), 47.

20. Weales, *Religion in Modern English Drama,* 164. For the charge of cerebralism, see Spanos, *Christian Tradition,* 166.

21. Anne Ridler, introduction to *Image,* lvi.

222   GEORGE RALPH

symbolic event."[22] Cavaliero echoes this understanding of *Seed of Adam*: "The human setting for the Incarnation is . . . not so much the historical moment as the timeless need." But such collapsing of linear (and, as Lessing and others would argue, dramatic) time is not limited to this particular nativity play. Cavaliero sees it as characterizing *Cranmer*, in which Williams seeks to "make the past truly present. . . . Williams's solution is to abolish time, place, and external events." This is accomplished in part "through a stylized symbolism in the manner of Bertolt Brecht."[23] James G. Dixon notes that the large book of dates and incidents whose pages were turned by a child during the original production of *Cranmer* was "designed to provide the audience with a framework for weathering the episodic nature of the plot."[24] In "cinematic" fashion (Cavaliero, 41), Williams's scenes shift suddenly "between the extremes of seriousness and fun, repugnance and joy."[25] Ridler characterizes Williams's method as "dialectical" (vii)—again suggesting a similarity to the German dramatist Brecht. On the other hand, dialectic is a complex mode of linearity; and perhaps "perpetual paradox" would more aptly describe Williams's dramaturgic practice.

As one might expect—and as in medieval example—the drama of ideas produces characters who are frequently given to declamation. This propensity has already been cited with reference to the early *Scene from a Mystery* and the relatively early *The Rite of the Passion*. A few examples can serve to illustrate this continuing feature of Williams's dramatic work. In episode 2 of *Judgement at Chelmsford* the bloodthirsty (or fire-thirsty) Hopkins and Stearne give voice to their own unsavoriness, as in Stearne's

> he predestinated me to be a remarkable finder of witches. I am a man of no learning, it is true; I have not read many wise books; I do not know what they did in France and High Germany. I am a simple man, good John, but I hope I can recognise evil when other people commit it: the Lord bless us all! (*CP*, 86)

The means for this self-revelation, it is true, is somewhat more economical

---

22. Heath-Stubbs, *Charles Williams*, Writers and Their Work, no. 36 (London: Longmans, Green, 1955), 33.

23. Cavaliero, *Poet of Theology*, 46, 41. Sibley suggests one significant respect in which Williams shares Brecht's ideal of theater. "Religious plays, . . . to Williams's mind, should stir up discussion and argument by a thoughtful treatment of real issues" (*CW*, 7). She has reference to Williams's essay "Religious Drama," in which he speaks with approval of "a drama of ideas," "the speculative intellect," and the importance of "always asking questions" even and especially of doctrine (in *Image*, 55–59).

24. Dixon, "Charles Williams and *Thomas Cranmer* at Canterbury," in *Seven: An Anglo-American Literary Review* 5 (1984): 41. Dixon also calls attention to this device as "somewhat Brechtian."

25. Sibley makes this point with respect to *Grab and Grace* (*CW*, 33).

AN AUDIENCE IN SEARCH OF CHARLES WILLIAMS

than that which Shakespeare must employ in the lengthy aside, as when, in *Othello,* for example, Iago expresses his villainy. In episode 3 of *Chelmsford,* following a highly theatrical "whirling belligerent dance" (95, stage direction) symbolizing the controversy over the Tyndale Bible translation, the Abbot of Colchester and Rose Allen step forward in turn to unburden themselves in presentational, expositional fashion of their respective personal histories. In act 1 of *The House of the Octopus* several of his followers endeavor to convince the priest Anthony to flee for his life. Their dialogue soon becomes a longish expository debate. Finally even the Flame cries "O peace, peace!" (258–61).

Williams's characters are often given to speaking in concepts rather than conversation because, of course, many of the characters *are* to some extent concepts. Ridler maintains that, while Williams never abandons characters as symbols, he comes eventually to give them "local life."[26] Elsewhere she remarks that in *Seed of Adam* especially "he has succeeded in making his characters both archetypal and particular."[27] Cavaliero considers that in *Cranmer* "the characters are representative less of qualities or humours than of capacities and attitudes" (41). According to Heath-Stubbs, Williams departs from his morality play precursors in that his characters, "though personifications, are by no means abstractions."[28] It is arguable, though, that here Williams remains squarely *in* the morality tradition, on the grounds that "abstraction" is no more accurate a description of the medieval dramatic characters.[29] The most theatrically effective and engaging of Williams's incarnated concepts might best be described by the term William Arrowsmith applies to Euripides' view of the gods as the "personified necessities"

---

26. "He had begun with purely symbolic figures—an early unpublished masque, for instance, has the Fool, Chaos, Earth, and Love as characters—later, he attempted naturalistic characters, but they hardly exist as individual beings. As he continued to write, however, he became able to give his symbolic figures local life" (Ridler, in *Image,* lvi). Hadfield offers a useful analysis of the early masques in *Exploration,* 61–72.

27. Ridler, introduction to *Seed of Adam and Other Plays,* by Charles Williams (London: Oxford University Press, 1948), vii. Spanos suggests, with reference to *Chelmsford,* a relationship between archetypal/particular characters and Williams's treatment of time: "He presents the individual experience of the present in the context of historical events that are at the same time archetypal or paradigmatic, thus rendering the present and the past actions analogous and continuous" (*Christian Tradition,* 77).

28. Heath-Stubbs, introduction to *CP,* x.

29. On the point, see Arnold Williams, *The Drama of Medieval England* (East Lansing: Michigan State University Press, 1961), 145: he demonstrates that the characters of morality plays are not "personified abstractions," but rather figures "capable of generalized application."

GEORGE RALPH

of existence.[30] The problem remains, in any case, whether, as Pickering observes in regard to *Cranmer*, figures "representing forces" can serve effectually Williams's attempt to present "a study of the characters, of the way they act and react, misleading because the majority of them embody an idea and act as mouthpieces rather than developing individual characters."[31]

A sampling of characters as types might usefully begin with *The Rite of the Passion* (1929), in which Caiaphas and Pilate and Herod function as symbols of, respectively, "religion, and government, / and the wonder of a show"—or of the corruptions of Custom, Service, and Desire.[32] The three Kings of *Seed of Adam* (1936) represent the same principles as those of the early *Scene from a Mystery,* and the imagery employed in their respective speeches is similar. Melchior and Gaspar have in both pieces switched their traditional gifts, and roles, though in the later play Melchior seems somewhat more enamored of esoteric philosophy than of the arts. They are also rather more exotic, with Gaspar (King of Gold) introducing himself as Tsar of Caucasia and Melchior (King of Frankincense) as Sultan of Bagdad. Many members of a contemporary audience are likely to be put off by Williams's use of the convention of the third King as "a Negro" (*CP,* 150). This black King of Myrrh—not in this play identified as Balthasar, but referred to simply as The Third King—is connected with death; his "Negress" mother, Mother Myrrh, is Hell.[33]

Judgement at Chelmsford (1939) opens with a scene reminiscent of the "Parliament of Heaven" of a typical medieval morality such as *The Castle of Perseverance.* A kind of trial is to take place at the gates of Heaven to determine whether the See of Chelmsford merits a place alongside Canterbury, Rome, Constantinople, Antioch, and Jerusalem. The Accuser, as

---

30. Arrowsmith, introduction to *The Bacchae,* in David Grene and Richmond Lattimore, eds., *The Complete Greek Tragedies, Volume IV: Euripides* (Chicago: University of Chicago Press, 1958), 537. Browne refers to *Cranmer*'s Skeleton as "a symbol of the Necessary Love which compels the Christian" (*Four Modern Verse Plays,* 12). Dixon quotes Alice Mary Hadfield on the Skeleton as "Necessity" and further characterizes him as "a tireless Hound of Heaven" ("CW and *Cranmer,*" 43).

31. Pickering, *Drama in the Cathedral,* 207.

32. *Three Plays* (London: Oxford University Press, 1931), 156, 153–54. The Herald who proclaims the lesson which this drama is about to impart is again a direct borrowing from medieval models.

33. Sibley likens the Third King to the later dramatic personifications Skeleton, Accuser, and Flame as "a paradoxical figure; they are all figures of contradiction or pain and yet, at the same time, messengers of God." The King of Myrrh, then, is both "symbol of man's hopelessness" and "the way of Return to Paradise" (*CW,* 27–28). Hadfield makes a like comparison in describing the King as one of those characters "who in timelessness comment upon the play's action in time" (*Exploration,* 80–81).

AN AUDIENCE IN SEARCH OF CHARLES WILLIAMS

prosecuting attorney, like the figure Death of *Everyman* proclaims his role.

> I stand
> at the right hand of all men in their hour of death;
> but also they may see me at any hour. Their breath
> catches, their blood is cold, they remember their sins.
> They see what they have made of their lives.

(CP, 72)

Contemplation, who does not appear on stage, is referred to as a person (71, 74). The five elder Sees make their self-introductions, as does St. Cedd, who is to act more or less as counsel for the defense.

Sibley comments that the "light" in *Terror of Light* (1940), while not actually a character in the play, is akin to the Flame of *The House of the Octopus* in representing the Holy Spirit.[34] Other characters do serve symbolic functions, Saul, for instance, representing the law, and Simon gnosticism. At the conclusion of the play Mary identifies each of the three apostles—Peter, Thomas, and John—as the foundations of the church, each in his distinctive aspect as, respectively, the common man, the skeptical intellect, and saintly inspiration.

The initial tempters of the radio drama *The Three Temptations* (1942) are Herod, representing material wealth, Pilate, power and fame, and Caiaphas, comfortable and status-conferring religion. Following their worried discussion of the threat of John the Baptist's public teachings about a new kingdom, and John's baptizing of Jesus, The Evil One confronts Christ with the points of view expressed by the three leaders of state and church. The temptations are those of Matthew 4:3–10.[35] One of Williams's more engagingly dramatic scenes is that between Judas and the rulers Herod, Pilate, and Caiaphas. Here the characters exchange genuine dialogue, and sound like real down-to-earth individual human beings. Particularly fascinating is Herod, who has something like a double vision, of both heaven and hell, as he consciously and cynically chooses the latter. Interestingly, he alone does not join in the terror-stricken "What has happened?" of Caiaphas, Pilate, and Judas in response to Claudia's

> The sun is out; thick darkness is all about,
> in and beyond your souls.

(CP, 400)

---

34. Sibley, *CW,* 39–40.

35. An interesting comparison may be made to T. S. Eliot's use of the same passage in his 1935 Canterbury Festival play *Murder in the Cathedral.* In part 1 three of the four Tempters who appear to Thomas Becket present versions of the biblical tempter's enticements. In part 2 they return as accuser-knights, employing the same arguments in justification of their assassination of the archbishop.

226 GEORGE RALPH

At the same time, there is constant emphasis on Judas's morality-like identity as Everyman, in Sibley's words "a reflection of most people's timid conformity and silent betrayal of their own best insights."[36]

The speeches exchanged between the Marshal and the Prefect near the beginning of act 2 of *The House of the Octopus* (1945) seem particularly difficult to enliven theatrically. The images employed by the Marshal are indeed striking, but the lengthy scene is essentially static, serving the purpose of developing the symbolism of "the cephalopodic process" (*CP,* 278). The Octopus, P'o-l'u, does not—and no doubt, so abstract a symbol is it, cannot—appear as a character. But as a presence it broods over the drama as a kind of apotheosized narcissism. And several means are utilized to depict the effects of "the spiritual octopus clutching a man's soul" (307), as when at the start of act 3 the chorus surround Anthony and gradually enclose him in a suffocating embrace. Assanti, through the course of the play, becomes increasingly a human embodiment of cephalopodism.[37]

Certainly the most interesting and innovative of Williams's personified concepts or forces are the Skeleton of *Cranmer* and this figure's successors, the Accuser of *Chelmsford* and the Flame of *Octopus.*[38] Joan Beatrice Gloria Barratt perceives the Skeleton as corresponding to T. S. Eliot's Tempters in *Murder in the Cathedral,* as their "function of externalizing inner conflict for the benefit of the audience is taken over by the skeleton figure of the Figura Rerum, the shower-forth of things, who, being Archbishop Cranmer's alter ego, shows his 'incredulous Thomas' what he already knows, can foresee the grim consequences of present decisions, and puts the audience forcibly in mind of them while the causes are being enacted."[39] Pickering, however, finds that the Skeleton functions as a good deal more than Cranmer's alter ego. His analysis is instructive and, incidentally, indicative of the complexity which may befuddle an audience.

---

36. Sibley, *CW,* 35.

37. The character reminds one of Wentworth, in Williams's novel *Descent into Hell,* who gradually sinks into and indeed becomes the hell of his own choosing.

38. These personae may be prefigured in the Satan of *The Rite of the Passion.* Cf. Hadfield, *Exploration,* 80–83; Spanos, *Christian Tradition,* 79; Cavaliero, *Poet of Theology,* 41; Sibley, *CW,* 124, 147. Reference has previously been made (see n. 33) to the notion that the Third King in *Seed of Adam* functions also as such a "jawbone of the ass," "the Judas who betrays men to God," "Christ's back" (Skeleton's self-descriptions in *Cranmer,* in *CP,* 13, 35, 54). Shideler further declares the Virgin Mary of *The Death of Good Fortune* to be a "counterpart of the Flame" (*CW,* 34). A clear precursor to these personifications is the medieval figure of Death.

39. Barratt, "The Canterbury Festival Plays: Their Moral Choice and Its Consequences," *Canterbury Cathedral Chronicle,* no. 77 (April 1983): 16–17.

AN AUDIENCE IN SEARCH OF CHARLES WILLIAMS

> He is . . . a macabre dancer, a playful Vice who is also Death, Chorus to historical events and apparent foe who reveals himself as a friend to the protagonist. Finally he is an extension of Cranmer's own personality, the non-rational part of Cranmer's being which Cranmer rejects. The Skeleton is thus by nature indefinable. . . . It is . . . extremely important not to see the Skeleton as simply another character, either real, as in the case of the King, or representative, as with the Priest or the Preacher.

Spanos believes that the Skeleton's purpose is to lead Cranmer on a spiritual journey which "is roughly analogous to the archetypal 'progress' from the aesthetic to the moral and finally to the religious phase of the existential Christian described by Søren Kierkegaard."[40]

Spanos depicts *Chelmsford*'s Accuser as similarly both the enemy and the lover of the protagonist—in this case the See of Chelmsford.[41] *Octopus*'s Flame relates to the priest Anthony as does the Skeleton to the archbishop Cranmer, frequently turning to irony statements offered by the central as well as by other characters. In Spanos's terms, he accompanies, defines, and finally guides Anthony's Kierkegaardian movement through self-delusion, weakness, and error, to spiritual insight and courage. Like the Skeleton, and like their medieval predecessor Death in *The Castle of Perseverance*, the Flame turns at times to assail the audience with searching questions and dire warnings, such as:

Oho, my people,

can you bear us? can you hear us? can you see us? are
    your hearts pure
to endure everywhere the speech of heaven and us?
do you die daily and live daily in us?
are you consumed and consuming?—Or are you content
to get someone else to die instead of you?
Apostates!

(*CP*, 314–15)

An advantage in the appearance *on stage* of such supernatural characters is that they can, incarnated in flesh-and-bone actors, the more easily be accepted as "real." A danger in the device is that these characters become didactic and in a narrative role allow the playwright an easy way out of providing genuine dramatic action. Williams dances with the temptation, but on the whole manages to redeem his omniscient spokespersons from this theatrical vice. But in the speeches of these figures Williams's thought and language tend to be the most severely compacted, however ingenious and theatrically fascinating the figures otherwise may be.

---

40. Pickering, *Drama in the Cathedral*, 222; Spanos, *Christian Tradition*, 116.

41. Spanos, *Christian Tradition*, 78.

228   GEORGE RALPH

It is Williams's use of language, admittedly brilliant, which can cause a theatre audience its greatest difficulty. With their internal rhymings and cryptic puns and allusions, Williams's lines of dialogue may tax the actor as well as the audience. According to Spanos: "At their best, Williams's sentences are complicated, their rhythm unusual, his verse difficult to read; the demands that he makes on an actor are greater than those of any other modern writer of theatrical verse."[42] Robert Speaight, who played Cranmer in the 1936 Canterbury Cathedral production, says that "the shorthand of Williams's poetic style makes unfair demands upon [our attention]."[43] Ridler contends that Williams's verse is frequently unsuccessful in what T. S. Eliot termed the "auditory imagination," particularly when he employs technical or "textbook" words.[44]

E. Martin Browne once related an experience with directing a touring production of a comedy by Christopher Fry. Dreading nothing more than "dead spaces," every actor learns to hold dialogue when an audience begins to laugh, and to resume just before the laughter has fully subsided. This cast, however, soon discovered that Fry's wit required some moments for audience members to comprehend the joke before responding to it. According to Browne, it was only at the end of a year of performing the work that the actors could confidently suspend action and dialogue at the appropriate points and be assured that there *would* be a response from the audience.[45] This same challenge is presented by a typical Williams script—except that appreciative reflection is likelier than laughter to be the reaction, resulting unavoidably in that "dead space" in the action.

Pickering insists that Williams's verse "demands powers of immediate comprehension and retention that are beyond most audiences" and quotes Bonamy Dobrée's assertion that his verse "has to be pondered."[46] Commenting on *Seed of Adam*, Spanos points to elements in Williams's

---

42. Spanos, *Christian Tradition*, 163.

43. Speaight, *Christian Theatre* (New York: Hawthorn, 1960), 129. Speaight refers to Williams's dramatic method as "expressionist" (129), while Pickering calls it "impressionistic" (*Drama in the Cathedral*, 206)! Although Speaight raises questions regarding the audience's ability readily to penetrate the language of *Cranmer*, he apparently does not agree that the actor is so discommoded. Dixon quotes him as finding Williams's lines "easy to speak" ("CW and *Cranmer*," 45).

44. Ridler, in *Image*, lxix.

45. Browne, conversation with the author and other Union Theological Seminary students, 1959. Browne mentions, with specific reference to *Cranmer*, that Williams's "kaleidoscopic compression of history" is similar in technique to that of Fry's *Curtmantle* (E. Martin Browne and Henzie Browne, *Two in One* [Cambridge: Cambridge University Press, 1981], 102).

46. Pickering, *Drama in the Cathedral*, 212. The quotation of Dobrée is from "Poetic Drama in England Today," *Southern Review* 4 (1938): 595.

AN AUDIENCE IN SEARCH OF CHARLES WILLIAMS 229

dramaturgy which depend "not on dramatic inevitability but on intellectual analysis."[47] Shideler remarks regarding Williams's writing in general that "later passages illuminate and fulfil the earlier ones," and that "the best way to read anything that Williams wrote is first to skim it in order to see his whole pattern, and only then settle down to a careful reading."[48] Insofar as this may be said to apply to the dramas, it must be added that the proposed method is not an option for one attending a stage production.

It is not the case that Williams was incapable of providing dramatic lines which can be more immediately apprehended. A survey of his works reveals throughout both theatrically obfuscating and theatrically felicitous dialogue. In a piece as early as *The Rite of the Passion* the iambic pentameter is ragged, like Shakespeare's, making possible a somewhat more conversational tone. Both syntax and English expressions are archaic, suggesting the medieval roots of this drama, and the *abab* and couplet rhyme schemes are employed. But at times the lines can be read fairly naturally, when consistent end-stops do not occur. What creates variety is not the characters so much as the verse, with its changes in meter, as when the minstrel suddenly switches from pentameter with:

> Three kings rode in to Bethlehem
> from Zion hastily:
> when Joseph opened door to them
> they entered in all three.
>
> *(Three Plays,* 144)

Language and image communicate effectively in Mary's "wine" speech (147–48). The image is extended and expanded at the resolution of the play in Love's echoing of the "wine" theme (189).

Ridler points out that from *Cranmer* onwards Williams abandoned blank verse "in favor of the new *Taliessin [through Logres]* rhythms." Dixon compares the new verse form to that of Gerard Manley Hopkins: "As with Hopkins, one often gets a *sense* of Williams's lines before one comprehends them." One notes, of course, that Hopkins was not a dramatic poet. Cavaliero provides a concise and useful characterization of the versification in *Cranmer.*

> Instead of regular stresses and elaborate metaphors Williams writes a vigorous rhythmical verse which varies the beat of the decasyllabic line with one strung on five irregularly placed stresses inlaid with rhymes. In this play he attempts a

---

47. Spanos, *Christian Tradition,* 165. He makes the further point, in regard to *Cranmer,* that "the speeches of the various characters tend to be undifferentiated, each revealing the same verbal idiosyncrasies" (121–22).

48. Shideler, *CW,* 9.

GEORGE RALPH

marriage between poetic and colloquial idiom. His speed and concentration, however, are almost his undoing, for the language is too knotted and succinct; there are not enough concessions to the naturally sluggish ear.[49]

At the very beginning of the play, on Cranmer's entrance, a passage of theological sophistication and density is preceded by a Latin phrase (*CP*, 4–5). (Mary's first words in *The Death of Good Fortune* are in Latin [179], while the Angelic Chorus and the Archangel in *Seed of Adam* serve up a healthy dosage of Hebrew [158]!) Shortly after the Skeleton has made his appearance, he unburdens himself of a packed series of difficult images, complete with Williams's internal rhyming, as a commentary on human-kind's corrupt ways (11–12). He repeats this sort of attack a bit later, after Anne's death, with such lines as:

> With the grand hydroptic desire of humane learning,
> as says a priest of Paul's, bended and boned
> to my frame, a master of this same wisdom,
> and a greater than he, another John than Donne,
> felt Christ's feet spurning such learning.
>
> (17)

> Are words wiser than women or worship? safer,
> securer, purer? will you hierarchize the glancings
> of everywhere the translucent golden-tinctured wafer
> on men's eyes, the webbed light of the glory
> wherein is the angle of creation? along those lines,
> up and down my sides, communion and adoration
> flow and ebb and flow.
>
> (18)

And so through the death of Henry (25), the confrontation between the Lords and the Commons (30), to the "I am Christ's back" speech near the end of the drama (54). At the same time, with an economy and directness of phrase and a clarity of image and idea, Williams's telescopic language

---

49. Ridler, in *Image*, lxiii; Dixon, "CW and *Cranmer*," 40; Cavaliero, *Poet of Theology*, 41. Heath-Stubbs offers a similar, though briefer, description: "In *Cranmer* Williams breaks with blank-verse rhetoric, and develops his peculiar technique of the irregularly stressed line with occasional internal and end rhymes . . . apparently owing something to Hopkins" (*CP*, ix).

Regarding Williams's attempted colloquialism, Ridler claims: "It is true that his language never became a colloquial language: he used a poetic diction to the last, but it became un-mistakably his, and . . . it does give the necessary illusion of colloquial speech" (introduction to *Seed of Adam and Other Plays*, vi). It is significant that the lines Ridler chooses to cite ("Surely that is Gabriel, that old gossip of heaven?" and "The house is full of things, and none right") are from *The House by the Stable*, a play which, along with its sequel *Grab and Grace*, has here yet to be discussed.

AN AUDIENCE IN SEARCH OF CHARLES WILLIAMS 231

effectively dramatizes the death of Queen Anne (14). Again, the scene of Cranmer's recantation is handled deftly and without unnecessary opaqueness, as the Queen, the Bishop, Cranmer, and even the Skeleton speak in a relatively straightforward manner (50–53).

Seed of Adam, in the same year as Cranmer, continues (as do the subsequent dramas) the internal rhyming. Williams also here revives the "thy-thou" language, presumably to produce a more elevated—or liturgical—tone, as in certain of Mary's speeches (*CP,* 159–60) and in many of the choral recitations. Numerous lines tax the auditor's ability to absorb and sort out the imagery and allusions. Salient examples are Joseph's response to his betrothal to Mary (157) and his depiction of her as one "in love" (159–60), Mary's reply to the Third King's announcement that Mother Myrrh plans to eat her (168), and the Third King's peroration on the birth of Christ (170–71).

Mary opens *The Death of Good Fortune,* despite Heath-Stubbs's supposition that the play is intended "to accommodate . . . a popular audience,"[50] with a long speech evincing Williams's near-riot of elusive imagery and religious notions. Her function in the play, nevertheless, remains of interest. As something of an Accuser or Flame,[51] she positions herself more or less outside the action, to play the role of narrator and commentator. But then, as the play's denouement nears, Williams draws her into the action to converse directly with the other characters.

For the most part *Judgement at Chelmsford* affords language somewhat easier to assimilate than do many of the plays. Rhyme and metrical schemes are varied in a way which prevents the verse from becoming as tedious as otherwise it might. The use of prose, as for example shortly after the beginning of episode 1, enables the characters to exchange dialogue which is conversational and even individually differentiated. The humor in such a scene as this between the Priest and a bevy of his parishioners avoids farcical exaggeration and is believable. During the interchange even so abstract a character as the See of Antioch manages a "human" ironical aside (*CP,* 80). On the other hand, in the opening of the Prologue Chelmsford slides from a picturesque description of Essex into a kind of tumult of image and idea. The Accuser manages speeches both turgid and excessively condensed to rival those of *Cranmer*'s Skeleton, and St. Cedd answers him in kind (82–83). Even "regular" characters are at times given to hyperbolic dialogue, as with the man at the start of episode 3.

In *Terror of Light* Williams briefly abandons verse in favor of prose. But it is at times a rather stilted prose, as in Peter's

---

50. Heath-Stubbs, in *CP,* x.

51. See above, n. 38.

232 GEORGE RALPH

Since it is so, since he is lost, and since your son chose twelve, it seemed to us that perhaps there should be twelve. We cannot be the bodyguards of his person; we were useless when it came to the point, and now his person is gone; well, and one of the twelve is gone. But do you think it would be wise to make a substitute for Judas of one of our friends, to complete the twelve points? (*CP*, 330)

Or when Mary in mid-sentence suddenly utters a short formal paean:

I told you that you were very young in this new life. I have had thirty-three years of it [*breaking out*]—blessed for ever and ever and ever be He who made it. (331; bracketed direction in the original)

And there is like stiffness in the exchange between Saul and Magdalen. (The situation, and the discourse, are perhaps redeemed in the Virgin Mary's admonition: "Sir, you are talking about a great many irrelevant things" [333].) Again, Mary moves back and forth between a conversational mode and something like high chant in her predictions for Judas, the apostles, and herself (369–70). Williams makes interesting use, it may be noted in passing, of Peter's traditional reputation as a preacher in the disciple's homily delivered to Simon the Magus (354–55).

The prose opening of *The Three Temptations* achieves a genuinely conversational tone, but the play—predominantly in verse—includes such a sentence (to be delivered by an actor) as the Evil One's

> Your drink vinegar, your bed cruel wood,
> your fame a criminal's—an obscene lost thing;
> and if then you mean to take comfort in God—
> no, even there you shall grow lost and obscene,
> seen by yourself as the sin worse than any
> you shall seem to yourself to have done all I will
> and had, more than all men together, skill in iniquity.
>
> (CP, 390)

In the final drama, *The House of the Octopus,* the language is on the whole more readily graspable than is the case with the majority of the earlier works. The Flame, of course, as one of Williams's "personified necessities," is as usual exempt from the rule of linguistic (and hence histrionic) simplicity and clarity.

If the medieval mystery, miracle, and morality plays informed Williams in the construction of some of his most dramatically and theatrically difficult devices, the morality in particular also inspired him in discovering the means to surmount the hurdles otherwise confronting his audience. Spanos finds that *The Death of Good Fortune, The House by the Stable,* and *Grab and Grace,* all based on morality models, "represent a significant development of Williams' dramatic method. They reflect his effort to naturalize, to humanize his actions, and to transform the rhetoric of his previous dramatic

AN AUDIENCE IN SEARCH OF CHARLES WILLIAMS 233

verse into the poetry of the spoken word, the high into the low style."
Referring to the same three plays, along with *Seed of Adam*, Hadfield
comments: "When [Williams] used allegory, his principle was that the idea
must spring from the allegorized person, and not the person from the
allegorized idea." It could be argued surely that this characterization of
Williams's effective concretizing of the general or abstract applies most
particularly to *The House by the Stable* (1939) and its sequel *Grab and
Grace* (1941). Cavaliero regards the characters of these two dramas as
"appropriately realized as types and fully alive as individuals, so that the
plays' message is organically, not arbitrarily, presented." Spanos has it that
Stable and *Grace,* "squarely in the medieval dramatic tradition of figural or
sacramental realism," present characters which "are not . . . personifications
of abstract ideas; they are highly individualized without loss of their generic
attributes." And, Spanos continues, these characters speak a new kind of
theatrical dialogue. "It is obvious that Williams' dramatic verse has also
undergone a change in these plays, a simplification and humanization
analogous to that of the action."[52]

Appearing in the same year as *The House by the Stable, Judgement at
Chelmsford* might at first seem in its near-static, pageant-like nature something of a regression from earlier dramatic works, notably *Thomas Cranmer
of Canterbury* with the latter's greater particularity of character and concept.
In fact, however, in *Chelmsford* Williams is further exploring the possibilities of the conceits of the morality play as opposed to those of the masque.
The experimentation attains fruition in *The House by the Stable* and *Grab
and Grace.*

The passing reference by Satan in *Scene from a Mystery* to Gabriel's
presence in man's house is broadened in *Seed of Adam* whose "scene is
before the house of Adam" (150), and it is fully realized in *Stable,* which
takes place within Man's house as well as his stable. And, indeed, Gabriel
is resident in the house of Man, offering the guidance available essentially
through the Old Testament law. In *Seed of Adam,* according to Williams's
own designation in the subtitle a "nativity play" (and thus traditionally an
episode in the mysteries), the features are more those of a morality, with the
dramatis personae at least on their way to realization as individuated
characters. Yet in this regard *Stable* constitutes a marked advance. *Seed of
Adam*'s Adam, for instance, representing both the First Father and an
Everyman figure, must engage in some clumsy explanations of how the
other characters are his children, as well as appear on stage at one point as
a historic person, Caesar Augustus. This conceptual and theatrical awkward-

---

52. Spanos, *Christian Tradition,* 166; Hadfield, *Exploration,* 143; Cavaliero, *Poet of
Theology,* 49; Spanos, 171, 176.

ness is avoided in *Stable*'s and *Grace*'s more distinctly morality-play protagonist Man.

The device of the multiple setting, which originated in the Middle Ages, is called for in the production of *Stable*. Man's house and the stable are both represented on stage, enabling action to occur alternately or simultaneously in both locales. The figures, while personifications, are also distinct dramatic characters. Whereas Williams found character self-introductions necessary through *Seed of Adam* and beyond,[53] here a character's nature and purpose are revealed through interaction with others. Genuine conflict, rather than formal debate, is possible, as when Man demonstrates his foolish bravado in threatening Hell, or in the dice game the two of them play.

In contrast to the prolix and thickly-symboled opening monologue typical of Williams's other dramas, *Stable* begins with dialogue which is clear and concrete, conveying the requisite exposition in conversation. "You are Man, the lord of this great house Earth, / or (as its name is called in my country) Sin," simpers Pride. "Thus endures my love for my own Pride," says Man (*CP*, 197, 198). The names given to the characters permit further instances of trenchant plays on words. After Pride argues against providing shelter for the peasants Mary and Joseph, for example, Man explains to Gabriel "my Pride will not stomach it" (204). The language remains simple and direct, theatrically immediate. This realistic convention is broken only by Mary's recitation of the Magnificat. Pride interrupts that recitation at points with what is intended as an ironic reversal of the gospel passage, but in doing so she is forced to enter into the same formality of speech. The effect, while possibly arresting, seems strained. Mary once again waxes liturgical in diction in concluding the play with a couplet, part of which is identical to her opening statement in *The Death of Good Fortune*.[54]

The treatment of such concepts as "hell" and "soul" might seem simplistically conventional. But their very concretization, the former as a person and the latter as a jewel which has been allowed to tarnish, is what makes for ready communication of idea through theatrical performance. Throughout *The House by the Stable* Williams ingeniously weds theatrical convention to theological premise or scriptural event, as in the one case when Hell and Man (with some assistance from Gabriel) gamble for Man's soul, and in the other when Mary and Joseph arrive at the "inn" (Man's house) and are lodged in his stable. There is no need for explanatory narrative delivered from outside the action.

---

53. It might be noted, however, that in *Seed of Adam* Williams has somewhat alleviated the tedium of this device through his division of the chorus into two parts, creating upon a character's entrance the impression of dramatic progression. In *Stable* and *Grace* he finds no need at all for a chorus.

54. The clause is: "substance is love, love substance" (*CP*, 179 [*Death*], 215 [*Stable*]).

AN AUDIENCE IN SEARCH OF CHARLES WILLIAMS 235

The setting for *Grab and Grace* is identical to that for *The House by the Stable*, facilitating the performance of the two one-acts as companion pieces, though there is in the second play no clear need for the stable. But *Grace* also lacks *Stable*'s references to parts of the house and to its furnishings, and thus *Grace* would appear to take place outdoors on the grounds adjacent to Man's dwelling. It is the convention of the multiple set that the neutral stage area extending before the particular scenes or "mansions" becomes a part of that depicted locale through which an entrance has been made. It is possible that the stable can be found convenient for Pride and Hell in hiding from Faith and Gabriel, and later for the two villains to conceal Faith whom they have trussed in a sack.

Occasionally a less than universally accessible vocabulary marks the dialogue, as when Pride's consideration of how best to approach Man includes the lines

> I am sure that some antipodean rumour
> reached us of his altered humour; that he likes now
> prayer and servile monochromatic designs.
>
> (*Grab and Grace*, in *CP*, 220)

But by and large Williams's language here remains as theatrically viable as that of *Stable*. Often a word play may be missed by some (or even many) in the audience, but the naturalness of the dialogue obviates the need for the auditor to engage in the distracting exercise of trying to comprehend what is going on. The allusion is there, but it is not necessary to "get it" in order to continue to follow the play's action. Finally recognizing her, Man exclaims: "By my soul, it is Pride" (223). As she endeavors to bind Faith, Pride complains, "She is so supple" (233). A number of ironies are rendered in a delightfully direct manner.

> PRIDE: And tell me, dear Man, how you are faring in Religion.
> MAN: Well, I am trying to lead the Christian life.
>   It is not easy, is it, Gabriel?
> GABRIEL: Sir,
>   I do not think you have found it too difficult.
> PRIDE: To lead the Christian life is always difficult.
>   How we have to work! digging, building,
>   giving alms, prayer.
>
> (225)

Faith offers a thought-provoking definition of wrong-headed "public prayer":

>   I do not mean
> praying with others present, but rather that sedate
> praying to oneself, with oneself too as listener;

236 GEORGE RALPH

> a ubiquitous trinity of devotion the temple-Pharisee
> practised long and successfully.
>
> (228)

When Pride asks Hell for "a better belt," her receipt of Jezebel's colorful one represents her need to appear more attractive to counteract Faith's and Grace's bids for Man's attention (234). At the same time, this action is *dramatically* motivated, in that her original rude Pilgrim's cord has been used to bag Faith, and her cloak will no longer stay together.

Grab and Grace introduces some of Williams's most intriguing personified concepts. Pride, man's paramour of *Stable,* returns, accompanied again by her brother Hell, this time in her "Christian" guise of Self-Respect. Faith is an attractive young woman given to singing, Grace a mischievous boy given to whistling. Their theological relationship is defined by Gabriel: "This boy, whom we call Grace— / he is part of Faith's household, and she of Man's" (*CP,* 224). Gabriel is also, of course, of Man's household—that is, in his service, to provide strength and support. The point is not left only to Gabriel's remark, but is clarified further through the dramatic action. Grace (proceeding from heaven), who at one point trips Hell, when thrown into a lake cannot be drowned. Faith (the human response to grace), however, can be tied up in a sack for a time. Yet she is able, finally, to free herself, for as Grace comments: "Faith in a bag is Faith at her best!" Gabriel then sets the matter straight with "No; / even Faith must flag when she is stifled, / and Faith with vision is wiser than Faith without" (238).

In a discussion of modern morality plays, including these two by Williams, Marvin Halverson concludes that "one might properly assert that there are two types of moralities: a morality of works and a morality of grace. The one is medieval and Catholic. The other is contemporary and Protestant."[55] In *Stable* and *Grace* Williams manages successfully to rework the old morality genre into a refreshingly sprightly and "graceful" contemporary theatrical idiom. To be sure, his dramatic thought and method continue to reveal a specific theological framework. But an appreciation of these dramas does not require that an audience be well schooled in religious doctrine. And it is not at all remarkable that any serious dramatist should write from the perspective of his or her convictions. The medieval drama was preeminently a popular form of art and entertainment. In *The House by the Stable* and *Grab and Grace* Williams sets aside a number of his rhetorical idiosyncrasies to produce a theater which can speak to a relatively

---

55. Halverson, ed., *Religious Drama 3* (Cleveland and New York: World Publishing, 1959), 11. Halverson oversimplifies the matter, particularly in his characterization of the medieval "Catholic" version as concentrating exclusively on "works." The distinction is nonetheless quite useful.

broad audience. The question of course can still be asked as to whether it is possible to put new wine into old wineskins. Williams's willingness to take that risk has, in this instance, accomplished the end of enabling an audience to experience his unique and fascinating angle of vision. And produced some amusing as well as edifying drama.

Rhetorical Strategies
in Charles Williams's Prose Play

John D. Rateliff

Of all Charles Williams's serious work, none has been so neglected as has his drama. Williams himself regarded his plays very highly, as is shown by his fictional self-portrait in *Descent into Hell* as Peter Stanhope, that latter-day Shakespeare beloved by the London stage and intelligentsia alike.[1] But whereas Williams believed he would be remembered as a great poet and playwright,[2] critics interested in his work have focused primarily on his novels, his theology, and his influence on other writers.[3] This is a great pity, because Williams's plays are perhaps his most interesting work. Nowhere else are his ideas presented so clearly; nowhere else is Williams's iconoclastic imagination so vividly revealed.

---

1. Humphrey Carpenter describes Stanhope as "a character undoubtedly based on what Williams would have liked to be" and notes that the only significant difference between the author and his fictional persona is the fame and recognition Stanhope had received (*The Inklings* [Boston: Houghton Mifflin, 1979], 107). The degree to which Williams identified himself with Stanhope is shown by his adopting that name as a pseudonym for the next play he wrote after *Descent into Hell, Judgement at Chelmsford* (1939).

2. As early as the mid-1930s he had appointed an official biographer, Raymond Hunt, to whom he passed along any letters he received from notable literary figures like C. S. Lewis, W. H. Auden, G. K. Chesterton, et al., for eventual inclusion in the biography that, Williams believed, would establish him in his rightful place as one of the preeminent men of letters of the twentieth century. Williams's letters to Hunt are now held at the Wade Center at Wheaton College; I am grateful to Dr. Lyle Dorsett, former curator, for having granted me access to these papers for my research.

3. This imbalance would probably not have occurred had T. S. Eliot followed through on his promise to provide a study of Williams as a dramatist to *Essays Presented to Charles Williams,* the memorial festschrift that appeared two years after Williams's death. Unfortunately the essay, mentioned in several of C. S. Lewis's letters to Eliot now at the Wade, was never completed or published. Perhaps the intense dislike Lewis, the volume's editor, felt for Eliot and all his works played some part in its nonappearance. It is more likely, though, that the combination of overwork, poor health, and the string of bereavements that descended on Eliot from 1945 through 1947, chronicled in chapter 14 of Peter Ackroyd's *T. S. Eliot: A Life* (New York: Simon and Schuster, 1984), was the true culprit.

Because most of his plays were written with very specific audiences in mind, they afford especially favorable texts in which to examine his rhetoric. A particularly interesting case is *Terror of Light,* which was produced in 1940 but not published until after Williams's death. It may well be Williams's best play, the culmination of his stagecraft and the most comprehensive and satisfying presentation anywhere of his doctrines of Substitution and Coinherence. Certainly it deserves better than the critical neglect it has received. Contributing to this neglect has been a general failure to understand its rhetoric.

Williams's play is essentially what used to be called a Mystery play—that is, a dramatization of biblical events; in this case, scenes from the Acts of the Apostles. In the tradition of all such plays, from the Wakefield cycle to the Cornish *Ordinalia,* Williams has remained faithful to the biblical record but fleshed it out by adding elements and incidents of his own. In the process he has transformed a straightforward chronicle of what the Apostles said and did during the week of the first Christian Pentecost into a vehicle for his own ideas on the extent to which all Christians are involved in one another's salvation.

The great difficulty facing anyone who sits down to write a Mystery play is the same as that faced by playwrights in ancient Athens or authors of most "docudramas" today—the audience already knows the story, making it extraordinarily difficult to generate any sort of narrative suspense (or, indeed, audience interest) over the outcome. Although it is certainly possible for the playwright to alter the outcome—e.g., by having Barabbas crucified instead of Jesus, or by inventing a fictional detective who stops Lee Harvey Oswald seconds before JFK's motorcade passes by—the result is a work of fiction, of alternative history, and not at all a play of the sort we are considering here. The challenge in what Williams is undertaking is to restore a sense of the Apostles as people. It is in this sense that Williams is iconoclastic, turning the reverential and somewhat lifeless figures of Scripture lessons into believable characters, individuals in whom the reader or viewer can feel some sympathy and interest. As Dorothy L. Sayers said in the introduction to her own Mystery cycle, *The Man Born to Be King,* "we have fallen out of the habit of looking on Jesus and His disciples as . . . real people."[4] To "recover" a sense of these events as something that once really happened,[5]

---

4. Sayers, *The Man Born to Be King: A Play-Cycle on the Life of Our Lord and Saviour Jesus Christ* (New York: Harper & Brothers, 1943), 19.

5. It is relevant to note here remarks that Williams's friend J. R. R. Tolkien made in another context: "Recovery . . . is a re-gaining—regaining of a clear view. . . . We need . . . to clean our windows; so that the things seen clearly may be freed from the drab blur of . . . familiarity. . . . Of all faces those of our *familiares* are the ones . . . most difficult . . . to see

240   JOHN D. RATELIFF

Williams must first shatter the icons to shock us into rethinking the whole story. The most valuable rhetorical tool at his command for achieving this goal is also the most controversial aspect of this play: the use of colloquial language in the dialogue.

No feature of *Terror of Light* has been so universally condemned as has been its modern prose idiom, and no other element is so crucial to the play's success. It is the only one of all Williams's plays to be written in prose, not verse; the only one in which the characters speak in anything remotely resembling normal human speech. As far back as 1948 Anne Ridler asserted that Williams "was dissatisfied with *Terror of Light,* and intended some day to rewrite it in verse."[6] Even before the play had ever been published the pattern had been set and, thus encouraged, critics ever since have derided the play Williams actually wrote in favor of a hypothetical one which there is

---

with fresh attention" ("On Fairy-stories," in *Essays Presented to Charles Williams,* ed. C. S. Lewis [Oxford: Oxford University Press, 1947], 74). Not that Williams necessarily knew Tolkien's statement or consciously drew on Tolkien's ideas in writing his play, although he easily could have: "On Fairy-stories" was first written in March 1939 (Humphrey Carpenter, *Tolkien: A Biography* [Boston: Houghton Mifflin, 1977], 190–91), Tolkien and Williams met in September of that year, when the latter was transfered from London to Oxford for the duration of the war (Alice Mary Hadfield, *Charles Williams: An Exploration of His Life and Work* [New York and Oxford: Oxford University Press, 1983], 177), and *Terror of Light* was written for Pentecost the following year—i.e., May 1940 (Hadfield, *Charles Williams,* 191). Despite assertions to the contrary (Carpenter, *Inklings,* 120–21), all contemporary evidence supports the conclusion that Tolkien and Williams were friends. Not until long after Williams's death did Tolkien's attitude change: all of his harsh statements about Williams date from the 1960s. See my "'And Something Remains to Be Said': Tolkien and Williams," *Mythlore,* no. 45 (1986): 48–54.

6. Ridler, introduction to *Seed of Adam and Other Plays,* by Charles Williams (London: Oxford University Press, 1948), ix. So far as I know, no documentary evidence exists to support Ridler's statement—certainly none has been published, although Williams may have made the point to her in a still-unpublished letter. Significantly, Hadfield, in the section of her very carefully researched biography dealing with the composition of *Terror of Light,* makes no mention of any regret on Williams's part that he wrote the play in prose, nor of any desire to rewrite it in verse. Hadfield does, however, note that Florence Williams, attending the opening night performance of *Terror of Light,* "thought poorly of it and said so" (*Exploration,* 191). Williams thought very highly of his wife's judgment and is said to have abandoned his unfinished novel, *The Noises That Weren't There,* after she criticized that work (Carpenter, *Inklings,* 193). In the case of *Terror of Light,* Williams's reaction was to set to work at once to make a number of small changes—cutting a line here, adding one there (see note 11 of this article)—with the result that Florence was very pleased with this new version of the play (Hadfield, *Exploration,* 191). I suspect that Ridler's memory has played her false and that she has confused some comment Williams may have made at the time about the play's "needing revision" with the idea that it was the play's prose form that was at fault—an idea that cannot be traced to any published statement made by the play's author.

RHETORICAL STRATEGIES IN *TERROR OF LIGHT*   241

no sign he ever attempted. Sibley argues the play "must be looked on as a first draft, since he intended to rewrite it in verse." Cavaliero likewise stresses that the play "was to have been rewritten in verse" and thinks "it is a pity that it was not, for the prose is uncertain in tone, often lapsing into the stilted or the chatty." Heath-Stubbs reiterates the theory that "Williams intended its final drafting in verse" and believes that only the author's death "shortly" after the first performance prevented him from carrying out his intention.[7] Yet in point of fact just over five years intervened between the two events, during which time Williams wrote another three plays, a novel, a biography, the final volume of his Arthurian cycle, his book on Dante, and several theological works. In short, these were among the most productive years of his entire life, and if he had seriously felt the need to recast the play into verse he would no doubt have done so.

The simple truth is that Ridler's passing comment that Williams was "dissatisfied" with the play's prosiness has conditioned subsequent critical thinking to the point that no one has heretofore asked the obvious question: what function does the prose rhetoric have? Why did Williams depart from his usual practice in this, his fourteenth play? Every preceding play he had written had been in verse, as indeed were the three plays that followed, making *Terror of Light* a radical departure from his usual style, an experiment breaking wholly new ground. Nor does the "rough-draft" theory hold up when we realize that Williams thought highly enough of the play to have it staged.

It is important for us to remember that Williams was no closet dramatist: all but three of his plays were produced in his lifetime, an enviable record.[8] *Terror of Light* was, like most of his other dramatic works, commissioned for a specific occasion—in this case, by the Oxford Pilgrim Players, a group led by his friend and disciple Ruth Spalding, for their Whitsunday (Pentecost) production in May 1940.[9] If we assume Williams, an experienced dramatist familiar with the exigencies of the stage, had a purpose in writing this play as he did, in colloquial everyday speech, then it is difficult to avoid the conclusion that in breaking with his own tradition Williams knew exactly

---

7. Agnes Sibley, *Charles Williams* (Boston: Twayne, 1982), 37; Glen Cavaliero, *Charles Williams: Poet of Theology* (Grand Rapids, Mich.: Eerdmans, 1983), 50; John Heath-Stubbs, introduction to *CP*, xi; *CP*, 325n.

8. The exceptions were *The Masque of the Termination of Copyright, Judgement at Chelmsford*, and *Grab and Grace*. Of these, the latter two were commissioned but not performed because of difficulties arising out of the war (Hadfield, *Exploration*, 144, 202), while *The Masque* was written to close out the trilogy of roman à clef skits Williams came up with for his friends at Amen House.

9. Hadfield, *Exploration*, 191.

242 JOHN D. RATELIFF

what he was doing, and that the critics are faulting him for achieving precisely the effects he had in mind when he conceived of the play.

From this perspective, Heath-Stubbs's comments are particularly illuminating, since he sees clearly what Williams is doing but, starting from the a priori of Williams's supposed dissatisfaction with the results, is forced to interpret the play's greatest strength as a flaw:

> Reading [*Terror of Light*] as it stands, one realizes that the rather formal and mannered nature of [Williams's] verse-diction and metric had an important function. It distanced the dialogue of his plays, removing them, as it were, to a timeless dimension. The prose dialogue of his novels has often been rather sharply criticized for conveying a sentimental and even cozy quality—which is, one must add, in the sharpest possible contrast with the intense spiritual realism, as we may call it, of their themes. The same paradox confronts us in *Terror of Light* as it here stands. (*CP,* xi–xii)

Juxtaposed with Heath-Stubbs's perceptive observation on the way Williams used verse as a distancing device, Sayers's workmanlike comment that "technically, the swiftest way to produce the desirable sense of shock is the use in drama of modern speech"[10] helps us see that in this case Williams hoped to *collapse* distance, to bridge the nineteen-hundred-year gap between his audience and his characters. Only then can Recovery take place; only then can we conceive of ourselves thinking and doing the same things as those folk of long ago.

But did he succeed? What Williams did is a matter of record and can be demonstrated; whether he did it well requires an aesthetic judgment and is therefore something each reader must decide alone. A representative passage of dialogue, however, will give a flavor of the play as a whole:

> JOHN: Saul! My dear man. . . . How do you come here?
> SAUL: I was delayed at Antioch by my old trouble, and I very nearly turned back. . . . But I was anxious to see you[.]
> JOHN: . . . You will stay here, of course[.]
> SAUL: That is kind of you. But you have guests already—no, that is not the reason. . . . John, are you still in with these . . . Nazarenes?
> JOHN: Yes.
> SAUL: *Now*? Now, when he has been hanged?
> JOHN: O but such a lot more. You are behind-hand, Saul; it comes of living in provincial centres like Tarsus and Antioch. Now here in Jerusalem things *happen. (Thoughtfully)* You have no idea how much *has* happened.[11]

10. Sayers, *Man Born to Be King,* 7.

11. *CP,* 333–34. Throughout this paper I have followed the original text of *Terror of Light* in preference to the slightly revised version Williams did in response to his wife's criticisms; my reasons for doing so are (a) I believe the original text is better in most cases than the

Chatty? Yes, deliberately so. Stilted? Occasionally, but remember that these lines were written a half-century ago, and for an English audience; what sounded quite natural then could, through no fault of its own, hardly help seeming a little old-fashioned to a modern American reader. But even with these handicaps, the play contains a few gems that age has not tarnished, such as Luna's homey questions to Simon Magus (*CP*, 343), Thomas's sarcastic remark to Saul ("I do not myself care for this crucifying and stoning and mutilating people to make them see the light. . . . But many great and good men disagree with me"[362]), or Judas's spirited exchange with Peter (350). When we set lines like

JOHN: . . . Saul, have you ever felt an absolute, complete, and utter fool?
SAUL: No.
JOHN: M'm. You will. (337)

alongside dialogue from Williams's other plays, we see how great a gulf lies between. We can imagine two old friends talking and disputing the way Saul and John do, but has ever a woman in the agony of labor pains shouted out "Parturition is upon me!" as does Mary in *Seed of Adam*, Williams's best-known nativity play? One is the voice of a person, the other a ritualized expression put into the mouth of an abstraction. I, for one, much prefer the former.

Important as it is, the play's prose rhetoric is only one of the means by which Williams seeks to make us think of his characters as real people, and, ironically, his second method seems to have offended the few whom his use of modern language hadn't bothered, chief among them C. S. Lewis.[12] I refer, of course, to Williams's unorthodox characterization, which departs so far from hagiography as to suggest that John the Evangelist and Mary Magdalene might have fallen in love with each other after Jesus's death; that John had formerly been a Pharisee and close friend of Saul of Tarsus; that Thomas was an intellectual ("It is not so easy . . . to be devoted and intelligent, to trust God and keep your mind dry" [*CP*, 362–63]), as calm and rational as John is mystical and Peter impatient. These characterizations have

---

revision, and (b) much as Williams valued his wife's opinions, I am more interested in the play as he saw it than in the play as she wanted it to be. The differences between the two versions are minor, consisting mainly of a few lines being cut and a few more added in other places. The posthumous *Collected Plays* prints the final text, but since it includes the original readings as footnotes, this play offers a rare chance to compare two states of the same work—so far as I am aware, the only such case in all of Williams's dramatic work.

12. "We had an unusually good Inklings on Thursday . . . at which Charles Williams read us a Whitsun play, a mixture of very good stuff and some deplorable errors in taste" (C. S. Lewis to W. H. Lewis, letter of 4 May 1940, quoted in Carpenter, *Inklings*, 115). Carpenter goes on to note that "the play was called *Terror of Light*, and its chief 'error in taste' [from Lewis's point of view] was the invention of a romance between Mary Magdalen and St John."

244 JOHN D. RATELIFF

exactly the same effect as the casual dialogue; that is, they surprise us and they make us think. The only character that is an outright failure is that of the Virgin Mary, whose thoroughly traditional role as a calm, all-knowing font of wisdom stands out as a pious cliché against the lively background of Apostles, sorcerers, and ghosts that make up the rest of the cast.

By contrast, the most impressive characterization of all—that of Judas Iscariot—is also the most daring. The climax of *Terror of Light,* beyond any doubt, is the moment when the Ghost of Judas Iscariot, accidentally summoned from Hell by Simon Magus, appears on stage. Instead of the cowering, defeated spirit we might expect from a more traditional playwright, Williams's Judas is easily the most dynamic character in the play, well able to hold his own and trade insults with Peter:

> PETER: . . . What are you doing here, Iscariot?
> JUDAS: The Lord sent me, Peter. Do you know me still?
> PETER: I know you, traitor. Are you dead or alive?
> JUDAS: I am dead, apostate. Are you alive or dead?
> PETER: I am alive, by the Compassion.
> JUDAS: And I am dead by the Justice. What is the difference?
> PETER: . . . I repented in agony.
> JUDAS: Was the agony that left you alive greater than the agony that drove me to death? Was that why you were quick to choose another in my place? Someone who had never been offered a bribe.
> PETER: Traitor, none of us would have taken it.
> JUDAS: Apostate, you were not offered it. (*CP,* 350)

The parallel structure underlying this exchange is a good example of Williams's use of rhetorical devices to underscore his points—in this case, to suggest an identification between Peter and Judas. They are polar opposites, mirror images of one another who nevertheless share a good deal in common. Peter is Christ's spokesman on earth; Judas his representative in death ("He sends me on his errands there" [*CP,* 347]). Each has his own fold, each his own purpose in the divine scheme, as Judas recognizes: "I may be in hell, but even in hell I am an Apostle. . . . God has shut me out of heaven and I have shut myself out of earth, but Jesus has not taken away my apostolate" (347–48).

Startling and thought provoking as this is, it is really no more unorthodox than the romance between John and Mary Magdalene; Williams is yet again shattering our preconceptions by filling in gaps in the Gospel record in ways calculated to surprise us and force us to realize how much of what we think of as "gospel" is in fact merely tradition.[13] Considered this way, the portrait of Judas is the culmination of his efforts at "recovery."

---

13. A good example is the traditional identification of the woman who anointed Jesus' feet in Luke 7:36–50 with Mary Magdalene, an identification for which there is no scriptural authority whatsoever.

But Williams does not stop there. The true value of *Terror of Light* lies not in its considerable merits as an amusing and thought-provoking retelling of the gospel story—if this were the case, Williams would in effect have only provided us with a "translation" of an old story into more modern terms, an achievement doomed to become dated with the passage of time. Instead he gives us something new, turning the biblical account into a means of expressing his own most strongly held theological beliefs, in the moment that marks the high point of *Terror of Light,* the redemption of Judas.

Williams's great theological teaching centered on a sort of informal sacrament he called Substitution. For him, this went far beyond the biblical injunction to "bear one another's burdens": it was literally a means by which one person's woes, physical or spiritual, could be taken away by another person, who would then feel the fear or depression or seasickness or toothache in the original sufferer's place.[14] A startling idea, but again of a piece with Williams's heterodoxy—a word that, had it not already existed, would have had to have been invented to do justice to Williams's idiosyncrasies. But Williams went further, holding that not just pain or discomfort could be taken away by the mechanism of Exchange and Substitution: damnation itself could be negated, an idea that goes beyond heterodoxy into what less generous times would have called heresy.[15]

There are at least four occasions in Williams's work (two of them in this play) where the living interfere with the fate of the dead: the redemption of the suicide through Pauline Anstruther's actions in *Descent into Hell;* Virgil's deliverance through the intervention of all the latter-day Christians

---

14. More details on how Williams conceived Substitution to work can be found in the novel *Descent into Hell.* For a real-life example as opposed to a fictional one, see Lois Lang-Sims's account of a Substitution Williams ordered her to undergo (Lang-Sims, ed., *Letters to Lalage: The Letters of Charles Williams to Lois Lang-Sims* [Kent, Ohio, and London: Kent State University Press, 1989], 53–54).

15. Heresy is a strong charge, and one not to be entered into lightly; however, it is hard to see how else one can describe his belief that humans can achieve salvation through each other and not directly through Christ. In addition, Williams engaged in practices that were strictly forbidden by both the Catholic and Anglican Churches: although a layman who had never undergone any form of ordination, he regularly heard confessions and imposed penances, sometimes including corporal punishment (e.g., spanking) on his disciples (see Lang-Sims, *Letters to Lalage,* 47, 60, 68). He founded his own order of disciples, the Companions of the Coinherence, and, although insisting that he was merely the first among equals, expelled any member who questioned his orders (Lang-Sims, *Letters to Lalage,* 80). Finally, he often referred to himself using the first person plural, a form usually reserved for the reigning monarch or pontiff but also used by bishops when speaking in their official capacity; presumably Williams adopted it in his self-appointed guise as head of his own spiritual order. These activities pass beyond any accepted definition of heterodoxy and can only be described as heretical.

246 JOHN D. RATELIFF

who loved his work in "Taliessin on the Death of Virgil"; the rescue of Luna, Simon Magus's medium, through Mary Magdalene's willingness to share her fate in *Terror of Light;* and Judas's escape from "the compulsion of [his] own act" (i.e., his despair and suicide) in the same play, again through Mary Magdalene.[16]

One need not, however, agree with Williams's beliefs to be moved by the moment in the play when Mary Magdalene asks, "Judas, I have been angry with you till now. . . . Will you . . . forgive me?" Judas replies, "I am returning to death; if there is any life anywhere and I find it, I will live it" (*CP,* 352). In Williams's metaphysics, the damned are eternally trapped by their own actions; only the actions of others can break them out of the sterile round of their existence. By releasing Judas from the inability ever to change again, Mary opens the door to his eventual salvation.

Virtually alone among Williams's work, *Terror of Light* holds out the hope of universal salvation to the entire cast. In stark contrast to Williams's usual tendency to provide a number of "object lessons," people who reject Coinherence and thus end up in the outer darkness—as do Sir Giles Tumulty in *Many Dimensions,* Evelyn in *All Hallows' Eve,* Assantu in *The House of the Octopus,* and Wentworth in *Descent into Hell*—the "villains" of *Terror of Light* (Saul of Tarsus, Simon Magus, Luna, Judas) all either find redemption and join the fold or, in the case of Saul, soon will. Coinherence by its very nature stresses the community of believers and their dependence

---

16. *DH,* 226-29; *TTL,* 31-32; *CP,* 357, 351–52. It might be objected that these examples should not be taken seriously, since they occur in a novel, a poem, and a play, respectively, and not in Williams's "theological writings." This view, however, does Williams a grave injustice, assuming as it does that he considered his fiction, poetry, and drama less important than his religious essays and literary criticism—a view his letters to Hunt (see note 2 of this article) do not support. Williams's work was all of a piece; whether he was writing a poem, an essay, or a biography, he made what he was writing a way of spreading his ideas to others.

Oddly enough, it is almost always through women that Substitution occurs in Williams's works, either because he thought, through some lingering Victorianism, that women were more capable of self-sacrifice than men, or because of the historical accident that almost all of his own disciples, the Companions of the Coinherence, were women (one of the very few exceptions was Raymond Hunt, the "Dinadan" of the Taliessin poems). In addition to the examples cited in the text, we might note two cases of the dead reciprocally helping the living: the ghost Alayu taking Fr. Anthony's fear in *The House of the Octopus* and Lester's helping Betty escape from Simon the Clerk's control in *All Hallows' Eve.* It is also a woman, Chloe Burnett, who is the means of the Stone of Suleiman returning where it belongs in *Many Dimensions.* For a negative example, Damaris Tighe's refusal to recognize any common ground with the madman Quentin (for which, given the circumstances, it is hard to blame her) causes all kinds of severe repercussions on both him and herself in *The Place of the Lion.* I can only think of one example of a man fulfilling a similar function in one of Williams's works, the Archdeacon in *War in Heaven;* Williams's overwhelming tendency was to assign such roles to his female characters.

on one another, and *Terror of Light* portrays such a community far more successfully than does any other work by an Inkling—more realistic and detailed than Taliessin's household in the Arthurian poems, less idealized and more believable than the group at St. Anne's in Lewis's *That Hideous Strength*. For the first time, Williams's vision is revealed as humane and all-inclusive, able to see the ways a suicide, a sorcerer, and a Pharisee can all enter into the New Life and become part of that community, giving and receiving the Joy that is at its heart. This is indeed the Way of Affirmation. There had been hints of it before—when he showed in *Judgement at Chelmsford* that the Devil is only Devil's Advocate in the end, or in *Seed of Adam* that even Hell itself can be turned into a willing servant of God's will—but never before had the concept been worked through so consistently and convincingly. Peter's justice drives Judas back into the outer darkness; Mary's forgiveness and request to be forgiven in turn open a path by which he can reenter the Light. Similarly, Peter is quite willing to leave Luna's soul trapped in hell and Simon a grief-stricken and broken man over her loss; only Mary's gesture of self-sacrifice frees Luna and leads both Simon and Luna into the newly founded community of believers.[17] In most of his works, Williams is upholding Peter's standards, separating with ruthlessness and precision the sheep from the goats and the wheat from the chaff, and providing a detailed description of the horrible fate of those rejected; in *Terror of Light* a more charitable—dare one say more Christian?—spirit presides. Through a rhetoric of recovery and a vision of reconciliation we are given both an entertaining play and the single most attractive explication of Williams's thought. What reader could ask for more?

17. This detail, by the way, is not of Williams's invention; although most people do not remember it, the original Simon Magus of the scriptural account (Acts 8:9–24) repents. The character of Simon gives Williams a chance to bring some of his occult preoccupations into the play; the ceremonies Simon performs and the language he uses are very similar to those used by the Golden Dawn, the magical order to which Williams belonged prior to his leaving it to found the Companions of the Coinherence. Although in later life Williams hid his earlier involvement with the Golden Dawn (Lang-Sims, *Letters to Lalage,* 18–19), scenes such as this one throughout his work show that the time he spent there had a permanent influence on his work. By redeeming Simon Magus, Williams may on a private level be baptizing his own early occultism and putting it at the service of his faith. The degree to which *Terror of Light* is a "kinder, gentler" work than most of Williams's opus is shown by the damnation a similar figure, Simon the Clerk, suffers in *All Hallows' Eve.*

Thomas Cranmer
and Charles Williams's Vision of History

Clifford Davidson

Following the success of T. S. Eliot's *Murder in the Cathedral* at the Canterbury Festival in 1935,[1] E. Martin Browne was invited to indicate a choice of author for the next year's play. He recommended Charles Williams,[2] and the result was *Thomas Cranmer of Canterbury,* a play that, like Eliot's, was a treatment of an archbishop of Canterbury who had suffered persecution and death.[3] Williams's subject, again like Eliot's, is closely related to the liturgy, for he uses chants and psalms from the Book of Common Prayer—a work that must, of course, be identified with the hero of his play—and it also carefully explores the relationship between Church and state. The resulting play, however, develops quite different dramatic strategies—in form Williams thought of it as a masque, while the verse he adopted at the suggestion of Anne Ridler was uniquely new[4]—and is concerned with making its effect in ways entirely different from those Eliot used in *Murder in the Cathedral.*[5] Most strikingly, *Thomas Cranmer* lacks the impersonality and objectivity of Eliot's Canterbury play, for it is at once a highly personal work and a play that was intended to have a broader

---

1. For a useful survey of the Canterbury Festival plays, see Kenneth W. Pickering, *Drama in the Cathedral* (Worthing: Churchman, 1985).

2. E. Martin Browne and Henzie Browne, *Two in One* (Cambridge: Cambridge University Press, 1981), 101.

3. The acting edition, reduced by numerous cuts so that the play might fit into the hour and one-half allotted to it at the festival, was entitled *Cranmer of Canterbury* (Canterbury: H. J. Goulden, 1936). In this article, however, I quote from the unabridged text as it appears in *CP,* 1–59.

4. Anne Ridler, introduction to *Image,* lxiii. On the influence of Gerard Manley Hopkins's verse, which Williams had seen through the press in 1930, see ibid., lxi–lxii.

5. For Eliot's handling of dramatic material in his play on Archbishop Thomas Becket, see my "T. S. Eliot's *Murder in the Cathedral*: Reviving the Saint Play Tradition," in Clifford Davidson, *On Tradition: Essays on the Use and Valuation of the Past* (New York: AMS Press, 1992), 135–50.

CRANMER AND WILLIAMS'S VISION OF HISTORY 249

application in its presentation of history. In Williams's drama, history is indeed interpreted as a process in which the Christian vision is worked out and revealed, though the revelation is imperfect and ambiguous in any given moment or in any given age. The play's rhetorical structure must therefore not step aside from the ambiguity inherent in the events of Archbishop Cranmer's career, while at its center is hieratic experience that cannot be explained but that nevertheless affirms transcendence.[6]

It is clear that a naturally weak hero rather than one with the strength of a Becket was the personal choice of the playwright.[7] Alice Mary Hadfield describes Williams's sense of loss and angst at this time in his career —elements that led to his personal affirmation of images and a renewed effort to discover the transcendental in the material world and its events.[8] Such an angle of vision gives a particularly poignant meaning to the words of the Collect for the fourth Sunday after Trinity sung by the Singers at the opening of the play since this prayer is in part a request that, through the guidance of God who is the sustainer of all things, "we may so pass through things temporal, that we finally lose not the things eternal" (*CP,* 3). For the protagonist of the play will in the course of the drama indeed pass through things temporal to his terrible end, and yet he will rise to his martyrdom with a quite uncharacteristic resolution that validates certain aspects of his work, especially his reformation of the eucharistic service and his translation of the traditional Christian rituals into English.

Williams's presentation of his protagonist is carefully contrived to set him off against both Protestants and Catholics who are characterized by their utter certainty with regard to doctrine and practice. Cranmer, who had been an undistinguished scholar at Cambridge (and a lover of horsemanship, as early documents also indicate),[9] is from the beginning sketched as a moderate man, honest in spite of his vacillation and the Erastianism that made him defer to secular authority again and again throughout his career.

---

6. As John Heath-Stubbs has commented, "to Williams, a hieratic view of reality, more akin to that of earlier ages, was a living experience. From his boyhood days ritual was of central importance to him; ritual centered in the liturgy of the Church, at the heart of which lay an affirmation of a transcendent order made actual by incarnation and sacrament" ("The Posthumous Career of Charles Williams," *New Republic,* 11 June 1966, 20). And for Williams the liturgy that mattered personally was contained in the *Book of Common Prayer* which Cranmer had done so much to shape in the sixteenth century.

7. On weak characters who achieve strength in Williams's novels, see Ridler, in *Image,* xlvii–xlviii.

8. Alice Mary Hadfield, *Charles Williams: An Exploration of His Life and Work* (New York and Oxford: Oxford University Press, 1983), 136.

9. *Narratives of the Days of the Reformation,* ed. John Gough Nichols, Camden Society, 77 (1859; reprint, New York: AMS Press, 1968), 239.

250 CLIFFORD DAVIDSON

He stands in contrast to priest and preacher whom we first meet in the opening scene. Wearing vestments and black Geneva gown in the Canterbury Festival production,[10] these two represent surely

> the ruinous nonsense of the mind,
> that men come mightily to believe their causes,
> because of their mere rage of controversy,
> and without morality to believe in morality.
>
> *(CP, 28)*

Cranmer does not shout as they do,[11] nor does he accuse loosely. Later, as archbishop, he is remorseful for his role in the matter of the "Nun of Kent" (17), Elizabeth Barton, whose visions were regarded as too politically dangerous to allow her to go unpunished,[12] and he treats the staunchly Catholic Vicar of Stepney with a gentleness that his accusers find astounding. The Protestant Preacher, echoing words originally spoken by one Underhill,[13] insists, "Were I Archbishop, I would fast unvicar him; / and put sharp sentence on such rogues as he." Then, in words that ironically point to Cranmer's own martyrdom, the Preacher adds: "If it come to their turn, they will show us none / of this foolish favour" (39–40).

Their turn does come, of course, and Cranmer's Erastianism must in the end break down when confronted with a queen who is determined to put him to death in spite of his recantations, which for him represent the temptation of continued life instead of burning. King Henry in the play claims that his power is derived directly from heaven: "The will of the King is as the will of God" *(CP,* 9). Cranmer accepts this view of kingship, and indeed it is his expression of this opinion that initially obtains for him his position as primate of England. Nevertheless, while "the King's law might run savingly through the land," as Cranmer at first thinks (6), royal absolutism might also lead him into a suspension of his best judgments in response to a teleology that is directed to the crown as if to God.

Queen Mary insists on the authority of the crown as fully as had her despotic father, but she uses it tyrannically against those of her people whom

---

10. James G. Dixon, "Charles Williams and *Thomas Cranmer* at Canterbury," *Seven* 5 (1984): 44.

11. In *Dove,* 162, Charles Williams comments on the self-righteousness and "clamouring" of the Reformers, who, he suggests, "declaimed like the Communist leaders of our own day." Hence, while his attitude toward the major Reformers is respectful, lesser Protestant agitators obtain less sympathy from him.

12. On the Holy Maid of Kent, see Francis Gasquet, *Henry VIII and the English Monasteries,* 7th ed. (London: G. Bell, 1920), 35–44.

13. John Strype, *Memorials of the Most Reverend Father in God, Thomas Cranmer* (Oxford: Ecclesiastical History Society, 1848–54), 2:82.

CRANMER AND WILLIAMS'S VISION OF HISTORY 251

she sees as dangerous. Her claim to be like a god—a link, therefore, between the authority of heaven and those who should obey as if they were heeding the behests of God himself—makes Cranmer despair and see himself as sinning "whatever I do" (*CP,* 51). In this pathetic state, he decides to recant more fully: "They may be right; they are, / for they say they are, they are sure, they are strong" (52). He has suffered the humiliation of his degradation at the hands of the Bishop (historically, his defrocking was carried out by Bishops Bonner and Thirlby, the former harsh and cruel, the latter deeply upset by the ghastly ritual)[14]—a very brief scene, which here nevertheless may owe a little to the structure of the deposition scene in Shakespeare's *Richard II*—and, having in his integrity failed to profit from the dissolution of the monasteries or his position as the primate of England, he goes to his execution as impoverished as a common criminal. At the conclusion, when Cranmer runs to his martyrdom, we might be tempted to borrow words from Horatio: "If aught of woe or wonder, cease your search" (*Hamlet,* V.ii.363).

Williams's method throughout is to adapt and change the language of his sources into the dialogue of a poetic drama; thus, for example, the final speech of Cranmer at Oxford as he recants his recantations is a highly condensed version that nevertheless very carefully retains the core of meaning present in the original. The speech of the Bishop (*CP,* 56) has the essence of the nastiness of Dr. Cole's sermon (preached, because of the weather, inside the church of St. Mary the Virgin) which the former archbishop heard from a low platform on which he was forced to stand,[15] and which in Williams's version accuses him of having stolen "from England the food of the soul." The Bishop's insistence that "it is needful that he burn / to make equilibrium with the Lord Cardinal John [Fisher] / who died for defending as this man for destroying" is proof that the execution will be purely and simply retribution for past deeds in the realm. Historically this sermon may have inspired Cranmer to become firm in his resolution to recant his recantations and to offer first to the fire his right hand with which he had written his recantations. For Williams, the decision seems to come at a slightly earlier point, when the Skeleton urges Cranmer to "run hastily to meet me" (55). The play ends not with the burning outside in the street not far away beside Balliol College but with the confusion that follows Cranmer's last speech. He speaks a final sentence (one found in Williams's sources but here presented as an echo of a sentence spoken by

14. Strype, *Memorials,* 3:22–23.

15. Strype, *Memorials,* 3:245ff. See also D. M. Loades, *The Oxford Martyrs* (New York: Stein and Day, 1970), 230, 232; the woodcut from Foxe's *Acts and Monuments* showing Cranmer on the platform is also reprinted by Loades, fig. 8.

252 CLIFFORD DAVIDSON

the Skeleton)—"If the Pope had bid me live, I should have served him" (59)[16]—and rushes away to his martyrdom. A review of the Canterbury Festival production in the *Canterbury Cathedral Chronicle* commented on the final segment of the drama: "The growing oppression of a trap closing in on Cranmer and on the mind, forcing out the reluctant desperate truth; black-gowned and masked Executioners with flames in their hands; Cranmer running, stumbling into the arms of the Skeleton, the final appalling clarity and then the cries, 'Speed! Speed!' and the rush of the flames down the aisle and Cranmer pursued by the Skeleton flying after them."[17]

Cranmer's character represents a mixture of wheat and tares (to use the biblical metaphors so important to Williams) that will be sorted out only in the end and only by a divinity that exists beyond and above the mere man. That his weaknesses have made him prey to other, more determined men, whether rapacious members of the aristocracy or ideologically oriented clergy, establishes Cranmer as a victim and thus makes his martyrdom a real act of imitation of Christ—an imitation that, especially when we keep the scene of the Agony in the Garden in mind, sets off the archbishop from the zealously and rigidly Protestant Latimer and Ridley, who had lost their lives to the queen's bonfires not long before. There is no doubt that Williams saw Mary's persecution as the terrible thing that it was.[18] In his essay "Church and State" (1939) he would write: "The Church is the knowledge of the mystical substance of man spiritually—in corruption and in redemption, and in neither can men be separated from each other until the heavenly division between tares and wheat, goats and sheep. But the wheat and the sheep were never encouraged by Christ to do the dividing" (*Image,* 116–17). At the same time, the state has certain and conflicting claims on men, and these may be legitimate. But clearly for Williams the idea of persecution was abhorrent, and in his presentation of the events of history during the lifetime of Archbishop Cranmer he as a playwright insisted on asking the right questions to illustrate the tensions existing between the claims of a merciful God and those of the secular state. These were certainly appropriate questions to be asking in the 1930s, and they remain appropriate today. But

16. See the letter written by Williams to *The Guardian* (10 July 1936) in defense of this final speech by Cranmer (quoted by Dixon, "CW and *Cranmer,*" 48). Williams was responding to an attack on the play by the Reverend V. T. Macy, rector of St. Nicholas, Canterbury.

17. *Canterbury Cathedral Chronicle,* no. 24 (1936): 14, as quoted by Dixon, "CW and *Cranmer,*" 49.

18. For an assessment of the effect of the persecution under Mary and of Cranmer's martyrdom in particular, see Loades, *Oxford Martyrs,* 234–60. A more sympathetic view of her reign is entertained by Eamon Duffy, *The Stripping of the Altars* (New Haven: Yale University Press, 1992), 524–64.

CRANMER AND WILLIAMS'S VISION OF HISTORY 253

thus also Williams establishes the historical framework in which martyrdom might take place—a martyrdom that, along with other events of the latter part of Queen Mary's reign, subsequently had a very great effect on English history and on the history of the Church.

A sense of turmoil, of action and reaction, is pervasive in *Thomas Cranmer,* but it serves as background to the archbishop's struggles against the lords, his compromises, his defense of those threatened by the secular state, and his true work, which was to reform the liturgy of the Church of England. Perhaps not enough emerges of the losses the Church suffered in the Reformation, which applied a nominalist aesthetic to religious art and effected a devastating campaign against the visible scenes and images that had formerly stimulated the people's religious fervor.[19] Indeed, in his historical biases Williams seems to be fairly conventional to the extent that he seems not to anticipate recent revisionist historians who recognize the importance of late medieval piety for the establishment of Protestantism, though in a way he seems to understand the developments of the sixteenth century quite correctly in terms of loss as well as gain. He recognizes that the Protestantism that gained ascendancy in England was to discourage the principle of coinherence for nearly two generations after Cranmer's death, while widespread efforts were also made during these decades to restrict access to the way of the affirmation of images. Still, as he explains in *The Descent of the Dove,* the Church in England did not entirely turn away from spiritual awareness, and in spite of it all "between the 'slight column' of Calvin counter-weighing the ocean-mass of Trent, the Church of England pursued her odd (but not, for that, necessarily less sacred) way, still aware of herself as related to all the past, and to the ceremonial presences of Christ" (*Dove,* 185).[20] Herein his historical vision is markedly different from the positivism normally to be expected in the writing of history by professional historians.

We thus come here to the central issue of Cranmer's role in the Reformation as Williams sees it. It is indeed a far more significant issue in Williams's view than is the matter of Church-state relations or of obedience within either the ecclesiastical or the secular hierarchies, for it involves the interpenetration of such ordinary things as bread and wine by the sacred

19. See Clifford Davidson, "The Anti-Visual Prejudice," in *Iconoclasm vs. Art and Drama,* ed. Clifford Davidson and Ann Eljenholm Nichols, Early Drama, Art, and Music, Monograph Series (Kalamazoo, Mich.: Medieval Institute Publications, 1989), 33–46.

20. It should be noted that recent revisionist interpretations of the English Reformation provide a view of this period that in part corroborates and in part differs from Williams's view; see, for example, J. J. Scarisbrick, *The Reformation and the English People* (Oxford: Blackwell, 1984).

254   CLIFFORD DAVIDSON

itself. The point is made very clear in *The Descent of the Dove* (185), and in his Canterbury drama he has Cranmer say to the lords that the King had wanted

> a ritual for communion, that men should find
> by nourishment on the supernatural, the natural
> moving all ways into the supernatural,
> and the things that are below as those above.
>
> (*CP*, 26)

This is not in fact Cranmer's view of the Eucharist,[21] the rite that stands at the center of Catholic and Anglican worship, but it does precisely express Williams's concern to place the rite of communion as central to his own incarnational theology. For Williams the Eucharist is the "great Rite . . . where the co-inherence is fully in action: 'He in us and we in Him'" (*Image*, 154).

A bishop early in the play goes in procession "with acolytes and incense" around the stage as Cranmer complains that the Church has shut its eyes "on the steep sacramental way, / for it beats its heart in a half-sleep" while "multiple show and song / throng in its dreams the bare step of the Lord / and are adored in comfortable fearful respect" (*CP*, 4–5). The crucial passage, however, is the statement that "now are means of communion adored / yet dyked from approach" (5). In the late Middle Ages, the Eucharist had been indeed more of an occasion for adoration than for reception or communion.[22] The important act of worship for the layman was to be in the presence of the rite as it was celebrated and to *see* the Host at the elevation after its change into the true body of Christ. The *Lay Folks Mass Book* gives a representative late-medieval view. At the sacring bell, "then shal thou do reverence / to Jhesu Crist awen presence" with raised hands while kneeling, "for that is he that Judas salde, / and sithen was scourged and don on rode, / and for mankinde there shad his blode."[23] The

---

21. Interestingly, the statement as set forth in Williams's play comes closer to Cranmer's final recantation, which affirmed: "I say and beleve that our Saviour Christ Jesu is really and substancially conteined in the blessed Sacramente of the Aultare under the fourmes of breade and wine" (*All the Submissyons, and recantations of Thomas Cranmer* [London, 1556], sig. B2ʳ).

22. Williams sees the adoration of the Sacrament in the context of late medieval religion as a perversion through excess. Then "self-circling adoration" (*CP*, 5) had become in his view an end in itself rather than a proper function in worship. Hence adoration is not different from the principle of love, which in its perversion turns back upon the individual in self-love instead of radiating outward to another. Communion is an expression of legitimate love and is necessarily balanced with adoration in its proper sense.

23. *The Lay Folks Mass Book*, ed. Thomas Frederick Simmons, EETS, 71 (London, 1879), 38 (B text).

CRANMER AND WILLIAMS'S VISION OF HISTORY 255

book tells the worshipper to "biholde this sacrament" and to pray in its presence until the canon is completed, then to follow with personal prayers and with attention to the celebrant at certain times (e.g., when the Lord's Prayer and the Peace are spoken).[24] There was no encouragement for the layman to receive communion, for normally the congregation communed but once each year.

Cranmer specifically rejected "adoration" of the Host,[25] just as he had rejected the veneration of devotional images and the use of candles placed before such images. The medieval view upholding the adoration of the Eucharist is represented in the play when Queen Mary comes to the throne and the Singers sing *Tantum ergo sacramentum,* which is the hymn at the Benediction of the Blessed Sacrament at the Feast of Corpus Christi.[26] But Cranmer's response was not like that of the other reformers since, in spite of certain of his theories of the nature of the Eucharist, he never ceased to value it as an "effectual" sign of grace and, indeed, he preferred the idea of

24. *The Lay Folks Mass Book,* 38–56.

25. The term *oblation* had been included in an earlier draft of the Prayer Book of 1549, but it was removed from the final version. See G. J. Cuming, *A History of the Anglican Liturgy* (New York: St. Martin's, 1969), 67.

26. The music used for this Latin hymn in the Canterbury Festival production was taken from the *Antiphonale Monasticum* (Tournai: Desclée, 1934), 1259, where the tone is identified as *Alter Tonus.* Production notes identifying the music apparently used for the Canterbury production are housed among the E. Martin Browne manuscripts in the Bodleian Library at Oxford. The other music for the production included solo intoning and chanting by the singers as well as two-part music, presumably polyphony; both "Blessed is he that cometh" (*CP,* 3) and the English *Gloria Patri* at the end of the drama are designated as "2-part." Some of the chants, including settings of Psalms 72.1–4 (7), 22.1–3 (37), and 88.1–2, 5, 18 (49–50) in the Prayer Book version, were to be sung from an unidentified "Green Book." The *Dies irae* (53) was from *The English Hymnal,* 2d ed. (Oxford: Oxford University Press, 1933), no. 351. The singers are shown in a photograph published in the *Canterbury Cathedral Chronicle,* no. 24 (July 1936): 11; the illustration shows two adult men, one of whom is the precentor, at the head of a procession in the Chapter House; the other singers were boys of varying ages. The names of the precentor and the singers are published in the program distributed at the festival performances, for which see Pickering, *Drama in the Cathedral,* 343. A letter by Browne to Alan Wickes on 26 June 1979 also gives directions concerning the music to be used at a revival of the play in that year; the collects were to be sung to the "usual intonations" by a solo male voice; the psalms "to whatever plainsong tones you think appropriate," the *Benedictus* and *Gloria* to plainsong or polyphony, the *Tantum ergo* and *Dies irae* to plainsong melodies, and the litany and preface to melodies "as used in worship." Browne comments: "It could be done with one precentor and a small group of boys, or a second man—but you'll judge what's best." Music for the psalms, probably for this reading, appears among Browne's manuscripts. I am grateful to the Department of Western Manuscripts and Mrs. Audrey Browne for the opportunity to examine these dramatic records in the Bodleian Library.

256   CLIFFORD DAVIDSON

daily communion,[27] which was to be received kneeling.[28] In Williams's play, the lords, in their reaction to the Book of Common Prayer, jibe, "What is this, Archbishop, about kneeling / to a memory, to a past day, to creatures and men?" (*CP*, 41). The elevation of the Host was forbidden by the rubrics,[29] but in Williams's opinion kneeling was the more significant gesture in the presence of the Eucharist. And, more important, Cranmer had not only preserved the ancient rites but had opened them up for the participation of the lay faithful on a frequent basis. His influence thus comes down to the present day, for at the most recent Lambeth Conference (1988) Archbishop Robert Runcie could say, "As we bishops come together, I thank God that we form a *communion:* not an empire, nor a federation, nor a jurisdiction, nor yet the whole Church, but a Communion—a fellowship based on our gathering at the Lord's table, where we share 'the means of grace and the hope of glory'."[30]

To be sure, Cranmer's whole view of the Eucharist was less important to Williams than were certain aspects of that view. The nominalism of his approach to the problem of Christ's body in its relation to the elements of the Eucharist[31]—a view that in his own day was characterized as Zwinglian by his enemies[32]—hardly could appeal to Williams, whereas the Reformer's incarnational theology, which was quite inconsistent with nominalism, was another matter. In spite of himself, therefore, Cranmer was one who in the

---

27. Cuming, *History of Anglican Liturgy,* 109, citing Cyril C. Richardson, *Zwingli and Cranmer on the Eucharist* (1949), 21, 30, 34.

28. See the second Prayer Book of 1552, which specifies the way of receiving communion "in their handes kneeling" (*The First and Second Prayer-Books of King Edward the Sixth,* Everyman's Library [London: Dent, 1910], 389).

29. The Prayer Book of 1549 commands that there should be no "eleuacion, or shewing the Sacrament to the people" (*First and Second Prayer-Books,* 223).

30. *Times* (London), 18 July 1988, 14.

31. For a highly useful summary of the problems involved in Cranmer's view of the Eucharist, see Cyril C. Richardson, "Cranmer and the Analysis of Eucharistic Doctrine," *Journal of Theological Studies* 16 (1965): 421–37. In particular Richardson carefully surveys Cranmer's Protestant insistence on the body of Christ as an empirical object, an opinion that the archbishop falsely claimed to be consistent with the Church Fathers. This understanding of Christ's body, dependent as it was on a nominalist view of things, is at the opposite pole of belief from the realist view implicit in Williams's writings, especially in his insistence on the doctrine of coinherence. Nor could Cranmer's nominalist view of the elements as "self-enclosed, empirical objects of the Nominalist tradition" have had any appeal for Williams, for this kind of thought attempted to overthrow "the whole fluid, mystical, substantial way of thinking, whereby the divine can impregnate the natural" (427).

32. John Foxe, *Acts and Monuments* (1563), introd. George Townsend, 8 vols. (1843–49; reprint, New York: AMS Press, 1965), 8:57.

CRANMER AND WILLIAMS'S VISION OF HISTORY   257

end stood on the side of the affirmation of images.[33] So long as Cranmer's incarnational theology preserved its base in philosophical realism and the Eucharist itself remained a sacrifice of sorts (implied in the words from the Prayer Book[34] spoken by Cranmer: "Although we be unworthy, through our manifold sins, to offer unto thee any sacrifice" [*CP*, 33]), the element of adoration could be restored historically in spite of certain aspects of the theology of the one responsible for the preparation of the Prayer Book. Instead of *things said* as in the Zwinglian and Calvinistic services on the continent and in Scotland, the Anglican Church retained the Eucharist as a *thing done*. "The things said are the accompaniments of something done," Williams has said in his review of G. W. O. Addleshaw's *The High Church Tradition*, and further, the Eucharist is a specific kind of rite or thing that is done. As noted above, it involves *sacrifice* (*Image*, 122–23). In *Thomas Cranmer*, the point is extended in ways implicitly suggested by the Prayer Book, which implies the sacrifice of individual believers as well as of Christ on the cross.[35] Indeed, this is emphasized by the Singers, who, at the end of Part One of the play, intone the words from the Book of Common Prayer: "Here we offer and present unto thee, O Lord, ourselves, our souls and bodies, to be a reasonable, holy and lively sacrifice . . ." (*CP*, 36).

Williams's statement to his friend Mrs. Hadfield concerning the Eucharist is therefore extremely important:

> I think the Sacrament is more than images; how and after what mode is another matter. I think the elements are drawn into him at the moment of the flesh-death-resurrection. The method of the union is obscure enough, and I'm a little inclined to agree that if there is nothing but He there, there is hardly a sacrament. . . . I will genuflect and adore the Presence, because it seems to me consistent with the general movement that he should so have withdrawn creation into him. On the other hand, I am shy of the arguments; the Rite which culminates in an adorable Mystery of co-inherence will serve for me![36]

She reports: "Charles went almost every Sunday to the Eucharist. It was the centre of his thought and so of his life."[37] It was also, we might add, at the center of Williams's historical vision in his play about Thomas Cranmer.

33. The point is made by Hadfield, *Exploration*, 136.

34. Here and elsewhere Williams quotes from the text of Prayer Book in use in his time rather than from the versions of 1549 or 1552.

35. See Cuming, *History of Anglican Liturgy*, 79.

36. Quoted by Hadfield, *Exploration*, 212.

37. Hadfield, *Exploration*, 212. See also Pickering, *Drama in the Cathedral*, who likewise emphasizes this point with reference to the playwright: "To theologians like Charles Williams . . . the experience of Christ's continuing presence in the sacraments was the central concern of the Church" (201).

258   CLIFFORD DAVIDSON

Williams therefore may be said to have shown in the play his gratitude toward Cranmer for his efforts in preserving the traditional rites and in translating them into English for the understanding of all the people. The playwright saw in the archbishop's martyrdom the heroism of one who, like himself, was not entirely clear about the nature of the Eucharist but who insisted upon the rite itself in a form that did not break so very much from tradition. The presence of ambiguities in the contemporary Book of Common Prayer—ambiguities that had been present since 1549[38]—not only failed to engage Williams in any attempt to think out his own theological position in this regard but also in fact worked instead to inspire him to make ambiguity of meaning into an integral part of his historical vision in the play. But ambiguity of meaning in the play also extended into a symbolic level with the introduction of a role quite different from the others.

The one character in the play with no objective basis in history is the Skeleton—a role played in the production at the Canterbury Festival by none other than E. Martin Browne himself, who could say that the part "gave me a satisfaction more complete than any other in my acting career."[39] By his very nature the Skeleton is marked by ambiguity, for though he is Death he is also something much more. He is a *double* being, in fact initially conceived by Williams as two separate characters symbolically representing the opposites of Death and Life.[40] As Browne indicates, "the Skeleton is uncompromisingly death, but as clearly bears the promise of life. Only through death did Christ pass into life, and his follower has to travel the same road."[41] The passage through life to death and beyond, however, is not depicted in the manner of allegory; instead, the events of the play, as the actor Robert Speaight (who played Cranmer in the Canterbury Festival production) recognized, take on a powerful expressionistic quality.[42]

The model the playwright had in mind for the Skeleton may well, however, have been the figure of Death in the allegorical drama *Everyman,* for in that play the traditional shape of this representation comes to the protagonist with the news that he must go on a journey which will take him beyond this life.[43] In *Everyman,* Death, who owes something to Satan in

38. See Cuming, *History of Anglican Liturgy,* 81.

39. Browne and Browne, *Two in One,* 105–7; see fig. 17 for a photograph of E. Martin Browne as the Skeleton.

40. Ridler, in *Image,* xxxv.

41. Browne and Browne, *Two in One,* 104.

42. Robert Speaight, *Christian Theatre* (New York: Hawthorne Books, 1960), 129.

43. Williams's *Thomas Cranmer* seems actually to have been influenced either directly or indirectly by a particular production of *Everyman.* This was, as Pickering notes, Poel's production with its figure of Death in the guise of a skeleton (*Drama in the Cathedral,* 209). The Skeleton's appearance in the Canterbury Festival production also seems to have been

CRANMER AND WILLIAMS'S VISION OF HISTORY 259

Job, is in function a messenger as well as a necessity in his allegorical meaning, and hence there is no escaping from his summons to a reckoning. On the title page of the undated sixteenth-century editions of *Everyman* printed by John Skot[44] he is pictured in the traditional manner as a cadaverous and bony form rather than simply as a skeleton, and the scene in the woodcut depicts him in a cemetery. So, too, Williams's Skeleton has associations with the pit, with Gehenna (*CP,* 11), and he comes to men to announce to them their death, as he does when he touches King Henry to let him know it is time for his earthly journey to come to an end (*CP,* 24).

Like the Death of the play *Everyman* and the depiction in the woodcut on the title pages of Skot's editions, Williams's Skeleton further must be seen as connected to the well-known series of late medieval illustrations of the Dance of Death. Several clues indicate that the playwright had this motif in mind—e.g., the touching of the victim at the moment when he is to die, as noted earlier, and the suggestion of the Dance as he is led away (*CP,* 25). In series showing the Dance of Death in the visual arts, the figure of Death also commonly comes to arrest individuals of various social classes whom he will carry off to heaven, purgatory, or hell. In the scene of the Bishop's sermon, immediately prior to Cranmer's scheduled execution, the Skeleton, like Death in a woodcut by Holbein,[45] actually copies the preacher's gestures and thus mocks him (56). Then, too, as the instrument of death that has overtaken Archbishop Warham, the Skeleton had been able to give the crozier to King Henry, who could then give it to Cranmer (9); in the end, however, it is again the Skeleton who will take this emblem of his high ecclesiastical office away from him (49). Because there is a vacancy on account of death, Cranmer, though twice married,[46] can be made primate of England; because of the Skeleton's summons in the conclusion of the play, he will rush off to his own martyrdom. Like the Death of the medieval series, the Skeleton is indeed a gatherer of souls (56), but he has also been

influenced by the costume of Poel's Death; see the photograph illustrating the former in Browne and Browne, *Two in One,* 105, and the latter in Robert Speaight, *William Poel and the Elizabethan Revival* (London: William Heinemann, 1954), Pl. facing 224.

44. A. W. Pollard and G. R. Redgrave, *A Short-Title Catalogue . . . 1475–1640* (London: Bibliographical Society, 1926), Nos. 10605 and 10606.

45. *The Dance of Death by Hans Holbein the Younger: A Complete Facsimile of the Original 1538 Edition of Les simulachres & historiees faces de la mort,* introd. Werner L. Gundersheimer (New York: Dover, 1971), 36. There is a panel of painted glass at St. Andrew's, Norwich, which illustrates Death coming to arrest a bishop, but because Williams did not have an acute visual sense it is unlikely that he would have known this pertinent example from the visual arts.

46. Nothing is said about the archbishop's marriages in the play by Williams, however.

260   CLIFFORD DAVIDSON

the creator of opportunity for Cranmer, who to be sure accepted the appointment to the see of Canterbury reluctantly. Nevertheless, the place of the archbishop in history, in the working out of a design of the Holy Spirit, requires precisely the intervention of the ambiguous principles—principles that also illustrate a dialectic or, in Anne Ridler's words, "a clash of opposites"[47]—represented by the Skeleton.

The Skeleton thus drives Cranmer to an unconditional surrender to his destiny,[48] in this case of the greatest historical significance for the English Church. The ambiguity of the character of the Skeleton cannot disguise the view that, as the program notes at the 1936 Canterbury Festival indicated, the Skeleton is "essentiality—the bare bone of fact eternally behind all the ideas and words of men, the fact which is both life and death, the fact, to face which is the only way to the Love of God."[49] He is both negative and positive at once—"the Judas who betrays men to God" (*CP*, 35). As an "indweller" in the household of man, he is "the delator of all things to their truth" (34). And his name is, in its Latin form, "Figura Rerum" (34). As such—though he is "without face or breath"—he is in the end to be perceived as "Christ's back" (54), the reverse of the incarnate God who took on humanity in order that hope might be born of despair. And he, too, is ultimately a minister of God, who in Williams's view is most fully revealed when encountered on a ground of skepticism.[50]

Through the assistance of the Skeleton, therefore, loss is converted to historical gain, and this is so when weakness has been transformed to strength. The Skeleton has tempted Cranmer to "restore communion" in the belief that it is Christ's will (*CP*, 9), and he has been present throughout the play's action as it expresses the historical vision of a remarkable playwright who saw the visible and invisible worlds coinhering and the highest deeds of humankind as acts of substitution in which they suffered for others, often for men and women not yet born. The topic of Williams's play is thus *martyrdom,* the surrendering of one man's life so that others might through him have a channel to devotion, in this case using the English rite. The topic of martyrdom was indeed an appropriate one for Williams, since he had spent his childhood from the time he was seven at St. Albans, where the

---

47. Anne Ridler, ed., *Seed of Adam and Other Plays,* by Charles Williams (London: Oxford University Press, 1948), vii, as quoted by Dixon, "CW and *Cranmer,*" 42.

48. The point is an important one, and it may have been influenced by Williams's reading of Søren Kierkegaard, whose *Philosophical Fragments* was in press at the Oxford University Press in 1936; see Hadfield, *Exploration,* 124–25. See also Williams's commentary on Kierkegaard in *Dove,* 212–18.

49. Quoted in "The New Canterbury Play," *Times Literary Supplement,* 20 June 1936, 512.

50. See Ridler, in *Image,* xli.

CRANMER AND WILLIAMS'S VISION OF HISTORY 261

shrine of Britain's protomartyr had been restored in the cathedral less than a generation before.[51] Still, Williams's martyr was a thoroughly different kind of man from the early convert who reputedly was the first in Britain to give his life for the faith. This was apparently deliberate rather than accidental. As noted earlier, Cranmer's weakness reflected the weakness that the playwright seems to have felt in himself at this time. Just as Cranmer's royal crutch that had guaranteed his survival would in the end collapse, so had Williams's personal life lost the "Second Image" of love that had given him happiness and stability.[52] The personal experience of the playwright is therefore subsumed into the interpretation of history. But history, after all, is made up of the personal, of loss, of conditions that establish heroism through unexpected and unwanted demands that are unconditional. Yet paradoxically loss may be gain, and the Skeleton, an emblem of nothingness or death, might be the source of new life grounded in Being.

51. On the shrine of St. Alban, which was restored from the fragments in 1872, see the commentary in Charles Wall, *Shrines of British Saints* (London: Methuen, 1905), 35–43. Charles Wall was Charles Williams's uncle, who had helped his mother to set up her artists' supply shop in St. Albans; see Hadfield, *Exploration*, 4, 6–7.

52. Ridler, in *Image*, xxvi–xxvii, and Hadfield, *Exploration*, 136.

PART V

History, Theology, Criticism

History as Reconciliation:
The Rhetoric of *The Descent of the Dove* and *Witchcraft*

Robert McColley

> To make our decisions in faith is to make them in view of the fact that no single man or group or historical time is the church; but that there is a church of faith in which we do our partial, relative work and on which we count.
>
> (H. Richard Niebuhr)[1]

> We shall not cease from exploration
> And the end of all our exploring
> Will be to arrive where we started
> And know the place for the first time.
>
> (T. S. Eliot)[2]

In everyday conversation *history* means past events, whether momentous or trivial. To serious thinkers it may also mean the record of humanity up to the present, obviously unknowable in all its particulars yet leaving evidences enough to yield some meaning to those who would study and ponder it. Or *history* can mean that which historians—not merely Ph.D.-bearing academics but anyone who undertakes to write extensively and coherently about the past—produce between the covers of books or learned journals. Benedetto Croce wisely called history "present thought about the past." It is in this sense that this essay treats the two most important historical writings of Charles Williams; mere facts, even ordered chronicles, have no power in themselves either to reconcile or to inflame partisanship. The writing of real history does have such power, and it is, unfortunately, most often used to advance the interest of a party or a nation. Though he was biographer, critic, playwright, novelist, poet, and theologian, Williams was also, quite seriously and successfully, a historian—one who marshaled significant facts, placed them in an interpretive framework, and made meaning out of the seeming

---

1. Niebuhr, *Christ and Culture* (New York: Harper & Brothers, 1951), 256.

2. Eliot, *Little Gidding* (1942), in *The Complete Poems and Plays* (New York: Harcourt, Brace, 1952), 145.

266 ROBERT MCCOLLEY

chaos of near-infinite data. He wrote on behalf of peace, both between contending parties of Christians and between Christians and the rest of humankind.

Charles Williams wrote his two most famous histories after he had reached full intellectual maturity. *The Descent of the Dove* appeared in 1939, *Witchcraft* in 1941. His work at the Oxford University Press, far from wasting his energies, seems to have endowed him with a thorough historical as well as literary culture; certainly his thought ranged easily over centuries and civilizations, somewhat in the fashion of Arnold Toynbee's. Williams's biographies, too original in method and message to deserve their classification as honest potboilers, were also histories, which treated a span stretching from the late fifteenth century (*Henry VII*) to the Restoration (*Rochester*). Williams qualifies as an outstanding historian despite the haste with which he wrote his books and his apparent reliance on printed sources and published scholarship. To an unusual degree he had the ability to identify with the life and thought of earlier ages; he had an impressive amount of that which should be implied by the words *historical imagination.* There remains, nevertheless, the striking difference between Williams's biographies and histories and those of almost anyone else, whether Christian or otherwise. Williams keeps one aware of eternity as the foreground to human temporality. The effect redeems the past and informs it with meaning in a way that nineteenth- and twentieth-century schools of objective and scientific history cannot. Williams reminds us that we live with the consequences of our ancestors' deeds as we also are the consequences of their marriages. So much our secular historians must know, but Williams, with his sense of multiple schemes of time, invites us to share the agonies and triumphs of our predecessors—in brief, to live in them as they live in us. Historical coinherence affirms a spiritual as well as a biological kinship of all people through the ages.

Williams brought to the study of history the crucially important dimensions of supernatural time, but he did not neglect more easily verifiable phenomena. Whatever his sources of information, Williams had powerful critical and discriminating faculties, by means of which he grasped the essential issues in historical conflict and, proximately, the motives of human agencies. He could, like the rest of us, make minor errors: in his account of the Salem witchcraft trials he credits Cotton Mather with a more important role in the proceedings than he actually played (a common error in secondary accounts) and identifies the Reverend Mr. Parris's slave Tituba as an American Indian;[3] she was in fact a daughter of Africa, by way of the West Indies, and was married to a Native American. On the other hand, Williams

---

3. Williams, *Witchcraft* (London: Faber and Faber, 1941), 284–85, 278.

sees the Salem episode in such a wide context that he makes a point missed by most historians better informed about local events: what distinguished the people of Massachusetts was not that they had a witch-hunt in the late seventeenth century but rather that they early and thoroughly repented of having had one.

Charles Williams was an accomplished poet and critic long before he displayed his gift for writing history; it seems to have ripened in the mid-1930s, while he was editing histories and writing his historical biographies. The verse-play *Cranmer* shows a fine and subtle understanding of the Reformation in England. The martyrdom, or punishment, of Cranmer also reminds one of a fictional counterpart, the fiery execution of Pauline Anstruther's ancestor in Williams's novel *Descent into Hell.* Compared with its five predecessors, that novel is more convincing in the old sense of being "true-to-life" exactly because in it Williams so well portrays the world of our mortal experience. Curiously, the character in the novel who actually descends into hell, Lawrence Wentworth, is no satanic power seeker in the fashion of Nigel Considine in Williams's first novel (*Shadows of Ecstasy*) or Simon the Clerk in his last (*All Hallows' Eve*); he is rather a mediocre professional historian for whom the past serves only as a source of intellectual puzzles and personal aggrandizement. Williams is not so harsh as to consign to perdition all historians whose work is mediocre and self-serving: Wentworth's descent results from more serious failings, yet his shortcomings as historian reflect his basic selfishness, his unwillingness to enter sympathetically the lives of others, past or present.

The Descent of the Dove and *Witchcraft* have much in common; both take in the entire Christian era from antiquity to (virtually) the present; both display a remarkable power of synthesis and interpretation; both are rich in anecdotes that serve to give faces to the characters and life to the generalizations. Each book emphasizes an important side of the two millennia of Christian history. Williams reports on much that is evil, in effect if not intent, in *Dove,* and he reports some redeeming characters and acts in *Witchcraft.* On the whole, however, the central theme of the one book is obedience to "our Lord the Holy Spirit," man and God cooperating in the history of redemption. The theme of the other is the human effort, beginning with the Fall, to be in power and self-sufficiency a sort of god.

The Descent of the Dove appeared when Williams's central and unifying concept of coinherence was perhaps more meaningful to him than ever before. During the early months of 1939 he finally decided to establish, however informally, "the Order of the Co-inherence," and even dedicated *Dove* to "the Companions of the Co-inherence." *Witchcraft* must, by its subject matter, be a different kind of book. It concerns itself with people who seek power for its own sake, whether they be those who undertake the practice of black magic—and such there certainly were—or those dedicated

268   ROBERT MCCOLLEY

to catching and punishing witches—not always "witch hunters," in today's unfavorable sense, but often something rather worse. Furthermore, the writing of *Witchcraft* coincided with the darkest days of the Second World War, so far as denizens of the United Kingdom were concerned. Charles Williams found his close network of personal and professional acquaintance centered at Amen House in London entirely disrupted. Most of the men and women he knew best went to different wartime posts, and he himself moved to Oxford. To be sure, the Inklings, led by C. S. Lewis, welcomed him and arranged for lectures, to the great enlargement of his following. But taken altogether these benefits do not appear to have compensated for the many personal separations, the awareness of advancing age, and the stresses of wartime existence. How much these personal and historical factors accounted for the far more subdued and cautious usage of *Witchcraft* is, of course, beyond our present calculation; the hunch advanced here is that their influence was considerable.

Williams did not originally think of the two books as complementary. Two different editors, at different publishing houses, suggested the books at two different times; it was, in fact, T. S. Eliot who urged Williams to write *Witchcraft,* for Faber and Faber. The differences between the two books are sufficiently great that each should be considered on its own terms, especially with respect to its rhetoric. In spite of the solemn and holy subject matter, or perhaps because of it, Williams chose to write *The Descent of the Dove* in a detached and witty style. Indeed, it must be set down as the most immediately striking characteristic of his rhetoric that he is usually off-hand and casual when discussing the most serious issues. Early in his first chapter Williams refers to Jesus as "a certain being." He then uses the pronoun *it* rather than the conventional, reverently capitalized *He:* "It had a very effective verbal style, notably in imprecation, together with a recurrent ambiguity of statement. It continually scored debating-points over its interlocutors. It agreed with everything on the one hand, and denounced everything on the other." And so on through several more paradoxical sentences, ending with "It did disappear—either by death and burial, as its opponents held, or, as its followers afterwards asserted, by some later and less usual method" (*Dove,* 2–3). The odd thing about this mode of expression is that it does not strike one as frivolous or irreverent; rather, it seems a practical method by which Williams, though confident of his own understanding, is nevertheless always aware of the finite, limited, and imperfect nature of even the most astute human thought on transcendent subjects. Williams's near-flippancy, far from undermining his examination of the most serious episodes of church history, tends rather to lighten an otherwise crushing weight of seriousness. The habit of style, including the idiosyncratic referring to Jesus Christ as "Messias" here as in his other books, may also awaken some readers to full attention where conventional usages would not.

The touch may be light, even casual, but Williams never belittles or demeans. Indeed, he is often most courteous and respectful when discussing the enemies of the Church, as in his discussion of Roman persecutions: "The 'good' Emperors had come to regard Christianity as an evil, as all tolerant and noble non-Christian minds tend to do. . . . Gods, and the nature of the Gods, are likely to be better understood by sinful than by stoical minds" (*Dove,* 28). And beyond courtesy, Williams could extend praise to enemies of the Church. The prime example of this is his positive view of Voltaire, the first man in over a millennium to level an attack against the Church pure and simple, not just against heresies and corruptions within a Church he wished to purify: "He wrote across the brain of all future Christendom, '*Écrasez l'Infame.*' Christendom will be unwise if ever she forgets that cry, for she will have lost touch with contrition once more" (202).

Williams's courtesy becomes a matter of critical tactics and high strategy when dealing with the Church's insurgent controversialists and reformers. He establishes his distinction between the two Ways—the Affirmation of Images and the Rejection of Images—with the appearance in antiquity of the desert Fathers, incomparable masters of Rejection, and he maintains his respectful understanding of both Ways throughout the book, even though it remains clear which he prefers. He credits the Emperor Constantine (not usually admired in recent histories of the Church) and other founders of medieval Christendom with reconciling the Church to time. He remains remarkably free of blame or partisanship while noting the separation of the Eastern and Western Churches and, centuries later, the Great Schism that produced multiple popes in the West. There is scarcely any leading character in the history of the Reformation that he treats with anything less than full respect, which includes a fair statement of each reformer's thoughts and deeds. He notes that in the year 1534 Martin Luther completed his German Bible, St. Ignatius Loyola and St. Francis Xavier took their vows, and John Calvin began his *Institutes:* "In that great age of *Homo,* with its magnificences of scholarship, architecture, art, exploration, war, its transient graces and terrene glories, it pleased our Lord the Spirit violently to convulse these souls with himself" (*Dove,* 172). Williams has correcting criticism as well as praise for these heroes of the Reformation and Counter-Reformation, yet he meant exactly what he said, however casually: God the Holy Spirit was in each of them. "*The Exercises* was the title of Loyola's manual; 'this life is an exercise,' wrote Calvin. That those two masters should have been opposed was, humanly speaking, tragic" (173). Williams goes on to deplore, with characteristic economy of statement, the wars, cruelties, and martyrdoms of the historic Reformation.

270 ROBERT MCCOLLEY

For readers, Christian or otherwise, who wish heartily to condemn the persecutions, exclusions, and bigotries of churchmen through the ages, Williams has neither denials nor apologies, but a forthright portrayal of that dreary record. He will modify the legends of atrocities only when convinced to do so by the best of secular scholarship, as in the case of the Borgias. But rather than explain away the record of evil done by Christians, he turns it to instructive, cautionary purpose: the universality of the Church has always left it open to the worst of men and women, and the doctrines and rites of the Church will not prevent any of us from falling, like Adam and Eve, into rebellion against its founder.

The last two chapters of *The Descent of the Dove* are the most difficult to understand; any serious attempt at explaining them in language more simple and didactic than Williams's would take considerably longer than the chapters themselves, so nothing of the kind will be attempted here. Williams entitled these chapters "The Quality of Disbelief" and "The Return of the Manhood"; in them he summarizes the situation of Christianity in the modern world in language perhaps a bit less playful than that used in the earlier chapters. All the other qualities remain, however, and none so much as his generous appreciation of those who have attacked Christian beliefs. This is most unqualified in his treatment of the new professional scholarship: "Never before had the serious critical and historical arguments against Christianity had a chance to be properly put forward; never before had they had a chance to be—not answered, for what arguments of the kind can ever be answered? but—understood and enjoyed" (*Dove,* 221). To be sure, Williams cannot resist an ironic sketch of certain hypotheses that have resulted from the Higher Criticism: "The humanitarian Jesus appeared, with the fearful and fiend-like face of St. Paul looking over his shoulder, and hypnotizing the simple credulity of the early Church into accepting Oriental mysteries. Presently indeed there was nothing left but St. Paul, for the historic Jesus vanished altogether, and St. John was resolved into Plato" (220).

All this is clear enough sailing, but when Williams on the one hand praises the return of doctrine in the early nineteenth-century missionary and antislavery activities, and the honest dogmatism of new sects and divisions, and on the other commends the nearly nihilistic skepticism of Kierkegaard and the revolutionary indignation of Karl Marx, one is more than a little baffled as to where human agency and "our Lord the Holy Spirit" are assumed to be at work. I am annoyed that Williams, so original in most of his thought, is so conventional (for an English intellectual of his generation) in propagating the century-old view of the new upper class of capitalist managers as robber-barons and oppressors of the masses. My annoyance is not because that class is without fault but rather because only under the

HISTORY AS RECONCILIATION

hegemony of that class has mankind for the first time attained something close to an objective understanding of the creation, universal education, and political rights. But even Charles Williams cannot see both sides of every question, and this one was far from the center of his interests. Nor did appreciation of Marx make him an advocate of Marxism; Williams is altogether true to his own beliefs in his pronouncement on the worker's paradise of Lenin and Stalin:

> The intended material salvation of sensuality had, inevitably, one temporal limitation; it could not redeem the past. That [Communist] co-inherence could not reach the millions who had died in their misery; the Republic of the future was to be raised on their bones. That could not be helped. But the City of Christendom had declared that all must be capable of inclusion—unless indeed they deliberately preferred a perpetual exile. (*Dove,* 229-30)

To the now historical but then contemporary question of whether the regime in Soviet Russia or the regime of National Socialism in Germany was worse, Williams had a clear answer: "The Body and Blood of Christendom had been declared to be divine, human, and common; the body and blood of Communism were thought to be human and common; the body and blood of the new myth were merely German. It set itself against the very idea of the City; it raised against the world the fatalistic cry of Race" (230).

But Williams's penetrating views of the totalitarian states on the eve of the Second World War were also side issues. His praise of skepticism, of unbelief, of the honest pursuit of truth for its own sake sets Williams somewhat apart from most leading Christian apologists, the more so because of his intense awareness that official church leaders must be dogmatic; the institutional church cannot very well propagate the ideas of its enemies. The true Church, the body of all believers throughout the ages, presumably always present to God, therefore exists in a different intellectual milieu, as well as a different kind of time, from temporal churches. Serious, studious, and sincere doubters and skeptics, whether within or outside the institutional church, whether trying to reform or discredit it, seem in Williams's view to be positively essential to the mission of the Church through the linear time of human history.

Williams's idea of "The Return of the Manhood" may be explained in two complementary ways: first, though mankind knows perfect freedom only through the grace of God, transmitted in and through his Church, each soul must be free to seek that freedom by rational inquiry; second, the democratic, egalitarian, and humanitarian impulses of the modern world have restored (in this, at least, prompted by the Holy Spirit) to the Church the possibility of a genuine coinherence embracing all humanity. Though in 1939 barbarians had conquered much of the known world and seemed fully capable of conquering the rest, *The Descent of the Dove* strikes a remarkably

272   ROBERT MCCOLLEY

optimistic note overall. This is in part because Williams has no notion that
"modern thought" has in any important sense disproved, or made irrelevant,
any essential Christian belief; there is, in his appreciation of earlier ages of
Christianity, no nostalgia and certainly no longing to return to these earlier
ages. More important is the certitude Williams balances against his sense of
the conditional and relative; Christendom's "only difficulty will be to know
and endure [the Holy Spirit] when he comes, and that, whether it likes it or
not, Messias has sworn that it shall certainly do" (*Dove,* 233). The book
ends with a Postscript, modestly and tentatively recommending an informal
"Order within the Christian Church" to combat (the word is mine, Williams
uses no such militant term) "our present distresses, of international and
social schism" by reaffirming the divine principles of exchange, substitution,
and coinherence (236).

   Witchcraft, as suggested earlier, differs in style and mood from *The
Descent of the Dove.* Long familiar with the world of books and ideas of his
own time and place, Williams could assume a certain acquaintance with the
epochs of history discussed in *Dove.* But in an age in which intellectuals had
in large measure ceased to believe in any supernatural orders of existence,
he wrote *Witchcraft* for readers who knew little or nothing of the subject.
Most of the serious studies of Williams have been written by people either
devoted to him personally (for example, C. S. Lewis and Alice Mary
Hadfield) or entirely sympathetic to his thought (for example, Glen
Cavaliero). All seem eager to minimize Charles Williams's interest in the
occult and diabolical and to insist that *Witchcraft* "is not 'exciting' or
horrible" and that his "interest was primarily psychological."[4] Williams
himself supports this view with the disclaimer in his Preface: "No-one will
derive any knowledge of initiation from this book; if he wishes to meet 'the
tall, black man' or to find the proper method of using the Reversed
Pentagram, he must rely on his own heart, which will, no doubt, be one way
or other sufficient." He further denies any wish "to titillate or to thrill," his
sole aim being to write as accurate a history as possible (*Witchcraft,* 9). The
profession is sincere, yet misleading. However objective and dispassionate
the treatment, one cannot write a book that catches the essence of "the
Goetic life" and its kindred ways without describing, however briefly, much
that is horrible. Those who find such things titillating or thrilling will
therefore find them so wherever set down, without regard for the intention
of the author; it is, after all, another case of the dangers inherent in free will.
No doubt Williams succeeds, and succeeds admirably, in telling no more
dreadful details than his subject demands; in treating his subject, however,

---

   4. Hadfield, *Charles Williams: An Exploration of His Life and Work* (New York and
Oxford: Oxford University Press, 1983), 196; Cavaliero, *Charles Williams: Poet of Theology*
(London and Basingstoke: Macmillan, 1983), 143.

HISTORY AS RECONCILIATION

he assumes that his readers can stand to face parts of the human record both horrible and disgusting, and that at least some knowledge of such things is probably better than complete ignorance of them.

Witchcraft covers the same two millennia of human history as *The Descent of the Dove,* though it begins with backward glances at antiquity and locates its first instances of divination, conjuring, and necromancy in the pagan world of the Roman Empire. Belief in sorcery is much older than Christianity, and the Christian Middle Ages, far from being the age of superstition, actually achieved a great reduction in superstitious beliefs and practices (apart from those related to orthodox Christianity) for several hundred years. But the Middle Ages did develop doctrines and legends concerning the Devil, a shadowy figure in the Bible and the early Church, and generally prepared civilization for the enormous growth and variety of interest in all sorts of supernatural as well as natural phenomena that characterized the Renaissance. The beginning of the modern era began also the Catholic Inquisition and a host of Protestant imitations thereof; the people of Europe exposed or discovered, tortured, tried, and convicted witches by the hundreds of thousands in the sixteenth and seventeenth centuries. Then, with remarkable swiftness, most people ceased to believe in the whole dreadful business. Or rather, as Williams carefully shows, certain brave souls began remonstrating against the type of evidence brought against alleged witches. The belief in particular cases of witchcraft diminished first; as cases became rare and remote, belief in the thing itself then weakened.

Broadly speaking, Williams achieves two notable purposes in this book. He makes it perfectly clear that there were witches—that is, men and women who deliberately undertook, by means of rituals, spells, and conjuring, to do harm to their enemies or to advance their own fame and fortune. Of course, one hardly needed statutes against witchcraft to punish the worst of these, whose guilt was confirmed beyond reasonable doubt. The proof against them was in the fact that they had poisoned, kidnapped, tortured, or murdered their victims; concerning such acts there were always laws enough. What such deluded people believed can only be partially reconstructed, but Williams makes fairly good sense of it.

His second and more important purpose, however, is not to expose witchcraft but to expose the series of errors by means of which the leaders of church and state came to allow, or even encourage, the mass witch-hunts. Once the process had started, two things especially fueled the fires. One is familiar to those of us who teach, in courses concerning colonial North America, the unfortunate business at Salem Village in 1692: the acceptance of testimony from unbalanced children who complained of being tormented by apparitions of the accused. The idea was that spectral manifestations

274 ROBERT MCCOLLEY

could not appear unless so willed by those whose images flew through the night and entered bedchambers. The people of Massachusetts were, for a time, hopelessly but not untypically gullible; they did not, however, go on to the next and even worse error: seeking more evidence of witchcraft by torturing everyone under suspicion until they accused others.

Charles Williams affected skepticism and agnosticism about so many things that it becomes difficult, sometimes, to maintain that he was exactly what he claimed to be, a perfectly orthodox, believing Christian. In *Witchcraft* he makes that same "quality of disbelief" already celebrated in *The Descent of the Dove* into the principle by means of which the horrors of witchcraft finally ended. Perhaps many of Williams's readers have been as surprised as I to find that the counterattack of Christian reason and charity began with the insistence of the Spanish Inquisition that strict rules of evidence be followed in cases of witchcraft. A further gain came with the work of a particular Inquisitor, Alonzo Salazar de Frias, "who was also intelligent and good." Sent in 1611 to investigate a particularly deadly outbreak of witch-finding and punishing in Navarre, he concluded, after exhaustively reviewing evidence in hundreds of cases, "I have not found even indications from which to infer that a single act of witchcraft has really occurred" (*Witchcraft,* 251–52). It took a hundred years for the rest of Europe to follow the good example of Salazar de Frias, but follow it eventually did. *Witchcraft* ends with a summary (305–9) of "that perverted way of the soul which we call magic" (9) and then with a powerful reminder that those who consciously fight the Devil's evil may themselves be devilishly evil: "If ever the image of the Way of Perversion of Images came into common human sight, outside the Rites of the Way, it was before the crowds of serious Christians who watched a child, at the instance of pious and intelligent men, scourged three times round the stake where its mother was burned" (311).

The contents and style of the two books thus having been reviewed, what, by way of summary, should be said about the rhetoric Charles Williams employs in them? The view of rhetoric taken here will be a broad, simple, and traditional one: it is, as Aristotle discovered, the art of ethical persuasion. Secondarily, it ideally employs devices that will succeed in persuading. In *The Descent of the Dove* and *Witchcraft* Charles Williams argues for his spiritual idea of coinherence in several important ways. As the Church reconciled itself to time in the early Middle Ages, modern Christians need to reconcile themselves to a past that secularists (most notably Marxists, but also many other varieties of modern reformers, many of them confessing Christians) characterize only as a prelude to the moment of liberation we are now experiencing or, if only some revolution or transformation succeeds, will experience. Psychologically sound and theologically essential, Williams teaches us to identify with our ancestors, making their concerns ours, their errors and sins as well as their inspirations and mercies. One can scarcely be reconciled to what one neither knows nor understands. More than polite manners are involved in finding the good elements in practically every historical protagonist and movement. To do this illustrates repeatedly the true doctrine that evil is no simple opposition of good but rather is its misuse, distortion, or corruption. If among the inspirational figures in history are some we count as especially on an opposing side—some Borgia Pope, or Grand Inquisitor, or Luther or Calvin, or Voltaire, or Lenin—it is especially important that we are reconciled to them; not in the sense of subscribing to all they said or did but rather in separating their good from whatever corruption of it followed in their own actions or in those of their followers.

It would not do to score points for one's own favorite denomination, doctrine, or theologian in such a recovery of the Christian past; however, one cannot simply approve of everything, in equal degree. The light touch in *The Descent of the Dove,* the subdued and cautious understatement coupled with appropriate sympathy in *Witchcraft,* serve to convince the reader that Williams—whether we agree with him in detail or not—aims at reconciliation rather than victories or vindications. Gnosticism was the first major heresy within Christianity because "men were not responsible for each other. The Gordian knot of the unity was cut, and the bits fell radically apart" (*Dove,* 25–26). Gnosticism, to put it another way consistent with the teaching of Charles Williams, struck at the doctrine of the Incarnation. God became man, taking on flesh that all flesh might be redeemed. This marriage of the supernatural with the natural exists in supernatural as well as natural time; hence "living Christians" are linked with past and future, heaven and earth.

Most Americans of my generation became acquainted with the writings of Charles Williams through first reading C. S. Lewis. Lewis lived, imaginatively, in bygone ages; his own never figured in his scholarship and only rarely in his fiction. His one novel set in contemporary England, *That Hideous Strength,* actually presents a counter-Utopia in which, unconvincingly though entertainingly, literary, legendary, and fabulous types (not all of them, to be sure, virtuous) representing tradition save the world from scientists and technicians (a few of whom are nevertheless virtuous) representing modernity—i.e., our present world. One must read Lewis's letters and occasional papers for reassurance that he even noticed the world of people and events stirring around him and was capable of occasional shrewd observations concerning it. Lewis's strength lies in his ability to state Christian doctrine clearly and convincingly and to stir us to spiritual self-discipline. But his sincere desire to heal the divisions in Christianity was at

276   ROBERT MCCOLLEY

least partly at war with his broad hostility to things modern and his longing, marvelously expressed, for fantasy visions of an unfallen world or a world redeemed. In the terms of H. Richard Niebuhr, Lewis stood with the sectarians who understand Christ as standing against a corrupt human culture and redeeming mankind from it. His rhetoric, if not his logical formulations, urges us to escape from history rather than redeem it.

At the beginning of this essay I quoted the Fourth Quartet of T. S. Eliot, "Little Gidding," because it reminds us, with peculiar eloquence, that Christian history—history contemplated in faith—is not merely instructive but is centrally important to knowing ourselves. Also quoted at the outset and now mentioned again is H. Richard Niebuhr's *Christ and Culture*. It is the only modern book I know which treats the history of Christendom (the terms *history* and *culture* are virtually interchangeable for Niebuhr—he means *culture* in the sense of all purely human achievement) with an irenic impartiality equal to that of Charles Williams in *The Descent of the Dove*. Both works rest on rock-solid, essential Christianity, and both breathe an admirable gentleness of spirit. But how extraordinarily different is the rhetoric of the diffident, witty, anecdotal, epigrammatic Williams from that of the earnestly and Germanically philosophical Niebuhr, pleasingly clear in diction but always systematic and logical in pursuing his thought. The theologian no doubt makes better sense of history, and that is his praiseworthy advantage.[5] But Williams also has an advantage, presenting us with the history itself, alive with meaning. Here is a duality in which one can indeed relish opposites.

---

5. For example: "The kingdom of God is transformed culture, because it is first of all the conversion of the human spirit from faithlessness and self-service to the knowledge and service of God. This kingdom is real, for if God did not rule nothing would exist; and if He had not heard the prayer for the coming of the kingdom, the world of mankind would long ago have become a den of robbers" (Niebuhr, *Christ and Culture,* 228–29).

The Theological Rhetoric
of Charles Williams: A Peculiar Density

B. L. Horne

In 1959 when Alice Mary Hadfield published her biography of Charles Williams she remarked of *The Forgiveness of Sins* that she "could never read this book. . . . Or, I have read it but never been able to remember it. There is much in it, but it is a tired book."[1] Twenty-four years later in *Charles Williams: An Exploration of His Life and Work* this disparaging assessment was not repeated; however, the book, though treated with greater sympathy, was disposed of in less than two pages. This attitude toward *The Forgiveness of Sins* is not unusual. Much has been made of Williams's other major theological essays *He Came Down from Heaven* (1938) and *The Descent of the Dove* (1939) and even of *Witchcraft* (1943), but little has been said about *The Forgiveness of Sins*; there is even some doubt about whether it should be considered "major." Readers of all kinds seem to find it unsatisfactory and problematic, its content difficult and its prose mannered. It seems to have neither the intellectual coherence of *He Came Down from Heaven* nor the stylistic lucidity of *The Descent of the Dove*.

Like much of Williams's work, the book was written to commission. In this case it was the publisher Geoffrey Bles who provided the author with his subject—though Williams seems to have had some initial misgivings about the title. Nonetheless, the idea interested him and presented him with an opportunity to develop aspects of the theological vision that had already been adumbrated in his first sustained piece of theological writing, *He Came Down from Heaven*. Williams even incorporated a long quotation from that first book in the third chapter of *The Forgiveness of Sins*. It is, perhaps, because of the closeness of the connection between the two essays that Faber and Faber were persuaded of the propriety of publishing them in a single volume in 1951. The intentions of the publishers were, no doubt, commendable, i.e., to restore "to circulation all of his [Charles Williams's] principal

---

1. Hadfield, *An Introduction to Charles Williams* (London: Robert Hale, 1959), 178.

theological books,"[2] but the action has had its unfortunate consequences. The title chosen for the volume was *He Came Down from Heaven,* a title that by implication relegated the later essay to the position of an appendix. Furthermore, the title page itself reinforces this impression because, although the words "The Forgiveness of Sins" do appear, they are printed in smaller type beneath "He Came Down from Heaven." Of course, there is good reason for bringing the two essays together in a single volume, as there is undoubtedly a strong and vital theological link between them, but *The Forgiveness of Sins* is much more than an afterthought: it is one of the most profound and original contributions that have been made to English theology in this century. It is, for all its defects, at least the equal of *He Came Down from Heaven,* and its prose style is quintessentially that of its creator.

That there are defects must be acknowledged at the outset; and in identifying them the reader may begin to understand why *The Forgiveness of Sins* has been considered a difficult book and why Hadfield originally described it as "tired." First, there is the extensive use of quotation. It is puzzling that Williams thought it necessary to incorporate so long a passage from one of his own works, which inevitably gives the impression of someone whose energy is flagging. In addition, no other work by Williams includes so many words by so many other authors. Thomas Aquinas, Dante, Julian of Norwich, Shakespeare, Blake, Wordsworth are all prominent, and the seventh chapter contains whole paragraphs from the writings of William Law—writings that, fine as they are, add little to the development of Williams's own argument. Second, there is the question of the organization of the material. The yoking together of William Blake and the Lady Julian in the seventh chapter is arbitrary and, in the end, clumsy. The discussion of Blake's poetry, fascinating and illuminating though it is, is only marginal to the theological purpose and is disproportionately substantial in a book of this kind and length.

Finally (and here we begin to approach the theme of this essay) there is the style of Williams's prose: his unique manner of verbal self-expression—what will be called his "rhetoric." His distinctive "habit of speech" in nonfictional prose is more obviously on display in *The Forgiveness of Sins* than in many of his other works; we see it at its best and at its worst, and it gives us the opportunity of identifying with greater ease both its strengths and weaknesses. "In a writing of any complexity, a confusion of style is likely to be part of a confusion at a more substantial level."[3] Williams's style was never confused, nor was his thought, but his writing is undoubted-

2. See the publishers' blurb on the front flap of the dust cover of the volume.

3. W. K. Wimsatt, *The Verbal Icon: Studies in the Meaning of Poetry* (Lexington: University Press of Kentucky, 1967), xiii.

THE THEOLOGICAL RHETORIC OF CHARLES WILLIAMS   279

ly complex. The style is one that is highly conscious of itself—I do not say self-conscious, for that might suggest a criticism I do not intend. At its worst it is mannered, overwrought and opaque; at its best it is decorated with allusion, formal and rich. For all its formality, it can be unpredictable and ironic. It is, above all, characterized by a peculiar quality of "density"; in the following pages I shall try to describe how this density is achieved.

I

In his history of English rhetoric, *The Movement of English Prose,* Ian A. Gordon observes that by the end of the eighteenth century three styles of prose writing had "been evolved" which "have remained the basis for virtually all later writers." They are "the speech-based prose . . . to which the present-day reader can return with little fear of meeting archaism or obsolescence"; the "neo-Quintilianic rhetoric which was to provide the model for most 'serious' writing in the nineteenth century"; and "romantic" prose "marked by the continuous use of syntactical and metaphoric devices designed to excite an affective response."[4] If this characterization of English is correct and can be taken as a useful description of styles in the twentieth as well as the nineteenth century, in which category does one locate the theological rhetoric of Charles Williams?

The most obvious choice might be the second, on the grounds that this is "serious" writing. It is, after all, theology, and it addresses itself to subjects that are the most serious that can be imagined. It is also, like the neoclassical writing of the eighteenth century, deliberately shaped and often formal. However, its shape—its use of periods and its arrangements of antitheses and parallelisms—only occasionally resembles that of the masters of this type of rhetoric, Samuel Johnson and Edward Gibbon. It does not possess the regular "beat" of neoclassical prose; it is, as I have already said, syntactically unpredictable. To use a musical metaphor, Williams hardly ever writes in "common time"; the rhythm of his sentences is constantly changing. Nor does he consciously introduce Latinisms into his text: his vocabulary is eclectic and, even when he is writing theology, usually owes more to the language of the English poets than to the texts of the ancient world. There is, furthermore, a sense of the rhetoric's being original, unique, conscious of and delighting in its strangeness in a way that the neoclassicists would have thought vulgar. The author of *The Forgiveness of Sins* is not the pupil of either Aristotle or Quintilian, even though there are times when his prose seems to be obedient to their demands.

Perhaps, then, it belongs in the first category. Theology need not adopt

---

4. Gordon, *Movement* (London: Longman, 1967), 151–52.

the rhetoric of neoclassicism; even at its most serious it can be written in a "speech-based" prose. His close friends C. S. Lewis and Dorothy L. Sayers both wrote like this, as did several other outstanding modern English theologians, such as J. H. Newman, G. K. Chesterton, and A. M. Farrer. The clear intention and achieved result of all these writers was lucidity, the kind of lucidity that is the aim of the scientist. They are, as T. S. Eliot observed of Dante, "easy to read." "The thought may be obscure, but the word is lucid, or rather translucent."[5] Their style, when writing theology, tends towards the simile rather than the metaphor: in the interests of clarity they open out and exclude rather than fold in and compress. Although all of them wrote poetry, they put away the techniques of poetry when they wrote theology. Williams did not. Indeed, it is precisely as a poet that he perceives and frames the questions of theology, and this disconcerts the reader used to other kinds of theological discourse. Though striving for accuracy of thought at all times, his rhetoric does not attempt nor desire the accuracy of the syllogism, and he seldom pursues an argument, as a scientist would, by exclusion: "It is *either* this or that: if it is *this* it cannot be *that*." Instead, we see a constant attempt at inclusion: "It is *both* this and that: being *this* need not exclude being *that*." "In English poetry words have a kind of opacity which is part of their beauty,"[6] and the rhetoric of Williams in *The Forgiveness of Sins* is full of words used in the manner of a poet who understands the possibilities of their opacity. So while Gordon says truly that the "present-day reader" need have "little fear of meeting archaism or obsolescence," the reader can still remain perplexed by the writing, in which words that are apparently part of everyday speech are placed in extraordinary contexts, appear in unusual juxtapositions, and follow rhythmic patterns quite unlike those of ordinary speech.

There is the third possibility: romantic prose. Much of Williams's writing could legitimately fall into this category. Some remarks Ian Gordon makes about the great orator Edmund Burke are apposite here. Burke is portrayed as the exemplar of the romantic stylist, and Gordon notes that Burke achieved his effects by "the use of evocative imagery and of a sentence made up of short co-ordinated elements."[7] Both these devices are conspicuous in Williams's rhetoric, but they are not the usual instruments of the theologian. They are, however, the instrument of the preacher whose intention, quite blatantly, is frequently, if not invariably, the "exciting of an affective response." We must tread carefully here: there is something of the

---

5. Eliot, *Dante* (London: Faber and Faber, 1929), 18.

6. Eliot, *Dante*, 18–19.

7. Gordon, *Movement*, 148.

THE THEOLOGICAL RHETORIC OF CHARLES WILLIAMS   281

orator, if not exactly the preacher, in Williams's theological rhetoric, but the desire to "excite the affections" is always tempered by intellectual rigor, the determination of accuracy, and the presence, from time to time, of an irony that is not usually present in sermons. What, however, confirms our perception of Charles Williams as the writer of "romantic" prose comes by another route. Gordon, having described the style of Burke, goes on to observe that his rhetorical devices are the "common property of a group of his contemporaries, notably the writers of the sentimental and terror novel" (148). This seems, at first, unlikely to throw much light on Williams's rhetoric; but Glen Cavaliero has recently shown how Williams's novels are rooted in this tradition of English fiction.[8] His nonfictional prose works can be shown to have a discernible family resemblance to their fictional siblings. It must never be forgotten, either, that the sensibility of Williams (the "structures" of his thought and feeling) was that of a poet; it was from poetry and toward poetry that his imagination grew and tended. Whatever the form—drama, biography, novel, history, theology—it is permeated by this poetic sensibility. Although Williams's prime purpose in the theological essay is persuasion by intellectual argument, it is impossible for him to perform this task except as a poet and, therefore, impossible for him not to excite feeling even when engaged in the act of rational persuasion.

II

Four major rhetorical devices in *The Forgiveness of Sins* give Williams's theological discourse its unique quality, its peculiar density: the adjective, the metaphor, the "inserted" clause and semicolon, and the antithesis.

1. The adjective

Not for Williams the abhorrence of the adjective; adjectival phrasing is one of the chief characteristics of his style. Every student of rhetoric is aware of the dangers of this kind of writing, especially in prose that is meant to persuade by argument. In feeble or disingenuous oratory the frequent use of adjectives (or adverbs) usually has the effect of blurring the outlines of the thought and giving the impression of dishonesty; one will seek to convince by decking out meager thoughts with colorful descriptions. At best an overuse of this sort conveys only the conviction of the orator. However, this is true only of feeble oratory. In the best romantic prose the adjective is a

---

8. Cavaliero, *Charles Williams: Poet of Theology* (Grand Rapids, Mich.: Eerdmans, 1983), 54ff. Cavaliero draws an interesting comparison between Walter de la Mare and Charles Williams: "Inconclusiveness is the essence of his [de la Mare's] style. Williams, however, concentrates on achieving precision" (55).

282 B. L. HORNE

tool that can be used not just to heighten emotion but also to draw more vividly and accurately the picture that is intended. So it is in *The Forgiveness of Sins,* as in this typical passage: "That web of diagrammatised glory, of honourable beauty, of changing and interchanging adoration, depended for its perfection on two things—the will of God to sustain its being and its own will to be so sustained" (chapter 3; *FS,* 18).

The theological position with its intellectual clarity and emotional force is carried not only by the metaphor of the web with which the passage begins but also by the adjectives "diagrammatised," "honourable," and "changing and interchanging." They make not for imprecision and obscurity of thought: just the opposite, they make the thought more luminous. Here, in an extraordinary set of juxtapositions, Williams brings together four adjectives in three "sets." "Glory"—a noun either almost without content in many writings (so vaguely do some write about it) or a word with a multitude of possible meanings—is here exactly conceptualized. It is to be thought of and seen as a diagram: a clear and definite construction with constituent parts and interstices that can be identified. It is the adjective that bears the intellectual weight of the statement as it takes up the metaphor of the web and indicates what is latent within that metaphor. Running through this diagram are the shafts of that special form of love known as "adoration." The adjectives for this noun catch up the statement made on a previous page: "It was to be a web of simultaneous interchange of good" (16), and there is a swift reference, too, to the phrase "counterchange of joy" (10). The concept of adoration is here extended by the adjectives, and what might have been thought proper only to Divinity is presented as the possible (perhaps necessary) experience of all parts of creation. Finally, with the qualification of beauty as "honourable," beauty is placed in the context of honor. Williams takes a word whose natural milieu is either that of social ethics or that of social order to make a statement not only about beauty but also about goodness; it suggests a world in which truth, goodness, and beauty are inseparable.

Not all of the adjectives in *The Forgiveness of Sins* possess this same concentrated power, but Williams never uses an adjective carelessly or dishonestly, merely to raise the emotional temperature or cover up a shallowness of thought. When, for example, he writes, "Chastity is the obedience to and the relation with the adorable central body" (*FS,* 24), he is enunciating a precise theological position: human beings are "made in the image of God," but Christ *is* the image of God so they are made "in him." As Christ was the possessor of a human body, so that body is, by definition, adorable, and being "made in him," the bodies of human beings are potentially part of the glory that was his and so are also worthy of adoration. The sentence is peculiarly dense in both its thought and its style. Similarly,

THE THEOLOGICAL RHETORIC OF CHARLES WILLIAMS 283

the phrase "awful responsibility" in the sentence "The awful responsibility of the First Cause remains with the First Cause" (28) condenses an entire theological debate. It is primarily a statement about justice and the relationship of God with his creation. (It is the kernel of the later essay "The Cross.")[9] The responsibility that God has, as the creator of the universe, is one that can only be contemplated with wonder and terror by creatures who know something of the meaning of responsibility (aw[e]ful in one sense) and the painful price justice can exact when that for which one is responsible goes wrong (awful in another sense). The deliberate ambiguity enriches the sense by condensing a number of thoughts into a single phrase.

One adjective is perhaps used too frequently, but it is of great significance for the rhetoric: it is the adjective *high,* as in "the high Day of Atonement" (*FS,* 40); "It may . . . be supposed that so high, so original, a miracle" (49); and "the high dignity . . . of our nature" (57). Williams uses this word to suggest both power and strangeness but also to recall the formal address of medieval chivalry and the titles of the medieval world. The language of religion has retained a few of these titles—the Lord (for God or Jesus Christ) and Our Lady (for the Blessed Virgin Mary)—but it has allowed the adjectives that would have been the natural accompaniments to these titles to disappear. Williams's religious rhetoric preserves at least one of them: "high." But it is opaque in that it depends for its meaning upon something that is not present in the text. It alludes to Williams's own doctrine of the hierarchical nature of life, and if this is not understood, the adjective will seem an empty flourish, portentous and teasing but, in the end, conveying very little.

2. The metaphor

If Williams's rhetoric can be characterized as adjectival it must also be characterized as metaphorical. The theology is not presented in abstract terms that may then be supplemented by concrete illustration (although there are examples of that); it is carried by metaphor.[10] That is, the theology is contained in the metaphor. Williams does not use the striking image, as do most theologians and philosophers, primarily as an illustration of a point that could, in theory, be grasped without the concrete image or example. In Williams's rhetoric the metaphor cannot be omitted or replaced without altering or damaging the theological vision.

We have already noticed the image of the web in the third chapter of *The*

---

9. (1943: original title "What the Cross Means to Me"); reprinted in *Image,* 131–39.

10. An example of the "simple" illustration can be found on page 73: "But, that being so, there can be an added power; as it were, the oxygen to the mountain-climber."

284 B. L. HORNE

Forgiveness of Sins. It was one of Williams's favorite metaphors for the integrity of the whole created order, and it is one of the central images of this book.

> Sin had come into the great co-inherent web of humanity; say rather that all the web burst into sin, and broke or was antagonised within itself; knot against knot, and each filament everywhere countercharged within itself. (chapter 3; *FS,* 26)

The image is one of his solutions to the problem of writing coherently and intelligibly about the mystery of that total interdependence he called co-inherence. The web, with its suggestions of intricacy, intellectual pattern, delicacy, fragility, beauty, complexity, fitted his purpose admirably. It became an irreplaceable element in his theology, and because it is a metaphor it gives the theological statements in which it appears a peculiar density. If the passage just quoted had to be (and could be) explained, spelled out in terms of rational discourse, it would, even in the hands of a skillful theologian, take several pages. Moreover, the metaphor, being a metaphor, is both opaque and expansive. When the rational explanation has been provided there is no more to be said: it is either accepted or rejected, and a counterargument can be produced. But the metaphor does not yield to argument; one cannot grasp its content by intellectual effort or perceive its implications all at once.[11]

Other metaphors inhabit the essay: the diagram (*FS,* 7 and 18), the flame and the fire (89), the city (24, 80, 84), light (107 and 111). Most of them have already appeared in previous theological writings, most particularly in *He Came Down from Heaven.* One, however, is original—the metaphor of "weight," which is introduced so late in the essay that it is easy to pass over its significance. "The metaphor which our Lord used has a particular aptness —it is the taking up, the carrying, the Cross, not the being crucified; it is the intolerable *weight* of the duty, and not its agony, which defeats us—'the *weight* of glory'" (112–13; emphasis in the original). The reader only realizes in time, as the metaphor expands in the imagination, that this image has been underlying and informing much that Williams has been saying about the practice of forgiveness throughout the book. Only now has it sur-

---

11. "Metaphor subverts order or confuses categories in order to create or to adumbrate a new order. . . . Metaphors result, then, from an impasse between the lexical possibilities of a word and the inapplicability of those possibilities to a particular sentence. This impasse is transcended by the release of a new meaning that rescues the sentence from meaninglessness. Metaphor forces the sentence, then, to jump tracks, to uncover a new pertinence despite the impertinence, the calculated or unconscious error. The word is affected by the new meaning. . . . By virtue of its metaphoric dimension, language not only submits to innovation; it often accomplishes it apart from our awareness" (Wesley A. Kort, *Story, Text, Scripture* [University Park: Pennsylvania State University Press, 1988], 78–79).

THE THEOLOGICAL RHETORIC OF CHARLES WILLIAMS   285

faced. Contained within it is the opposite notion of "lightness/ease." When dealing with forgiveness in Shakespeare, Williams contrasts the weight and gravity of Isabella's pardon with the speed and lightness of Imogen's:

> There is the deliberate . . . act of Isabella; pardon corresponding to penitence, and penitence demanding penalty as pardon offers freedom: a union of passions, but a grave and deliberate union. (12–13)

> And this too is, artistically, the cause of his phrasing of the speed of pardon; he would not have it heavy. But the realistic style reflects a realism: this is what the loveliest pardon is . . . . (11)

When he moves into the strictly theological discussion the same contrast is presented. "To prefer another's will to one's own . . . to become another's will by means of one's own . . . is indeed the necessary thing for love" (*FS*, 72) and is indeed one of the most difficult things in human experience; it is "heavy." It may be glorious, but it is often experienced as an almost intolerable burden, as "weight." "The penance of our life is too heavy" (100). Yet Williams insists throughout on the opposite possibility of pardon being practiced with swiftness and ease: like Imogen's, carried lightly and offered with a kind of gracious speed. The reader is led into this complex theological and psychological mediation by the metaphor that sustains it; though that metaphor's actual significance emerges only at the very end of the essay.

3. The semicolon and the inserted clause

These two devices are grouped here because Williams usually uses them to achieve a similar effect; indeed they frequently appear in the same sentence, where the semicolon introduces the clause that begins with an "insertion." The insertion is really an exclamation; the rhythm of a sentence is broken or interrupted by the insertion of a small exclamatory phrase: "or rather," "or at least," "must one say," "as it were," "say rather." These insertions are quite deliberate; they are part of his rhetorical technique and make his writing distinctive. The reader is thrown off balance by these phrases. The prose does not have the regular movement that is the feature of most nonfictional writing. The sentences advance in darts and rushes; the rhythm speeds up and slows down unexpectedly. The "syllogistic" pattern of philosophical and theological prose, proceeding from premise to premise in measurable periods, is abandoned and replaced by something more urgent. One might have expected that the intellectual content would have become less clear and more diffuse in this rhetoric, for the frequent use of the device normally creates a sense of hesitation, diffidence, tentativeness, even uncertainty. Not so here. Williams uses these exclamations to introduce an amplification of the thought with which the sentence began. A second thought is coupled to the first with such speed that the reader is forced to consider both at the same time. For example: "The Atonement made possible the forgiveness of sins; or at least made it possible after the best manner" (*FS,* 100). This is an extraordinarily complex and "dense" sentence. Its theological elements are (a) the doctrine of the Atonement, i.e., the reconciliation of God and man in the life and death of Jesus Christ; (b) the forgiveness of sins, i.e., the recognition that in any kind of reconciliation the exercise of pardon on the part of someone is the focal point; (c) the machinery of reconciliation, i.e., how the desired state is actually achieved; (d) the suggestion that other ways of achieving the end might have been used. I can think of no other theologian who would have described the crucifixion of the Son of God as the "best possible manner" for opening up the way to the exercise of pardon. It is the suddenness with which the direction of the sentence changes that surprises and concentrates the attention of the reader: the theological proposition with which it begins is abruptly qualified and enriched by the practical application. In eighteen words Williams both enunciates the doctrine and indicates the way in which the doctrine "works." And the effect is made possible by the exclamation, the inserted clause.

The semicolon is used to much the same effect: for the purposes of surprise and enrichment. A statement is made, complete in itself; but the period is not closed by the expected full stop, it is elaborated by means of the semicolon. It is as though thought is organic, continually unfolding. Nothing is allowed to be discrete. "It is the choice of a God, not of a man; we should have been less harsh. We should not have created because we could not have endured; we could not have willed; we could not have loved" (*FS,* 100). The sentence unfolds by means of the clauses introduced by the semicolon, which signals not so much an alteration as an addition, an enlargement of the original concept. Far from creating an impression of a loosening of the material, the semicolon increases the tension and "contracts things into a span." This device is used more frequently in *The Forgiveness of Sins* than in any other nonfictional prose work by the author. The very density of this prose may be one of the reasons so many readers find it a difficult book.

4. The antithesis

In the twelfth section of the *Rhetoric* Aristotle tells us that the elements that make a speech graceful are antithesis, metaphor, and animation. We have already dealt with metaphor in Charles Williams's prose, and the kind of animation Aristotle has in mind does not concern us here. Antithesis does, however, and Williams is intensely aware of the power that antithetical writing can exercise. His most famous utterance is, after all, a supreme

THE THEOLOGICAL RHETORIC OF CHARLES WILLIAMS   287

example of antithetical rhetoric: "This also is Thou; neither is this Thou." In *The Forgiveness of Sins* the antithesis usually appears in two variations: the antithesis of paradox and the antithesis of contrast.

All theologians have been forced to face the question of paradox and introduce it into their writings; it is simply an inescapable part of a language that has to relate the conjunction of the natural and the supernatural. Religious language is inevitably the attempt to convey the ineffable in the principal medium of human communication, words. Charles Williams is doing nothing new in expressing himself in paradox, but his way of using the device betrays a particular delight in this form of speech. At the beginning of the sixth chapter he introduces the theological problem of the relationship between faith and morals: "We must not cease from our own labour because the glory is seen free in another; but neither must we cease to admire the glory because the labour is all that we can feel in ourselves" (*FS,* 69). We notice the antithetical balance of the sentence immediately: it is like a mirror, the second part reversing the first in its repeated and subtly altered phrases: "We must"/"neither must we"; "our own labour"/"labour is all"; "another"/"ourselves"; "glory . . . seen"/"glory . . . [felt]." The antitheses enable the thought to be compressed into so short a span, and the paradox increases the density: its meaning can be approached and teased out but never fully explained. The same theological point, that we are the free and undeserving recipients of grace and yet have, by our own will and efforts, to appropriate the grace (a point that has been the cause of endless debate throughout the Christian centuries) is made in a much terser paradox later. "This does not rule out the necessity of what was said before about acts; say, Do, and add, But do not do" (93). Its reverse appears six pages later: "Say, Do not do; and add, And then do." At its worst, the paradox is nonsensical and merely a statement that is self-contradictory. At its best, it is the expression of a recognized ambiguity—whether in life or in the texts, the coexistence of two things that apparently contradict and exclude each other. Williams was particularly sensitive to this state of ambiguity, both in life and in texts. His two major works of literary criticism focus on the experience of "contradiction" in the life and imagination of the poet.[12] His discussion of the Fall in *He Came Down from Heaven* (repeated in *The Forgiveness of Sins*) revolves around the notion of ambiguity: the consequence of the rebellion of Adam and Eve is the experience of "contradiction," the knowledge of good "as antagonism" (21). This is a deathly and terrible paradox. The Atonement achieves the "reversal" of the Fall, bringing life out of death and turning the terror into joy. However, the paradoxical

---

12. *The English Poetic Mind* (1932) and *Reason and Beauty in the Poetic Mind* (1933).

nature of human experience does not disappear: now it is not that good is known as evil but that evil is known as good. The practice of forgiveness is both the cause (on God's part) and the consequence (on humankind's part) of the Atonement. The paradoxical rhetoric perfectly expresses the paradoxical fact.

The second variation of the antithetical mode is less startling. Here the effect is more like that of an antiphon: a statement is made and is followed by one that contrasts with it not by way of contradiction (the paradox) but by way of looking at the proposition from another angle. "He who professes only nature may be rewarded with the best of nature, perhaps with more than nature; he who professes more than nature, if he does not practise it, may be left with neither" (*FS*, 75). This surely is a sentence Aristotle would have considered graceful. The balance is arrived at by the repetition of words and phrases; interest arises out of the way they are contrasted; and satisfaction from the almost identical number of syllables in each part of the sentence. The antithetical mode, in this case, also makes for linguistic and semantic density.

III

This brief analysis has not been offered as an exhaustive study of Williams's rhetoric in *The Forgiveness of Sins*; other features—such as the dialectical mode of question and answer, the deliberately formal and ceremonious styles of address, the use of the pun—have not been discussed. I have merely sought to identify the ways in which the unique density of his prose has been achieved; and the density of the style is at one with density of the theological vision. It has not been my task to scrutinize the theology of the essay, but I would claim that it is inconceivable that this theology could have been communicated in any other way—that is, in a different kind of rhetoric. Williams himself was aware of this and in the sixth chapter of the book has something to say about the relationship between form and content:

> Love must carry itself beautifully; it must have style. It may seem absurd, in such high matters, to use so common a literary term, and yet there is hardly any word so useful. Style, in literature, is an individual thing. *Le style, c'est l'homme même*—style is the man himself. (*FS*, 82)

The style of Williams's writing is the style of the theology, and the idea of density is crucial to both: this is at the center of his method and his vision.

Many interpreters of Williams's work seem to detect—or at least show a desire to find—a dualism in his thought and imagination: evil against good; darkness against light; natural against supernatural. I think this kind of interpretation is profoundly mistaken. For all his interest in witchcraft and the occult, for all his use of images of supernatural conflict in his novels,

Williams's imagination and thought are monistic, as the theological essays demonstrate. The whole created order belongs to God; his attributes (justice, love, mercy, pity) penetrate it and sustain it; he is the cause of its existence and therefore responsible for that existence in all its ugliness, wickedness, and perversity as well as in all its beauty and goodness. Evil has no real existence; there is only the good to know. There is about the universe a fundamental integrity that cannot be destroyed, however much it is perverted. It is for this reason that Williams was so attracted to the writings of the Lady Julian of Norwich and could make sense of her oft-quoted but seldom understood phrases "All shall be well" and "All manner of thing shall be well."[13] This is the vision of Christian monism, and the theological method is the method of inclusion. It rarely proceeds by exclusion: either/or; it must, if it can, proceed by incorporation: both/and. Apparently disparate and even contradictory experiences must, somehow, be brought into conjunction with one another. And for the presentation and articulation of this Christian monism Williams forged his unique monistic rhetoric.

13. Julian of Norwich, *Revelations of Divine Love,* chap. 27.

The Caroline Vision
and Detective-Fiction Rhetoric:
The Evidence of the Reviews

Jared Lobdell

"He always boiled an honest pot"—thus T. S. Eliot[1] of his friend Charles Walter Stansby Williams (1886-1945), M.A. (Hon.)—and his detective-fiction reviews represent one of the longer-simmering pots. They date from the Ghetto Age of detective-story reviewing, when the daily papers devoted an occasional review column to detective fiction, stipulating no more than one paragraph per book. This Ghetto Age coincided with the so-called Golden Age of British mystery and was in fact its corollary.

Williams's reviews, in the *Westminster Gazette* and its successors, begin in 1930 and end in 1935.[2] Over the six years, there are some eighty-three columns, which, taken together (as they will be in my forthcoming book *English Mysteries: Charles Williams and the "Golden Age" Detective Novel*), provide one of the best critiques of the genre, for all their scrappiness. They also provide an excellent lead-in to Williams's understanding of detective-fiction (including "thriller") rhetoric and vision, and it is to this that my essay here is directed.

Before turning to what Williams said, I should like to suggest my own view of the genre, formed largely before I read his reviews but not immune from his influence. After all, in his essays collected in *The Image of the City* there are statements that echo some of the statements in these reviews, and I think as well that I detect some influence of Williams's views in C. S. Lewis's writings on narrative—but on that I will not insist.

Histories of detective fiction, or of mystery fiction usually contain an unexplained gap between Poe, who is deemed to have invented the genre (if

---

1. Introduction to *All Hallows' Eve,* by Charles Williams (New York: Pellegrini & Cudahy, 1948), xii.

2. Since Lois Glenn has provided a detailed catalog of Williams's detective fiction reviews (*Charles W. S. Williams: A Checklist* [Kent, Ohio: Kent State University Press, 1975], 24–38), I content myself in this essay with just enough information to identify the references.

THE CAROLINE VISION AND DETECTIVE-FICTION RHETORIC   291

that is what it is), and Doyle, who is deemed to have brought it very nearly to perfection. Lately it has been suggested—and in my view very largely demonstrated—that this gap has its origin in improper categorization and that the genre we should have been looking at all along is what the Victorians called sensation or sensational fiction.[3] I shall use it as a starting point for a consideration of Charles Williams as a critic of such stories, of "thrillers" that descend, in right line, from the shilling shocker.

At the outset, it would perhaps be wise to define roughly (if no more) what we mean by *genre*. Perhaps a recent handbook said it best in stating that established genres "carry with them a whole series of prescriptions and restrictions, some codified in the pronouncements of rhetoricians and others less officially but no less forcefully established by previous writers," and that the writer in the genre must always be making a declaration of indebtedness to or a conscious declaration of independence from those predecessors.[4] Our expectations, and thus our understanding of the work, are keyed by our knowledge of its (stated or intended) genre, including its rhetoric.

It is reasonable to call detective stories a kind of mythic comedy, in order to catch at least an echo of Northorp Frye's *mythos* of comedy. Recalling Frye's four great *mythoi*—springtime's comedy, summer's romance, autumn's tragedy, and winter's irony—with their contrapuntal motion,[5] I wish to suggest here that while science fiction is ironic and hivernal,[6] detective fiction is comedic and vernal. The place of fantasy in this formulation is a matter I have dealt with elsewhere[7] and doubtless will again (indeed it is dealt with toward the end of the essay): for the present, however, our concern is with comedic movement—indeed, a particular kind of comedic movement.

This may seem a roundabout way of getting at the work of Charles Williams, but we shall make up on the swings what we lose on the roundabouts, and it is in any case as well to set the groundwork firmly before trying to catch that elusive and mercurial author within our bounds. The point to which I am leading up, as those familiar with Northrop Frye's

3. R. F. Stewart, . . . *And Always a Detective* (Newton Abbot: David & Charles, 1980), chap. 1.

4. Heather Dubrow, *Genre* (London: Methuen, 1982), 9ff.

5. Frye, *Anatomy of Criticism* (Princeton: Princeton University Press, 1957), chap. 1.

6. See James Blish, "Probapossible Prolegomena to Ideareal Fiction," in *The Tale That Wags the God,* ed. Cy Chauvin (Chicago: Advent Publishers, 1987), 72–82, esp. 74.

7. In a series of papers given at annual meetings of the Wisconsin Science Fiction Convention, as for example, "The Spenglerian City in James Blish's *After Such Knowledge,*" *Extrapolation* 32 (1991): 309–18.

292 JARED LOBDELL

The Myth of Deliverance will already have noted, is that sensation fiction, and particularly detective fiction, fulfilled the same function for, and demanded the same responses from, the reading public in Victorian England that the popular comedic plays fulfilled and demanded in Shakespeare's day. Here is Professor Frye:

> In a famous chapter of the *Poetics* (xi), Aristotle speaks of reversal and recognition (*peripeteia* and *anagnorisis*) as characteristic of what he calls complex plots. . . . Sometimes the effect [of what Frye calls the "and hence" story, as opposed to the "and then" story] seems to reverse the direction of the action up to that point, and when it does we are normally very close to the end. Hence a reversal of the action often forms part of an *anagnorisis,* a "recognition," depending on how much of a surprise it is. Thus in a detective story the identifying of the murderer is a "discovery" in the sense that we realize he is a murderer for the first time: it is a "recognition" in the sense that, if the normal conventions of the detective story are being preserved, he is already a well known and established character.[8]

This anagnorisis is in fact a staple of Victorian popular fiction as well as of Shakespearean comedy: one need only think of the stolen or runaway child motif in, for example, G. A. Henty, or indeed the whole matter of *Lady Audley's Secret,* or (to come into Edwardian times) the double anagnorisis of the first of the Father Brown stories. It could even be said that the anagnorisis is the sensation of the sensation fiction. But how does this tie in with Frye's myth of *deliverance*?

By the myth of deliverance, Frye means (roughly) the story pattern whose essential drive is toward liberation, "whether of the central character, a pair of lovers, or the whole society" (p. 14). The comedy, or the detective fiction, is a ritual enactment of this pattern of deliverance, highly conventionalized. The point is thus not in the guessing "Whodunit?" but in the reader's participation in the denouement, the anagnorisis.

But we have been speaking of *detective* fiction, and it may be reasonably asked, what is the position of the detective in all this? R. F. Stewart has suggested a possible answer: the "detective" in the phrase "detective fiction" refers originally not to the character (Dupin or Sergeant Cuff), but to the fact that a process of detection occurs within the story.[9] In other words, early detective fiction had a person or persons engaged in the process of detection—who might therefore be called by the name *detective*—but the story did not center on the person of the detective to the same degree that

---

8. Frye, *The Myth of Deliverance: Reflections on Shakespeare's Problem Comedies* (Toronto: University of Toronto Press, 1983), 4.

9. Stewart, *Always a Detective,* 71ff.

THE CAROLINE VISION AND DETECTIVE-FICTION RHETORIC   293

Chesterton did with Father Brown or Doyle (most of the time) with Sherlock Holmes. (Even Poe paid less attention to the *personalia* of his detective than Doyle did to that of his—though I recognize that this statement is something of a judgment call.)

Nonetheless, an increasing tendency toward detective omniscience in detective fiction was there, and this raises an interesting point. It cannot be successfully argued that this tendency came about as a result of, or even in parallel to, an increasing detective omniscience in the "real world"—No. It seems rather that Sherlock Holmes and his successors are, like the disguised Duke in *Measure for Measure* or Prospero in *The Tempest,* stage managers or "deputy dramatists,"[10] whose function is to ensure that "everything comes out all right in the end"—which is to say, to enact the myth of deliverance. As I have elsewhere observed, using T. A. Shippey's term, Sherlock Holmes may be taken as a "calque" of the Victorian detective on the White Magician.[11] He is a type raised to the dignity of an archetype.

If all this is true, as I believe it is, we can see that Miss Sayers and her colleagues in the Detection Club were acting by a just instinct when they formalized (some would say "overformalized") the conventions of their genre.[12] This does not mean that the country-house or "Golden Age" English mystery is *per se* a better thing than the American hard-boiled or "Black Mask" mystery: both, after all, are conventionalized, and both accord with their national myths of deliverance. This, I think, may lie behind the dictum of Henry James that the most mysterious of mysteries (those participating most in the essence of mystery) are those that lie at our own door, so that Lady Audley drives Udolpho from our minds. "What are the Apennines to us or we to the Apennines? Instead of the terrors of Udolpho, we are treated to the terrors of the cheerful country house and the busy London lodgings."[13]

"Terror" is not, in my view, *le mot juste,* though it points the way to a possible Aristotelian catharsis and thence at least toward the communal aspects of the deliverance. But what is involved may better be called *mystery* than *terror*: if it were terror only, no one would reread *The Hound of the Baskervilles*. The first time I read it, I was twelve and terrified (and in a

---

10. Frye's term, in *Myth of Deliverance,* passim.

11. Lobdell, "Calquing and the Problem of Sequels in Edwardian Fiction," awaiting publication in the proceedings of the 1983 Marquette Conference on Tolkien. Cf. T. A. Shippey, *The Road to Middle-Earth* (London: Allen and Unwin, 1982), 77–78.

12. Howard Haycraft, ed., *The Art of the Mystery Story: A Collection of Critical Essays* (1946; reprint, New York: Carroll & Graf, 1983), 194–96, prints Father Knox's rules for the Detection Club (1928).

13. Quoted in Stewart, *Always a Detective,* 45.

294 JARED LOBDELL

strange house): I read it differently now, but I read it, and the fact that I know the outcome does not alter my pleasure in the ritual enactment of the myth. But James did have his finger on the importance of tying the story to the world (though I think the mythic world) of the reader.

Let us here consider Charles Williams on the question of pattern, its relation to realism, and perhaps to the self-critical or self-referential mode we referred to above, particularly as it led to the technique of those particular detective-story authors that Julian Symons calls the *farceurs*.[14]

Although Williams once praised whimsicality (15 April 1931), he inveighed against signs of "chats and chuckles" in the books of G. D. H. Cole and Margaret Cole (4 November 1930). But in a way, this is one of the few cases in which he speaks out against any kind of consciousness of the book as a book, a made thing, an artificial creation. It is not that he is playing the kind of tongue-in-cheek game that Father Knox played with the rules of detection for the Detection Club. But there is an exaltation of pattern, and not of "chats and chuckles," in his recognition that the status of reality and realism in detective fiction and the "thriller" is a subordinate one. If it were not, what would we make of a statement like this (24 December 1930): "The setting in Africa is pleasantly unusual, the English are pleasantly usual, and the Africans are pleasantly mysterious, so that the whole book is pleasantly satisfying"?—of a murder story, remember. Or when he speaks (2 March 1931) of "a really satisfactorily agonizing death for" a charming murderess?

In reviewing Collin Brooks's *Three Yards of Cord* (17 June 1931), Williams says at the end that it is "not real, but very good." He divides detection and thrillers (taken as a single category) into four types (22 October 1931)—the whole passage is worth quoting, almost as much for Williams as journalist as for Williams as critic: "'There are nine-and-sixty ways of constructing tribal lays, and every single one of them is right.' A list would be useful for advanced criticism; in the elementary classes we are confined to four. They are fact, fable, faerie, and fantasy."

It can scarcely escape notice that three of these four stand over against fact. To be sure, fable can be told with realistic detail (as in *Animal Farm,* to take a relatively recent example), and so can fantasy, whatever that may be. In fact, as Tolkien pointed out, if you are to make the rare and beautiful blue moon to shine or put fire in the belly of the cold worm, you had best do it with an accumulation of realistic detail. And if you enter the realm of

---

14. Symons, *Mortal Consequences: A History—From the Detective Story to the Crime Novel* (New York: Harper and Row, 1972), 114–16.

THE CAROLINE VISION AND DETECTIVE-FICTION RHETORIC   295

faerie, be sure that it is strictly an earthbound realm.[15] But, for all that, realism of story inheres not in these three: what inheres is pattern, even myth.

It is this pattern that, if "directly controlled by intense poetic passion," can produce a classic (7 April 1932). But even a lighthearted or irrational romp can work. Of one such, Williams writes (5 July 1932), "His murderers pop in, and his victims pop off, and Mme Storey pops round, and the whole thing is clearly incredible and therefore in its clear insanity fascinating." Or of Jefferson Farjeon's *Ben Sees It Through* (21 December 1932), it "is a pantomime," and it "has all the knockabout glory of the perfectly irrational. . . . Mr. Farjeon at his best attracts with perfect nonsense and thrills with fairy tales."

Or of another story (5 June 1933), "It is quite unconvincing, but it is unconvincing in the right way. There is something very near imagination in it." Of *Murder on the Orient Express* (17 January 1934), "a piece of classic workmanship; almost unbelievable, but exquisite and wholly satisfying." Perhaps the best summing up of Williams's view of detective fiction and the "thriller" is given in a review published 26 July 1933: "The danger and delight of these stories is (1) the immediate awareness of the form and the choice of the author in the form, and (2) the vitality of the characters by whom the form exists."

Recall the earlier statement in this essay that genre is conventionalized to permit uses that are either statements of indebtedness or statements of independence. If one looks at the history of the English country-house detective novel, one finds in the farceurs simultaneous statements of indebtedness and independence, what might be seen as a fuzzy delineation between action within the genre and commentary on it. And this has been true not only of farceurs, though they (and Edmund Crispin in particular) may be the best examples of it. The earliest Gideon Fells are simultaneously within the locked-room or puzzle subgenre and commentaries on it, as well as on G. K. Chesterton. In fact, if one looks at the timing, it is almost as if the genre awaited only the advent of its most conventionalized, most magicianlike, most pattern-bound, and most (therefore) purely mythic detective before its practitioners began their experimentation and independence (or forays into independence) and commentary-within-genre.

The detective I refer to is, of course, Dame Agatha Christie's Hercule Poirot, and the importance of the point for consideration here is that it establishes the years 1930 to 1935 as a time (in England particularly) in

---

15. "On Fairy-Stories" [originally the Andrew Lang Lecture in 1938], first published in *Essays Presented to Charles Williams*, ed. C. S. Lewis (London: Oxford University Press, 1947), 50–51.

which the use of the genre was unstable and even shifting. We are accustomed to thinking of the interwar period as the Golden Age of the English detective story, and in a way it was, but what a vast congeries is encompassed in that Golden Age. In 1930, the year Charles Williams began his detective reviews, Conan Doyle had but lately finished with Sherlock Holmes (and at the beginning of the year was, like Holmes, alive in Sussex), Chesterton had Father Brown stories still to go, *Trent's Own Case* was still in the future, Anthony Ruthven Gethryn was at the height of his career, Lord Peter short of his, and Thorndyke and the Humdrums (as Julian Symons has called them) were going strong.[16] Monsignor Knox, first of the farceurs, was publishing stories about the Indescribable, but in that he was distinctly avant-garde.

By 1935, when Williams did the last of his newspaper reviews, left-wing detective writers (Day Lewis and Christopher Caudwell) were in place, the Humdrums were beginning to die off, Chesterton was in the final year of his life, J. I. M. Stewart was writing as Michael Innes, Gethryn's creator had crossed the Atlantic to Hollywood, and, for two memorable experimental books (one of which Williams reviewed with considerable perspicacity), Anthony Berkeley had become Francis Iles. Of course, Williams did not confine his reviews to British authors—Ellery Queen and John Dickson Carr and Q. Patrick and S. S. Van Dine and Dashiell Hammett all make their appearance. Nor did he review only the experimenters: J. S. Fletcher, John Rhode, R. A. J. Walling, G. D. H. Cole and Margaret Cole, Jefferson Farjeon, and Gethryn's Philip MacDonald all make their multiple appearances.

In his entertaining *Snobbery with Violence,* Colin Watson remarks that in the so-called Golden Age, "book reviewers settled into an attitude of good-natured, if slightly supercilious, tolerance. They too had fallen in with the notion of detective stories being in a class quite separate from 'legitimate' literature. . . . Editors provided a segregated hutch for mystery novels, where they could be dealt with, a whole litter of twenty or thirty at a time, by means of a sentence apiece."[17] Charles Williams's reviews in the *Westminster Chronicle & News Gazette* and its successors, from 1930 into 1935, may be considered a kind of minihutch, as he reviewed three or four (occasionally five or six) books at a time and, rather than the sentence apiece suggested by Watson, more often gave them a paragraph apiece—or two, or three.

Watson goes on to say that there "evolved for this purpose a special style of reviewmanship. It was (and is) slightly facetious in flavour, crisp and

---

16. See Symons, *Mortal Consequences,* 114.

17. Rev. ed. (London: Eyre Methuen, 1979), 98.

insubstantial, like lettuce" (98). Williams's reviews are occasionally facetious, as he was occasionally facetious elsewhere: sometimes the facetiousness is akin to Chestertonian paradox. But he is less facetious than many reviewers, and far more substantial. In fact, he is the only one of the "hutch" reviewers I can think of who kept firmly in mind the position of the mystery novel *sub specie aeternitatis*. That is one reason for reprinting as well as analyzing his reviews; that and the light they cast on his own novels, mostly written during this time from 1930 to 1935.

The confines into which detective fiction reviews were squeezed during the Ghetto or Golden Age of detection provide us with a Charles Williams we may find it difficult to recognize at first glance. As he said of one of his favorite authors in the genre, we are (in reading Williams on detection) "never quite sure whether at bottom [he] is a wit, a moralist, or an occultist" (on H. C. Bailey, 29 December 1933). This is the epigrammatic Charles Williams, of relatively simple diction and light and pleasant rhetoric.

Williams's own perception and the need to say something intelligent and arresting about a book in one paragraph (all he was usually given) make it particularly fortunate that he was writing at the time of shifting genre use. It is my contention not only that he was fully cognizant of the sensation-fiction origins of detective fiction but that he was conscious also of the anagnorisis involved (as I hope my quotations will show). And here I would pause to make what may seem to be two digressions, but they really are not.

First, I want to shift attention back to my earlier remark on the place of "fantasy" in all this. And I want to suggest that, if we take one highly restrictive definition of fantasy, we can identify the comedic anagnorisis with the eucatastrophe of faerie. Let me remind you of the relevant passage in Tolkien's essay:

> But the "consolation" of fairy-stories has another aspect than the imaginative satisfaction of ancient desires. Far more important is the Consolation of the Happy Ending. . . . I will call it the *Eucatastrophe*. . . . The consolation of fairy-stories, the joy of the happy ending: or more correctly of the good catastrophe, the sudden joyous "turn," . . . this joy, which is one of the things which fairy-stories can produce supremely well, is not essentially "escapist," nor "fugitive." In its fairy-tale—or otherworld—setting, it is a sudden and miraculous grace. (81)

Second, I wish to call to your attention a curious phenomenon: the detective fiction writers mentioned above have, many of them, fairly close relationships to the writers habitually thought of as mythopoetic. The relationships range from identity (Chesterton and perhaps Sayers) to familial relationships (Philip MacDonald as George MacDonald's grandson), to friendship and influence (Bentley with Chesterton and—*vide* his fondness for the clerihew—Tolkien), to possession of the mythopoetic talent (Doyle), to shared Oxford (Stewart, Crispin—in one of whose books C. S. Lewis

298   JARED LOBDELL

appears as a character[18]—and, of course, Day Lewis, who beat out CSL for Professor of Poetry). It cannot be claimed that the world of the interwar detective story moved far apart from the world of the mythopoetic. Or, if you like, from the world of the fantastic (but it is not necessarily part of that world).

Nor, given both what we have said and what Tolkien said about the eucatastrophe, should we expect to find any great distance between them. For, in a way, it might be claimed that the vaunted "intellectualism" of the detective story (or the detective novel) comes down to this: the authors are fundamentally concerned, particularly in the time of Williams's reviews, with a set of patterns, a mythos if you like, involved in deliverance, involving a joyful anagnorisis—but (and here we follow James) centered on the familiar rather than on the strange. That is, the intellectualism consists in the embodiment of intellectual concerns in a "popular" form. But the concerns are popular as well, as Watson's book makes clear.

The distinction between the strange and the familiar, which seems simple enough with Burke and Alison in the eighteenth-century context (and even with James in the nineteenth),[19] tends to give way as we press on it in the twentieth. But perhaps we might say that the conventions of detective fiction put it into the realm of familiarity as a genre. In such a way the conventions of the Greek theater made the action familiar to the playgoers, for all the obvious artificiality of what happened on stage. This is a case parallel to the demand for pattern, as against realism.

I know of only one case in which Williams specifically considered the question of detection-fiction rhetoric. In a review of an utterly forgettable novel by Guy Morton (10 June 1934), he notes that it "would be a better book if Mr. Morton had not introduced a false rhetoric of action." There is also a passage in which he says that "without exciting words, there is not and cannot be any excitement in crime" (23 August 1932), though this is capable of more than one interpretation.

However, his use of allusion should give some clues to his assumption of the audience's background and, therefore, of appropriate rhetoric, insofar as rhetoric is not determined entirely by genre. Our search for these indications of the audience Charles Williams saw for detective fiction and for "thrillers" lies not only in the direct allusions but also in the concealed allusions with which his reviews are sprinkled. We are not surprised, of course, to find

---

18. Crispin, *Swan Song* (1947), chap. 8, as cited by Humphrey Carpenter, *The Inklings* (Boston: Houghton Mifflin, 1979), 208.

19. Edmund Burke, *A Philosophical Enquiry into the Origin of Our Ideas of the Sublime and the Beautiful* (London: R. and J. Dodsley, 1757); Archibald Alison, *Essays on the Nature and Principles of Taste* (Dublin: P. Byrne et al., 1790). On James, see note 24 of this article.

THE CAROLINE VISION AND DETECTIVE-FICTION RHETORIC 299

Miss Jane Marple (on her first appearance, in *Murder at the Vicarage*) hailed as Mother Brown, with G. K. Chesterton's Father Brown as her implied counterpart (14 October 1930). When author J. S. Fletcher is described as standing "to great detection as the other Fletcher stood to Marlowe" (17 November 1931), the audience is expected to know how the Fletcher of Beaumont and Fletcher stood to Christopher Marlowe in the gallery of Elizabethan and Jacobean dramatists.

When Williams echoes the Horatian ode, "Eheu! fugaces, Posthume, Posthume, / labuntur anni," (6 November 1930, "even though, Posthumus, we are all growing old": *Odes* 1.24) some, at least, of his readers must have been expected to grasp the allusion. When he says of a novel (25 August 1931), "The story goes into top gear up the Hill Difficulty," the allusion to Bunyan is expected to strike home.[20] When he says (7 April 1933), "It is no longer sufficient to look in your heart and write," we may catch the allusion to Sidney's first *Astrophel* sonnet ("Fool! said my Muse to me, Look in thy heart and write!") and he would expect us to catch it. In the same review, he refers to a "novel whose center is intellectual sensation and only its circumference physical." The concealed allusion is to the definition of God as a circle whose center is everywhere and circumference nowhere (it was a favorite allusion of Williams), but whether he expected this to be recognized I neither know nor would want to guess.

Similarly, when he says (26 July 1933), "Beauty, fortunately, in this respect, is no longer truth," the reference to Keats is evident to us and I suppose to his original readers. When he says that "'something lingering with melted lead or boiling oil in it' was wanted," we recognize *The Mikado* and assume his original readers would, too. But when he says (18 March 1931), of *Malice Aforethought,* that Dr. Birkleigh "determines and dares and does murder his tyrannical and unpleasant wife," are we or is anyone really expected to catch an echo of Kit Smart's *Song to David,* "Seers that stupendous truth believed / And now the matchless deed's achieved / Determined, dared, and done"? (I think we are.)[21]

It is here necessary that we carry out three tasks. First (and simplest), we should ask, and try to answer, the question of whether an examination of Williams's reviews in this area will help us understand Williams and his views of the appropriate rhetoric for, and the underlying vision in, popular detection fiction and the "thriller." (It will certainly help us understand the canons of Golden Age detective fiction, but that is another story.) The

20. Similar expectations are evident in John Buchan, *Mr. Standfast* (1919), and in Dorothy L. Sayers, *Busman's Honeymoon* (1937).

21. Smart, *A Song to David* (1763), final stanza, as adapted for congregational use in *Songs of Praise*, ed. Percy Dearmer (London: Oxford University Press, 1925).

300 JARED LOBDELL

answer to this is quick and easy and comes (perhaps surprisingly) by way of Sax Rohmer, as we will shortly see.

Second, we should see what it is that Williams looked for in detective fiction. What elements, for him, determined whether a book was good or bad? (It is also of interest to see whether his judgments have stood the test of time: so far as I can tell, they have, though some authors he liked—notably H. C. Bailey and R. C. Woodthorpe—are in need of reprinting and critical resuscitation.) We have already noted the demand for pattern and the assumptions implied by allusion.

Third, we should look at the classifications and taxonomies Williams used to help him reduce the blooming buzzing confusion of the golden ghetto to order. This will lead naturally into the point about "a false rhetoric of action" noted earlier. These classifications and taxonomies are highly revealing for an inquiry into the aesthetic of Williams's own supernatural "shockers" (or "theological thrillers"), besides providing some hitherto unused clues on the Golden Age aesthetic.

We begin—and indeed virtually end—our first and briefest inquiry with a comment in a review of Sax Rohmer's *The Bride of Fu-Manchu* (29 December 1933). "There are some few absurd books of my own which exist only because one evening, having finished one of Mr. Rohmer's, I said suddenly to myself, 'I also will write a novel.' It wasn't, when finished, much like any of his, but can one now seethe the mother in the kid's milk?"

This passage illustrates three points. The first is that Sax Rohmer (Arthur Sarsfield Ward) was Williams's inspiration as a novelist: he was also Williams's coeval and contemporary in the Order of the Golden Dawn, but his mark as inspiration is more significant here. It makes clear that Williams was deliberately writing in the tradition of the "shilling shocker" (though by now they were seven-and-six). The second point is that the reviewer's persona is the traditional self-deprecatory one going back to Chaucer in the *Prologue*—a reference that, had he made it, Williams would have expected his readers to "get" (as he expected them to "get" Bunyan's *Pilgrim's Progress* and even Kit Smart's *Song to David*). And the third point is precisely in both this wide frame of reference and the smile which Williams shared with the discerning reader and with which he knocks the ball to the boundaries of the frame: "seethe the mother in the kid's milk" is a humorous turnabout of the biblical injunction against seething the kid in its mother's milk[22] and may even refer obliquely to the then-growing popular use of *kid* to mean "child."

What Williams looked for principally in detective fiction was style. (This

22. Exod. 23:19 et al.

THE CAROLINE VISION AND DETECTIVE-FICTION RHETORIC   301

from the creator of a style that might itself be described as fortunately inimitable—but the contradiction is apparent, not real.) Without multiplying examples needlessly, I note several cases in which he exalts the need for style. Of a novel by Anthony Abbot (Fulton Oursler), for example (2 March 1931), he writes "Mr. Abbot's is certainly an ingenious mind; what such a mind needs now is only—O everlasting cry!—style, style, and always style." In another review (17 June 1931), he speaks of "an ingenuity of style that keeps hinting at dark possibilities." Of Glen Trevor's (James Hilton's) *Murder at School,* "No compliment can be too handsome for style" (1 January 1932). Of the forgotten novel *The End of Mr. Davidson* (27 April 1932), "It is a perfectly simple book, with the simplicity of pure style." Of Ellery Queen's *The Greek Coffin Mystery* (28 July 1932), "If his verbal style lacks something, his spiritual style is perfect." Of a novel by Jefferson Farjeon (13 December 1932), "This excellent opening demands something finer (stylistically) than Mr. Farjeon gives us." Of a subsequent book by Ellery Queen (14 June 1933), "Mr. Queen is in danger of denying style by overstating one element of style," and "we demand from him not a solution but a story." The element of style Queen is overstressing is indicated in Williams's opening line to this paragraph, "A reader does not read to discover the criminal but to discover the book." Of Philo Vance in *The Dragon Murder Case* (17 January 1934), "Culture does not consist of knowing a lot of unusual facts. It implies a style of intellect to which Mr. Vance is a stranger."

Shortly thereafter, of a novel by David Sharp (2 February 1934), Williams writes, "Mr. Sharp, on the other hand, has a plot that only his persuasive style can carry. The plot is fairy, but the style is real." Five months later, in reviewing a novel by Father Ronald Knox, he refers to Father Knox's "keen sense of the sanctity of style" (4 June 1934). And, in one of his last detective-fiction reviews (3 August 1934), "There is about [*The Bell is Answered*] a flavour of intelligence: that subtle thing which is style, which is culture, which is irony and common-sense." Perhaps the strongest statement of all concerns Martin Porlock (Philip MacDonald), "Mr. Porlock's first novel has style; it has therefore inevitably everything else" (7 October 1931).[23] Further, "Style can only afford to be dramatic about profound spiritual crises, if then" (13 February 1933), which speaks also to the question of rhetoric.

From these comments, I think it evident that, in the mind of Charles Williams, style, though connected with verbal felicity, is something much more like an innate sense of the fitness of things. It is connected with

---

23. The book referred to is *Murder in Kensington Gore;* its title in the United States is *Escape.*

302   JARED LOBDELL

culture (a much more difficult word to define) and it is connected with rhetoric, which is, after all, that part of writing which is linked to verbal felicity: also, of course, the fitness of things includes the fitness of rhetoric to pattern or plot.

Thus, pure style would in detective fiction be a perfect fitness between rhetoric (or technique generally) and pattern or plot. Note that in his praise of Trevor's *Murder at School,* Williams says not that "no compliment can be too handsome for his style," but that "no compliment can be too handsome for style." Like the butterflies and serpents of *The Place of the Lion,* style is an absolute: there is a Platonic Form of style for detective fiction or sensation fiction or "thrillers"—and we can reasonably believe there is a proper rhetoric.

We might now look at the characteristics and taxonomies to which detective fiction is linked, and then to the ways in which Williams generally makes sense of the genre whose products he is reviewing. We find that there is, in his reviews, a constant sense of the bounds of the genre and of its nature—in short, of its definition, in both senses of that word. He notes (11 June 1930) that "every thriller ought to have at least two different kinds of excitements—that of getting to the climax, and that of the climax itself." The excitement thus lies in the story and in its denouement or eucatastrophe—in peripeteia and anagnorisis.

The initial distinction (the climax and getting to the climax) is one dichotomy. Early on in his reviewing, Williams draws a second, between breathlessness and brain (7 July 1930), though this will not allow him to accept in full Canon Whitechurch's distinction between thrillers and detective stories (13 December 1932), while acknowledging that every "clear-minded honest follower of the true path down clues of matches, ciphers, shoe laces, and postcards will enjoy Mr. Whitechurch."

Williams also remarks (30 July 1930) that "to be like ourselves is a miracle—in a detective novel." He praises a book for presenting real people in "real surroundings—ladders and tennis courts and so on" (4 June 1930). He argues for an achievement in which "the mystery is felt to be produced by [the author's] people and not the people by the mystery" (26 August 1930). He notes that, in a police procedural, "pattern is seen much more clearly as a pattern than when a single mind does all the work." (This of a novel "too extreme for realism but not for pattern"—3 September 1930.) To a book by M. P. Shiel, he says, he responded with "a fascinated irritation. It is unbelievable and it is alive" (21 October 1930). He acknowledges a "personal passion" for books of a particular kind: "They are circumscribed; they have a pattern; they have unity" (9 February 1931). Of course, this is not Aristotelian unity, but a unity by pattern.

So at the outset of his reviewing (which is also the outset of his career as

THE CAROLINE VISION AND DETECTIVE-FICTION RHETORIC   303

a novelist, marked by that one of his novels—*War in Heaven*—which most closely approximates a detective thriller), Williams is seeking a kind of realism of execution, combined with perfection of pattern, in ordinary surroundings. (He comes down on the side of Henry James, as against H. G. Wells.)[24]

Let us turn now to the question of vision. In his review of *Malice Aforethought* by Francis Iles (Anthony Berkeley Cox), Williams calls the story that of a "commonplace crime, but no doubt hell is commonplace" (18 March 1931). Of a novel of Christopher Bush three months later (17 June 1931), he remarks that the author "reminds us of the chaos round the corner and writes a thrilling story in doing it." He speculates in September (16 September 1931) that perhaps "we must take a life for a life, but the compensating life must be freely offered." Of a book by Philip MacDonald (Williams's most often reviewed author), he says "Mr. MacDonald makes not our flesh, but our souls creep" (17 November 1931). Six weeks later he issues a dictum (7 January 1932) that "the more sense of infinity, the better the story."

David Sharp's *I, the Criminal*, he says, "introduces us to the spiritual reason of thrills. I feel as if Mr. Sharp had explained the universe by accident in writing an amusing, happy, and restless book" (28 July 1932). And of another Philip MacDonald book, the next year (26 April 1933), he writes that "before he told me I knew who the madman was, and at that moment a ray of the real sun broke upon his goblin world. But what goblins! What a marvellous capacity for shaking one's soul up." (We will come back to the real sun and the goblin world in our discussion of reality in detective fiction and thrillers.)

I have wondered, in reading a review of 5 June 1933, if Williams was punning: "As the man is dead it might seem not very much to matter but it is always the immaterial that matters so frightfully" (actually, "frightfully" could be a pun, as well as "immaterial"). But this is by way of a detour on the way to the review in which Williams lets himself go on the spiritual nature of detective fiction. The book, appropriately, is Dorothy L. Sayers, *The Nine Tailors* (17 January 1934). One contemplates with something akin to envy a reviewer whose column for the week included the new Sayers (*The Nine Tailors*), the new Van Dine (*The Dragon Murder Case*), and the new Christie (*Murder on the Orient Express*). In one morning.

---

24. See Robert Bloom, *Anatomies of Egotism: A Reading of the Last Novels of H. G. Wells* (Lincoln: University of Nebraska Press, 1977), 9–37 (chap. 1), esp. 9; Leon Edel and Gordon Ray, eds., *Henry James and H. G. Wells: A Record of Their Friendship, Their Debate on the Art of Fiction, and Their Quarrel* (Urbana: University of Illinois Press, 1977), passim.

304   JARED LOBDELL

Laughter and pity and terror, clarity and mystery, inform all these things, and as Miss Sayers's mastery moves on to its climax in the tower of the church where the refugees, admirably ordered by a mortal and immortal ritual, find shelter, the book becomes in itself a kind of judgment.

The powers of earth and air denounce and encourage, and below them lies the wide sweep of waters. There is nothing supernatural—unless indeed we and our life and all our art are supernatural, as some have held.

But it is the reflection of our dark and passionate life itself which those waters hold and those bells proclaim. It is a great book.

That is the most favorable review of any book in his years of reviewing detective fiction. Next perhaps is his review of Philip MacDonald's *Escape,* and next to Miss Sayers in *The Nine Tailors,* his favorite author is H. C. Bailey in anything. Here is Williams on Bailey's *Mr. Fortune Wonders* (29 December 1933):

He can do a murder, no doubt; but the evils he really hates are pride, hate, cruelty. He seems sometimes almost to imagine spiritual sin, and his cherubic Reginald Fortune thrusts at it like a real cherub.

In five of these stories he arranges for death or life at his will. You do not like or dislike them because they are good crime, but because they are good Fortune, and because that means something like good fortune in the world.

These two paragraphs, by the way, show the punning and allusive Williams and the epigrammatic Williams. Because the cherubim of popular art are *putti,* fat, cheerful, and childlike, Mr. Fortune is cherubic, as we speak of a cherubic countenance. Because the cherubim of the Old Testament are fierce and winged lions, he thrusts like them. Without knowledge of the background, there is no pun and little sense to the epigram. The "good Fortune" pun requires less arcane knowledge.

But for our present purposes, it is important that all this is testimony to what Williams considers the nature of the detective-story vision. (The assumption that the readers of his reviews will understand his allusions speaks, of course, to his rhetoric, as noted earlier, or rather to what he deems the appropriate rhetoric for thrillers and detective stories.)

Here I pause to note something that has occurred to me in reading Williams's reviews. The claim, advanced particularly by C. S. Lewis, that Williams could make goodness interesting is in fact a claim which could be made on behalf of a host of Golden Age detective novels, and which is implicit in Williams's call simultaneously for character that determines action and for action that falls within the patterns appropriate for the genre. The interest in character—if there is an interest in character—is directed not toward the villain but toward the detective hero. It is Peter Wimsey or Jane Marple or Gideon Fell that we love, or at least follow avidly, and not their virtually anonymous adversaries. Most of the time. (But in one of Inspector

THE CAROLINE VISION AND DETECTIVE-FICTION RHETORIC   305

French's cases, his wife wept when a particular murderer was hanged.)[25]

Moreover, Sherlock Holmes may have begun as a cocaine addict, and C. Auguste Dupin was doubtless addicted to some drug or other (his creator certainly was), but for all their silly-assery, Wimsey and Albert Campion and Reggie Fortune (particularly good Fortune, but he is not of quite that ilk) are uncomplicatedly good. Granted that the early Fu Manchu is uncomplicatedly evil, and his opponents uncomplicatedly incompetent, the general rule is that Heaven conquers Hell. (As Williams said in another context, "Hell is always inaccurate.")[26]

It was Williams's peculiar genius to strip this mythic comedy of its pretensions to a purely earthbound existence, to recognize and set forth its essence (I might even say its quintessence), and to see the *visio Caroli* concerning, if not Piers Plowman, then at least ordinary Englishmen (but "we have never met an ordinary mortal") among the principalities and powers of comedic redemption. Only the first-published of his books retained the form of a detective story, but they all derive from that origin. What Williams has said about rhetoric and vision in that context is of no less value in looking at his fiction than in looking at that of Sayers or Bailey or MacDonald.

Williams listed fantasy as one of the four principal—indeed elementary —ways "of constructing tribal lays" for the tribe of the "thriller" or detective fiction reader. I find this of particular interest, for reasons that should become clear and that have a great deal to do with rhetoric and vision. For fantasy as a craft (which is what a tribal poet practices) has rigorous requirements for subcreation: if the writer is indeed to make the rare and beautiful blue moon to shine, or to put fire in the belly of the cold worm, then he or she must manage that elvish craft of *enchantment;* there, in that word, is the key.

Was Williams wrong in linking fantasy and detection fiction—which includes detective fiction and "thrillers"? Let us see. We know that for the quality of fantasy we have the craft of enchantment, the power of the strange and otherworldly, and the sudden joyous turn, the eucatastrophe. For the genre of detective fiction, we have the conventions of the genre (and the detective process), the power of the familiar and the this-worldly, the magician conventionally on stage, as it were, and then the sudden turn, the anagnorisis. Both promise deliverance, in a way, but in what different ways.

And yet, is this not where the goblin world comes in? And what of Chesterton? Has he not shown, with Father Brown, that the quality of

---

25. See Williams's review published 15 March 1934.

26. "John Milton," in *Image,* 30 (originally published as an introduction to *The English Poems of John Milton,* World's Classics Series [London: Oxford University Press, 1940]).

306   JARED LOBDELL

fantasy can inhere within the conventions of detective fiction? Rather as his master Dickens showed that the quality could inhere within the conventions of the English sporting tale? To this I can think of two answers, both of which are, I believe, in accord with Williams's views.

First, with the appearance of Sam Weller, the "angel in gaiters," Dickens and *Pickwick* begin to burst the bounds of the genre, and the same kind of thing might be said of Father Brown and Chesterton as the stories progressed—and still more of some of GKC's other detective stories. And second, there is a distinction to be drawn between *Mooreeffoc* fantasy and creative fantasy. Here is Tolkien again:

> *Mooreeffoc* is a fantastic world, but it could be seen written up in every town in this land. It is Coffee-room, viewed from the inside through a glass door . . . and it was used by Chesterton to denote the queerness of things that have become trite. . . . But it has, I think, only a limited power; for the reason that recovery of freshness of vision is its only virtue. (pp. 56–57)

This recovery of freshness of vision is not unlike anagnorisis. Creative fantasy, on the other hand, in making something new, promotes delivery not merely from triteness (or from the unexamined life, perhaps—or should I say, from the mundane?) but out of all our sea of troubles to a new dry land. And this is far more like a full reversal or peripeteia, of action, of energy, of reality.

I think the Father Brown stories, still more *The Man Who Knew Too Much,* eventually test the conventions of the genre too severely, and the *Mooreeffoc* comes too automatically at the denouement, as in "The Vanishing of Vaudrey," for example. But in the best of the early stories, the very first, with its double anagnorisis, or "The Queer Feet" or even, a little later, that extravaganza in which a corpse is hung on a hat rack and a murderer 'a' babbled o' silver bullets—the detection is real and the deliverance is real, none the less so (indeed more so) for being salvation. For that also is deliverance.

Though creative fantasy may achieve a fuller peripeteia than *Mooreeffoc* fantasy, and though detective fiction without fantasy may be stronger on anagnorisis than on peripeteia, we must be careful not to formulate this statement in such a way as to give the impression that fantasy is one genre (stronger in peripeteia) and detective fiction another (stronger in anagnorisis). Detective fiction is, by our standards, a genre, but fantasy of either kind is not. It is a craft—like poetry, perhaps, or goldsmithing. Or at least it used to be, and was still in the days of which we are speaking here. And it is this of which Charles Williams speaks in his quadripartite division—fact, fable, faerie, and fantasy. (And only "thrillers" or Jefferson Farjeon's romances can enter even the lands bordering on faerie.)

Chesterton suggests that the quality of fantasy can indeed inhere in

THE CAROLINE VISION AND DETECTIVE-FICTION RHETORIC   307

detective fiction, as indeed it can only in mythic genres. But there are other kinds of reversal and discovery as well. Because there are other kinds, this discussion may seem another of my roundabouts, but it has a definite purpose here and a definite connection to Charles Williams. Because Tolkien wrote what is generally considered fantasy, and C. S. Lewis wrote children's stories (which are thought of as fantasy) and interplanetary novels (which are thought of as science fiction), and because Charles Williams was their wartime friend and also a writer (and a significant influence on Lewis), there is a tendency to think of him as a "fantastic" writer. Now it happens that I dispute the syllogism pretty much in toto, but what is important here is that detective fiction, and the sensation fiction from which it comes, be seen as a form of mythic comedy, as presenting the myth of deliverance but as only possibly (not necessarily) permitting the inherence of the fantastic—and even then, more often of *Mooreeffoc* than of creative fantasy.

For if we fail to realize this and if we do not seek to find out what Williams thought were the bounds and characteristics of the detective-fiction genre, we will not make the proper in-genre response to a detective novel that begins with these words:

> The telephone bell was ringing wildly, but without result, since there was no one in the room but the corpse.
> A few moments later there was. Lionel Rackstraw, strolling back from lunch, heard in the corridor the sound of the bell in his room, and, entering at a run, took up the receiver. He remarked, as he did so, the boots and trousered legs sticking out from the large knee-hole table at which he worked, but the telephone had established the first claim on his attention. (*WH,* 7)

Moreover, unless we are familiar with the genre, its conventions, its origins, its purposes, we might find it difficult to accept at face value, or even to understand the reasons for, Charles Williams's unequivocal statement that his novels began in emulation of Sax Rohmer. Before closing this essay, I should emphasize the point that when Williams found the vision of Heaven and Hell in the confines of detective fiction, he was not finding what was not there. He was rather stripping the core of the redemptive comedy for action, as it were, and honing the fineness of the edge for the rhetoric appropriate to Golden Age detective fiction.

After all, it might have been Lord Peter who imagined Shakespeare quiring to the young-eyed cherubim on the underground, and it certainly would have been in Lord Peter's character to have interrupted a disquisition on the proper plural of *rhinoceros* with the lines "The feet of your favorite Rhino / Are apt to leave marks on the lino." But in both cases it was Charles Williams, *in propria persona*.[27]

---

27. *Cherubim:* see Carpenter, *Inklings,* 95; *rhino:* Williams, "Sound and Variations," in *Image,* 54.

Is this important? Yes. The placing of Williams's restless intelligence within the reviewer's hutch not only confirms his choice of the theological thriller as the vehicle of his own expression but also goes a significant way toward illuminating what was in fact golden about the Golden Age. If we are to believe his reviews, the golden quality inhered in the style, and the style was a function of the rhetoric (almost the "light touch") of the stories, with their fundamental—even archetypal—pitting of the powers of light against the powers of darkness. No, make that the Light touch, and make it the Powers of Light, and the Powers of Darkness. Sun and Goblins. Or perhaps Son and Goblins. In either case, a little capitalization would not be amiss.

Not least on the fortunate meeting of Williams and detective-fiction reviewing.

Poetry, Power, and Glory:
Charles Williams's Critical Vision

Diane Tolomeo Edwards

"How many sermons, addresses, and talks have you read on what are usually called Moral Problems, that suggest what is really felt? The people to which you should go to find out are the great poets." Charles Williams offered this observation in 1940.[1] He argued that the energies of great poetry speak to those who intuit or desire a world larger than the one their senses convey and who are intensely aware of the frequent contradictions between what are often held up as moral ideals and the more immediate and real situations to which these ideals do not seem to apply. This is why poetry often touches a nerve, whereas moral debate can seem dry and insensitive. Williams's critical writings illuminate the link he found between poetry and the numinous and demonstrate how that link extends to include an incarnational view of language and a sacramental view of poetry.

In addition to his novels, poems, and theological and critical works, Williams also wrote numerous book reviews, addresses, and brief articles that deal with a literary text or concept and at the same time illustrate and invoke his own theological interests and beliefs. In his essays on poetry, his book reviews, and his other writings about literature, he does not measure what he reads against a set of theories he holds about literature. What he most often does is hold these works up next to a reality he perceives and judge them by how their vision matches that reality. His interest in poetry lay in whether a poet spoke the "truth," and he remained wary of a tendency to turn truth into a theory and, ultimately, watch it "rapidly degenerate into a thesis."[2] "Truth" here is obviously something more objective than an argument and exists independently of whether we find it attractive or even find it at all. But it does invite being sought and is capable of being mediated through a text, and this is one of the functions of the poet.

The idea of the poet as a seer (*vates*) and maker is at least as old as the

---

1. Williams, "The Recovery of Spiritual Initiative," *Christendom,* December 1940, 247.

2. Williams, *The English Poetic Mind* (Oxford: Oxford University Press, 1932), 195.

ancient poets who called upon their Muse for inspiration. As seers they were to receive insights and as makers they were to turn these insights into something that would communicate their inspiration to others. Whereas Sir Philip Sidney stressed the double-edged nature of poetry's ability to delight and instruct, the didactic element received comparatively little attention from Williams in his writings about poetry. But he agreed with Sidney's complaint against moral philosophers who speak in such abstractions that they cannot be understood.

More appealing to Williams was the emphasis the Romantics placed on the inspirational elements of poetry, yet, as John Heath-Stubbs rightly explains, "Williams's use of the term 'Romanticism' must be distinguished from the use of the word by some other modern writers. It does not, for him, mean an affirmation of emotional values to the exclusion of formal and intellectual ones."[3] It does, however, include the effect that great poetry has on the emotions and the power it has to touch the inner self, while not divorcing the heart from the head. In his earliest novel, Williams gives us a character who holds a new chair as professor of applied literature, the purpose of which is to "recall [England] from the by-ways of pure art to the highroad of *art as related to action*" (*SE,* 8; emphasis added). This connection is essential to understanding Williams's ideas about the nature of poetry and its transforming power in our lives.

The search for what is true is of central importance to Williams and is found throughout his critical work from the 1920s until his last writings. This should not surprise us, since Williams was a student of theology as well as of literature; in neither discipline did he receive formal academic training, which may help to account for the ease with which he shifted from the one to the other with no attempt to compartmentalize his ideas on either.

One important clarification may be needed at this point: having an interest in both theology and literature is not the same as imposing one's beliefs on what one reads and determining a work's greatness by how well the text matches the beliefs. Williams shows no patience with those who would attempt to impose a particular structure on the world, even if that structure were the Christian one with which he was himself sympathetic. Forcing a Christian interpretation on works of art that are evidently not Christian in their origins or values cannot result in renewed faith in God or in humanity. It does a disservice to both by misreading the art and imposing a theory when vision is what is demanded. Similarly, those "who accept unspeakable art or scholarship because the theme is Christian" also harm both artistic and theological values by watering down their vision because they are so

---

3. Heath-Stubbs, *Charles Williams,* Writers and Their Work, no. 63 (London: Longmans, Green, 1955), 18.

CHARLES WILLIAMS'S CRITICAL VISION

delighted to see Christian art in the marketplace. Taste, or "discrimination," may, and perhaps even must, lead one to prefer a tight argument that attacks one's fundamental beliefs to a vapid and confused argument that tries to support them.[4]

In a more direct way than do his novels, Williams's critical writings provide his readers with a clear opportunity to perceive his vision. When we read Williams's critical writings, we discover that he wrote almost exclusively on poets and their poetry and its effect on the reader. While Williams does not stress a reader-response approach to a text and does not espouse any particular literary theory, he keeps coming back to clear criteria of greatness, which include the impact felt by a reader as well as the vision that reader is asked to behold. Williams's critical writings define both the role of the critic and that of the reader, and he is cautious about the prospect of possibly ruining the impact of the original: paraphrase can remove the desired sense from a literary passage. In *Poetry at Present* (1930), he sees the critic as one whose attempt must be to recreate for his reader the experience of the text itself, but to do so in another medium. The "impulse" of the poet, on the other hand, is not chiefly "to communicate a thing to others, but to shape a thing, to make an immortality for its own sake."[5] Thus, while the poet does not consider the reader as someone to whom the poet must convey a message, the critic sees this task as an essential aim and tries to communicate not the text but the experience of the text. But since there is no singular "experience" of a text, all the critic has to recreate is his or her own experience, and so criticism becomes a personal statement that approaches the condition of poetry.

What is intriguing about much of Williams's criticism is that he so often usurps the role of the poet in his personal statements about poetry: he abandons the critic's role of recreating his own experience of a text and becomes instead the poet who creates a vision that makes us feel as if we are capable of great actions or emotions. In *The English Poetic Mind,* Williams argues that this is the role of great poetry, to awaken in us an awareness of our capacity for change and to cause us to recognize the "hiding-places of the power and of the glory" (199). Here is one instance of this sort of prose, in the last paragraph of one of Williams's reviews:

> Our idolatry has destroyed complexity in Milton. We have not willingly admitted that he could smile. Eve in "sweet austere composure," Satan "stupidly good," at whom he did smile, have been imposed on him as his own image. His

4. Williams, review of *Christian Discrimination,* by George Every, *Theology* 42 (1941): 183.

5. Williams, *Poetry at Present* (Oxford: Oxford University Press, 1930), vii; *English Poetic Mind,* 5.

312 DIANE TOLOMEO EDWARDS

intellectual background therefore has been robbed of half its proper scope, as his noise (by our organ-notes) of its softness and shyness. Only Wordsworth ever got drunk in his honour, and justly. For the Forms of Wordsworth, which are his Solitaries, are poised at points of a world consistent with this world and with them—the Leech-Gatherer, the Soldier. But Milton's Forms, when they are Solitaries, are often in motion; they are on journeys through a further universe imagined as intensely as Wordsworth imagined this. "Stupidly good," we have turned the 'feeling intellect' of Wordsworth to our exterior daffodils and sunsets and the visionary power of Milton to the granite of our interior folly; we have not yet begun investigation.[6]

Surely this passage shows us something of Williams's vision of great poetry. It tells us very little about Tillyard's book: though the review is positive, its five paragraphs defend Milton, and Tillyard, against Milton's opponents, and discuss, not "the Miltonic setting," which is Tillyard's topic, but Milton's sense of greatness, laughter, and rhetoric. One-fifth of the review, the passage quoted above, is perhaps Williams the poet more than Williams the critic speaking, if, indeed, we can separate the two. He is here seen fulfilling his own characterization of the poet, and also of the reader of poetry: "It is [the reader] as well as the poet who proceeds from a sense of unknown modes of being to the search for the hiding-places of man's power" (*English Poetic Mind*, 199). The descriptions of Wordsworth's and Milton's "Forms" invite the reader to consider further the intersection of intellect and vision not only in the poetry but also, and perhaps even especially, in one's own life. To fail to see Milton's "visionary power" is to fail to see his poem at all. And to say that Wordsworth's poetry is about clouds and daffodils is to ignore where the images intersect with the "further universe": "Wordsworth, praised too often and too entirely for his Nature poetry, was concerned primarily with the soul of man."[7] This is the concern of all great poetry, and the poet's skill is determined by how successfully this concern is made concrete in the poem. Alice Mary Hadfield recollects that in Williams's lectures "he told us how the voicing of a grief or love or despair can strengthen the mind by lucidity and lead to a vision able to make sense of it, and give daily ability to hold to it and even grow into it."[8]

The demand that the text makes on the reader in this respect is not the same thing as reader-response criticism; its approach is not theoretical, and Williams is interested in the poet's vision as well as the reader's response

6. Williams, review of *The Miltonic Setting*, by E. M. W. Tillyard, *Criterion* 17 (1938): 740.

7. Williams, "The Commonwealth in English Verse," *Contemporary Review* 124 (1923): 232.

8. Hadfield, *Charles Williams: An Exploration of His Life and Work* (New York and Oxford: Oxford University Press, 1983), 110.

to it. Reader and writer, or reader and text, do not interact in a subjective manner but must together engage in looking outward to a meaning that is larger than both. The possibility is then raised that the values of our culture might be "re-energized" by "spiritual grace."[9] Poetry is therefore not an intellectual exercise but something that can put us in touch with who we are and whence we came. It deals with momentous things and is not reducible to dissection of metaphors and analysis of word games.

In his *A Myth of Shakespeare,* Williams imagines a dialogue between Shakespeare and Marlowe in which Marlowe asks about poetry, "Will, is it real or is it fantasy?" and continues,

> All we mean by poetry—
> That's the great question; is it a good game
> Played with sweet fellows for companions
> With the mere game for gaining, and their praise—
> Or is it more—a knowledge beyond earth's,
> More than the tales of godhead, a divine
> Motion of all our hearts towards ecstasy,
> And our blood beating with the beating world?[10]

It is clear which of these visions of poetry belongs to Williams, and he is anxious in his critical writings to explore what it is in great poetry that achieves "knowledge beyond earth's." In doing so, the role of the poet is not to be obscured. But neither is the poet simply one of our fellow companions playing a "mere game" with us, and the art cannot exist solely for its own sake.

Yet Williams also insisted on the primacy of the text as "the existing thing, the image we have to deal with," enriched by, but not subordinate to, its literal and allegorical meanings.[11] That poetry cannot be paraphrased in prose (though there can indeed be poetic prose) was a basic premise of Williams's attitude toward the great English poets, by whom he almost always meant Shakespeare, Milton, and Wordsworth. But it is certainly not the quality or the details of the poet's life that encourage "a divine motion of all our hearts towards ecstasy," nor does psychobiography play a part in arriving at an understanding of a poem's dynamics. Williams's review of a book that attempted to portray "authorship humanized" suggests that "the book has the smallest resemblance to a stone closing the entrance to the dark resting-place of a god."[12] Such an approach obscures those "hiding-places

---

9. Williams, "Recovery," 244.

10. Williams, *A Myth of Shakespeare* (Oxford: Oxford University Press, 1928), 46–47.

11. Williams, *The Figure of Beatrice* (London: Faber and Faber, 1943), 45.

12. Williams, "The Picturesque Approach to Literature," review of *The Human Approach to Literature,* by William Freeman, *Supplement to the Week-End Review,* 25 March 1933, 340.

314   DIANE TOLOMEO EDWARDS

of power and glory" that great poetry reveals. By focusing on the poet rather than on the poetry, the stone stands in front of the place where the god rests. Williams concludes: "This is the danger of humanising; the humanised poet becomes more important than the poetry, and poetry becomes something terribly like a relaxation. But poetry, Wordsworth has told us, is power. The picturesque tends to conceal the 'hiding-places of power.'"[13] We are meant to be drawn to the poetry, not in any New Critical sense of ignoring the author altogether but as a meeting place between creator and vision, a place in which the creator points to the vision and guides us closer to it rather than pointing to himself or herself and asking for our admiration. The poet acts as Virgil to the reader's Dante, showing the way to things hitherto unseen and, finally, abandoning the reader to see the vision unassisted. For this reason, Williams recommended that Hadfield begin her reading of Dante with the *Paradiso,* "so that [she] should grasp the aim of the whole journey, the celestial glory that moved the verse and drew the travelers onwards from the fearful beginning."[14] The vision can transcend the immediate and personal and awaken in the reader a sense of the numinous even if the reader is unprepared for such results in reading a poem. This awakening is where poetry and theology intersect most clearly.

Williams gives an example of this in Wordsworth's *Prelude,* a poem he often turns to for elucidation of matters concerning the making of a poem and the relationship among the poem, personal vision, and the transcendent. While acknowledging that that poem is full of personal experience (though Williams carefully distinguishes between author and persona), he emphasizes: "But that is not the immediate point. An experience *of that kind* is here the subject of the poetry—it happens to be his own, which is interesting to the biographer but unimportant for poetry. His poetry is here concerned to discover, to express, to define, a particular state of being. . . . Poetry is here awakening in us our sense of our capacity for 'change and subversion.'" And a year later, Williams again clearly delineated the difference between Wordsworth "as a personal poet and a psychological problem" and William, the persona through whom we may explore "the poetic effect of the poem," and staunchly allied himself with the "Williamites."[15] Once again we discover that poetry has a mission and that great poetry demands a response from its readers, but not arbitrarily. The discovery of the "hiding-places of the power and of the glory" is its true aim and effect.

13. Williams, "The Picturesque Approach," 342.

14. Hadfield, *Exploration,* 128.

15. Williams, *English Poetic Mind,* 26; *Reason and Beauty in the Poetic Mind* (Oxford: Oxford University Press, 1933), 17.

CHARLES WILLIAMS'S CRITICAL VISION

One way to explore these "hiding-places" is to look at how Williams differentiates between the imaginations of lesser and greater poets. For him, both sorts agree about the importance of undertaking work on one's own soul, but they differ in how they try to pierce the protective walls around the soul's hiding place. There is a division "between the poets to whom Liberty was a name and a mist, and those to whom it was a meaning and a road. The former have always tended to desire an immediate earthquake; the latter a more wearisome, a more *bourgeois* pilgrimage."[16] The poets to whom Williams applies this distinction are Shelley and Wordsworth: Shelley wishes for an inner earthquake, Wordsworth takes us on a pilgrimage. Both, however, understand the power of poetry, which moves us and sends a tremor to our innermost being. Alice Mary Hadfield recounts the time Williams asked her, "If you were offered the choice of never feeling that shudder at great verse again or never drinking a glass of wine again—would you hesitate?"[17]

Williams amplified this idea in *Reason and Beauty in the Poetic Mind.* He presents there the idea that the harmony of poetry "can induce harmony" in its reader (171). That tremor or thrill which poetry induces may, wrongly, convince us that we can appropriate its "divine phrases for our self-definition." But this is to make the transcendent a servant of the ego. Instead, we are to respond to it submissively and "we adore and obey the Reason, Power, and Beauty which are to be freely served and freely loved. In that sense a regained paradise is open to us" (172). For in that way the transcendent is afforded the opportunity to enter creation freely and engage in the work of re-creation, which includes both the making of verse and the shaping of the individual soul. The poet can help unite human nature and divinity by engaging in the act of creation.

In *Reason and Beauty,* Williams gives an instance of the relationship between nature and transcendent Reality in his description of the storm in *King Lear,* which is not interpreted as signifying the voice of Heaven but as "more nearly the condition in which a character moves; it is the echo of the voice of earth" (141). Lear's condition does not here undergo a supernatural judgment, yet "the voice of earth" that cries out in Lear's storm is the presence in the play of the transcendent as perceived in the created realm. When Lear awakens to the tensions between life and death, sanity and madness, the play achieves its vision in the "bringing together of separate things in a thing inseparate" (*English Poetic Mind,* 85). Language at such a level has an incarnational dimension to it as diverse elements are drawn

---

16. Williams, "Commonwealth," 233.

17. Hadfield, *Exploration,* 110.

into a unitive vision. The vision of a great poet becomes embodied or incarnated through the language of the poem and the reader may perceive it in a mediated form. Rather than imposing our reductive systems on the external world, such art forces us to attend to *natura rerum,* to things as they are, envisioning a "complete universe" (*Reason and Beauty,* 133) rather than avoiding certain of its aspects. It draws into our selves a vision that is larger than our individual egos, and when it does so it may well cause us to tremble even if we cannot say why. Williams pointed out that this was a significant difference between us and the Elizabethans: "For us all strangeness, most adventure, and in a growing sense all space, must be found within. It is rather in ideas of the world than in the world that novelty and familiarity must lie, and it is by the recognition of the inner in the outer that most of us find satisfaction, by the accommodation of the phenomenal world to our beliefs and consistencies" (*Poetry at Present,* 60–61). This suggests that perhaps we should instead be looking to recognize the outer in the inner, that vision rather than theory is what is most needed in the modern age.

There is also necessary a corresponding movement, without which we run into the danger of contemplating only the vision of the poem itself. In a review of Owen Barfield's *Romanticism Comes of Age,* written near the end of his life, Williams continues to assert that "later and feebler semi-Romantics" have not believed that the question needs to be asked concerning "how is it that you live and what is it you do?"—a question Williams likens to "the more ancient Grail-question, 'Of what is it served?'" The modern age relies too often on "the meddling intellect" and not enough on what Wordsworth called "the feeling intellect," which includes "an act of will, a choice in belief, a decision."[18] Hadfield asserts that Williams "shrank from no feeling, he accepted all intellectual examination," even as he struggled to unify head and heart in his life.[19] This definition of the feeling intellect removes it from too close a connection to the emotions and puts it closer to deliberate choice, making poetry allied to religion in its demanding "an act of will." It also resists poetry that makes us feel as if something has been written simply to impose a pattern on the text. What it does give us is a glimpse of the transcendent: even though a poem must embody its vision through its language, it can still point us beyond itself to the very source of creativity. In the last analysis, poetry offers correlations among head, heart, and spirit in ways similar to, yet unlike, religious experience.

18. Williams, "The Romantic Imagination" (review), *New English Weekly,* 10 May 1945, 34.

19. Hadfield, *Exploration,* 132.

CHARLES WILLIAMS'S CRITICAL VISION 317

In one of his discussions of religious drama, Williams offers a succinct summary of how poetry should relate to religion, not as "a meddling intellect" but as a medium in which what is inherent in our human nature finds its correlation in great art. He argues that "the only design which we can bear in art is that which arises from within."[20] We may not recognize the process as it occurs, but we will perceive the correspondence when it is presented to us. The "invention" (in the sense of discovery) poetry undertakes can highlight those aspects of experience that could easily serve the religious intention of religious drama in a poetically credible manner, by pointing us to the transcendent Reality even while telling us a story. Frequently, this is achieved through indirection, so that "the images will not be of the central idea so much as of something connected with the centre."[21] We see this in the *Second Shepherds' Play* in the Wakefield cycle and also in Williams's own nativity plays (*Seed of Adam, The House by the Stable,* and *The Death of Good Fortune*), all of which direct our attention to unconventional aspects of the story of the Nativity but ultimately use the myth to go beyond story to universal truths.

Besides such invention, the poetry must also display an appropriate complexity of diction, since having a good subject is not reason enough to write a poem or play. But because of the nature of language as a semiotic system, the language of a poem can attempt to point to "that untrappable thing"[22] by combining sound, sense, and idea in a complex richness. This is especially notable in verse like that of Gerard Manley Hopkins, in which "the intellect goes speeding to sound the full scope of the imaginative apprehension" and often gets "left behind" because it cannot keep pace.[23] The intellect need not always catch up with the imagination, however, since vision does not rely on it alone. But sometimes the "idea" is left out entirely because of the artist's fear of questioning or appearing to question dogmas. Yet, argues Williams, "it is we [Christians] who should be attacking, questioning, disputing. The cry of the Blessed Virgin '*How shall these things be?*' is our signal; the scepticism of S. Thomas was a part of the Apostolic College, and the scepticism preceded the answer."[24] This need not mean that all art must be intellectual, but it must be recognized that the intellectual freedom to question yet simultaneously accept dogma can create the style

20. Williams, "Notes on Religious Drama," *Chelmsford Diocesan Chronicle* 23 (May 1937): 75.

21. "Notes on Religious Drama," 75.

22. "Notes on Religious Drama," 75.

23. Williams, introduction to *Poems of Gerard Manley Hopkins,* ed. Robert Bridges, 2d ed. (London: Oxford University Press, 1930), xi.

24. "Notes on Religious Drama," 75.

318 DIANE TOLOMEO EDWARDS

necessary to the wedding of poetry with religion. Both contain contradictions, and both invoke "unknown powers," whether natural forces and supernatural occurrences as in Shakespeare or the interpenetration of the physical and paranormal worlds Williams presents in his own novels.

The interpenetration of the natural and supernatural realms is often a given in both poetry and theology. Williams seemed to believe that poetry usually does a better job than theology in demonstrating this, however. The language of theologians tends to be "one-sided": "Their terms ought to be ambiguous; they ought to carry meanings at once in time and outside time. It cannot be done" (*FS*, 17). Theologians are limited by language because their vocabulary must necessarily be drawn from figurative language when they attempt to describe God. Poets, however, work primarily in this realm already and, whether they acknowledge it or not, participate in the metaphysical. Like theology, poetry can suggest rather than define, but unlike theology it does not have to appeal to a language outside itself. It appeals to the imagination as well as to the intellect, much as religious symbols and sacraments do, but it is not limited to their concrete forms. Of course in ritual the symbol is not the god, any more than it is in poetry, for if it were, "what godhead remains to be symbolized?"[25] Williams told "Celia" (Phyllis Jones) in a letter to "examine your own admirable mind and tell me if you believe that the imagination of Dante accepted something you wouldn't accept for a minute; and that not in the mere accidentals of science but in his very vision of the universe."[26] Poetry shows us a vision of the universe through the medium of words; in this sense it may be considered an incarnational art insofar as it transforms ideas into concrete images, but these images remain in the mind rather than meet the eye.

Thus, it may be truer to Williams's beliefs to reverse this incarnational model and regard poetry rather as something full of *vestigia,* or footprints, that lead us to the transcendent rather than as evidence of the numinous in our midst. Citing the metaphysical poets, Williams ascribes to them a kind of sacramental progression: "To begin with a flea and end with God is almost the habit of English verse; though both the flea and God are sometimes—as in Shakespeare—given different names" (*English Poetic Mind,* 207). St. Augustine used almost the same image when he wrote that the immaterial and material meet in creation and "evoke praise to the Creator . . . even in the case of the tiniest fly."[27] This is entirely consistent with the verse in the Athanasian Creed which Williams cited as "the very

25. Williams, "Trial by Symbols" (review), *Week-End Review,* 12 August 1933, 168.

26. Quoted by Hadfield, *Exploration,* 116.

27. Augustine, *City of God,* 22.24; trans. Henry Bettenson (Markham, Ont.: Penguin, 1986), 1072.

maxim of the Affirmative Way" (*Dove*, 59), namely, that Christ is both God and Man "not by conversion of the Godhead into flesh, but by taking of the Manhood into God." Thus, "all images are, in their degree, to be carried on; mind is never to put off matter, all experience is to be gathered in" (59). A sacramental rather than an incarnational role may be assigned to poetry that observes the law of the Affirmation of Images and uses all created things, including itself, to point to a higher Reality.

In a speech Williams gives to Shakespeare in his *Myth of Shakespeare,* we can see this law encompassing the created physical realm (the sun) and hear Williams, via Shakespeare, asking how to extend this law to his writing:

> What's beyond?
> What's in the sun's self, the vastidity
> And circumambulation of that world
> Which lights the rest? I don't misjudge my play.
> There's freshness in it, youth and decent age;
> But the last secret—but age touched with youth,
> Ripeness of being, ripeness of poetry;
> No longer life transmuted into words,
> But words transmuted into life. . . .
>
> (97)

The writing of poetry (and plays, and all else) conveys life through words, but clearly what Williams here envisions is the profounder act of using language in such a way that its quickening powers point to the source of life much as the light on the earth directs our gaze upward to the sun. Language contains power, but there is a power beyond language that is both its source and its life.

Perhaps we are meant to connect this passage with the ending of the *Paradiso* and its acknowledgement of the Love that moves the sun and other stars. The Love there referred to is the creative Word made flesh, which has also raised "the Manhood into God." Not surprisingly, Williams finds this act of raising the everyday into the realm of the divine most clearly accomplished in the writings of Dante, through which he developed much of his "theology of romantic love." Beatrice is regarded as "the ordinary girl exalted into this extraordinary. . . . The union of flesh and spirit, visible in her (or him), is credible everywhere; indeed, that union, which so much poetry has desired to describe, is understood as more profound and more natural than the dichotomy . . . which has separated them" (*HCD*, 98). Earlier it was stated that "the feeling intellect" necessitates "an act of will," and the sort of poetry that has attempted to describe the union of flesh and spirit must acknowledge the power of the will as well as the emotions. So when Williams writes about the final lines of the *Paradiso,* he stresses that

320   DIANE TOLOMEO EDWARDS

the important element is not just the Love that moves the stars but also, and even greater, the fact "that Love rolled his own desire and will" which is higher than the sun and other stars. The Power that empowers the sun is the final vision of the *Paradiso*. Yet, of course, the sun and other stars "have their poetic place" as "they allow the mind to relax (if such a word may be used of such a state) towards the creation."[28]

This, then, is where Williams's "critical vision" is grounded. To express the inexpressible through the medium of language is the difficult task set before the greatest poets. They cannot dramatize pure abstractions, "which is why," asserted Williams, "if Christianity were not true, it would have been necessary, for the sake of letters, to invent it." He elaborates this further in what is probably his clearest statement about the relationship between theology and art: "It [Christianity] is the only safe means by which poetry can compose the heavens, without leaving earth entirely out of the picture. The Incarnation, had it not been necessary to man's redemption, would have been necessary to his art" (*Reason and Beauty*, 119). Williams was here discussing Milton's difficulty in depicting God in a dramatic narrative, and he admitted that the character of God in *Paradise Lost* was not always entirely convincing. But, he added, "in the *psychological* poem things are easier; for there the part of God is but a personification of something else. He—as best he can—personifies the mystery of heaven" (120; emphasis added). The character of God, while essential to the poem, is clearly not God, who, nevertheless, is personified as a means of alerting us to the greater Reality that cannot be described or personified. Heaven as a state is, ultimately, what all great art points to and awakens in its audience. The tingling spine is a symptom of a spiritual nerve that has been touched, and the nerve can be stimulated by grief, sorrow, delight, or joy. Because Heaven is a state that cannot in itself be either conceived or depicted, it is best understood through vision rather than theory, and what is best able to awaken that vision is great art, because Heaven's "properties and nature must be reckoned by things on earth and are perhaps more like them than is thought" (121).

"As above, so below" is one of the maxims of the Affirmative Way.[29] Poetry that, while it may be visionary in nature, remains private is not able to direct its readers to understand the correspondences it might itself perceive. To see the "above" in the "below" where we live is the achievement of the greatest art. Williams once referred to living as "acted poetry,"[30] and it is through this connection that great poetry usurps the

28. Williams, *Figure of Beatrice*, 225.

29. Williams, *Figure of Beatrice*, 10.

30. Williams, *Poetry at Present*, 173.

position of those sermons and addresses that do not connect with life as it is really lived. Awakening the inexpressible transcendent within us and stirring it to action is, ultimately, where the greatest art achieves its highest realization and invites us to partake, even if only for a moment, in sharing its vision of things as they really are in that state of being we all recognize as the destination of our journey.

Concordances

Citations from Charles Williams's books in this volume are normally from the earliest published versions. Page numbering in the later editions often differs greatly. As an aid to locating references, the following tables list the contents of certain books by chapter, and initial pages of each, in selected editions.

AH   *All Hallows' Eve*

    I.   London: Faber and Faber, 1945. 206 pp.
    II.   London: Faber and Faber, 1947 (4th impression). 240 pp.
    III.   New York: Pellegrini & Cudahy, 1948. xix, 273 pp.
        New York: Noonday Press, 1963. xix, 273 pp.
        Grand Rapids, Mich.: William B. Eerdmans, 1981. xix, 273 pp.

		I	II	III
	[Introduction *by T. S. Eliot*]			ix
1.	The New Life	7	7	1
2.	The Beetles	23	26	23
3.	Clerk Simon	42	49	50
4.	The Dream	54	63	66
5.	The Hall by Holborn	75	88	95
6.	The Wise Water	91	107	117
7.	The Magical Sacrifice	109	129	142
8.	The Magical Creation	132	154	172
9.	Telephone Conversations	154	180	202
10.	The Acts of the City	182	212	240

DH   *Descent into Hell*

    I.   London: Faber and Faber, 1937. 305 pp.
    II.   London: Faber and Faber, 1949. 222 pp.
        Grand Rapids: William B. Eerdmans, 1965. 222 pp.
    III.   New York: Pellegrini & Cudahy, 1949. 248 pp.

		I	II	III
1.	The Magus Zoroaster	9	9	3
2.	Via Mortis	29	24	20

323

CONCORDANCES

3.	Quest of Hell	45	35	33
4.	Vision of Death	69	52	53
5.	Return to Eden	102	76	80
6.	The Doctrine of Substituted Love	123	91	97
7.	Junction of Travellers	154	113	123
8.	Dress Rehearsal	172	126	138
9.	The Tryst of the Worlds	208	152	168
10.	The Sound of the Trumpet	241	176	196
11.	The Opening of Graves	258	188	210
12.	Beyond Gomorrah	290	211	236

GT　　　　　　　　　　　　　***The Greater Trumps***

- I. London: Victor Gollancz, 1932. 287 pp.
- II. New York: Pellegrini & Cudahy, 1950. xi, 268 pp.
  New York: Noonday Press, 1962. xi, 268 pp.
- III. London: Faber and Faber, 1954. 230 pp.
  Grand Rapids, Mich.: William B. Eerdmans, 1976. 230 pp.
- IV. London: Sphere Books, 1975. 203 pp. (The Dennis Wheatley Library of the Occult)

		I	II	III	IV
	[Preface *by William Lindsay Gresham*]		i		
	[Introduction *by Dennis Wheatley*]				5
1.	The Legacy	7	3	7	9
2.	The Hermit	29	24	25	24
3.	The Shuffling of the Cards	44	38	37	34
4.	The Chariot	63	56	52	47
5.	The Image that did not move	80	72	66	59
6.	The Knowledge of the Fool	104	95	85	76
7.	The Dance in the World	111	102	91	81
8.	Christmas Day in the Country	127	118	104	92
9.	Sybil	151	141	123	109
10.	Nancy	164	153	133	118
11.	Joanna	183	171	148	131
12.	The Falling Tower	199	186	161	142
13.	The Chapter of the Going Forth by Night	210	196	170	149
14.	The Moon of the Tarots	237	221	191	168
15.	The Wanderers in the Beginning	251	234	202	177
16.	"Sun, stand thou still upon Gibeon"	270	252	217	190

CONCORDANCES   325

HCD   *He Came Down from Heaven*

    I.   London: Heinemann, 1938. xi, 147 pp. (I Believe Series, no. 5)
        Grand Rapids, Mich.: William B. Eerdmans, 1984. [iv], 147 pp.

FS   *The Forgiveness of Sins*

    II.   London: G. Bles, 1942. v, 123 pp.
        Grand Rapids, Mich.: William B. Eerdmans, 1984. [iv], 123 pp.

    He Came Down from Heaven and The Forgiveness of Sins

    III.   London: Faber and Faber, 1950. 200 pp.

		I	II	III
He Came Down from Heaven				
1.	Heaven and the Bible	1		9
2.	The Myth of the Alteration in Knowledge	13		17
3.	The Mystery of Pardon and the Paradox of Vanity	32		29
4.	The Precursor and the Incarnation of the Kingdom	58		46
5.	The Theology of Romantic Love	83		62
6.	The Practice of Substituted Love	114		82
7.	The City	134		95
The Forgiveness of Sins				
1.	Introduction		1	107
2.	Forgiveness in Shakespeare		5	111
3.	The Sin of Adam		15	119
4.	The Offering of Blood		35	134
5.	Forgiveness in Man		52	147
6.	The Technique of Pardon		69	160
7.	Forgiveness and Reconciliation		92	177
8.	The Present Time		109	190

MD   *Many Dimensions*

    I.   London: Victor Gollancz, 1931. 317 pp.
    II.   London: Faber and Faber, 1947. 269 pp.
        Grand Rapids, Mich.: William B. Eerdmans, 1965. 269 pp.
    III.   New York: Pellegrini & Cudahy, 1949. 308 pp.
    IV.   Harmondsworth: Penguin, 1952. 254 pp.

		I	II	III	IV
1.	The Stone	7	7	3	7
2.	The Pupil of Organic Law	20	18	16	17
3.	The Tale of the End of Desire	43	38	39	36
4.	Vision in the Stone	60	52	56	49
5.	The Loss of a Type	75	65	71	61

326 CONCORDANCES

6.	The Problem of Time	101	87	96	82
7.	The Miracles at Rich	120	103	115	98
8.	The Conference	136	116	130	110
9.	The Action of Lord Arglay	149	127	143	120
10.	The Appeal of the Mayor of Rich	169	144	163	137
11.	The First Refusal of Chloe Burnett	187	159	181	151
12.	National Transport	205	174	198	165
13.	The Refusal of Lord Arglay	222	189	215	179
14.	The Second Refusal of Chloe Burnett	246	209	238	198
15.	The Possessiveness of Mr. Frank Lindsay	260	221	252	209
16.	The Discovery of Sir Giles Tumulty	276	235	268	222
17.	The Judgement of Lord Arglay	290	247	282	233
18.	The Process of Organic Law	310	263	301	248

PL   *The Place of the Lion*

    I.   London: Victor Gollancz, 1931. 288 pp.
    II. London: Victor Gollancz, 1947. 175 pp.
    III. New York: Pellegrini & Cudahy, 1951. 236 pp.
    IV. London: Faber and Faber, 1952. 206 pp.
         Grand Rapids, Mich.: William B. Eerdmans, 1965. 206 pp.

		I	II	III	IV
1.	The Lioness	7	7	3	9
2.	The Eidola and the Angeli	22	16	15	19
3.	The Coming of the Butterflies	43	29	33	34
4.	The Two Camps	60	39	47	46
5.	Servile Fear	77	49	61	58
6.	Meditation of Mr. Anthony Durrant	93	59	74	69
7.	Investigations into a Religion	103	65	82	76
8.	Marcellus Victorinus of Bologna	118	74	95	87
9.	The Fugitive	131	82	106	96
10.	The Pit in the House	149	93	121	109
11.	The Conversion of Damaris Tighe	173	107	141	126
12.	The Triumph of the Angelicals	192	118	156	139
13.	The Burning House	213	131	174	154
14.	The Hunting of Quentin	232	142	190	167
15.	The Place of Friendship	250	153	205	180
16.	The Naming of the Beasts	268	164	220	192

CONCORDANCES

SE   *Shadows of Ecstasy*

   I.   London: Victor Gollancz, 1933. 287 pp.
   II. London: Faber and Faber, 1948. 224 pp.
        Grand Rapids, Mich.: William B. Eerdmans, 1965. 224 pp.
   III. New York: Pellegrini & Cudahy, 1950. 260 pp.

		I	II	III
1.	Encountering Darkness	7	7	3
2.	Suicide while of Unsound Mind	25	21	20
3.	The Proclamation of the High Executive	42	34	36
4.	The Majesty of the King	57	46	50
5.	The Neophyte of Death	86	68	76
6.	The Mass at Lambeth	112	88	100
7.	The Opening of Schism	136	106	122
8.	Passing through the Midst of Them	157	122	141
9.	The Riot and the Raid	173	134	155
10.	London after the Raid	203	158	183
11.	The House by the Sea	213	166	192
12.	The Jewels of Messias	238	186	215
13.	The Meeting of the Adepts	256	200	232
14.	Sea-Change	278	217	252

TTL   *Taliessin through Logres*

   I.   London: Oxford University Press, 1938. viii, 96 pp.

Region   *The Region of the Summer Stars*

   II. London: Nicholson & Watson, 1944. 55 pp. (Editions Poetry
       London)
   III. London: Oxford University Press, 1950. viii, 61 pp.

Arthurian Torso: Containing the Posthumous
Fragment of **The Figure of Arthur** *by Charles Williams and*
a Commentary on the Arthurian Poems of Charles Williams by C. S. Lewis

   IV. London: Oxford University Press, 1948. viii, 200 pp.

Combined editions

   V.   *Taliessin through Logres and The Region of the Summer Stars.*
       London: Oxford University Press, 1954. xii, 96, viii, 61 pp.
   VI. *The Arthurian Poems of Charles Williams, Taliessin through*
       Logres and The Region of the Summer Stars. Cambridge: D. S.
       Brewer, 1982. x, 96, vi, 61 pp.

328 CONCORDANCES

VII.   *Taliessin through Logres, The Region of the Summer Stars, and Arthurian Torso.* Grand Rapids, Mich.: William B. Eerdmans, 1974. 384 pp. ("One-volume edition")

AP   VIII.   Part 1, "The Published Volumes," of *Arthurian Poets: Charles Williams*, ed. David Llewellyn Dodds. Cambridge: D. S. Brewer, 1991. (Arthurian Studies, 24) Pp. 17–145. (Published simultaneously in paperback, Woodbridge, Suffolk: Boydell Press.)

	I/V/VI	VII	VIII
[Introduction *by Mary McDermott Shideler*]		5	
[General Introduction *by David L. Dodds*]			1
Taliessin through Logres			
Prelude	1	19	21
Taliessin's Return to Logres	3	21	23
The Vision of the Empire	6	24	25
The Calling of Arthur	14	32	31
Mount Badon	16	34	33
The Crowning of Arthur	19	37	35
Taliessin's Song of the Unicorn	22	40	38
Bors to Elyane: The Fish of Broceliande	24	42	39
Taliessin in the School of the Poets	27	45	41
Taliessin on the Death of Virgil	31	49	44
The Coming of Palomides	33	51	46
Lamorack and the Queen Morgause of Orkney	38	56	50
Bors to Elayne: On the King's Coins	42	60	53
The Star of Percivale	46	64	56
The Ascent of the Spear	48	66	58
The Sister of Percivale	51	69	61
The Son of Lancelot	54	72	64
Palomides before His Christening	64	82	71
The Coming of Galahad	69	87	75
The Departure of Merlin	75	93	80
The Death of Palomides	78	96	82
Percivale at Carbonek	81	99	84
The Last Voyage	84	102	86
Taliessin at Lancelot's Mass	89	107	90
Note	95	111	92

	II	III/V/VI		
The Region of the Summer Stars				
Preface	6	vii/vii/v	117	97
Prelude	7	1	119	99
The Calling of Taliessin	10	5	123	102
Taliessin in the Rose-Garden	23	21	139	114
The Departure of Dindrane	29	29	147	120
The Founding of the Company	34	36	154	125

CONCORDANCES

The Queen's Servant	39	42	160	130
The Meditation of Mordred	43	47	165	134
The Prayers of the Pope	46	50	168	137

	IV	VII
Arthurian Torso		
Introductory (C. S. Lewis)	1	185
The Figure of Arthur (Charles Williams)		
1. The Beginnings	5	189
2. The Grail	13	197
3. The Coming of the King	24	208
4. The Coming of Love	45	229
5. The Coming of the Grail	60	244
Williams and the Arthuriad (C. S. Lewis)		
1. Preliminary	93	277
2. The Establishment of Arthur	97	281
3. The Golden Age in Logres	113	297
4. The Beginning of Separations	128	312
5. The Grail and the Morte	158	342
6. Conclusions	187	371

WH   ***War in Heaven***

    I.   London: Victor Gollancz, 1930. 288 pp.
   II.   London: Faber and Faber, 1947. 256 pp.
            Grand Rapids, Mich.: William B. Eerdmans, 1965. 256 pp.
  III. New York: Pellegrini & Cudahy, 1949. 290 pp.
  IV. London: Sphere Books, 1976. 205 pp. (The Dennis Wheatley
           Library of the Occult)

	I	II	III	IV
[Introduction *by Dennis Wheatley*]				5
1. The Prelude	7	7	3	7
2. The Evening in Three Homes	16	15	12	14
3. The Archdeacon in the City	31	29	28	25
4. The First Attempt on the Graal	44	40	41	34
5. The Chemist's Shop	62	56	59	47
6. The Sabbath	76	69	74	57
7. Adrian	86	78	85	64
8. Fardles	104	94	103	77
9. The Flight of the Duke of the North Ridings	123	111	122	90
10. The Second Attempt on the Graal	139	125	139	101
11. The Ointment	160	143	160	115

12. The Third Attempt on the Graal	185	165	186	133
13. Conversations of the Young Man in Grey	212	189	213	152
14. The Bible of Mrs. Hippy	230	205	231	165
15. "To-night thou shalt be with Me in Paradise"	236	210	237	169
16. The Search for the House	248	271	249	177
17. The Marriage of the Living and the Dead	263	234	265	188
18. Castra Parvulorum	279	248	281	199

Contributors

BERNADETTE LYNN BOSKY trained in English literature at Duke University and taught there and at Durham Technical Community College. She is now a full-time free-lance writer covering topics ranging from self-esteem to Renaissance alchemy; her articles on Charles Williams appear in *Mythlore* and in a volume of selected papers from the International Conference on the Fantastic in the Arts.

GLEN CAVALIERO is a member of the Faculty of English at the University of Cambridge and a fellow of the Royal Society of Literature. His publications include *Charles Williams: Poet of Theology* (1983) and *The Supernatural and English Fiction* (1995).

ALICE E. DAVIDSON is vice president of corporate finance at the Canadian Imperial Bank of Commerce in Houston, Texas. After completing her M.A. and Ph.D. in English at Indiana University with a dissertation on Charles Williams, she earned an M.B.A. in finance there in 1983.

CLIFFORD DAVIDSON is professor of English and medieval studies at Western Michigan University. He is also coeditor of *Comparative Drama* and executive editor of the Early Drama, Art, and Music project in the university's Medieval Institute. His *On Tradition: Essays on the Use and Valuation of the Past* (1992) deals with the Gothic Revival, the Ecclesiological movement, and T. S. Eliot, among other topics. His publications also include *Illustrations of the Stage and Acting in England to 1580* (1991), other books, and numerous articles and reviews.

DAVID LLEWELLYN DODDS was at Merton College, Oxford, as a Rhodes scholar, served for three years as president of the Oxford C. S. Lewis Society, and oversaw the beginning of the restoration of the Lewis house, The Kilns, as its curator. He is the editor of both the *Charles Williams* and *John Masefield* volumes of Boydell & Brewer's Arthurian Poets series (1991 and 1994, respectively) and is the author of the entry on Williams as novelist in the *Dictionary of Literary Biography*. He has also read, and published, several papers on Williams, and on J. R. R. Tolkien, in England, Germany, Finland, and The Netherlands. He is currently working on a complete critical edition of Williams's unpublished Arthurian poetry and prose.

DIANE TOLOMEO EDWARDS is associate professor of English at the University of Victoria. She has published "Christian Existentialism in the Early Poetry of Charles Williams," in *Seven,* and "From Garden to City: Closure in the Bible," in *Mappings of the Biblical Terrain: The Bible as Text* (1990). Her areas of interest include Milton, biblical literature, and the literature of mysticism.

CATH FILMER-DAVIES is a lecturer in English at the University of Queensland, Australia, and an honorary research associate at the University of Wales, Lampeter, where she teaches in the Departments of English and Welsh for part of one term each year. She has published *Skepticism and Hope in Twentieth-Century Fantasy Literature* (1992) and *The Fiction of C. S. Lewis: Mask and Mirror* (1993), as well as editing *The Victorian Fantasists* (1991), and *Twentieth-Century Fantasists* (1992). She has also published many articles on aspects of literature and theory. Her most recent projects include completing a book on Welsh mythology and the gradual acquisition of fluency in the Welsh language.

VERLYN FLIEGER is associate professor of English at the University of Maryland, College Park, where she teaches courses in medieval literature, comparative mythology, and J. R. R. Tolkien. The author of *Splintered Light: Logos and Language in Tolkien's World* (1983) and of articles on Tolkien, C. S. Lewis (in *Word and Story in C. S. Lewis*), and E. R. Eddison, she is presently completing a book on time and dream in Tolkien's fiction.

JOHN HEATH-STUBBS, O.B.E., attended lectures given by Charles Williams at Oxford. He has taught at the Universities of Leeds, Michigan, and Alexandria (Egypt). A fellow of the Royal Society of Literature and a former president of the Poetry Society, he is the author of more than twenty books of poetry. His *Collected Poems* appeared in 1988. His awards include the Queen's Gold Medal for Poetry (1973) and the Commonwealth Poetry Prize (1989). In addition to articles and a booklet on Charles Williams—including "Charles Williams as I Knew Him" in the 1987 *Inklings-Jahrbuch*—he has written other works of criticism and edited several volumes, including *The Faber Book of Twentieth Century Verse* (1953). His autobiography *Hindsights* was published in 1993.

CONTRIBUTORS

B. L. HORNE is lecturer in systematic theology at King's College, University of London. He is the author of *A World to Gain: Incarnation and the Hope of Renewal* (1984) and the editor of *Charles Williams: A Celebration* (1995). His doctoral dissertation, "The Systematic Theology of Charles Williams," was completed in 1967 at London University. He serves as librarian of the Charles Williams Society.

CHARLES A. HUTTAR, professor of English at Hope College, Holland, Michigan, is the editor of *Imagination and the Spirit* (1971), coeditor of *Word and Story in C. S. Lewis* (1991), and author of many essays on Lewis, Tolkien, and Charles Williams, as well as numerous articles on sixteenth- and seventeenth-century British literature. He is currently completing a book on angels in the modern imagination.

ROMA A. KING, JR., is distinguished professor of English literature, emeritus, Ohio University, and a retired priest in the Episcopal Church. He is still active in teaching part-time at the University of Texas, Dallas, and as Canon in St. Matthew's Cathedral, Dallas. In addition to *The Pattern in the Web: The Mythical Poetry of Charles Williams* (1990), he has published three books on the poetry of Robert Browning and was general editor of Browning's *Complete Works*, in which he edited *The Ring and the Book* in three volumes (1985–89). He is cofounder and associate Editor of *Mundus Artium: A Magazine of International Literature and the Arts*.

JUDITH J. KOLLMANN is professor of English and chair of the department at the University of Michigan–Flint. She is coeditor of *Chaucerian Shakespeare: Transformation and Adaptation* (1983) and author of such reference articles as "The Centaur" in *Mythical and Fabulous Creatures* (1987) and "Sheridan Le Fanu" in *Dictionary of Literary Biography*. Her articles on Charles Williams have appeared in *Inklings-Jahrbuch*, *Mythlore*, *Kansas Quarterly*, *King Arthur through the Ages* (1990), and *Studies in Medievalism*.

JARED LOBDELL is the author of *England and Always: Tolkien's World of the Rings* (1981) and editor of *A Tolkien Compass* (1975, 1980). He contributed an article on C. S. Lewis to *Word and Story in C. S. Lewis*. He is preparing a collection of Williams's detective-fiction reviews.

STEPHEN MEDCALF is reader in English in the School of European Studies, University of Sussex. He has written a number of essays on the relation of Latin and Greek authors to English literature, on medieval English literature and on modern literature, including an article in *Word and Story in C. S.*

Lewis. He has recently edited the selected poems of G. K. Chesterton (*Poems for All Purposes*, 1994) and with the Reverend Gavin Ashenden is preparing a life of Charles Williams.

ROBERT MCCOLLEY is professor of history at the University of Illinois, Urbana-Champaign. He has published *Slavery and Jeffersonian Virginia* (1964, 1973) and is coeditor of *Refracting America: Gender, Race, Ethnicity, and Environment in U. S. History to 1877* (1993). He contributed an article on Mariana Griswold Van Rensselaer to the *Dictionary of Literary Biography* and is currently writing a book on her works. He has contributed to the *Encyclopedia of Black America, Critical Survey of Mystery and Detective Fiction, Encyclopedia of Colonial North America, Great Lives from History,* and other publications. He also regularly writes articles and reviews for *Fanfare, the Magazine for Serious Record Collectors*.

GEORGE RALPH is professor of theater and chair of the department at Hope College, where he regularly acts and directs in play productions. He also teaches a course in religion and drama. While at Union Theological Seminary he acted in E. Martin Browne's production of Charles Williams's *Thomas Cranmer of Canterbury*. He has a particular interest in Oriental drama, with study in Japan and Hawaii, and has also published numerous haiku and other poems in traditional Japanese forms, for which he has received several awards.

JOHN D. RATELIFF moved from Arkansas to Wisconsin fifteen years ago to work with the J. R. R. Tolkien manuscripts at Marquette University. He received his Ph.D. in twentieth-century English literature from Marquette with a dissertation on Lord Dunsany, the Anglo-Irish fantasist. He has been active in Tolkien scholarship for many years, helping to organize two major Tolkien conferences and delivering papers on Tolkien, Dunsany, the Inklings, and other fantasy writers. While at Marquette, he assisted in the collation of Marquette's holdings with those Christopher Tolkien was editing for volumes 6 through 9 of the History of Middle-Earth series. He is currently editing the manuscript of *The Hobbit* for publication.

PETER J. SCHAKEL, Peter C. and Emajean Cook Professor of English at Hope College, Holland, Michigan, is editor of *The Longing for a Form: Essays on the Fiction of C. S. Lewis* (1977) and of *Word and Story in C. S. Lewis* (1991). He is the author of *Reading with the Heart: The Way into Narnia* (1979), of *Reason and Imagination in C. S. Lewis* (1984), and of two books and many articles on Jonathan Swift and on verse satire in eighteenth-century England.

CONTRIBUTORS 335

GEORGE L. SCHEPER is professor of English and humanities at Essex Community College in Maryland, where he also directs the program Artifacts of Culture, named by the National Endowment for the Humanities as one of thirteen "exemplary programs in humanities for adults." He published *Michael Innes* in 1986 and is currently at work on a book on Tony Hillerman. Several NEH grants have supported his work in topics as varied as pre-Columbian cultures and the Bible in literature, on which his articles appear in *Semiotics 1990, A Dictionary of Biblical Tradition in English Literature, Analecta Husserliana, New England Quarterly,* and *PMLA.*

ANGELIKA SCHNEIDER received her Ph.D. from the University of Cologne, with a dissertation on Charles Williams's poetry. Her dissertation has been published in abbreviated form in the Boydell and Brewer Arthurian Literature series. Her contribution to the Charles Williams centennial symposium in Aachen appeared in the Inklings Gesellschaft *Jahrbuch.* She currently teaches English and Latin in a high school in Germany and serves as the Charles Williams editor for *Inklings: Jahrbuch für Literatur und Ästhetik.*

Index

Abercrombie, Lascelles, 194
Abraham, 140
Abstract and concrete words, 188
Ackroyd, Peter, 238n
Adam: naming the beasts, 29, 30, 136n, 139, 140; figured in *PL,* 30, 106, 107, 139; in *MD,* 78; as name for primordial androgyne, 139; and Eve, 270, 287. *See also* Fall; CW: Dramatic works: *Seed of Adam.*
Addleshaw, G. W. O., 257
Adjectives, 23, 281–83
Affective stylistics, 20, 23, 59–72, 279, 280–81
Affirmative Way. *See* Way of Affirmation.
Agee, James, 15, 59, 60n
Agnosticism, 85, 274
Aladdin, 77
Alban, St., 261
Alison, Archibald, 298
All Saints, Vigil and Feast of, 155–57, 159
Allegory: used by CW, 94, 155, 160n, 233; avoided by CW, 98, 258; in interpreting, 100–01, 313; in *Everyman,* 259. *See also* Characterization: symbolic.
Allingham, Margery, 305
Alliteration, 120, 187, 188–89, 191. *See also* Meter: alliterative.
Allusion, 57, 117, 128, 129, 228, 279, 298, 304. *See also* Bible; Dante; Intertextuality.
Alphabet, 177
Ambiguity: as a theme, 22, 249, 258, 260, 287; as rhetorical device, 23, 258, 283; as a stylistic fault, 54; needed in theological language, 66; as interpretive principle, 287. *See also* Contradiction; Multivalence.
Amen House, 241n, 268

Anagnorisis, 292, 297, 298, 302, 305–6
Anaphora, 55
Anderson, Angelee Sailer, 133n, 138n, 142n, 147n, 150n, 155n, 160n
Angels: in *PL,* 29–30, 110, 113, 202; in *DH,* 124–25; in Old Testament, 124, 139, 156, 304; in *TTL,* 204; in Claudel, 219n; mentioned by CW, 307. *See also* Gabriel.
Antichrist, 146–50
Antithesis, 23, 279, 286–88
Aphorisms: "As above, so below," 254, 320; "Know Love," 58, 130; "Know thyself," 58, 130. *See also* Epigrams; "This also is Thou . . . ."
Apophasis, 136–37n
Aporia, 21, 105–6
Apposition, 187
Aquinas, St. Thomas, 40, 100–01, 278
Arianism, 20
Aristotle, 31, 221, 274, 279, 286, 288, 292, 293, 302
Arrowsmith, William, 223–24
Arthur. *See* Myth: Arthurian.
Ascension of Christ, 157n
Ashenden, Gavin, 334
Association. *See* Stream-of-consciousness.
Assonance, 188–89, 207
Astrology, 167, 168–69, 174–75, 186
Athanasian Creed: as governing principle in CW's thought, 8, 19–20, 23, 28, 38, 39, 40–43, 145, 318–19; in *GT,* 143; quoted, 27, 143, 319
Atonement, 39, 286, 287. *See also* Redemption.
Atwood, Margaret, 136n
Auden, W. H.: influenced by CW, 8; on CW, 16n, 159n; letters to CW, 238n
Audience: CW's awareness of, 22, 239; CW's demands on, 22, 59, 64, 165, 190, 217, 218, 228–29, 231, 235, 236–37,

337

INDEX

298–99, 304, 312; responses to CW's writings, 24, 64–65, 105–07, 187, 217–20; effects on, 60–72 passim, 75, 85, 96, 105, 111, 115, 116, 127, 128, 130, 188, 208–9, 240, 242, 285–86, 311, 314, 316, 321; responses to ghost stories, 91, 97; of *Cranmer,* invited to worship, 219n; familiarity with stories, 239; response demanded by great poetry, 314. *See also* Affective stylistics.

Augustine, St., 8, 318

Augustus. *See* Caesar Augustus.

Austin, J. L., 144

Bacon, Sir Francis, 94

Bailey, H. C., 297, 300, 304, 305

Balance: as stylistic feature, 23, 105, 125, 127, 129, 130. *See also* Parallel structure; CW: Key words and images: balance.

Baptism, 72, 144, 153, 158, 159, 183

Barfield, Owen, 316

Barratt, Joan, 226

Barton, Elizabeth, 250

Beatrice. *See under* CW: Key words and images.

Beaumont, Ernest, 133n, 144n, 155n, 160n

Beauty, 27–28, 31, 33, 176, 282, 315

Beethoven, Ludwig van, 85

Belief: suspension of disbelief, 39, 115; audience's, 78, 79, 108, 231, 239, 247, 295, 302 (*see also* Audience); shaping force of, 316. *See also* Skepticism.

Bentley, E. C., 296, 297

Berkeley, George, 108

Bernard, St., 157

Bible: relation of Old and New Testaments, 30, 176, 233; stylistic influence on CW, 54, 55, 123, 197n; allusions to, 55, 218n (*see also list following, by book*); plays based on, 231–32, 239–47, 317 (*see also* CW: Dramatic works: Nativity plays); literary treatment of characters from, 219, 220, 224–26, 242–44; mentioned, 46. *See also* Adam; Angels; Cain; Calvary; Diction: religious; John, St.; Judas; Lord's Prayer; Magdalen, St. Mary; Mary, Virgin; Paul, St.; Peter, St.; Simon Magus;

Thomas, St.; Urim and Thummim.

—Genesis, 49, 135, 140, 159; Exodus, 95, 140, 156, 300; Deuteronomy, 123; Job, 104, 259; Psalms, 54, 157, 255n; Isaiah, 49; Ezekiel, 149; Gospels, 29, 84, 109, 111, 117; Matthew, 95, 140, 155, 157, 225, 252; Luke, 140, 148, 234, 244n; John, 80, 139, 171; Acts, 41, 148, 239, 247n; Pauline Epistles, 183; 1 Corinthians, 51, 184; Galatians, 245; 1 Thessalonians, 114; Revelation, 50, 52, 54, 56, 57, 95, 114, 156

Blackwood, Algernon, 93, 94, 98

Blake, William, 8, 104, 109, 111, 112, 278

Blank verse, 196, 229–30

Bles, Geoffrey, 277

Blish, James, 291n

Bloom, Robert, 303n

Boadicea, 31

Body. *See under* CW: Key words and images.

Boehme, Jakob, 111

Boies, J. J., 155n

Book of Common Prayer: of sixteenth century, 249n, 255n, 256; ambiguities in, 258; mentioned, 141, 142, 156, 217, 218n, 219, 248, 257

Booth, Wayne, 136

Borges, Jorge Luis, 7

Bosky, Bernadette, 18n, 20, 21, 134n, 146n, 147n, 148n, 155n, 331

Brecht, Bertolt, 222

Brewer, Elisabeth, 21n

Bridges, Robert, 199n

Brooks, Collin, 294

Brown, Robert McAfee, 62, 66, 142n

Browne, E. Martin, 217, 224n, 228, 248, 255n, 258, 259n, 334

Browne, Henzie, 228n, 248n, 258n, 259n

Browne, Sir Thomas, 61n

Browning, Robert, 333

Buchan, John, 299n

Buddhism, 154

Bulwer-Lytton, Edward, 91–92

Bunyan, John, 68n, 299, 300

Burke, Edmund, 280–81, 298

Bush, Christopher, 303

Cabala: imagery from, 92, 165, 169, 175.

See also CW: Key words and images: Sephirotic Tree; *Zohar.*

Caesar Augustus, 78, 233–34

Cain, 135, 174

Calvary, 31, 154, 175, 176. *See also* Christ: Passion of; CW: Key words and images: cross *and* skull; CW: Other works: "Cross, The."

Calvin, John, 253, 269, 275

Canterbury Festival, 22, 225n, 248. *See also* CW: Dramatic works: *Thomas Cranmer:* original production.

Capitalization, 80, 101, 191

Carpenter, Humphrey, 60n, 104, 238n, 240n, 243n, 298n, 307n

Carr, John Dickson, 295, 296, 304

Carroll, Lewis, 49, 51, 108

Castle of Perseverance, The, 224, 227

Caudwell, Christopher, 296

Cavaliero, Glen: quoted, 16, 63, 79, 81, 141, 161n, 221, 222, 223, 229–30, 233, 241, 281; mentioned, 17n, 18n, 20–21, 62, 80, 134n, 157n, 159n, 226n, 272, 331

Celia. *See* Jones, Phyllis.

Certitude, rhetoric of, 18, 20, 65

Characterization, 20, 45, 107, 129, 131, 141, 231, 233–34, 236, 239; symbolic, 220, 223–27, 234, 236, 258. *See also* Bible: literary treatment of characters from.

Charlemagne, 37, 38, 78

Chase, Lewis, 194n

Chaucer, Geoffrey, 53, 300, 333

Chesterton, G. K.: influence on CW, 7, 192, 297; letter to CW, 194, 195, 238n; and detective fiction, 293–99 passim, 305–7; on fantasy, 305–7; mentioned, 193, 280, 334

Chorus: in drama, 219, 234n

Christ: figured, in CW's works, 30, 49, 106, 157n, 174–75 (*see also* Substitution); Transfiguration of, 40; Passion of, 62, 153–55, 209, 211n, 257, 286 (*see also* Calvary); CW's impersonal way of referring to, 62, 268; parody of, 147 (*see also* Antichrist); imitation of, 153, 252; crucified by his own spouse, 155; "Christ the City," 208, 209; real presence, 257n; humanitarian Jesus, 270;

image of God, 282. *See also* Ascension; Incarnation; Kenosis.

Christie, Agatha: and occult, 105; mentioned, 295, 299, 303, 304

Church: body of Christ, 183; CW on, 269–71; mentioned, 201, 256

Church of England, 253. *See also* Book of Common Prayer.

Churchill, Winston, 135

Cinematic style, 222

Clarity: in style, 127. *See also* God: clarity in.

Claudel, Paul, 219n

Cliché, 48

Closure: postponement of, 21

Cnidos, 85

Coinherence: defined, 15, 180–81; central in CW's vision, 15, 22, 23, 39–40, 66, 70, 110, 113, 114, 154, 168–71, 178, 180–81, 256n, 267, 274–75; rejection of, 15–16, 49, 181, 183, 184, 246; modeled by CW's rhetoric, 19–21, 23, 61, 131, 181–91; poetry as image of, 39–40, 114, 181–82, 185–86; in human relationships, 48, 156, 246, 271, 275, 284; and substitution, 145, 155n, 272; Way of, 149; Companions of the, 152, 200n, 245n, 246n, 247n, 267, 272; across time, 153, 266, 271, 274–75; entry into, by death, 156; planetary movement as paradigm of, 168; violation of, 172; related to world view of modern science, 179–80; discouraged by Protestantism, 253; in Eucharist, 254, 257; and Communism, 271; mentioned, 24, 65, 161, 239. *See also* Community; Exchange; Percival; Perichoresis; Trinity.

Cole, G. D. H., 294, 296

Cole, Margaret, 294, 296

Coleridge, Samuel Taylor, 109, 110–11

Colie, Rosalie L., 61n

Collins, Wilkie, 292

Colloquial speech: rhetorical purpose of, 95, 241; illusion of, 230n; in dialogue, 230, 240. *See also* Dialogue; Rhythm.

Comedy: detective fiction as, 291–92, 297, 302

Comedy of manners: *DH* as, 116

Comma, 127, 128

Communion of saints. *See* Community.

340 INDEX

Communism, 271, 274.
Community: of believers, 156–57, 246–47, 256, 275; Palomides in, 183. *See also* Companions; Reconciliation.
Companions, 185, 219. *See also* Coinherence: Companions of the.
Compounds, 187
Conditional conjunctive, 115–19
Conjunctions: *and,* 122, 123–25; *or,* 126
Conquest, Robert, 18, 38
Conroy, Tom, 154
Consolation. *See* Eucatastrophe.
Constantine, 269
Contradiction: in poet's experience, 287
Contraries, 104, 109, 112. *See also* Dualism; Opposites; Paradox.
Contrast, 287
Conversation. *See* Dialogue.
Cornish drama. *See* Ordinalia.
Corporal punishment, 245n
Correspondence: hermetic doctrine, 21, 66, 167, 171–72
Counter-Reformation, 269
Courtesy, 23
Cox, Anthony Berkeley, 296, 303
Cranmer, Thomas: as historical personage, 249–60 passim. *See also* CW: Dramatic works: *Thomas Cranmer of Canterbury.*
Creation: relation to coinherence, 15; language as instrument in, 46, 177; reflects God's love, 64; visualized, 149; goodness of, 157–58, 159, 160, 177 (*see also* Matter); channeled through *Sephiroth,* 175, 177; divine, 286
Crispin, Edmund, 295, 297–98
Critchlow, Keith, 61n
Croce, Benedetto, 265
Croft, Edward, 134n, 136
Crofts, Freeman Wills, 304–5
Crowley, Aleister, 165
Crucifixion. *See* Christ: Passion of.
Culture, 276
Cuming, G. J., 255n, 256n, 257n, 258n
Curtis, Jan, 16n, 24n

Damnation, 97, 114, 138, 245. *See also* Salvation.
Dance of Death, 259
Dante: and Way of Affirmation, 8, 141; and romantic theology, 132–33; source

of "holy flesh," 171; *De Monarchia,* 181, 211; *Divine Comedy,* 44; *Inferno,* 44, 46, 97; *Purgatorio,* 51, 117, 126, 151n, 157; *Paradiso,* 137, 157n, 319–20; *Vita Nuova, La,* 120, 121, 133, 152; mentioned, 241, 278, 280, 314, 318, 319
Davidson, Alice, 20, 21, 331
Davidson, Clifford, 22, 137n, 146n, 147n, 149n, 150n, 248n, 253n, 331
Davies, R. J., 160n
De la Mare, Walter, 281n
Dearmer, Percy, 299n
Death: spiritual, 110; relation of dead to the living, 113, 125, 126, 153–54; relation to life, 120, 258; of Christ, 154 (*see also* Christ); salvation after, 154, 245–46; and immortality, 156–57; personified as dramatic character, 225, 226n, 227, 258–59. *See also* Dance of Death; Death-in-Life.
Death-in-Life, 109–11
Deconstruction: in *PL,* 106, 107
Democracy, 271
Derrida, Jacques, 103, 106
Detection Club, 293, 294
Detective fiction: reviewed by CW, 23, 290, 294–304; as genre, 23, 290–308; CW's view of, 294, 295, 299–303; rhetoric of, 298, 299–303; mentioned, 305, 334
Devil. *See* Satan.
Dialectical mode of question and answer, 288
Dialogue: "spiritual colloquy," 141; concepts rather than conversation, 223; both felicitous and obfuscating, 229; conversational, achieved, 229, 231–34, 235, 242–43. *See also* Colloquial speech.
Dickens, Charles, 306
Diction: archaic, 20, 53, 55, 220, 229, 231; in CW's rhetoric, 20, 119–21, 187–88, 191, 242, 279; idiosyncratic, 32–33; religious, 53–56, 191 (*see also* Liturgy: language of); unusual, 53, 119, 179; Latinate, 118, 279; of CW's early poetry, uninteresting, 193; poetic, 230n; simple vs. complex, 279, 317; mentioned, 22, 115
Didacticism: CW's avoidance of, 218, 227

INDEX

341

Dies irae, 255n
Discordance. *See* Dislocation.
Dislocation, 33; rhetoric of, 20, 75–77.
  See also Aporia.
Distancing, 242. *See also* Dislocation.
Dixon, James G., 222, 224n, 228n,
  229–30, 250n, 252n, 260n
Dobrée, Bonamy: on CW, 228
Docetism, 142, 160
Dodds, David Llewellyn, 16n, 22, 202n,
  203n, 214n, 328, 331–32
Donne, John, 19, 230
Doppelgänger. *See* Doubles.
Doubles: in *DH,* 42, 71, 116–121 passim,
  128; in *MD,* 86; Peter and Judas, 244;
  Skeleton, 258
Doubt: relation to faith, 15, 21, 112. *See
  also* Skepticism.
Douglas, Margaret, 193n, 197n, 199n, 212
Doyle, Sir Arthur Conan, 291, 293, 296,
  297, 305
Drama: within *DH,* 52, 55, 56, 114, 115,
  142; of ideas, 222; religious, CW on,
  317. *See also* CW: Other works: "Reli-
  gious Drama."
Dreams: and time travel, 82; and reality,
  108–9; in *DH,* 126; in *AHE,* 145
Dualism: metaphysical, rejected by CW,
  15, 23, 171 (*see also* Manicheism; Mo-
  nism; Paradox); moral, in CW, 145n,
  152; matter disvalued by, 176–77. *See
  also* Contraries.
Dubrow, Heather, 291
Dürer, Albrecht, 85
Duffy, Eamon, 252n
Dugan, Alan, 155n
Dunne, J. W., 20, 81–89 passim
Dunsany, Edward, 18th Baron, 334

East, Roger, 301
Ecology, 22, 160, 179
Eddison, E. R., 82, 332
Edel, Leon, 303n
Edwards, Diane Tolomeo, 23, 104n, 332
Einstein, Albert, 20, 81
Elevated tone, 231
Elgin, Don D., 134n
Eliade, Mircea, 145
Eliot, T. S.: influenced by CW, 8, 39; on
  CW, 15, 16, 20, 24, 33, 36, 59–60,

134n, 136, 218n, 290, 303; as CW's
  publisher, 32, 268; "objective correlative," 60; possible influence on CW,
  197; failure to contribute to CW fest-
  schrift, 238n; on Dante, 280; "Ash-
  Wednesday," 51; "Coriolan," 51; *Four
  Quartets,* 8; "Burnt Norton," 33, 39,
  102; "Little Gidding," 265, 276; *Murder
  in the Cathedral,* 22, 225n, 226, 248;
  mentioned, 72, 82, 99, 193, 228, 331
Emptying. *See* Kenosis.
Enlightenment, 17, 179–80
Enright, Nancy, 133n, 160n
Epigrams: in CW's style, 55, 140–41,
  149, 155, 160, 276, 287, 297. *See also*
  Aphorisms.
Erastianism, 249–50
Eternity, 47, 99, 168. *See also* Time: and
  eternity.
Eucatastrophe, 297, 298, 302, 305
Eucharist, 172–73, 200, 209–11, 218,
  249, 253–57. *See also* Liturgy: in CW's
  novels.
Euripides, 223
Eve, 136n, 311. *See also* Adam.
Every, George, 311n
Everyman, 225, 258–59
Evil: relation to good, 64, 136, 145–46,
  181, 275, 287–88, 289; problem of, 145,
  160n; origin of, 184. *See also* Fall;
  Good.
Exchange: relation to hierarchy, 19n; in
  DH, 39, 50, 57, 68, 69, 120, 153, 154;
  in *AHE,* 48, 152–53, 156, 158; in *GT,*
  144; through Christ, 154; rejection of,
  181; in *TTL,* 168, 181, 182–83, 185,
  186; in *FS,* 282. *See also* Coinherence;
  Substitution; CW: Other works: "Way
  of Exchange, The."
Existentialism, 104, 105

Faber and Faber, 277–78
Fable, 98, 294
Facetiousness, 297
Fact: vs. meaning, 23, 25, 129, 220, 265;
  as reality, 30, 52, 58, 62, 65, 96, 130,
  141, 152, 159, 161, 214, 260, 288, 294,
  306; rejection of, 46, 58, 135, 151; and
  fantasy, 116; "holy fact," 145
Fairchild, Hoxie Neale, 16n

342 INDEX

Faith, 99, 287. *See also* Doubt: relation to faith.
Fall: CW's analysis of, 64, 136, 145, 267, 287; symbolized in Pelles' wound, 175. *See also* Language: fallen.
Fantasy: Tolkien on, 76, 297, 306; as genre, 89, 100, 115, 298; relation to detective fiction, 291, 294–95, 297–98, 305–7; Chesterton on, 305–7; mentioned, 77, 121, 332
Farjeon, Jefferson, 295, 296, 301, 306
Farrer, Austin M., 280
Fathers, desert, 269
Faust myth, 160
"Feeling intellect," 15, 316, 319
Feminine and masculine: symbols of, 169, 175–76
Filmer-Davies, Cath, 21, 103n, 332
Firebird, 77
Fish, Stanley, 61n, 68n
Fletcher, John (Jacobean dramatist), 299
Fletcher, J. S., 296, 299
Flieger, Verlyn, 20, 23, 332
Forgiveness, 246, 284–85, 286, 288
Form, relation to content, 288
Formality: in CW's style, 189, 279, 288
Forster, E. M., 99
Fox, Matthew, 159
Foxe, John, 55, 251n, 256n
Freedom, 271. *See also* Will.
Freeman, R. Austin, 296
Freeman, William, 313n
Friendship. *See* Love.
Fry, Christopher, 228
Frye, Northrop, 291–92
Fundamentalism, 180

Gabriel, 104, 220, 233–36 passim
Galahad, 185, 204–5, 208, 209
Gardner, Helen, 194n
Gasquet, Francis, 250n
Gehenna. *See* Hell.
Genre: CW's choices of, 17, 20; definition of, 291. *See also* Detective fiction; Fantasy; Ghost story; Occult; Parable; Parody; Rhetoric: relation to genre; Vision: "visionary" genre.
Ghost story (genre), 20–21, 90–93, 97–98, 100, 102
Gibbon, Edward, 279

Gigrich, John P., 17n
Gilbert, R. A., 92n, 165–66
Gilbert, W. S., 299
Glenn, Lois, 16n, 290n
Glossolalia. *See* Pentecost.
Gnosticism: and literary criticism, 136; in *SE*, 147; in *AHE*, 148, 149, 158; magic as symbol for, 160, 161n; as heresy, 160, 275
God: relation to Coinherence, 15, 66, 181, 283; inexpressible 24, 175–76, 177, 185, 318, 320; Prime Mover, 31; beyond comprehending, 65, 80; in *DH,* 69; in *MD,* 79, 85, 88; clarity in, 95, 96, 101; union with, 165, 169, 175–76; asexual, 175; various names for, 177, 318; as ruler, 184, 189; figured as circle, 299. *See also* Athanasian Creed; Creation; Holy Spirit; Logos; Tetragrammaton; Theology: language of; Trinity.
Göller, Karl Heinz, 16n
Goethe, J. W. von, 108, 157
Golden Age (of detective fiction), 290–308 passim
Golden Dawn, Order of the, 104, 165–66, 247n, 300. *See also* Rosicrucianism.
Golgotha. *See* Calvary.
Good: and evil, CW sensitive to, 18; refusal of, 158; goodness made interesting, 304. *See also* Creation; Evil: relation to good; Matter.
Gordon, Ian A., 279, 280–81
Gothic style, 7, 160, 281, 293
Grace: conditions for, 51, 52; and numinous experience, 99; relation to magic, 145, 167, 172–73; regenerative, 168; as a dramatic character, 236; relation to free will, 271, 287; mentioned, 55, 134, 143, 170, 171, 188, 207, 255, 256, 313
Grammar: manipulation of, 70
Greek theater, 298
Gresham, William Lindsay, 324
Griffin, William, 41n
Gurdjieff, Georges, 81

Hadfield, Alice Mary: papers in Bodleian, 209n; quoted, 32n, 105, 153, 158, 217, 219, 224n, 233, 257, 277, 278, 312, 314, 315, 316, 318n; mentioned, 16n, 29n, 67n, 132n, 135n, 138n, 145n, 198n,

199n, 223n, 224n, 226n, 240n, 241n, 249, 260n, 261n, 272
Halverson, Marvin, 236
Hammett, Dashiell, 296
Hanger, Nancy, 153n
Hanshell, H. D., 17n
Haycraft, Howard, 293n
Heath-Stubbs, John: quoted, 104, 192, 193, 197, 221–22, 223, 230n, 231, 241, 242, 249n, 310; mentioned, 16n, 191, 332
Heaven, 47, 96, 138, 225, 305, 307, 320
Hell: life as, 46, 110; Arglay's vision of, 96–97, 101–2; inaccuracy of, 138, 149, 305; Harrowing of, 149, 155, 305; as character, 224, 234–35, 236, 247; Herod's choice of, 225; Gehenna, 259; mentioned, 37, 39, 186, 244, 307
Henry VIII, 218, 250, 259
Heresy, 134, 275. See also CW: and heterodoxy.
Hermeticism: as an approach to the supernatural, 92; occult tradition, 171, 175
Hierarchy: CW on, 18, 19n, 191; egalitarian, 62
Hillerman, Tony, 335
Hilton, James, 82, 301, 302
History: CW's concept of, 22–23, 249, 260; definitions of, 144, 265; schools of, 266; redemption of, 276. See also CW: as historian; CW: Prose fiction: DH: Wentworth.
Hitler, Adolf, 135
Holbein, Hans, 259
Holder, Robert C., 145n, 149n
Holy Spirit: in CW's drama, 225; in history, 260, 267, 269, 270, 272; mentioned, 214
Hopkins, Gerard Manley: resemblances to, in CW's style, 50, 53, 229; influence of, on CW, 198–200, 230n, 248n; edited by CW, 199; CW on, 317
Horace, 299
Horne, B. L., 23, 202, 333
Howard, Thomas, 16n, 18n, 67, 106n, 157n
Humor, 106, 231, 300. See also Wit.
Hunt, Raymond: CW's letters to, 200n, 212n, 238n, 246n; biographer of CW, 238n; encoded in TTL, 246n; mentioned,

193n, 194n, 197n, 212n.
Huntley, Frank L., 61n
Huttar, Charles A., 18, 133n, 143n, 146n, 147, 153n, 155n, 160n, 333
Hymns, 143. See also particular titles.

Icon (Byzantine), 141
Iconography, 149, 155. See also Dance of Death; CW: Prose fiction: AHE: paintings in.
Ignatius of Antioch, St., 155, 160
Illusion, 46, 49, 103, 105, 108–9, 120, 131, 150, 158, 180
Image: word as, 47. See also Way of Affirmation.
Imagery: reassessment of, by CW, 9; incarnational nature of, 27–43; in prose style, 101, 118, 129, 280; relation to coinherence, 181–87; as poetic device, 181–87, 199–203, 205, 211; in drama, 317. See also Occult; CW: Key words and images.
Imagination, 173, 209, 317, 318
Imago dei, 282
Incarnation: of God in Christ, 15, 28, 141, 167, 222, 320; as a universal principle, 19, 27, 29, 31, 36, 39–40; modeled in rhetoric, 20; underlying poetry, 23, 318; as paradox, 62; its theological implications, 70, 133n, 135, 143–44, 145, 159–60, 177, 178, 249n, 254, 256–57, 275; Palomides' rejection of, 176; in literary theory, 309, 315–16, 319, 320
Individuation, 106, 111
Ingraham, Vernon L., 214n
Inklings, 243n, 268. See also Lewis, C. S.; Tolkien, J. R. R.
Innes, Michael. See Stewart, J. I. M.
Inquisition, 273, 274, 275
Insertion, 285–86. See also Parenthesis.
Intertextuality, 21, 108–11. See also Allusion; Quotation.
Irony: in CW's writing, 18, 85, 227, 231, 235, 270, 279; CW on, 24n; and science fiction, 291
Irwin, W. R., 17n, 60, 61, 134n, 141n, 145n, 148n
Islam, 78, 80, 173, 176, 182

Jakobson, Roman, 20, 97n

344 INDEX

James, Henry, 50, 293, 298, 303
James, Montague Rhodes, 91, 93, 94, 96, 98
Jeffery, Richard, 198n
John, St., 219, 225, 242, 243, 270
John of Damascus, St., 171
John of the Cross, St., 152n, 155
Johnson, Samuel, 279
Jones, David, 8
Jones, Phyllis, 318
Joseph, St.: viewed as sorcerer, 148; mentioned, 31, 34, 35, 220, 229–35 passim
Judaism 178
Judas: participant in exchange, 155n; relation to Christ, 155n, 226n; characterization of, 225, 243, 244; as Everyman, 226; redemption of, 245–47; mentioned, 232, 260
Julian of Norwich, 54, 70, 71, 159, 278, 289
Jung, C. G., 71
Justice, 95, 97, 101, 126, 188, 244, 247, 283, 289

Kabbalah. *See* Cabala.
Kalevala, The, 77
Kazantzakis, Nikos, 155n
Keats, John, 85, 299
Kenosis: of language, 40–41, 136, 138–39, 140, 150; of self, 147, 148, 152, 155, 157–58, 161
Kierkegaard, Søren, 104, 227, 260n, 270
King, Francis, 21n
King, James Roy, 17n, 59–60
King, Roma A., Jr., 16n, 18n, 21, 165n, 173n, 333
Kinlaw, Dennis F., 142n, 159–60n
Kinnell, Galway, 154
Kipling, Rudyard, 192, 193
Knox, Ronald A., 293n, 294, 296, 301
Kollmann, Judith J., 18n, 21, 68n, 133n, 146n, 147n, 159n, 333
Kort, Wesley A., 284n

Lampert, Evgeny, 160n
Lang-Sims, Lois, 28, 200n, 245n, 247n
Langland, William, 305
Language: limitations of, 17, 24, 66, 136, 137, 190, 318; redemption of, 19, 139–61 passim; performative, 19, 21,

46–47, 110, 115, 133, 137n, 144, 145, 151, 158 (*see also* Creation); CW's theories of, 20, 44, 115, 133, 317, 319; ethical implications of, 20, 21, 44, 45–46, 115, 130; as theme in CW's writing, 39–40, 44, 115, 119; meaning inherent in, 40–41, 44, 47, 137–38, 152; relation to transcendence, 44, 45, 315–16, 317, 320; undoing of, 46, 150–51 (*see also* Kenosis; Tetragrammaton); primordial, 47, 133, 135, 138, 140, 151, 152; as semiotic system, 100, 317; prelapsarian (*see* primordial); fallen, 133, 138, 140, 152; difficulty of CW's, 227 (*see also* Audience: demands on); telescopic, 230–31; of religion, 283, 287. *See also* Diction; Imagery; Liturgy: language of; Logos; Nominalism; Precision; Silence; Syntax; Theology: language of.
Latimer, Hugh, 252
Law, 38, 63, 97
Law, William, 278
Lawrence, D. H., 142
Lay Folks Mass Book, 254–55
Le Fanu, Sheridan, 333
Le Guin, Ursula, 136n
Lee, George, 153n
Lenin, V. I., 275
Lessing, G. E., 222
Lewis, C. Day, 296, 298
Lewis, C. S.: Oxford lectures, 8; on CW, 17, 59, 145n, 197n, 203, 243, 304; communications to CW, 197n, 238n; relations with Eliot, 197n, 238n; friendship with CW, 268, 272; evaluation of, 275–76; influenced by CW, 290, 307; depicted in fiction, 297–98; *Dark Tower, The,* 83; *That Hideous Strength,* 247, 275; *Till We Have Faces,* 111–12; "Transposition," 41–42; mentioned, 23, 28, 72, 82, 109, 172n, 180, 280, 327, 329, 331–34
Lexis. *See* Diction.
Lilith: in *DH,* 40, 56; in G. MacDonald, 109–10
Linguistics. *See* Jakobson, R.; Language.
Literary criticism: principles of, 97, 136, 310; postmodern, 101n, 103, 136; recreates critic's experience of text, 311. *See*

also Deconstruction; Gnosticism; New Criticism; Postmodernism; Reader response criticism; Structuralism; *and under* CW: Other works.

Liturgy: language of, as performative, 21, 133, 139, 144–45; and the redemption of language, 141–42, 145; in CW's novels, 143–44, 153–59; and CW's style, 133, 142–43, 219, 231, 234; contrasted with history, 144; elements of, in drama, 219–20, 234, 248, 249, 255n; reform of, by Cranmer, 253. *See also* Book of Common Prayer; Eucharist; Magic: as antithesis of liturgy; Ritual; CW: Other works: "Liturgy, The."

Loades, D. M., 251n, 252n

Lobdell, Jared, 23, 291, 293, 333

Loewenstein, Andrea, 150n

Logos: as a form of God, 115

Lord's Prayer, 36, 38, 255

Love, 27–28, 48, 57–58, 130, 143, 147, 155, 161n, 185, 209, 234n, 285, 288; analogy to life of Christ, 27; for God, 28; relation to exchange, 50, 57; as name of God, 50, 220, 319, 320; vs. sloth, 51, 52; friendship, 107–8; in Dante, 121, 319; parody of, 147, 148n, 149–50; erotic spirituality, 160, 175; associated with coinherence, 182; destructive, 183; personified in drama, 220, 224n, 229; as adoration, 254n, 282; second image of, 261; attribute of God, 289. *See also* Romantic theology; Sexuality; CW: Key words and images: love.

Loyola, St. Ignatius, 269

Luther, Martin, 269, 275

Lytton. *See* Bulwer–Lytton.

Mabinogion, 173n

Macaulay, Thomas B., 192

MacDonald, George, 108–12, 297

MacDonald, Philip, 296, 297, 301, 303, 304, 305

Macy, V. T., 252n

Magdalene, St. Mary, 139, 232, 243, 244, 246, 247

Magic: relation to mystery, 21, 144–45, 148, 165, 166, 172; as source of imagery, 21–22, 29, 160–61n, 185–86; use or avoidance of, in fiction, 29, 31–32, 77,

92; as abuse of language, 40–41, 46, 134–35, 140, 146, 158 (*see also* Language: undoing); as antithesis of liturgy 144, 146, 147, 161 (*see also* Parody); hostility to nature, 160; white and black, 167, 172–73, 185–86, 267, 293; and salvation, 186; detective as magician, 293, 305. *See also* Simon Magus; CW: Key words and images: magic; Witchcraft.

Magic realism, 7

Malory, Sir Thomas, 185

Manicheism: in the Church, 142; CW opposed to, 145, 146, 159–60n, 160. *See also* Dualism.

Manlove, C. N., 134n, 138n, 142–43, 144, 159n

Marlowe, Christopher, 150, 299, 313

Martyrdom, 31, 49, 117, 249, 252, 258, 260–61, 269

Marx, Karl, 270–71

Marxism. *See* Communism.

Mary, Virgin, 55, 104, 153n, 157, 201, 219, 220, 225–34 passim, 243, 244, 283, 317

Mary I, Queen, 31, 250–51, 252n, 255

Masculine. *See* Feminine.

Masefield, John, 331

Masonic tradition, 165

Masque, 233, 248

Mass. *See* Eucharist; Liturgy: in CW's novels.

Mather, Cotton, 266

Mathers, MacGregor, 165

Matter: relation to spirit, 1, 15, 98, 114, 146, 167, 171; goodness of, 145, 147, 148n, 184 (*see also* Creation); CW's affirmation of, 180

Maxims. *See* Aphorisms; Athanasian Creed; Epigrams.

Maynard, Theodore, 193–94

McColley, Robert, 23, 334

McKinley, Marlene, 133n, 157, 159n

McMichael, Barbara, 60n

Medcalf, Stephen, 19–20, 21, 201n, 333–34

Medieval drama. *See* Morality plays; Mystery plays; Saint plays.

Medievalism: in CW's dramas, 22, 220, 222, 223–26, 229, 232–36 passim,

258–59

Memory, 85, 139

Merlin, 172–73, 185, 187, 189, 202n, 205, 208, 211

Metaimages: defined, 182; in CW's poetry, 185–86

Metaphor: CW's handling of, 23, 129, 186, 188, 283–85; as theme in "Et in Sempiternum Pereant," 98; required for certain subjects, 100, 318; in prose style, 279; in Aristotle's *Rhetoric,* 286. *See also* Imagery; Simile.

Metaphysical poets, 15n, 318

Meter: alliterative, 188; variety of, in *TTL,* 212; in *Judgement at Chelmsford,* 231. *See also* Blank verse; Rhythm; Stanzaic forms.

Metonymy, 117, 118, 129; human psyche as, 115

Metrical schemes, 231

Meynell, Alice, 193

Miles, Alfred, 198

Milford, Humphrey: CW letter to, 195

Milton, John, 61–62, 66, 147, 218, 311–12, 313, 320

Modern art, 180

Modernism: CW's attitude toward, 17, 180, 197–98, 316; and Christianity, 270, 272; and C. S. Lewis, 276

Monarchy: absolutist view of, 250–51

Monism: CW's, 21, 23, 145–46, 289; his rhetoric based on, 141n, 289. *See also* Dualism.

Montaigne, Michel de, 104

Moorman, Charles, 16n, 133n, 139n, 140n, 149n, 155n, 192, 193, 198, 211–12

Morality plays, 22, 220, 221, 223, 224–26, 232–34, 236

Morris, Charles, 61n

Morton, Guy, 298

Moses, 140

Multivalence, 20, 23, 50, 61, 66–70, 120, 186. *See also* Ambiguity.

Mystery, 20, 65, 114, 168, 171, 257; in *MD,* 79, 80; "the Mysterium," 90, 91, 92, 97, 101; in detective fiction, 293. *See also* Magic: relation to mystery.

Mystery plays 220, 233, 239

Mysticism: language of, 61, 136n, 152n;

in *MD,* 80; in Golden Dawn, 165; mentioned, 90, 104, 105, 180, 243

Myth: CW's use of, 17; source of images, 22, 155, 186; Arthurian, 54, 181, 182–83, 185–86, 199–200, 202n, 207n (*see also* CW: Key words and images: Grail; CW: Poetry; CW: Other works: "Figure of Arthur, The"); truth in, 167; of deliverance, 292, 298, 307; relation to fantasy, 306–7

Mythopoesis, 20, 297–98, 307

Mythos. See Frye, N.

Names: as more than signifiers, 47, 139, 152, 156, 177; for type characters in drama, 234. *See also* Adam; Tetragrammaton.

Narcissism: of Wentworth, 42; of Damaris Tighe, 137, 139; of King Arthur, 183, 210; of P'o-Lu, 226

Narratorial voice, 55–56, 94, 141, 143, 150, 151, 231

Nash, Paul, 42

Naturalism: in fiction, critique of, 100, 141

Nature. *See* Supernatural.

Nazism, 271

Negative Way. *See* Way of Rejection.

Neoplatonism. *See* Platonism.

Nesbit, E., 91

New Age, 180

New Criticism, 101n, 314

Newman, John Henry, 280

Nicene Creed, 156

Niebuhr, H. Richard, 23, 265, 276

Nietzsche, Friedrich, 99

Nominalism, 160, 253, 256. *See also* Realism: vs. Nominalism.

Norwich, St. Andrew's Church, 259

Novalis, 108–9

Oaths, 41, 46–47, 88, 140, 152

Obscurity, 56, 60, 69, 191, 280, 282

Occult: as source of imagery, 8, 21, 165n, 168–78 passim; as rhetorical device, 21, 165n, 166, 167, 178; as theme in CW's fiction, 75, 166; juxtaposed with the familiar, 77; CW's interest in, 81, 92, 160, 165–67, 247n, 272, 288; as a genre, 92; contrasted with "visionary," 92,

INDEX

93; central beliefs of, 166–67; relation to Christian beliefs, 167, 171. *See also* Cabala; Christie, Agatha; Golden Dawn.

Olympic Games: CW receives award, 194

Opposites: illusion resulting from sin, 128n. *See also* Contraries.

Order of the Coinherence. *See* Coinherence: Companions of the.

Order of the Golden Dawn. *See* Golden Dawn.

Ordinalia, 239

Orwell, George, 294

Oursler, Fulton, 301

Ouspensky, P. D., 81

Oxford Pilgrim Players. *See* Spalding, Ruth.

Oxford University Press. *See* Amen House; CW: Life.

Oxymoron, 61–64, 65, 66, 187–88

Pageant, 221, 233

Parable: genre, 92, 97

Paradox: in the nature of reality, 15, 121, 130, 131, 186, 261, 287; in CW's rhetoric, 18, 20, 23, 42, 49, 61–65, 72, 89, 101, 127, 186, 222, 224n, 268, 287–88, 297; as a necessary tool of language, 61, 287. *See also* Ambiguity; Contraries; Dislocation; Oxymoron.

Parallel structure: in sentences, 64–65, 129, 279; in dialogue, 244

Paranormal: in ghost stories, 90, 91–92

Parenthesis, 23, 128n. *See also* Insertion.

Parody: in plot of *DH,* 31; of the sacred, in *AHE,* 139, 140, 145, 146–48, 150–51, 155, 157–58; as genre, 146; of Modernism, in *WH,* 197. *See also* Antichrist.

Parsons, Geoffrey, 59, 160–61n

Pascal, Blaise, 122

Patrick, Q., 296

Patterson, Nancy-Lou, 150n

Paul, St., 219, 225, 232, 242–43, 246, 270. *See also* Bible.

Pauses, 129

Pellow, J. D. C.: diaries, 192n, 194n, 201n; letters of CW to, 193n, 194n

Pentecost, 41–42, 142, 151, 177, 239, 240n, 241

Pepys, Samuel, 42

Perception: alteration in, 94; fragmentation of, 180. *See also* Vision: vs. perception.

Percival: symbol of coinherence, 173; linked with pentagram, 173, 176, 185; mentioned, 152

Perichoresis, 170–71. *See also* Coinherence.

Peripeteia, 292, 302, 306

Personification. *See* Characterization: symbolic.

Peter, St., 149, 219, 225, 231–32, 243, 244, 247

Pickering, Kenneth, 217–18, 219n, 224, 226–27, 228, 248n, 255n, 257n, 258n

Pitt, Valerie, 66n

Plato: *Phaedrus,* 27; *Symposium,* 27–28, 29, 30, 31, 33, 36; his myths, 33, 36; mentioned, 67, 270, 302

Platonism: imagery from, 29, 77, 79, 92, 106

Poe, Edgar Allan, 110, 290, 292, 293, 305

Poel, William, 258–59n

Poet: functions of, 76, 180, 309–10, 311, 320. *See also* Contradiction; Poetry.

Poetry: CW's conception of, 17, 23, 39, 140, 309–21; CW's prose style resembles, 23, 115, 129, 280, 281, 311; power of, 25, 76, 310, 315, 319; its "relativity," 100; relation to Way of Affirmation, 133, 141–42; CW on, 309–21; great, its effect on reader, 311, 314–19; relation to religion, 316–20; enacted in life, 320–21. *See also* Coinherence: poetry as image of; Incarnation: underlying poetry; Poet; Sacramentality: of poetry; CW: Poetry; CW: Key words and images: verse.

Polysemy. *See* Multivalence.

Postmodernism, 8, 9, 17, 21, 22, 101, 103–4, 108, 112. *See also* Deconstruction.

Poststructuralism. *See* Postmodernism.

Potter, Phyllis: recipient of letter from CW, 179n, 190n

Pound, Ezra, 179

Power: quest of, 31, 146–47, 267–68; supernatural, 31, 78; abuse of, 134, 186. *See also* Kenosis: of self; Magic; Poetry: power of.

348 INDEX

Prayer: rhetoric of, 235–36
Precision, verbal: CW's concern for, 20, 44–53 passim, 67–68, 95, 119–21, 151, 152, 281n. *See also* Oaths.
Pre-Raphaelites, 192
Press, John, 17n, 179
Preternatural: in ghost stories, 90–91, 102
Prickett, Stephen, 108
Priestley, J. B., 81, 82
Pronouns, 54, 61, 70–71, 128, 268
Propinquity, 127
Prose: in verse drama, 231–32
Providence, 184
Punctuation, marks of, 128, 187, 189. *See also* Comma; Semicolon.
Puns, 94, 228, 288, 303, 304. *See also* Wordplay.

Queen, Ellery, 296, 301
Quintilian, 279
Quotation, use of, 278. *See also* Allusion.

Radcliffe, Ann, 293
Ralph, George, 22, 334
Ramakrishna, 51
Rateliff, John D., 22, 240n, 334
Rationalism. *See* Reason.
Ray, Gordon, 303n
Reader response criticism, 101n, 311, 312–13. *See also* Audience.
Readers. *See* Audience.
Realism: vs. Nominalism, 137–38, 256–57 (*see also* Nominalism); literary (*see* Naturalism).
Reality, limited apprehension of, 190, 268; relation of poetry to, 309
Reason, 96, 128, 134, 176, 177, 185–86, 315, 317; valued by CW, 271
Recognition. *See* Anagnorisis.
Reconciliation, 247, 286. *See also* Community; Forgiveness.
Recovery: of immediacy of historical events, 239, 242; of freshness of vision, 239–40, 306; rhetoric of, 247. *See also* Dislocation.
Redemption: of creation, 46; CW's concept of, 97; and *agape,* 107; history of, 267. *See also* Language: redemption of; Salvation.
Reductionism, 20, 23, 41, 42, 316

Reformation: CW on, 250n, 267, 269
Reilly, Robert J., 16n, 66n, 133n, 140n, 142n, 157n, 159n
Repetition: of syntactic patterns, 56; of words and phrases, 130, 187–88, 200, 205–11, 288
Reynolds, George, 151n
Reynolds, Sir Joshua, 149
Rhetoric: definitions of, 19, 23–24, 54, 115, 274; unavoidable, 19, 24, 136; CW's views on, 19, 134–37, 140; as noise, 132–33; cessation of, 132–33 (*see also* Language: redemption of); of faith, 134n; relation to sin, 135, 136 (*see also* Language: fallen speech); associated with magic, 140, 158, 161; contrasted with blessing, 158; relation to genre, 299–300, 302
Rhode, John, 296
Rhyme, 188–89, 212, 213, 220, 229, 231; internal, 189, 191, 212–13, 228, 229–30, 231
Rhythm: in prose, 100, 124, 141, 279, 280, 285 (*see also* Pauses); in poetry, 188, 189–90, 229; of ordinary speech, 189 (*see also* Colloquial speech)
Richardson, Cyril C., 256n
Ridler, Anne: on CW's fiction, 59–60; CW's letters to her, 192, 196, 197, 203–4; on his poetry, 195, 197, 198, 199, 206n; her role in CW's revising, 195, 196–97; on his plays, 221, 222, 223, 228, 229–30, 240, 241, 248, 260; mentioned, 16n, 64n, 65n, 145n, 155n, 214n, 249n, 258n, 261n
Ridley, Nicholas, 252
Rilke, Rainer Maria, 98
Risk, rhetoric of, 18, 75
Ritual: in CW's novels, 29; quality of style, 37, 53, 189. *See also* Liturgy.
Rohmer, Sax, 300, 305, 307
Romantic theology, 64, 132–33, 155. *See also* Love; CW: Other works: *Outlines of Romantic Theology.*
Romanticism, 180, 310, 316
Rosicrucianism, 92. *See also* Golden Dawn.
Runcie, Robert, 256

Sacramentality: central in CW's world-

INDEX

349

view, 15, 22, 23, 133, 160, 161; of language, 44, 139; "sacramental realism," 233; sacraments, 249n, 318; of poetry, 309, 319. *See also* Baptism; Eucharist; Incarnation; Supernatural: relation to natural.

St. Albans. *See* CW: Life.

Saint plays, 248n

Salazar de Frias, Alonzo, 274

Sale, Roger, 18, 24, 134n

Salem. *See* Witchcraft.

Salvation: and damnation, 58, 95, 101–2, 114, 115, 131, 246; relation to exchange, 96, 183. *See also* Atonement; Judas: redemption of; Magic: and salvation; Virgil: redemption of.

Satan, 146n, 147, 148n, 220, 225, 226n, 232, 233, 247, 258, 273, 311. *See also* CW: Dramatic works: *Judgement at Chelmsford:* Accuser.

Saul. *See* Paul, St.

Sayers, Dorothy L.: on CW, 17n, 24, 133n, 142n, 159n, 161n; on modern culture, 24; and detective fiction, 105, 280, 293, 296, 299n, 305, 307; on biblical drama, 239, 242; and mythopoesis, 297; CW on, 303–4

Scarborough, Dorothy, 91

Scarisbrick, J. J., 253n

Schakel, Peter J., 334

Scheper, George L., 19, 21, 335

Schiller, Gertrud, 149n, 155n

Schneider, Angelika, 17n, 18n, 21–22, 140n, 190n, 214n, 335

Science: relation to CW's vision, 80–81, 179, 183, 187; to magic, 161n

Science fiction: critique of, 85

Scott, Anne, letter from CW to, 212

Scott, Sir Walter, 91

Second Shepherds' Play, 220, 317

Seder, 155

Self: autonomous, denied, 17; in *DH,* 39, 71, 114 (*see also* Doubles); death to, 110; in *AHE,* 158; effect of poetry on, 316

Sellery, J'nan, 17n, 18n

Sells, Michael A., 137n, 152n

Selver, P., 194

Semantic fields: juxtaposition of, 188

Semicolon, 115, 123, 128–30, 187, 285–86

Sensational fiction, 7, 291, 299–300, 302. *See also* Gothic.

Sentence fragment. *See* Stream-of-consciousness.

Series, 115, 118, 121–28, 129, 187, 286

Setting (stage): multiple, 234, 235

Sexuality, 175–76, 184, 186

Shakespeare, William, 49, 155, 223, 229, 251, 278, 285, 293, 307, 313, 315, 318, 319, 333

Shanks, Edward, 193n

Sharp, David, 301, 303

Sheehan, John, 136n

Sheinkin, David, 175n

Shekinah, 78

Shelley, Percy, 315

Shideler, Mary McDermott, 16n, 18n, 67, 133n, 145n, 148n, 150n, 161n, 217, 226n, 229, 328

Shiel, M. P., 302

Shippey, T. A., 293

Shocker. *See* Sensational fiction.

Shuttleworth, Thelma: CW letter to, 195; mentioned, 172n, 198n

Sibley, Agnes, 64n, 80, 83, 84, 106n, 141n, 146n, 148n, 157n, 218n, 221, 222n, 224n, 225, 226n, 241

Sidney, Sir Philip, 299, 310

Silence, 39–40, 56

Simile: vs. metaphor, 92, 280

Simon Magus, 135, 139, 148–49, 232, 243, 244, 246, 247

Simons, Thomas G., 159n

Sin: relation to sexuality, 184; defined, 219. *See also* Rhetoric: relation to sin.

Sisam, Kenneth: letter to CW, 194

Sisyphus, 94, 95

Skepticism: in CW's thought, 18, 23, 65, 101, 103–4, 105, 106, 260, 270, 271, 274, 317; in *PL,* 21, 104, 105, 112; in *Thomas Cranmer,* 22, 260; in *MD,* 85; relation to faith, 103–4, 105, 109, 317 (*see also* Doubt); Christian, 104, 112; in C. S. Lewis, 111; in *SE,* 134

Skot, John, 259

Smart, Christopher, 299, 300

Socratic argument, 131

Solomon: as magician, 185; in *TTL,* 208. *See also* CW: Prose fiction: *MD:* Stone.

350

INDEX

Space, 40, 113, 117, 186. *See also* Time: and space.

Spacks, Patricia Meyer, 16n, 60, 66, 134n, 141n, 148n

Spalding, Ruth, 241

Spanos, William V., 17n, 220–21, 223n, 226n, 227, 228–29, 232–33

Speaight, Robert, 228, 258, 259n

Speech acts. *See* Language: performative.

Speed: as an element of rhetoric 52. *See also* CW: Key words and images: speed.

Spencer, Kathleen, 60–61, 64, 65n, 67

Spengler, Oswald, 134

Spirit. *See* Matter: relation to spirit.

Stained glass, 155, 259

Stanzaic forms, 212, 213

State, secular, claims of, 252

Stevenson, Robert Louis, 7

Stewart, J. I. M., 296, 297, 335

Stewart, R. F., 291, 292, 293n

Stoner, Oliver, 301

Stream-of-consciousness, 127–28

Structuralism, 101

Strype, John, 250n, 251n

Style: idiosyncratic, 50, 57, 268, 278; four types, 125; elevated, 191 (*see also* Diction: religious; Liturgy: and CW's style); compacted, 227; of *Dove,* playful, 268, 270, 275; CW's criterion in judging detective fiction, 300–02; defined, 301–2

Subjectivity: portrayal of, 98; in scientific observation, 179. *See also* Affective stylistics; Stream-of-consciousness.

Substitution, 49, 66, 70, 96, 153–56, 158, 239, 245–46. *See also* Exchange.

Supernatural: in CW's fiction, 7, 60, 77–78, 98, 113, 116; CW attuned to, 15; intrusive, in CW's early writing, 19; relation to natural, 29, 54, 70, 76, 90–92, 113–14, 118, 120, 125, 127, 169, 186, 260, 287, 288–89, 315, 318; definition of, 90, 92; treatment of in fiction, 99–100, 105. *See also* Hermeticism; Paranormal; Preternatural.

Surrealism, 8, 95, 202–5

Swedenborg, Emmanuel, 111, 160n

Swift, Jonathan, 334

Syllogism: simulated, 130–31; abandoned, 285

Symbol: vs. image, 47; CW on 133, 137, 318. *See also* Imagery.

Symbolists, 180

Symons, Julian, 294, 296

Synesthesia, 203

Syntax: in CW's rhetoric, 22, 55, 56, 61, 69, 116, 128, 131, 187, 207, 229; mentioned, 171, 279

Taliessin, 173–74, 181, 182, 183, 185, 201, 211, 247

Talmud, 159n

Tantum ergo sacramentum, 255

Tarot, 30, 31, 37–38, 51, 54, 67, 77, 79, 113, 143–44, 153

Tennyson, Alfred, Lord, 207n, 210n

Tetragrammaton: reversed, 46, 150, 152, 160; in *MD,* 79

Text: question of its primacy, 101n, 313

Theology: language of, 66, 101, 135, 138, 150n, 279–80, 285, 287, 288, 318; and art, 280, 318, 320; not to be imposed on literary text, 310

Theosophy 165

"This also is Thou; neither is this Thou," 64–65, 101, 140, 287

Thomas, St., 219, 225, 243–44, 317

Thomas, Dylan: influenced by CW, 8

Thriller. *See* Sensational fiction.

Tillyard, E. M. W., 312

Time: CW's handling of 17, 20, 155, 186, 221–22, 223n, 224n; coevality of past, present, future, 31–32, 84, 87, 88, 113, 117–18, 153–54, 186, 219, 221–22, 266, 271 (*see also* CW: Key words and images: now *and* speed); relation to eternity, 66, 114, 130–31; in *MD,* 79–80, 83–89; and space, 80, 94, 99, 120, 186, 221; theories of, 80–82, 85, 89; and consciousness, 82, 86, 94; movement without change, 94–95; CW's conception of, 98–99; association with death, 101; redemption of, 153; "infelicity of," 203–4; supernatural dimension of, 242, 266, 271. *See also* Time travel.

Time travel: in fiction, 83, 92; in *MD,* 84–88

Tolkien, Christopher, 83, 334

Tolkien, J. R. R.: on fantasy, 76, 294–95, 306; influenced by J. W. Dunne, 82–83;

INDEX

friendship with CW, 83, 180, 240n; his style, 124; on Recovery, 239–40n; associated with E. C. Bentley, 297; on eucatastrophe, 297, 298; *The Lord of the Rings,* 83, 124, 207n; "The Lost Road," 83; "On Fairy-stories," 76, 239–40n, 295n; *The Silmarillion,* 77; mentioned, 20, 180, 307, 332, 333, 334

Toynbee, Arnold, 266

Transcendence: affirmed by CW, 17, 101, 249; and poetry, 313–18 passim, 321. *See also* Sacramentality.

Transformation (occult theme), 173–78

Trent, Council of, 253

Trinity: relation to coinherence, 15, 39, 170, 173; doctrine of, 133n, 171; parodied, 148; as macrocosm 171

Trowbridge, Clinton W., 133n, 153n, 157n

Types. *See* Characterization: symbolic.

Udall, Nicholas, 221

Unity, doctrine of, 61, 114, 178, 187

Urang, Gunnar, 17n, 59, 60n, 62, 67, 69, 133n, 134n, 141n, 144n, 146n, 148n, 154n, 155n, 160n

Urim and Thummim, 85

Van Dine, S. S., 296, 301, 303

Van Eyck, Jan, 156

Via . . . See Way . . .

Viewpoint: in narration, 56, 68, 70, 71, 143, 150n

Virgil: as magician, 172; redemption of, 245–46; mentioned, 208, 209, 211, 314

Vision: CW's, described, 15–16, 24, 61, 133, 168; and poetry, 23, 309, 312, 316, 318, 320; relation to fiction, 59; "visionary" genre, 92, 93; vs. perception, 106; theophany, in *TTL,* 210; of detective fiction, 299; vs. theory, 316; mentioned, 19–24 passim, 140n. *See also* History: CW's concept of; Sacramentality.

Vocabulary. *See* Diction.

Voltaire, F. M. de, 104, 269, 275

Wagner, Richard, 147

Waite, A. E., 21n, 92n, 165–66, 169n, 172, 175n, 177

Wakefield cycle, 239

Walker, Peter, 218n

Wall, Charles (CW's uncle), 261n

Walling, R. A. J., 296

Walsh, Chad, 16n, 72n, 145n

Wandall, Frederick S., 16n

Watkins, Vernon, 17n

Watson, Colin, 296–97, 298

Way of Affirmation, 9, 66, 105, 112, 133, 141–42, 147, 150n, 185, 247, 249, 253, 257, 269, 319, 320

Way of Coinherence. *See* Coinherence: Way of.

Way of Negation of Images. *See* Way of Rejection.

Way of Perversion, 146, 149, 274

Way of Rejection, 105, 144, 147, 152n, 158, 185, 269

Weales, Gerald, 218, 221

Weathers, Winston: "The Rhetoric of Certitude," 18, 65, 125, 134n, 141n; "The Rhetoric of the Series," 121–22, 125

Weinig, Sister Mary Anthony, 160n

Wells, H. G., 8, 303

Westerman, Nancy, 110

Wheatley, Dennis, 324, 329

Whitechurch, Victor L., 302

Will: of God, 85, 87, 247, 282; freedom of, 87, 181, 272, 287

Williams, Arnold, 223n

Williams, Charles: critical reputation, 16–18, 134n, 238, 272, 277; published reviews of his work, 17n, 194, 252, 260n; negative criticism of, 18, 24n, 32, 38, 48, 54, 55, 56–57, 60, 69, 75, 134n, 141, 160n, 187, 190, 229–30, 231–32, 241, 278–79 (*see also* CW: and anti-Semitism); self-image as poet and playwright, 238; fictional self–portrait, 238; revising, 240n, 242–43n (*see also below under* Poetry)

—and anti-Semitism, 150n; on capitalism, 270; and heterodoxy, 21, 104, 111–12, 180, 243–47, 245, 274; as historian, 22, 253, 265–76 (*see also* CW: Dramatic works: *Thomas Cranmer*); as iconoclast, 238, 239–40; as journalist, 294; on Milton, 147n; as theologian, 23, 39, 93,

352 INDEX

133, 180, 218–19, 277–78, 310; on his own writings, 190, 212–14. *See also* Allegory; Coinherence; Detective fiction; Dualism; Fall; Hierarchy; History; Irony; Language; Matter; Occult; Redemption; Reformation; Rhetoric; Sacramentality; Time; Vision; Women.

—KEY WORDS AND IMAGES: **accuracy,** 45, 138–39, 146; **annunciatory,** 55; **arm,** 182, 205–8, 209; **Babel,** 68; **balance,** 29, 44–45; **beasts,** 29–30, 138, 139, 200, 201–2; **Beatrice,** 132–33, 153, 157, 319; **blessing,** 72, 124–25, 151, 158–59, 161, 176–77, 204; **blood,** 72, 174–75, 176, 183, 185, 187; **body,** 21, 22, 36, 37, 40, 41, 118–19, 169–70, 171, 174–75, 175–76, 183–84, 200–01, 203, 205, 207, 211, 282 (*see also* arm; hand; *main entry* Matter: goodness of); **Broceliande,** 170, 173, 183, 200, 202n (*see also* beasts); **butterfly,** 29, 33–36, 140; **Byzantium,** 37, 172 (*see also* Empire); **Camelot,** 173, 187, 189, 190, 202n; **Carbonek,** 170, 173, 189, 190, 202n, 203; **Caucasia,** 27, 170, 184, 189, 190, 200, 224; **circle,** 168, 299; **City,** 16, 43, 46-50 passim, 65, 69, 71, 101, 114, 127, 149, 156–57, 158, 159, 186, 208, 209, 271, 284 (*see also* Logres); **color(s),** 35, 186, 188, 210 (*see also* rose); **constellation** (*see* sickle); **cosmos,** 168–69, 171; **Cross,** 48, 154, 155; **dance,** 18, 30, 35, 37, 39, 52, 56, 71, 142, 143, 168, 184, 218, 223 (*see also main entry* Dance of Death); **diagram,** 169, 284 (*see also* geometry); **dreadful,** 119, 121; **eagle,** 29–30, 177, 178; **Eden,** 139, 155; **Empire,** 37–38, 169–76 passim, 183–84, 186, 200–01, 205–6, 211; **eyes,** 173, 176, 188; **fearful,** 119, 121; **flame/fire,** 49, 58, 72, 95, 124, 126–27, 135, 173, 175, 176–77, 188, 225, 251–52, 284; **geography,** 168–69, 183, 190, 206–7 (*see also particular names*); **geometry,** 168–69, 190; **glory,** 35, 72, 88, 97, 121, 140, 143, 282, 284, 287, 311, 314; **gold,** 142, 200; **Gomorrah,** 57–58, 149; **Grail,** 29, 43, 54, 77, 113, 153, 166, 174–75, 185, 186, 198, 205,

206, 207, 209–11, 316; **granite,** 170, 171; **hallows,** 207, 209, 211; **hand,** 70–71, 206, 207–11; **hazel,** 22, 172, 186, 208–9, 211; **high,** 283; **Jerusalem,** 57, 149, 170, 175, 184, 224; **joy,** 41, 46, 49, 63, 119, 121, 127, 214, 247, 282; **largesse,** 172; **Lateran** (*see* Rome); **leaves,** 126–27; **light,** 40, 88, 190, 247, 284; **lion,** 29–30, 33, 50, 51, 106, 110, 112, 187, 304; **Logres,** 170, 173, 174, 182, 183, 185–86, 197, 200, 202n, 206, 207, 210; **London,** 32, 42–43, 69, 114, 149, 157, 159; **love,** 41, 46, 48, 49, 52, 57–58, 148, 156, 209, 231 (*see also main entry* Love); **lucidity,** 97, 101; **luxury,** 53; **magic,** 21, 22 (*see also main entry* Magic); **Mercy, the,** 52, 54; **milk,** 188, 210; **money,** 158; **moon,** 168; **mountain(s),** 117, 126, 203; **now,** 96–97, 98–99, 101; **peace,** 41, 46, 49, 63–64, 149, 223; **pentagram,** 21, 168, 173–75, 176, 177, 185, 272; **P'o–Lu,** 172, 184, 186, 226; **Porphyry Stair,** 176–79; **propinquity,** 119–20; **rain,** 72, 157; **Republic,** 32; **Rome,** 37, 78, 114, 171, 172, 173, 211, 224; **rope,** 48; **rose** (color), 72, 157, 170, 214; **roses,** 211; **Sarras,** 101, 173; **Sephirotic Tree,** 21, 168, 169–70, 173, 175–78; **serpent,** 29–30, 136; **sickle,** 206–7, 209; silver, 200; skull, 116–17, 118; **speed,** 29–30, 50–53, 56, 186, 252; **stairs,** 21, 118–19, 202 (*see also* Porphyry); **terrible good,** 49, 63, 64, 67, 119, 121; **unicorn,** 30, 144, 186, 200, 201–2; **verse,** 208; **way,** 68; **web,** 15, 70, 143, 282, 283–84; **weight,** 284–85; **wine,** 157, 229; **wish,** 87–88; **Zion** (*see* Jerusalem); **zodiac** (*see main entry* Astrology). *See also* Christ: figured; Imagery; Magic; Occult.

—LIFE: childhood home, St. Albans 31, 260–61; awarded 1924 medal, 194; membership in Rosicrucian order, 92 (*see also* Golden Dawn); church attendance, 249n, 257; illness in 1933, 198; angst in mid-1930s, 249, 261; work at OUP, 104, 266 (*see also* Amen House); move to Oxford, 240n, 268; lectures in

INDEX

353

Oxford, 268; his life reflected in his works, 261

—Works:

—Dramatic works, 7, 22, 217–61; theology in, 218–19, 234; music in, 219, 255; nativity plays, 220, 221–22, 233, 317; masques, 223n; demands on actors, 228; neglected, 238; written for specific audiences, 239; most produced in CW's lifetime, 241; function of verse in, 242; mentioned, 194. *See also particular titles:*

Chapel of the Thorn, The, 202n, 203n

Chaste Wanton, The, 202n

Death of Good Fortune, The, 219, 226n, 230, 231, 232–33, 234, 317

Grab and Grace, 222n, 230n, 232–33, 235, 241n

House by the Stable, The, 219, 220n, 230n, 232–35, 317

House of the Octopus, The, 135, 137, 138, 153, 154, 213, 214n, 219, 220, 223, 225, 226, 227, 232, 246

Judgement at Chelmsford: liturgy in, 219–20; relation to morality play, 221, 224–25, 233; language in, 222–23, 231; Accuser, 224–25, 226, 227, 231, 247; written under pseudonym, 238n; not performed, 241n

Masque of the Termination of Copyright, The, 241n

Myth of Shakespeare, A, 313, 319

Rite of the Passion, The, 146n, 219, 220, 221, 222, 224, 226n, 229

Scene from a Mystery, 220, 222, 224, 233

Seed of Adam, 22–23, 157, 219–24 passim, 226n, 230, 231, 233–34, 243, 247, 317

Terror of Light, 22, 134–35, 139, 149, 153, 155n, 218–19, 220, 225, 231–32, 239–47; CW's revisions in, 242n

Thomas Cranmer of Canterbury, 217–29 passim, 248–61; Skeleton, 146n, 218, 224n, 226–27, 231, 251–52, 258–61; original production of, 217, 218, 222, 228, 248n, 250, 252, 255n, 258, 260; style of, 192, 196, 229–30, 248; CW's handling of history in, 267; mentioned, 22

Three Plays, 192, 196. See also *Chaste Wanton, The; Rite of the Passion, The;* and under CW: Poetry.

Three Temptations, The, 225–26, 232

—Poetry, 21–22, 165–214; Arthurian, 7, 27, 158n, 180–81, 192n, 194–214, 246n, 247; changes in style, 22, 190–214, 229, 233; early poetry, 22, 27, 166, 192, 193–96; evaluation of, 190–91, 228; later: develops features found in earlier style, 192, 199–200, 202, 203, 205; drafts and intermediate versions, 194–97, 200–01, 202n, 203–7, 208–9, 212–13; relation of private and public in, 199–200; planned but uncompleted, 212, 213; mentioned, 66. *See also particular titles:*

Advent of Galahad, The (unfinished cycle), 196, 199, 200–01, 203, 206, 207, 214n

Heroes and Kings, 166, 194, 196

Region of the Summer Stars, The: public reading of, by CW, 8; evaluation of, 190–91; its style different from that of *TTL,* 190–91, 192, 211–14; unified structure of, 192; composition of, 212; editions of, 327–29; mentioned, 165, 166, 184, 241. *See also individual poems as follows:* "The Calling of Taliessin," 169–70, 172–73; "Taliessin in the Rose-Garden," 168, 169, 174, 176, 206, 209n, 211, 213; "The Departure of Dindrane," 212; "The Founding of the Company," 170, 189; "The Queen's Servant," 211; "The Meditation of Mordred," 186; "The Prayers of the Pope," 183, 185

Silver Stair, The, 166, 199, 202

Taliessin through Logres: end-papers map, 170, 175, 183; epigraph, 181, 211; evaluation of, 191; its style, 192, 211–13, 229; growth of, 195; editions of, 327–28; CW's notes on, *see under* CW: Other works; mentioned, 165, 166, 167, 172, 201, 212–13. *See also individual poems as follows:* "Prelude," 168–69, 189, 190, 196, 209; "Taliessin's Return to Logres," 188, 195, 196n, 205–7, 208–9; "The Vision of the Em-

354 INDEX

pire," 171, 172, 181, 183, 184, 185, 187, 188, 196n, 197, 211; "The Calling of Arthur," 187, 188, 189, 196n, 204n; "Mount Badon," 182, 189, 207, 208; "The Crowning of Arthur," 183, 186, 187, 189, 196n, 200, 210; "Taliessin's Song of the Unicorn," 199, 200, 213; "Bors to Elayne: The Fish of Broceliande," 182, 188, 209; "Taliessin in the School of the Poets," 170, 178, 185, 187, 195, 208; "Taliessin on the Death of Virgil," 246; "The Coming of Palomides," 182, 183, 187–88, 206, 207, 209n, 210; "Lamorack and the Queen Morgause of Orkney," 183, 187, 188, 189, 206, 207–8, 210; "Bors to Elayne: On the King's Coins," 188, 208, 209; "The Star of Percivale," 182, 197n, 208, 210, 213; "The Ascent of the Spear," 182, 188; "The Sister of Percivale," 182, 203, 208, 211; "The Son of Lancelot," 169, 186, 188, 208, 209, 210, 212, 213; "Palomides before His Christening," 183, 187, 197n, 202, 203; "The Coming of Galahad," 173–74, 195, 208, 210, 212; "The Departure of Merlin," 196; "The Death of Palomides," 176–77, 178, 187; "Percivale at Carbonek," 196, 203–5; "The Last Voyage," 185, 188, 195, 208, 212; "Taliessin at Lancelot's Mass," 154, 173, 188, 189, 196, 210–11
Three Plays (poems printed in volume), 192, 194, 202n
Windows of Night, 97

—Prose Fiction, 19–21, 44–161; typical characteristics of, 78; later novels, 99; magicians as villains in, 172; weak characters who achieve strength in, 249n; mentioned, 7, 75, 300, 318. *See also particular titles:*
All Hallows' Eve: language in, 21, 40–42, 44, 46–48, 53, 141, 144–45, 150–53, 155, 158–61; relation to *DH*, 32; magic in, 32, 40–41, 69, 144–50, 152, 155, 158, 160–61, 172; coinherence in, 40, 46–48, 65; attack on reductionism, 41–43; paintings in, 42–43, 66–67, 149; rhetorical techniques in, 65, 69, 71; damnation and salvation in, 68, 69,

96–97, 246, 247n; ending of, 71–72, 159–60; handling of supernatural in, 92; concept of rhetoric in, 132, 134; liturgy in, 144–45, 153–58, 161; substitution in, 154–55, 246n; editions of, 323; mentioned, 56, 133, 135, 138, 140, 267
Descent into Hell: language in, 21, 46, 48, 49–50, 68–69, 115, 140; rhetorical techniques in, 21, 62, 71, 113–31; and haunting, 31, 116–17; absence of magic, 31–32; Pauline, 31, 39, 40, 42, 49–50, 52, 55–57, 64, 68, 69, 71, 114, 116, 119, 120, 121, 128, 141, 245; Wentworth, 31, 39–49 passim, 57–58, 64, 68, 93, 97, 114, 119, 120, 127–28, 129, 138, 139n, 140, 151, 202, 226n, 246, 267; Battle Hill, 31, 49, 52–53, 55, 114, 116–18, 154; Stanhope, 49, 52, 55, 64, 68, 114, 115, 116, 121, 123, 141, 142, 238; Margaret, 52, 55, 56, 58, 69, 114, 120, 126, 140, 141, 154; "speed" in, 52, 56; style in, 55–58; oxymoron in, 63, 64, 67, 119, 121; handling of supernatural in, 93, 113–14, 116; contrasted with CW's earlier fiction, 113, 267; liturgical structure, 153–54; surrealism in, 202; substitution in, 245; editions of, 323–24; mentioned, 186n. *See also* Doubles; Drama; Time: coevality.
"Et in Sempiternum Pereant," 20, 90, 93–102; Tumulty, 95 (*see also MD*)
Greater Trumps, The: Platonism in, 29, 30–31, 92; Nancy, 30, 31, 67, 68, 70–71, 141, 142, 143–44; Fool, 33, 51, 53, 67, 142; ritual in, 37–38; dance, 37, 168; Sybil, 51, 142, 143, 151; language in, 67, 68, 151; syntax in, 69; occult in, 92, 166; exchange in, 144; imagery in, 201; editions of, 324; mentioned, 77, 113. *See also* Tarot.
Many Dimensions: rhetoric of dislocation, 20; title, 20, 80–81; Stone of Suleiman, 20, 29, 54, 63, 68, 70, 77, 78–80, 81, 83–89, 113, 153; Arglay, 20, 63, 68, 78, 80, 82–83, 86–88, 93, 167 (*see also* "Et in Sempiternum Pereant"); Chloe, 50, 63–64, 68, 70, 80–88 passim, 246n; "speed" in, 50; oxymoron in, 63–64; Tumulty, 68, 83–88 passim, 172, 246 (*see also* "Et in Sempiternum Pereant");

INDEX

layers of meaning in, 68; syntax in, 70; paradox in, 83; relation to occult, 92, 166, 167; editions of, 325–26

Noises That Weren't There, The (unfinished novel), 240n

Place of the Lion, The: skepticism in, 21, 103–12; Platonism in, 29–30, 33, 36, 67, 92, 106; Anthony, 30, 33–35, 51, 53, 65, 67, 105–8 passim, 112, 138, 139, 140, 151; T. S. Eliot on, 33; dislocation in, 33; rhetorical analysis of, 33–36, 65–66; "speed" in, 50, 51; elevated diction in, 53; obscurity, 56; Damaris, 65–66, 67, 105, 106, 107, 111, 112, 137, 138, 139–40, 151, 246n; characterization in, 107–8; relation to heterodox traditions, 108–12; language in, 137–38, 139, 140, 151, 152; liturgy in, 144; occult in, 166; imagery of, 201–2; editions of, 326; mentioned, 55, 77, 113, 141, 302. *See also* Deconstruction; Postmodernism; CW: Key words and images: butterfly, eagle, lion, *and* unicorn.

Shadows of Ecstasy: Roger Ingram, 61–62, 66, 134, 136; Considine, 134, 146–47, 267; concept of rhetoric in, 134, 136–37; liturgy in, 143; occult in, 166; editions of, 327; mentioned, 29, 141, 148n

War in Heaven: Graal, 29, 77, 113; language in, 32–33, 44–45, 54, 141; Batesby, 32, 45; Persimmons, 44–45, 172; Archdeacon, 45, 54, 144, 246n; religious diction in, 54; paradox in, 64; occult in, 92, 166; style of, 94; liturgy in, 144; parodies Modernism, 197; composition of, 201n; substitution in, 246n; relation to detective fiction, 303, 307; editions of, 329–30

—Other works: autobiographical sketch, 200n; biographies, 266; book reviews, 23, 257, 290, 294–305, 308, 309, 311–12, 313–14, 316, 318; criticism, 7, 23, 76, 309–21; lectures, 8, 197, 199n, 212, 312; letters, 190, 192–200 passim, 203–4, 212–14, 246n, 252n. *See also particular titles (those asterisked are collected in* Image*):*

"Anthropotokos,"* 146, 152

"Antichrist and the City's Laws,"* 146n, 147

Arthurian Commonplace Book, 27, 198

"Blake and Wordsworth,"* 109, 145n

"Church and State,"* 252

"Commonwealth in English Verse, The," 312, 315

"Cross, The," 24n, 135, 154, 283

Descent of the Dove, The, 266, 267–72, 273–77 passim; 104, 142, 155, 156, 159n, 160, 250n, 253, 254, 260n, 277

"Dialogue on Hierarchy, A,"* 18

English Poetic Mind, The, 287n, 309, 311, 312, 314, 315, 318

"Figure of Arthur, The," 148n, 153n, 327, 329

Figure of Beatrice, The, 121, 132n, 137–38, 141n, 313, 320

Forgiveness of Sins, The, 277–89; quoted, 64, 135, 143n; editions of, 325; mentioned, 23, 24, 66, 70, 136, 138, 146, 159n, 218n, 318

"Gerard Hopkins,"* 198

"Growth of a Poet's Mind, The," 76

He Came Down from Heaven, 65, 104, 132n, 135, 136, 146, 150, 154n, 277, 284, 287, 319; editions of, 325

Image of the City and Other Essays, The, 290. *See also particular titles (asterisked in this list).*

"Image of the City in English Verse, The,"* 154n

"Index of the Body, The,"* 19, 138, 140, 159, 167, 169–70, 171, 178

Introduction to *Poems of Hopkins,* 199n, 317

"John Milton,"* 138, 305

Letters to Lalage, 28, 37, 200n, 245n, 247n

"Liturgy, The,"* 142, 144, 257

"Making of *Taliessin,* The,"* 137, 184, 200, 208, 212–13

"Notes on Religious Drama," 317

"Notes on *Taliessin through Logres,*" 172n, 173–74n

"Notes on the Arthurian Myth,"* 185, 201

Outlines of Romantic Theology, 27, 137, 155, 160n

"Picturesque Approach to Literature, The," 313–14

INDEX

Poetry at Present, 197n, 311, 316, 320
Reason and Beauty in the Poetic Mind, 98–99, 100, 287n, 314, 315–16, 320
"Recovery of Spiritual Initiative, The," 309, 313
"Redeemed City, The,"* 67, 145
Religion and Love in Dante, 132n, 133n
"Religious Drama,"* 222n
Rochester, 266
"Romantic Imagination, The," 316
"Sensuality and Substance,"* 142, 159
"Sound and Variations,"* 307
"Taliessin through Logres. Notes for C. S. Lewis," 197n
"Trial by Symbols," 318
"Way of Affirmation, The,"* 138, 142n
"Way of Exchange, The,"* 16n, 147, 254
"What the Cross Means to Me." *See* "Cross, The."
Witchcraft, 36–37, 148, 150n, 266–68, 272–75, 277

Williams, Florence ("Michal"): CW letters to, 212, 213; her influence on CW, 240n, 242n; mentioned, 199n
Williams, Mary (CW's mother), 261n
Wimsatt, W. K., 278n

Winship, George P., Jr., 17n, 60, 69, 134n, 137n, 141n, 145n, 160n
Wit: in CW's style, 268, 276. *See also* Humor.
Witchcraft: witch-hunts, 222, 273; Salem trials, 266–67, 273–74. *See also* CW: Other works: *Witchcraft*
Women: in CW's thought, 169, 174–75; substitution through, 246n
Woodthorpe, R. C., 300
Woolf, Virginia, 91
Wordplay, 20, 48–50, 235. *See also* Puns.
Words. *See* Diction; Language; CW: Key words and images.
Wordsworth, William, 9, 15n, 20, 76, 77, 89, 156, 278, 312–16 passim
World War II, 268
Wright, Elizabeth, 138n, 140n, 142n, 143, 146n, 150n, 152n, 155n

Xavier, St. Francis, 269

Yeats, W. B., 51, 165, 193

Zohar, 172
Zwingli, Ulrich, 256